The Essential
Carlstadt

Andreas Bodenstein (Carlstadt) in Professional Garb.

The Essential Carlstadt

Fifteen Tracts by
Andreas Bodenstein von Carlstadt

Translated and edited by
E. J. Furcha

PLOUGH PUBLISHING HOUSE

Published by Plough Publishing House
Walden, New York
Robertsbridge, England
Elsmore, Australia
www.plough.com

Plough produces books, a quarterly magazine, and Plough.com to encourage people and help them put their faith into action. We believe Jesus can transform the world and that his teachings and example apply to all aspects of life. At the same time, we seek common ground with all people regardless of their creed.

Plough is the publishing house of the Bruderhof, an international community of families and singles seeking to follow Jesus together. Members of the Bruderhof are committed to a way of radical discipleship in the spirit of the Sermon on the Mount. Inspired by the first church in Jerusalem (Acts 2 and 4), they renounce private property and share everything in common in a life of nonviolence, justice, and service to neighbors near and far. To learn more about the Bruderhof's faith, history, and daily life, see Bruderhof.com. (Views expressed by Plough authors are their own and do not necessarily reflect the position of the Bruderhof.)

ISBN: 978-0-874-86270-6

Grateful acknowledgement is made to the Universitatsbibliothek, Basel, for permission to reproduce images on page 2, 50, 128, and 168.

Page 268, original at the Metropolitan Museum, New York, reproduced in Karl-Adolf Knappe, Dürer, (Secaucus, New Jersey: Well Fleet Press).

Hand lettering by Jan Gleysteen.

Library of Congress Cataloging-in-Publication Data pending.

*To my students, 1968-1994,
with gratitude and affection*

Classics of the Radical Reformation

Classics of the Radical Reformation is an English-language series of Anabaptist and Free Church documents translated and annotated under the direction of the Institute of Mennonite Studies, which is the research agency of the Anabaptist Mennonite Biblical Seminaries, and published by Plough Publishing House.

1. *The Legacy of Michael Sattler.* Trans., ed. John Howard Yoder.

2. *The Writings of Pilgram Marpeck.* Trans., ed. William Klassen and Walter Klaassen.

3. *Anabaptism in Outline: Selected Primary Sources.* Trans., ed. Walter Klaassen.

4. *The Sources of Swiss Anabaptism: The Grebel Letters and Related Documents.* Ed. Leland Harder.

5. *Balthasar Hubmaier: Theologian of Anabaptism.* Ed. H. Wayne Pipkin and John Howard Yoder.

6. *The Writings of Dirk Philips.* Ed. Cornelius J. Dyck, William E. Keeney, and Alvin J. Beachy.

7. *The Anabaptist Writings of David Joris: 1535–1543.* Ed. Gary K. Waite.

8. *The Essential Carlstadt: Fifteen Tracts by Andreas Bodenstein.* Trans., ed. E. J. Furcha.

9. *Peter Riedemann's Hutterite Confession of Faith.* Ed. John J. Friesen.

10. Sources of South German/Austrian Anabaptism. Ed. C. Arnold Snyder, trans. Walter Klaassen, Frank Friesen, and Werner O. Packull.

11. *Confessions of Faith in the Anabaptist Tradition: 1527–1660.* Ed. Karl Koop.

12. *Jörg Maler's Kunstbuch: Writings of the Pilgram Marpeck Circle.* Ed. John D. Rempel.

13. *Later Writings of the Swiss Anabaptists: 1529–1592.* Ed. C. Arnold Snyder.

Contents

Preface to the New Edition

Most accounts of the Radical Reformation begin with Andreas Bodenstein von Carlstadt (alternately Karlstadt), the first individual to challenge Martin Luther's interpretation of scripture and promote a form of reformation that differed from Luther's. While Luther was in hiding after the 1521 Diet of Worms, Karlstadt became the leader of a group that introduced practical reforms in Wittenberg in accordance with Luther's understanding of the gospel. Upon his return to Wittenberg in March 1522, Luther rolled back most of these reforms and denounced those who had tried to impose them on people who were not yet ready for such changes. Two years later Karlstadt would break decisively with Luther over the understanding of both baptism and the Lord's Supper.[1] In his enormously influential work *Against the Heavenly Prophets* (1525), Luther mocked and vilified his former colleague, creating a caricature that has endured to the present. Although Karlstadt rejected Thomas Müntzer's advocacy of violence, Luther criticized both men for claiming guidance from the Spirit rather than from the written Word of God. Heinrich Bullinger would repeat the association of Karlstadt with Müntzer in order to place the origins of Anabaptism in distant Saxony rather than in his own church in Zurich. Karlstadt spent his final years as a Reformed theologian teaching at the university of Basel, but his reputation as a Radical Reformer, nascent Spiritualist, and associate of Müntzer has continued into the twenty-first century.[2]

Luther's condemnations had such a deep and abiding influence on the historical interpretation of Karlstadt that Hermann Barge's favorable biography of Karlstadt caused a storm of protest when it was published in 1905.[3] The longevity of this negative image was due in part to the difficulty scholars had in finding and reading Karlstadt's own writings. Alejandro Zorzin has highlighted Karlstadt's importance as a pamphlet author,[4] yet until relatively recently only a few of his works were readily available to modern readers. Ironically, the easiest works to find were those included in Johann Georg Walch's edition of Luther's writings.[5] In the mid-1950s, Erich Hertzsch published eight of Karlstadt's vernacular pamphlets, although he contributed to further misunderstanding by transposing a page of Karlstadt's most influential work, his *Dialogue . . . on the Infamous and Idolatrous Abuse of the Most Blessed Sacrament*.[6] Over the final quarter of the twentieth century, individual pamphlets and sermons by Karlstadt were published within journal articles or included in edited collections of Reformation-era pamphlets.[7] Only recently, however, have long-standing efforts to produce a critical edition of Karlstadt's works and correspondence borne fruit, with the publication both in print and online of a first volume covering the period up through 1518.[8]

Until the publication of *The Essential Carlstadt*, Anglophone readers' access to Karlstadt's ideas was even more limited. Only a few of his pamphlets were available in translation. Ronald Sider included four tracts on the Lord's Supper and the pace of reform in *Karlstadt's Battle with Luther: Documents in a Liberal-Radical Debate*.[9] Karlstadt's pamphlet urging the removal of images was included in *A Reformation Debate: Karlstadt, Emser and Eck on Sacred Images*,[10] while Carter Lindberg published a translation of Karlstadt's *Dialogue on the Lord's Supper*, based on the faulty edition of Hertzsch.[11] The treatises translated by Edward Furcha in this volume therefore provided important new material for the study of Karlstadt's thought and influence.

Edward J. Furcha (1935–97) belonged to a circle of North American scholars, many of them from a dissenting church background, who contributed to the rapid growth of research on the Radical Reformation in the last third of the twentieth century. Born in Transylvania, Furcha immigrated to Canada with his parents, studied in Switzerland and the United States, and eventually became professor of religious studies at McGill University in Montreal.[12] Furcha's academic career was largely devoted to Reformation dissenters, beginning with his dissertation on Kaspar Schwenckfeld. Over the next thirty years he published translations of works by Schwenckfeld, Sebastian Franck, Hans Denck, and Huldrych Zwingli, in addition to this volume of Karlstadt's pamphlets. Furcha thus played an important role in exposing English readers to a range of voices critical of what became the established Protestant churches.

Like Lindberg, Furcha used Hertzsch's edition of Karlstadt's *Dialogue*, and he closely followed Lindberg's translation, which means that the version in this volume reproduces the transposed pages.[13] Although both *On the Removal of Images* and *Whether We Should Go Slowly* were already available in English, Furcha made his own translations of these tracts. The remaining twelve treatises were all new to English readers, and for five of these there is still no modern edition of their original German.[14] Furcha included two of Karlstadt's pamphlets concerning the Lord's Supper in this volume, and, as he announces in the introduction, he planned to publish the remaining pamphlets in a second volume produced together with Calvin Pater. Furcha's unexpected death in 1997 meant that this volume was never published, and it would be another fifteen years before Karlstadt's pamphlets on the Eucharist appeared in English translation.[15]

Furcha's selection of Karlstadt's writings stands out for its breadth of coverage. He chose pamphlets from every stage of Karlstadt's career, beginning with an early treatise on *Gelassenheit* (yieldedness) from 1520 and extending to an unpublished sermon preached in Zurich in 1534. His translations of Karlstadt's sometimes convoluted German is both colloquial and clear. Furcha did not give the German titles of the pamphlets because he intended the translations for a general audience. To make them easier to identify, I here provide a bibliography of the original German titles of Karlstadt's pamphlets:[16]

1. *Missive von der allerhöchsten Tugend Gelassenheit* (no. 24)

2. *Von Anbetung und Ehrerbietung der Zeichen des Neuen Testaments* (no. 40)

3. *Von Gelübten Unterrichtung* (no. 39)

4. *Von Abtun der Bilder* (no. 48)

5. *Sendbrief D. Andreas B. von Karlstadt meldend seiner Wirtschaft* (no. 47)

Research on Karlstadt has continued to grow since the publication of Furcha's translations. Alejandro Zorzin's brief biographical essay introduces Anglophone readers to the reformer's life,[17] and the published papers of two different conferences held in the 1990s provide a broad sampling of recent research on this "Reformation maverick."[18] Karlstadt's place within the early Wittenberg Reformation continues to draw the attention of German historians.[19] In contrast, English-language scholarship has looked at Karlstadt as a contributor to Reformation radicalism more broadly. Furcha himself contributed to the literature on Karlstadt with two short essays, the first comparing Karlstadt with Zwingli and the second highlighting the concern for internalized worship that underlay both Karlstadt's early advocacy of iconoclasm and his later emphasis on regeneration.[20] Recent studies have also examined Karlstadt's use of rhetoric[21] and highlighted the influence of both German mysticism and Erasmus's biblical scholarship on his thought.[22]

This republication of Furcha's translation is intended to familiarize a new generation of scholars with Karlstadt's life and thought, and it should spur further study of the first Reformer who dared to disagree with Luther.

Amy Nelson Burnett

Notes

1. Amy Nelson Burnett, *Karlstadt and the Origins of the Eucharistic Controversy: A Study in the Circulation of Ideas*, Oxford Studies in Historical Theology (New York: Oxford University Press, 2011). The importance of baptism became clear after Karlstadt was identified as the author of an anonymous pamphlet critical of infant baptism; see Alejandro Zorzin, "Zur Wirkungsgeschichte einer Schrift aus Karlstadts Orlamünder Tätigkeit. Der 1527 in Worms gedruckte 'Dialog vom fremden Glauben, Glauben der Kirche, Taufe der Kinder.' Fortsetzung einer Diskussion," in *Andreas Bodenstein von Karlstadt (1486–1541): Ein Theologe der frühen Reformation*, edited by Sigrid Looss and Markus Matthias (Lutherstadt Wittenberg: Drei Kastanien Verlag, 1998), 143–58.

2. A recent example of this pairing is Hans-Jürgen Goertz, "Karlstadt, Müntzer and the Reformation of the Commoners, 1521–1525," in A Companion to Anabaptism and Spiritualism, 152–1700, edited by John D. Roth and James M. Stayer, Brill's Companions to the Christian Tradition 6 (Leiden: Brill, 2007), 1–44.

3. Hermann Barge, *Andreas Bodenstein von Karlstadt*, 2 vols. (Leipzig: Brandstetter, 1905). For a survey of scholarship on Karlstadt that centers on Barge and his opponents, see Martin Kessler, *Das Karlstadt-Bild in der Forschung*, Beiträge zur historischen Theologie 174 (Tübingen: Mohr Siebeck, 2014).

4. Alejandro Zorzin, *Karlstadt als Flugschriftenautor*, Göttinger theologische Arbeiten 48 (Göttingen: Vandenhoeck & Ruprecht, 1990). Zorzin provides a useful chronological list of Karlstadt's printed works (273ff), which updates the standard Karlstadt bibliography, E. Freys and H. Barge, eds., *Verzeichnis der gedruckten Schriften des Andreas Bodenstein von Karlstadt* (Nieuwkoop: De Graaf, 1965 [1904]).

5. Johann Georg Walch, ed., *Dr. Martin Luthers Sämmtliche Schriften* (St. Louis: Concordia, 1881–1910); three of Karlstadt's eucharistic pamphlets are included in vol. 20. Walch's edition was first published in the eighteenth century.

6. Erich Hertzsch, ed., *Karlstadts Schriften aus den Jahren 1523–25*, Neudrucke deutscher Literaturwerke des 16 und 17. Jahrhunderts 325, 2 vols. (Halle: Niemeyer, 1956–57). The mistake makes it appear that Victus, who dropped out of the conversation earlier in the *Dialogue*, suddenly reenters the discussion, when in fact his contribution belongs to an earlier stage of the conversation. On the transposition error, see note 13 below.

7. Robert Stupperich, "Karlstadts Sabbat-Traktat von 1524," *Neue Zeitschrift für systematische Theologie* 1 (1959): 349–75; Calvin Pater, "Karlstadts Zürcher Abschiedspredigt über die Menschwerdung Christi," *Zwingliana* 14 (1974): 1–16; Hans-Peter Hasse, "Karlstadts Predigt am 29. September 1522 in Joachimsthal: Ein unbekannter Text aus Stephan Roths Sammlung von Predigten des Johannes Sylvius Egranus," *Archiv für Reformationsgeschichte* 81 (1990): 97–119; Hans-Peter Hasse, "Karlstadts Traktat 'De usura'," *Zeitschrift der Savigny-Stiftung für Rechtsgeschichte, kanonistische Abteilung* 76, 107 (1990): 308–28; Adolf Laube, et al., eds., *Flugschriften der frühen Reformationsbewegung* (1518–1524) (Vaduz: Topos, 1983); Adolf Laube et al., eds., *Flugschriften vom Bauernkrieg zum Täuferreich* (1526–1535) (Berlin: Akademie Verlag, 1992).

8. Andreas Bodenstein von Karlstadt, *Kritische Gesamtausgabe der Schriften und Briefe Andreas Bodensteins von Karlstadt*, Quellen und Forschungen zur Reformationsgeschichte 90/1–2 (Gütersloh: Gütersloher Varlagshaus, 2017–); http://diglib.hab.de/edoc/ed000216/start.htm.

9. Ronald J. Sider, ed., *Karlstadt's Battle with Luther: Documents in a Liberal-Radical Debate* (Philadelphia: Fortress, 1977).

10. Bryan D. Mangrum and Giuseppe Scavizzi, eds., *A Reformation Debate: Karlstadt, Emser and Eck on Sacred Images* (Toronto: Center for Reformation and Renaissance Studies, 1991), 19–39.

11. Carter Lindberg, "Karlstadt's Dialogue on the Lord's Supper," *Mennonite Quarterly Review* 53 (1979): 35–77. The letter from Orlamünde to Allstedt, by Karlstadt, is translated in Michael G. Baylor, ed., *The Radical Reformation*, Cambridge Texts in the History of Political Thought (Cambridge: Cambridge University Press, 1991), 33–35.

12. See Furcha's obituary by Joseph C. McLelland, *Sixteenth Century Journal* 28 (1997): 825–26.

13. The dialogue between Victus and Gemser from the middle of p. 614 through the middle of p. 616 belongs earlier in the dialogue and should be inserted near the bottom of p. 544, after Victus's statement ending with "for God is in hell as well as in heaven and fills all of creation."

14. Those five are the "Tract on ... Gelassenheit" (chap. 1), "Regarding Vows" (chap. 3), "Circular Letter" (chap. 5), "The Meaning of the Term Gelassen" (chap. 6), and "The Manifold, Singular Will of God" (chap. 8).

15. Amy Nelson Burnett, ed., *The Eucharistic Pamphlets of Andreas Bodenstein von Karlstadt*, Early Modern Studies 6 (Kirksville, MO: Truman State University Press, 2011).

16. The number in parentheses refers to the chronological checklist of Karlstadt's pamphlets in Zorzin, *Karlstadt als Flugschriftenautor*.

17. Zorzin, "Andreas Bodenstein von Karlstadt," in *The Reformation Theologians: An Introduction to Theology in the Early Modern Period*, edited by Carter Lindberg (Oxford: Blackwell, 2002), 327–37.

18. Sigrid Looß and Markus Matthias, eds., *Andreas Bodenstein von Karlstadt (1486–1541): Ein Theologe der frühen Reformation. Beiträge eines Arbeitsgesprächs vom 24.–25. November 1995 in Wittenberg* (Wittenberg: Drei Kastanien Verlag, 1998); and Ulrich Bubenheimer and Stefan Oehmig, eds., *Querdenker der Reformation: Andreas Bodenstein von Karlstadt und seine frühe Wirkung* (Würzburg: Religion & Kultur Verlag, 2001).

19. Jens-Martin Kruse, *Universitätstheologie und Kirchenreform: die Anfänge der Reformation in Wittenberg, 1516–1522*, Veröffentlichungen des Instituts für europäische Geschichte Mainz 187 (Mainz: Philipp von Zabern, 2002); Natalie Krentz, *Ritualwandel und Deutungshoheit. Die frühe Reformation in der Residenzstadt Wittenberg* (1500–1533), Spätmittelalter, Humanismus, Reformation 74 (Tübingen: Mohr Siebeck, 2014); see also Stefan Oehmig, "Die Wittenberger Bewegung 1521/22 und ihre Folgen im Lichte alter und neuer Fragestellungen. Ein Beitrag zum Thema (Territorial-) Stadt und Reformation," in *700 Jahre Wittenberg. Stadt, Universität, Reformation*, ed. Stefan Oehmig (Weimar: Herman Böhlaus Nachfolger, 1995), 97–130.

20. E. J. Furcha, "Zwingli and the Radicals: Zwingli and Carlstadt," *Fides et Historia* 25 (1993): 3–11; E. J. Furcha, "Iconoclast or Regenerator: the Work of Andreas Bodenstein in Reforming the Church of the Sixteenth Century," in *The Three Loves, Philosophy, Theology, and World Religions: Essays in Honour of Joseph C. McLelland*, edited by Robert C. Culley and William Klempa (Atlanta: Scholars Press, 1994), 159–69.

21. Neil R. Leroux, "Karlstadt's 'Christag Predig': Prophetic Rhetoric in an 'evangelical' Mass," *Church History* 72 (2003): 102–37; Neil R. Leroux, "'In the Christian City of Wittenberg': Karlstadt's Tract on Images and Begging," *Sixteenth Century Journal* 34 (2003): 73–105; Neil R. Leroux, "Why not now?: Karlstadt's 'Whether we should proceed slowly and avoid offending the weak in matters that concern God's will,'" *Reformation and Renaissance Review* 13 (2011): 33–62; see also the discussion of Karlstadt in Peter Matheson, *The Rhetoric of the Reformation*, (Edinburgh: T&T Clark, 1998), 59–80.

22. Vincent Evener, "Divine Pedagogy and Self-accusation: Reassessing the Theology of Andreas Bodenstein von Karlstadt," *Mennonite Quarterly Review* 87 (2013): 335–67, building on the earlier work of Hans-Peter Hasse, *Karlstadt und Tauler. Untersuchungen zur Kreuzestheologie*, Quellen und Forschungen zur Reformationsgeschichte 58 (Gütersloh: Gütersloher Verlag, 1993); Amy Nelson Burnett, *Debating the Sacraments: Print and Authority in the Early Reformation* (New York: Oxford University Press, 2019).

List of Illustrations

Abbreviations

ADB   *Allgemeine Deutsche Biographie*. Leipzig: 1875ff.

Barge I and II   Hermann Barge, *Andreas Bodenstein von Karlstadt.* Leipzig: 1905.

Bubenheimer   Ulrich Bubenheimer, *Consonantia Theologiae et Jurisprudentiae: Andreas Bodenstein von Karlstadt als Theologe und Jurist auf dem Weg von der Scholastik zur Reformation 1515-1522.* 1974.

CIC   *Corpus Juris Canonici*. Rome: 1918.

Barge/Freys   H. Barge and E. Freys, *Verzeichnis der gedruckten Schriften des Andreas Bodenstein von Karlstadt.* Zentralblatt fürs Bibliothekswesen XXI (1904), pp. 153ff., 209ff., 305ff.

Grimm   Jacob and Wilhelm Grimm, *Deutsches Wörterbuch.* dtv 1968ff.

Müntzer   Peter Matheson, ed. and trans. *The Collected Works of Thomas Müntzer.* Edinburgh: T & T Clark, 1988.

NCE   *New Catholic Encyclopedia.* New York: McGraw Hill, 1967.

Pater   Calvin A. Pater, *Karlstadt as the Father of the Baptist Movement.* Toronto: University of Toronto Press, 1984.

Sider   Ronald Sider, *Andreas Bodenstein von Karlstadt.* Leiden: Brill, 1974.

Williams   George H. Williams, *The Radical Reformation,* 3rd edition. Sixteenth Century Essays and Studies, 1993.

WA   *D. Martin Luther's Werke.* Weimar 1883ff.; reprint: Graz, 1964ff.

Z   *Huldreich Zwinglis Sämtliche Werke.* Berlin/Leipzig/Zurich, 1905ff.

ZW   E. J. Furcha and H. Wayne Pipkin, ed. and trans. *Huldrych Zwingli Writings.* Volumes I and II. Allison Park: Pickwick Publications, 1984.

Abbreviations of Biblical Books[1]

Old Testament

Gen	Genesis	2 Chr	2 Chronicles	Dan	Daniel
Ex	Exodus	Ezra	Ezra	Hos	Hosea
Lev	Leviticus	Neh	Nehemiah	Joel	Joel
Num	Numbers	Esth	Esther	Am	Amos
Deut	Deuteronomy	Job	Job	Ob	Obadiah
Josh	Joshua	Ps	Psalms	Jon	Jonah
Judg	Judges	Prov	Proverbs	Mic	Micah
Ruth	Ruth	Eccl	Ecclesiastes	Nah	Nahum
1 Sam	1 Samuel	Song	Song of Solomon	Hab	Habakkuk
2 Sam	2 Samuel	Isa	Isaiah	Zeph	Zephaniah
1 Kings	1 Kings	Jer	Jeremiah	Hag	Haggai
2 Kings	2 Kings	Lam	Lamentations	Zech	Zechariah
1 Chr	1 Chronicles	Ezek	Ezekiel	Mal	Malachi

Apocryphal/Deuterocanonical Books

Tob	Tobit	Song of Thr	Prayer of Azariah and Song of the Three Jews
Jdt	Judith		
Add Esth	Additions to Esther	Sus	Suzanna
Wis	Wisdom	Bel	Bel and the Dragon
Bar	Baruch	1 Macc	1 Maccabees
Sir	Sirach (Ecclesisticus)		
1 Esd	1 Esdras	2 Macc	2 Maccabees
2 Esd	2 Esdras	3 Macc	3 Maccabees
Let Jer	Letter of Jeremiah	4 Macc	4 Maccabees
		Pr Man	Prayer of Manasseh

New Testament

Mt	Matthew	Eph	Ephesians	Heb	Hebrews
Mk	Mark	Phil	Philippians	Jas	James
Lk	Luke	Col	Colossians	1 Pet	1 Peter
Jn	John	1 Thess	1 Thessalonians	2 Pet	2 Peter
Acts	Acts of the	2 Thess	2 Thessalonians	1 Jn	1 John
	Apostles	1 Tim	1 Timothy	2 Jn	2 John
Rom	Romans	2 Tim	2 Timothy	3 Jn	3 John
1 Cor	1 Corinthians	Titus	Titus	Jude	Jude
2 Cor	2 Corinthians	Philem	Philemon	Rev	Revelation
Gal	Galatians				

General Editor's Preface

The last three decades have witnessed a change in the understanding of the origins, nature, and development of the radical Reformation in general and the Anabaptists in particular. A growing awareness of the diversity and variety of the radical Reformers has emerged.

Essential to a grasp of the divergences and convergences of the early Anabaptists is the availability of the primary source materials of these Reformers. It has been the vision of the Institute of Mennonite Studies to make such sources available in English in the series Classics of the Radical Reformation (CRR).

The editions of CRR, though scholarly and critical, are intended also for the wider audience of those interested in the Anabaptist and free church writers of the late fifteenth, sixteenth, and early seventeenth centuries. The translations are intended to be true and polished, yet not excessively literal or wooden.

With this eighth volume in the series, we encounter a radical Reformer who was not an Anabaptist, but who has been widely credited with significantly influencing the early generations of the Anabaptists. Many themes that came to be distinctive among the Anabaptists were found first in the varied writings of Carlstadt.

We are grateful to Professor E. J. Furcha of McGill University for introducing this early radical Reformer to a larger reading public. These documents, most of which are translated into English for the first time, demonstrate that many of the concerns of the Anabaptists were shared widely during the early years of the Reformation.

—H. Wayne Pipkin, Editor, CRR
Institute of Mennonite Studies

Editor's Preface

To present Carlstadt's tracts we chose to render his German in as contemporary an English text as a translator's license permits without, we hope, having violated the original text or unduly misreading the author's intended meaning in the process of translating. In places where his intended meaning was not readily apparent, we have retained a key phrase of the original text and/or attempted a brief explanation in a note. However, we have kept explanatory notes to a minimum, primarily to avoid making the volume inordinately extensive and costly. To orient the reader, a brief explanatory note precedes each tract. Page references to the document from which each translation was prepared are included in square brackets [ ], indicating the end of a page in the original. Where the original has no pagination, the end of a page is indicated thus [//]. More seasoned specialists may want to skip these notes.

Work on this project has been enhanced by research grants from the Faculty of Graduate Studies and Research, McGill University, and by the helpful and willing cooperation of Dr. Heinz Peter Stucki of the Institut für schweizerische Reformationsgeschichte, Zurich, the Zentralbibliothek, Zurich and the Universitätsbibliothek, Basel. The translator is greatly indebted to his friend and colleague in scholarship, professor Calvin Pater of Knox College, Toronto, for willingly making his own translations of three of the tracts available as a reference point[1] and to Leszek Wysock, lecturer at Concordia University, Montreal, for providing most of the Latin translations. I am grateful to Michael A. King, Herald Press book editor, for fine work in seeing the volume through to publication. Last, but by no means least, I wish to acknowledge the cooperation of the Institute for Mennonite Studies and its associate director, professor H. Wayne Pipkin, in including this translation as volume 8 in the series Classics of the Radical Reformation.

Many hands, in addition, have assisted in preparing this volume. Among these Michael A. King must be singled out for his unstinting commitment to producing a well-crafted volume. His skillful help has made the task of translating and editing an enjoyable one and has contributed greatly toward minimizing errors or flaws. To all of the above and to my many students of Reformation history, I dedicate this volume with gratitude and affection.

—*E. J. Furcha*
McGill University

Introduction

Andreas Rudolff Bodenstein (Carlstadt), 1486-1541, from Karlstadt,[1] near Würzburg, Lower Franconia, deserves a prominent place in the honorable company of radicals of the Reformation. To make this seminal thinker and original Reformer accessible to a wider readership, we have translated fifteen tracts which represent his wide interests and show him at the cutting edge of several important issues of his day.

While traditional historiography has tended to dismiss Carlstadt as an enthusiast, several scholars in the twentieth century have been able to show his significance through careful studies of his life and by giving attention to his numerous publications. Hermann Barge's magisterial biography (published 1908 in two volumes) of this erstwhile colleague of Martin Luther at the fledgling Wittenberg University, was among the first modern studies to take Carlstadt seriously. It remains to this day an indispensable source for anyone wishing to make sense of Carlstadt's life and bring some clarity to his thought—a clarity that eluded Erich Hertzsch, among others.[2]

Barge carefully gathered fascinating material on Carlstadt, showing him to have been at once more progressive and significantly more conservative than his better-known contemporary Luther. The biography is all the more remarkable since Barge had to work from widely scattered sources and against fierce opposition from a few Lutheran scholars to his assessment of Carlstadt's place in the sixteenth-century Reformation of the church. Although minor corrections to Barge's *Karlstadt* have been made in recent years, the major thrust of the work has stood the test of time.

Since the Barge biography, numerous others have focused their attention on specific aspects of Carlstadt's work. Notable among these are U. Bubenheimer, C. A. Pater, R. Sider, and A. Zorzin. Many less detailed treatments by Reformation scholars of a variety of subjects relating to Carlstadt could readily be added.[3] To allow the reader a clearer picture of who he was, a brief outline of high points in his life is here drawn from existing biographies.

Carlstadt's Life

Carlstadt came from a small town in Lower Franconia, where he was raised in the medieval piety normative for what we might now call a middle-class family. He seems to have had clerical ambitions from an early stage of his life which brought him to the University of Erfurt (1499-1503), and to the University of Cologne (1503-1505) where for at least one year he was exposed to the teachings of Thomas Aquinas. At the newly founded university at Wittenberg, he obtained his master's degree in 1505 and some five years later his doctorate in theology. Since Luther earned his doctorate under Carlstadt, scholars presumed until fairly recently that he was Luther's elder colleague.

During a leave from the university (1515-1516), Carlstadt went to Rome. There he earned a doctorate in civil and canonical law to better qualify himself for ecclesiastical advancement. On his return to Wittenberg, he was made archdeacon, which obligated him to preach, to celebrate mass once a week, and to teach theology at the university.

His newly won insights—which he had gained largely as a result of his stay in Rome—soon led to conflicts with the hierarchy of the church. As early as 1518, he became embroiled in a conflict with John Eck, a brilliant scholar who stood for the absolute authority of the church at Rome. Among the 405 theses Carlstadt had drawn up for the debate, those stressing the absolute authority of Scripture in matters of faith and those questioning the infallibility of the church's councils stand out most prominently. A marked shift in theological emphasis away from Thomism to a distinct Augustinianism seems to have come between 1517-1519 with his commentary on Augustine's *De spiritu et litera*.

Tensions with his colleague Luther did not become acute until, in the wake of radical changes to liturgical practices in Wittenberg in 1521-1522, Carlstadt became suspect in Luther's eyes. He was eventually forced out of the territory of Electoral Saxony, although he had acquitted himself well of pastoral duties in the town of Orlamünde and seems to have been well liked by parishioners there.

On Boxing Day in 1521, Carlstadt became engaged to Anna von

Mochau, whom he married on January 19, 1522. Having openly broken his vows of celibacy, he had thus clearly stepped on the side of evangelical reform, since the right of priests to marry was an issue which pitted many an earnest cleric against the hierarchy.

For several years Carlstadt was forced to live as a fugitive, carefully balancing his evangelical faith and the desire to bring about radical changes in the life and work of the church with the need to support his growing family and to avoid imprisonment or death.

Employment through the Greatminster Foundation at Zurich in 1530 brought about welcome changes. Carlstadt ended years of wanderings, gained a new focus within the Reformed tradition, and eventually returned to academic work in 1534 in the city of Basel, Switzerland, where he remained until his death in December 1541.

This brief overview must suffice. However, for further details regarding Carlstadt's personal life and his activities, the reader is directed to Barge, Bubenheimer, Sider, and Zorzin. All provide reliable biographical data and are readily accessible in libraries and research centers.

Historical Contributions

Ulrich Bubenheimer's important monograph on Carlstadt the theologian and legal expert, published in 1977, shows him to have been an important link between scholastic thinking and reform activities.[4] The author followed up this study with a number of articles on Carlstadt's reform of congregational worship and the Christian life, on his relation to Luther, and on his reading of the late medieval mystic Johann Tauler. Bubenheimer also gets credit for the discovery of Carlstadt's year of birth. While many reference works still give conflicting dates, 1486 must now be seen as the correct year of his birth.

Calvin A. Pater argued in his *Karlstadt as the Father of the Baptist Movement* that the Reformer's contribution had far-reaching effects on Anabaptists and on all reform activities which valued discipleship and lay Christianity.[5] Pater has shown that, despite staunchly held positions on certain theological notions, lay persons and theologians alike had many more ideas in common than their occasional confrontations would suggest.

Other important aspects of this book are the author's argument for far greater kinship in essentials between the Anabaptists of Zurich and South Germany like Huldrych Zwingli and Reformers like Carlstadt; and an important realization. That realization is that Christians of the twentieth century who wish to take the radicals seriously must learn to value their insights without closing themselves off to the possibility that their alleged opponents shared common roots, drew from the same spiritual source, and worshiped the same God to whose Son they committed themselves.

Ronald Sider's monograph *Andreas Bodenstein von Karlstadt. The Development of His Thought 1517-1525* appeared almost concurrently with Bubenheimer's major work on Carlstadt. It is easily the best general study in English of Carlstadt's early years.[6]

Alejandro Zorzin, Karlstadt als Flugschriftenautor must be mentioned here as the most recent critical study of the Reformer's writings and of their dissemination and significance in the early sixteenth century.[7] Zorzin's analysis of Carlstadt's work shows as most significant the close connection between Carlstadt's life and his writing. Zorzin notes, for example, that crisis points in Carlstadt's life led to a reduction in his publishing. Sometimes he completely ceased publishing for prolonged periods. Zorzin observes six publication blocks between May 1518 and September 1525, interrupted by periods of varying length during which Carlstadt seems neither to have written extensively nor published through any of the printing houses at his disposal.

Carlstadt's Significance

Although Carlstadt has left us a literary legacy of some eighty publications, his work has never been given sufficient attention to merit a critical edition.[8] Apart from Sider's *Karlstadt's Battle with Luther*, only scattered translated excerpts from Carlstadt's tracts have appeared in journals or document collections.[9]

This volume is the first extensive collection of a cross section of Carlstadt's tracts to appear in English. A second volume, which will contain all of Carlstadt's eucharistic tracts, is currently in preparation as a joint project by Pater and Furcha. To date no other modern edition brings together in one volume as many of Carlstadt's booklets as this current volume does.

One reason for the relative neglect of Carlstadt is undoubtedly the fact that no Christian denomination has been able to identify him as its own. In denominationally oriented histories, Carlstadt has generally had a bad press for far too long to make publishing his writings an attractive undertaking. To both the Lutheran and the Reformed camps, Carlstadt has been somewhat of an enigma. Although by 1530 he seems to have been largely in tune with the aims of Zwingli and Bullinger in Zurich and was well received in Basel from 1534 on, his

German background may have posed an obstacle to his becoming fully accepted within the Swiss milieu.

Anabaptists, too, remained astonishingly distant, probably because Carlstadt lacked a clear stance on believers baptism. However, had they overlooked his return from being a lay Christian to serving as one of the "doctors" of sixteenth-century Protestants, they might have found in him much with which to resonate. Pater's analysis almost succeeded in showing Carlstadt's "paternity" of many Anabaptist tenets. Yet descendants of sixteenth-century Anabaptists have been slow to accept him as truly one of them in spirit, if not a card-carrying member of one of their conventicles or congregations. It is our sincere hope, then, that devoting a major volume in the series Classics of the Radical Reformation to Carlstadt's tracts will begin to redress the neglect his work has suffered for so long.

Much remains to be done, of course. Carlstadt's numerous writings ought to be collected in a critical edition. His correspondence must be sifted and gathered in one place. His exact place among the various agents of change and renewal in the sixteenth century needs still to be determined as we give him a careful and sympathetic hearing in the continuing process of charting his theology and ethics.

Carlstadt never had the good fortune of being heard as widely as he ought to have been, simply because the bad name he was given too often preceded knowledge of what he actually wrote or said; however, he certainly should be heard now. Today perhaps we can appreciate at last the useful, nonsectarian stance he chose to uphold in an age that seemed to thrive on partisan spirit and was incapable therefore of understanding a voice that sought to be heard above the clamor of conflicting interest groups.

Carlstadt is significant for a number of reasons. Most attractive perhaps is the manner in which he combines in his work the academic and the practical. Notable as well is his approach to ecclesiastical reform in full awareness that reforming the externals of the church will remain ineffective if not also accompanied by an inner transformation of its members to create a climate conducive to change and renewal.

While he does not unduly flaunt his learning by quoting patristic or medieval sources in detail, Carlstadt does show his extensive knowledge by allusions to canonical writings and by occasional references to saints and martyrs and to the theological nuances in the ancient doctors of the church. His knowledge of the Bible is impressive. He seems equally familiar with writings from the Old and New Testaments and quotes or paraphrases these frequently. While his interpretation of some biblical texts may be open to debate, there is no doubt about his familiarity with the Vulgate, the LXX, and probably German translations.[10]

He resonates with some of the notions of the mystics of the late medieval period such as Tauler, the *Theologia Germanica*, and Thomas à Kempis's *imitatio Christi*. However, he adapts these to formulate his own brand of evangelical Christianity which stresses inwardness, the ongoing work of the Holy Spirit, and regeneration as foundational to the reform of Christendom.

This independence of spirit is most fully apparent in his two tracts on *Gelassenheit* (documents 1 and 6 below), but comes to the fore also in the arguments he advances on the place of vows in Christian commitment (document 3), or in the shift in his understanding regarding the eucharist, which he unravels with some rhetorical skill in his "Dialogue on the Most Blessed Sacrament" (document 12).

As a result of Carlstadt's fresh approach to issues of theology and ethics, and because of his largely uncluttered style of writing, much of what Carlstadt had to say in his writings appealed to a number of his contemporaries who were concerned with the "inner experience" of the divine. Pietist thought of a later era may well have reaped some of the fruits of this inner experience in what was referred to as "true Christianity" (*wahres Christentum*); and the *Stillen im Lande* (the quiet in the land) may have patterned their lifestyle by the notion of *Gelassenheit* (yieldedness to Christ) he helped shape by his two tracts and many other references to it.

A. Zorzin has shown recently the relative success Carlstadt's publications enjoyed during his lifetime, as well as the fairly wide circle of readers he reached by publishing with different firms in at least eight cities.[11]

Carlstadt's stance was relatively moderate even in those heady years of reform in 1521-1522 during Luther's temporary absence at the Wartburg. Thus his involvement in iconoclastic activities must in retrospect be seen as having been determined by what he perceived to be the effect regenerate persons would have on ecclesiastical and social structures. He was not being guided primarily by strictly political, social, or hierarchical interests.

What seems to have mattered more than anything in his decision to participate in the removal from Wittenberg sanctuaries of so-called idols was his own inner yieldedness—Gelassenheit—to the perceived will of God and his concern for "weak consciences." These latter, he concluded, should—for their own and the church's good—no longer be exposed to the external temptations of having their old ways constantly before their eyes.[12]

In his theology and practice of the sacraments, notably baptism and the Lord's Supper, Carlstadt advances some important insights. His ability to undergo changes in worldview make him a most attractive Reformer in an age which was still largely dominated by intolerance toward divergent views and practices. A major impetus for Carlstadt's rethinking of the nature of the eucharist may well have come from the understanding of the relevant biblical passages advanced by Cornelius Hoen which also found acceptance, in part at least, with Huldrych Zwingli and Caspar von Schwenckfeld. The key was to be found in Hoen's reading of John 6 as significant for the "correct" interpretation of the intended meaning of the words of Jesus, "This is my body."

Like so many of his contemporaries, Carlstadt began his theological career firmly rooted in the scholasticism being taught in the early sixteenth century at Erfurt and Cologne. However, he was deeply affected by the observed worldliness of Rome and the profligate behavior of monks, priests, and prelates. As a result, he began distancing himself from scholasticism by turning to a religious internalizing which, because it drew on the language of the medieval mystics, has often been described as spiritualism or mysticism.[13]

What he intended, however, seems more akin to the New Testament idea of rebirth or regeneration than to the gradual ascent of the soul toward union with the divine, as the medieval mystics appear to have envisaged it. In his writings after 1523, this focus on regeneration comes to the fore and brings Carlstadt close to arguing for separate communities of regenerate people. What prevented him from going wholly in this direction remains an open question.

His exposure to Zwingli and Bullinger in Zurich and the relatively congenial academic and spiritual climate of Basel may well have played a significant role in his final accommodation to Reformed thinking as practiced in the two Swiss cities. He was welcomed into these circles for the last eleven to twelve years of his life.

However, Carlstadt remained his own person even in this last period of his life. Thus it would not be wholly appropriate, without further study, to equate Reformed thought and Carlstadt's thinking during the last phase of his theological development. It is clear, however, that he stressed the community of the spirit while acknowledging that ecclesiastical ordering has a rightful place. In Basel especially, he worked toward preparing ministers of the Word of God who would be firm in their knowledge of the Scriptures and be malleable under the guidance of the spirit of God. This would allow them, in turn, to point to Christ and act as spiritual midwives when hearers of the word learned to internalize it in appropriate ways.

To support the above sketch of the essentials in Carlstadt's thought, we have chosen fifteen key tracts of his (ranging from 1520 to 1534) which state in his own inimitable way what he considered essential in any reform of Christian life and practice. We limited our selections to his German tracts, since we believe his concern for common Christians was a dominant characteristic of his writing and publishing since at least 1520, perhaps as far back as 1518.

Furthermore, the tracts in this volume reflect a good sampling of the variety of issues he dealt with and provide us with a reasonably rounded understanding of his reform activities. Apart from the 1524 "Dialogue on the Most Blessed Sacrament" (document 12 below) and apart from material that appears in the *Main Points of Christian Teaching* of 1525 (document 14), we have not, however, included Carlstadt's writings on the sacraments.

The Essential Carlstadt

1

Tract on the Supreme Virtue of Gelassenheit[1]

Dr. Andreas Bodenstein from Karlstadt

[1520]

*Carlstadt wrote this tract in October 1520, shortly after the Papal Bull **Exsurge domine** and a letter from John Eck had been received in Wittenberg. Subsequent editions appeared in different printing shops in 1520 and 1521 (see Freys/Barge, numbers 38-42).*

*At this stage in his career, Carlstadt was still identified with Luther's reform work. However, the tone of the tract suggests that Carlstadt was beginning to rethink his position, probably inspired by notions transmitted from late medieval mysticism through such tracts as **imitatio Christi** by Thomas à Kempis and **German Theology** by an anonymous author. The radical changes hinted at were to bring about transformation in his attitude toward organized Christianity within the next three years. In 1523 Carlstadt published with a Wittenberg print-shop an even more detailed analysis of the notion of **Gelassenheit, The Meaning of the Term Gelassen and Where in Holy Scripture It Is Found** (see document 6 below, and Freys/Barge, 104, 105).*

The notion of Gelassenheit was widely used by other contemporaries, both traditionalists and Reformers. It was particularly popular among Anabaptists who expressed their "existentialist" commitment to the immediacy of the divine will to which they were prepared to submit themselves in total abandonment and to the exclusion of external human intermediaries.

In this as well as in the later tract, Carlstadt focuses on the dimension of physical and spiritual suffering, self-emptying, or self-denial before the overpowering presence of the divine. Since God's nature and will are perceived to be benevolent and graciously inclined toward the yielded person, Carlstadt implies that the ultimate outcome of being **Gelassen** *toward God is to receive divine approval and blessedness.*

The translation of this early Carlstadt tract was made from a photocopy of the volume located in Zentralbibliothek, Zurich.

Peace, joy, love and a strong Christian faith from God through our Lord Jesus Christ, I, Andreas Bodenstein, desire for my dear mother and all my friends. Amen.

I might well say now in deep anxiety, O God, my Lord, Creator, Redeemer, my refuge, my body and life, do not leave me [mar: Ps 12,[2] *tribulatio prima est*;[3] Ps 91:15. I will be with him in trouble. A Psalm of Invocation].[4] Do not leave me, for sorrow, trials, and temptations are very close to me. Nothing is closer to me than anxiety, and there is no one to rescue me except you alone, as you spoke through your true and unchanging word. "I will be with him in tribulation; I will redeem him from sorrow; and he shall praise me."[5] You also said, "Cry to me on the day of your suffering, misery, and pain and I shall help you."[6] Lord, you are a righteous and true God; your judgment and your promise are truth itself. Through this, your word, you comfort all believers. You desire no more than for me to believe in you, to believe that you are my Creator, my help, my Redeemer from all evil, and my Savior. You say, "If you can believe that I can and will help you, I shall help you." [mar: *credite quia accipietis*—"Believe that you receive it" Mk 11:23]. Yes, my God, all my comfort, heart, concern, and soul stands by you. How certain is the word of your truth; be mindful of that for the sake of your servant (yes, your small worm) [Mt 9:22, *Secundum fidem vestram fiat vobis*—"According to your faith be it done to you"]. In your promise you gave me all my hope [Ps 119:43; Ps 22; Ps 119]. This hope alone which my spirit received from your word, comforts me in my misery and sorrow. My Lord, do not leave me; do not ever take out of my weak heart the word of your true promise. [mar: Strong bulls][7] Stand by me with your help and redemption. For many calves and bulls surround me, my God, my Lord and my only help: Annas, Caiaphas, the scribes and hypocrites who do not give much attention to what your word and law contain and of what use they are. The pope, several cardinals and some bishops open their throats and yawn with their traps like wild roaring and devouring lions. The [//][8] Florentine lion[9] opens his mouth and is about to swallow me. Hear my cry now, O my God. Look upon my misery, assess for yourself what he is about to do to me; note my anxiety and redeem me. For the lion, along with several calves and bulls, is about to snatch my body and soul. I do not complain because of this temporal life (nature has nothing more noble, precious and dear than this miserable life), but rather because of my spiritual life [mar: Mt 10:28 . . . *nolite timere qui occidunt*—"do not fear those who kill the body"].

Undeservedly and without any merit on my part you have reborn me by the word of your truth, as is written, "He gave birth to us by the word of his truth that we might become his creatures."[10] In your word (i.e., in your promises and pledges), you bore us spiritually unto yourself, in faith, love, comfort, and hope, and you enlivened us.

If God had not enlivened us by his word [Ps 119;[11] Rom 10:6; Lk 1:25; Jn. 4:41], David would not have made this speech and prayer, "Enliven me, according to your word." Faith depends on your word. Paul wrote, "Faith comes from the hearing of the word," and Elizabeth verified this. Blessed are you for believing the word. Therefore, John the evangelist said, "The man or the official believed the words and promises of Christ and went away; and his son *[sic!]* stayed alive." Now, since faith is attached to the word of truth and since no one doubts that the righteous person lives by faith, it follows indisputably that we receive and attain to Christian life through the word of divine promise [Hab 2:4; Rom 1:16].

This life, Lord, (this most noble life which renews a person and brings about faith and every fruit pleasing to God, and which also makes us pleasing and acceptable to God, on which salvation is grounded, and without which we can expect nothing but hellish death) several calves and bulls want to take from me.[12] They are intent on killing my spirit which lives in your word [Mt 10:26ff.].

Because of them fear has enveloped me, as you yourself said, "Fear the one who kills the spirit." They say that I must renounce and deny your word and they threaten to cut me off, to ban and curse me, to rob me of honor and possessions, body and soul. Lord, the fat bulls surround me. And yet, this suffering is nothing compared to the suffering my spirit must face when they [threaten] to take the word of your promise out of my heart and understanding. Compared to death it is to be considered like a small festering [A ij] sore, or like a kernel of sand over against a mountain.

Therefore, Lord, look down from the heavens. Note my distress, suffering, and affliction, and my being spun around. I stand in hellish anguish, in pain of death, in hellish trials; with hands and feet I am nailed to your cross. Hear my lamentation and wailing and note what they are undertaking, how they stick out their tongues and how they shout like the Jews (at the cross), "He trusted in God, let him now save him, for he desired him" [Ps 22:8]. Do they not abominably say the same thing when they say that I ought to think on your word of truth and wait a while? If I fall from your word, I end up having fallen away and far from you. If I forget your promise, you, too, will not think of me. If I depart from your Scriptures, the devil with all his misfortune and evil will soon find me, torture me, and possess me forever. Therefore, help and redeem me.

I am solely comforted by Christ on the cross who also had to hear and suffer such robbers of God's word. I am further comforted that each tribulation washes away sin, if its pain is endured in faith [Tob 3:5] and has been accepted through hope in God [Jas 1:2ff.]. Thirdly, God tests and proves our faith through temptation. Fourthly, I rejoice that all suffering is a punishing rod with which the heavenly Father visits, cleanses, and beautifies his children. I am also constantly refreshed by the word of God which says that the living, merciful God descended into hell and ascended again. He castigates so that he might show mercy. The righteous Job says, "Do not despise or ridicule the punishment and pain of the Lord, for he wounds what he heals, he beats what his hand restores to health" [Prov 3:11f.; Heb 12:5f.; 1 Sam 1; Lam 3:31f.; Job 5:18].

God casts me into deep waters and makes all his rivers flow over me [Ps 23:2]; God pins me down in the mud with bulls and ruttish calves;[13] had God not led me there, they would not be able to do anything to me [Deut 31]. Should I despair then—since God averts his face from me and hides himself; since every evil has found me and burst in on me—lest he has forsaken me? That, in the judgment of the world, God is not with me? Far be it from me to believe that God has totally forsaken me.

Christ says, "O my God, why have you forsaken me?" [//] He laments to God, yet commends his spirit to him, saying, "Father, into your hands I commit my spirit" [Mt].[14] Why then should I despair? He names him "father" and calls on him, yet feels abandonment, nonetheless. So the word of God is true (when it says), "I am with you in sorrow and anguish, in pain and misery." Therefore, Christ in his suffering must ever be before my eyes and go ahead of me. Although God permits me to be beaten and ridiculed, boiled or roasted, broken on a wheel and torn to pieces, I know, nonetheless, that he is my God, that he is in control of my life and my suffering, and that he is my redeemer. Therefore, I will put my hope in him and cry unto him. And although he should kill and murder me (as Job says), I will hope in him, nonetheless. And though I should see with my own eyes how he stirs up Annas and Caiaphas, calves and bulls, lions and bears, and incites them against me, I shall call on him, nonetheless [Job 13:3].

Lord, my hope and consolation are in you. In you I have placed my hope; in you shall I hope. Therefore, do not leave me forever. Maintain me in your wholesome word. Firm me up and make me strong, according to your word and I shall live [Ps 119:33ff.]. Lord, do not dash my hope and expectation, and set me free from the jaws of the lion [Ps 22:21] and from the horns of unicorns who press in on me exceedingly greatly. They make of me a fable for the people and a laughingstock for everyone. They say that I am a stranger and alien to you. But, Lord, avert my eyes so that I cannot see the great evil of their great wickedness and unkindness [Ps 119:39, 134]. Then shall I have an answer for those who taunt me.[15] Let salvation be my portion according to your word. Then I will answer those same mockers,[16] "Yes, I trust in God's promise." Do not allow them to tear your word of truth out of my heart, so that one who loves your law and clings to your word and speech may depend and build on it and have great peace. Abundant peace to those who love the law.[17] They shall never be forsaken, although for a little while you [God] may appear to be strange and far away. As Job says [Job 19:9], "He robbed me of my glory and has taken away the crown of my head. He shattered me altogether and I perish. He took away my hope like that of a tree which has been uprooted. His wrath is kindled against me and he treated me like an enemy. Nonetheless, I know that my redeemer lives and I know [A iij] that I shall see him." This hope has been put in my bosom. I will cry unto him therefore, and hope; I shall do this as long as God's grace assists me to do so.

Therefore, my mother, brothers and sisters, uncles, cousins, brothers-in-law and sister-in-law, and all my dear friends in Christ, I beg of you, do not hurt and afflict yourselves because of the temporary shame, the tribulations and anxiety that surround me on all sides. I see two deaths before my eyes, one of which I must suffer. On the right, death threatens to destroy and kill my spirit and torture me forever. On the left, stands the death to my flesh. I must accept one of them. If I love and preserve my flesh by following the Florentine lion, my spirit is bound to fall away from the word of God and die eternally.

Is it not better then, since I must die, not to lose anything (except a short time in this life), to suffer the death of body and flesh and thus preserve the life of the spirit, rather than to love this perishable life of mine and spoil myself for all eternity? The righteous St. Andrew rejoiced in his heart that he was to die on a cross on account of his master Jesus Christ—and he was righteous and holy. Why should not this poor and great sinner, also desire to die, on account of the one who first died for my sin, my evil life, for my good and my benefit? If I flee physical death, the eternal hellish death shall destroy me—body and soul. Christ died in bitterness and he rose again so that he might sweeten death for us and remove its sting. I enquire by your conscience and by the strong and living God, and call on heaven and hell, trees and grass, wood and stone to be my witnesses, so that you will have to say and confess that, according to the word of God, I am bound to die. If I am bound to die, why then do you want to mourn over whether the lion or the fire shall destroy me? If you love God and your honor, you would encourage and admonish me, as did the mother of Symphorianus,[18] at the moment when the executioner leads me to the stake, saying, Son or cousin, be of good cheer. Is there a more precious way [//] to give up your life? For you will go from a miserable and perishable life to the divine and eternal life. Be of good cheer and fear not.

I know that you had rather I allowed myself to be murdered than that I should deny my territorial prince or that I should betray a city. Granted, I have temporal sustenance and much work from my territorial lord. But from there I receive physical and spiritual birth, daily life, temporal sustenance, honor, possessions, faith, hope, and the promise of eternal life. I know that he is my gracious lord when he makes me anxious. Should I then flee death when no one wants to rob me of that same lord and force me to diminish, deny, and reject his unerring word. [mar: *Scoma in papam*][19] This is what the tyrannical and alleged Pope Leo X dares to do. Would I not be an evildoer and traitor toward my most gracious Prince Elector[20] and suzerain if I should throw away and deny a letter (entrusted to me by His Grace and which I promised to handle)? How then can I renounce and reject Holy Scripture?

Through my godparents and sponsors (who lifted me out of baptism), I promised God and the Christian church to remain and die in the faith [mar: *Patrinos notat*—Note my godparents]. Now faith is contained in Holy Scripture as in an enclosed garden. How then can I recant Scripture without reneging on my oath and my faith? [mar: Fides hortus conclusus—Faith is an enclosed garden]

I let you know that often during my mature years I bound myself to Holy Scripture with oaths, never to depart from it. Should I now deny the articles which an unlearned Pope [*mar: Indoctus Papa*] condemns, but which I know to be grounded in Scripture, yes, more than that, several of which I can explain in words, sentences, and with my hand? Yes, why would you desire (something I should not attend to, anyhow) that I deny the same (to my eternal shame and harm), and break my many vows and oaths? I should be an evildoer with regard to all that is right and a fugitive knave and you, a dishonest friend if you were to think that I ought not endure fire and tongs. I do not want to negate any truth, especially not if I am under oath to it, even if all the devils along with the [//] pope were against me. God will surely help me to this.

Yes, some may say, the pope too understands the Bible quite well, but you have a raving, proud mind. To this I should answer, dear friend, I have the text of the Holy Bible which is so clear that not only a scholar, but also a layperson who hears it read, is able to understand it. In this way also I generally read my response and argument at Leipzig from the Bible and from the books of Augustine, Jerome, Ambrose, Bernhard, Gregory, Cyprian, Cyril, and others—to stop, flee, and avert from me any suspicion of heresy [mar: The Pope labels Augustine a heretic!].

My enemies hold this up to me to my shame, although I did it for the sake of my honor and in order to anticipate what I am now facing. Thus no one can say, "He understands Scripture according to his own lights," and the pope cannot condemn me as a heretic without also condemning the pillars of the Christian church, as I have just shown [mar: *Truculentus papa*—cruel father]. But as you shall note, this fierce raving person, Pope Leo X, never looked at a single one of them, yet seeks to force me away from the Bible, against God, right, and honor. He shall not accomplish this, even if he should light a fire as large as the entire earth.

Should you also fall prey to the lion and burden yourselves with unnecessary concern, you must know that my sorrow will be to your honor [Eph 4]. The apostles thanked God and left the Council of the Jews with joy because God considered them worthy of suffering for the sake of the name and word of Christ [Acts 5:41]. Why then should not I, too, and you with me, rejoice in suffering on account of our Redeemer? I know well that no suffering is worthy of the future glory. Therefore, rejoice with me that God called me to suffer on account of his word.

But, if you should become soft and undertake to keep me from it, I will say to you, as Moses said [Deut 33:9], "He said to his father and mother, I do not know you and to his brothers and sisters, I know nothing of you. And those who did not know their children, knew and kept your covenant, your word, and your judgment."

Therefore, I, too, shall leave you and if you should say, dear son or uncle, follow the pope, I will dare say, Who are you? [//] May God preserve me from you and your counsel. If a bishop's miter can protect me from error, then Christ inappropriately resisted Annas and Caiaphas. In this matter I know neither father nor mother. I follow divine Scripture alone—it cannot err; it cannot deceive me. Although I should have to endure shame, derision, poverty, and misery, I shall do so happily.

[mar: Archdiaconate: if I be found to have forfeited it] I will willingly divest myself of my archdiaconate and all the goods which I have; forgive father, mother, brothers, and sisters; and surrender [*Gelassen*] everything in body and soul which draws me away and distances me from divine promises. I know that I must be yielded [Gelassen], and that I must let go [Gelassen] of all creatures, and that I must not trust any angel who wishes to teach and bless me other than as delineated in the Bible [Gal 1:8f.]. Everything which an angel from heaven teaches, other than what is contained in Holy Scripture, is an abomination [*vermaledeiung*], dreaded and hateful, worthy of excommunication and banning before God. Why then should I fall for a person [mar: the pope] who has not studied Holy Scripture much, when he wishes to teach me contrary to that which is written in Holy Scripture?

But if the pope is righteous and a Christian, let him show me Scripture and overcome my teaching with the word of God. I have always taken my teaching from the Bible and can prove it through Scripture. I trust that almighty God shall give me grace so that I cannot depart from his word, although this might aggrieve all my enemies.

I recall the word of Christ who speaks as follows [mar: *Gladius*, Mt 10:34f.], "Do not think that I have come to bring peace to earth. I have come to send a sword—a sword which separates children from their parents, wives from their husbands, brothers from sisters, yes, the soul from the body." It is written [Rom 8:35-39], "The sword separates soul and body and places a person wholly and totally in the divine will, in love, hope, and faith, in such a way that neither derision nor need, neither sword nor danger, neither torture nor fire shall separate us from God." Innumerable sighs and pain arise in such a person when he [B] takes the sword properly into hands of faith. For this is the sword which now separates me from the pope and which shall separate the pope from Christendom, which Christ sent us and of which he wrote as follows [Lk 22:36; mar: *Qui habet tunicam vendat eam, et emat gladium, et ema relinquat propter verbum*—Let the one who has a mantle sell it and buy a sword, etc."].[21] But now in the beginning of death, whoever has a pouch or bag and who does not have a purse or bread basket, will sell his coat and buy a sword for it. What kind of sword is this? Hear what Christ says.

This is the sword: Scripture must be fulfilled. I observe then that Scripture is the sword which we are to purchase. And this same sword must be accomplished with suffering, blood, and death.

Yes Lord, it is right. On account of this same sword I have to surrender my bag, purse, clothes; in other words, the least and the externally greatest goods and everything else to boot [Mt 25]. My old Adam will probably whisper, "Ask God to remove the cup of death from you."[22] But the spirit will say, "My Lord, not as I, but as you will."[23] On account of the same sword, i.e., the word of God which separates me from father, mother, brother and sister and from all friendship, I dare say it.

Christ cannot be found amidst friendship, but in his temple within which his word rings out, so that the Pharisees and hypocrites, the pope and all his ninnies shall marvel and go nuts. In that same temple (which is a yielded person), God is;[24] Christ our Lord is found. In this case I shall not find Christ with you, my sorrowful friends, but you will write to me and sound off, "Dear friend, far be it from you to be captured, cut in pieces, and killed by the pope at Rome." Just as poor Peter said to Christ, "Lord, far be it from you that you should be captured, beaten, and killed by the Jews at Jerusalem" [Mt 26:33ff.]. You will thus hear badly. Although Peter had a sound, worldly, natural opinion, as he and other Christians might have, [//] Christ, nonetheless, said to Peter, "Get away from me, Satan, you devil, you obstructer. For you do not understand what God wills, but only what is human" [Mt 16:23]. In some such manner I shall answer you, if you dare say to me, "You had better stop what you are doing. Those who seek to bind you to the pope through the Word of God, are not well-disposed toward you. What if you had remained well and enjoyed honor!" You devils, depart from me, all of you, for you do not know what is of God.

[mar: John Hus] Did not the righteous, Christian, and highly learned Dr. John Hus receive and suffer a bitter sword?[25] They condemned him for his good, righteous teaching, the greater part of whose articles are found in Scripture. They placed on this strong martyr a miter full of painted devils, and they then burned him, and in this way ridiculed him. I fear that I may also become such a ridiculed bishop, though unmerited; my friends have a hard time swallowing this. But then Scripture comforts me with Christ speaking through his word, "You must not think that I have come to make peace; for I came to set a man against his father and a son against his mother."[26] Therefore, dear friends, I have to be against you, if you should try to draw me away from the word of God.

But why do you want to impute that the matter is right and Christian and so high that I am unworthy to suffer on its behalf? If you want to continue in your carnal love, I do not know you and am against you, as I am against the pope who is not my father, as he claims, but a wolf [mar: *Papa lupus, non pater*—The pope is a wolf, not a father]. Whoever loves father and mother more than me is unworthy of me.[27] Holy Scripture in which Christ lives and dwells as if being in a temple is available to me. But if I join the pope, I should leave Christ in Scripture [Mt 10]. And if you cling to the pope and I should want to attach myself to you, I would become odious to Christ and his enemy. Remember that the daughter of Jephthah [Judg 11:35ff] sealed her father's vows with her death. Why then should not I seal the vows of my godparents who pledged me to God at my baptism? Yes, not only must I detach myself from you, but from myself as well. I must have no regard for my body and soul [B ij].

[mar: The cross] I must wrong myself and be irksome and willingly face death. For Christ says, "Whoever does not take up his cross and follow me, is not worthy of me" [Lk 14:27]. The term cross means suffering, scorn, sneering, mockery, ridicule, death, and destruction. Yes, it means descending into the abyss of hell, yet in God's pleasure it also means that a kernel of grain must die unto Christ [Jn 12:24].

Now, since Christ says that we must take up the cross and follow him, it is necessary that in the end we are fastened to the cross (i.e., to misery and pain). Therefore, do not concern yourselves, even if I should be tied to a fire-grate and be burned. Was not Christ truly human and God, yet he was not ashamed to hang on the gallows and die.

Since on account of my old Adam I have no intention of running after the cross, nor do I especially long for the fire, therefore, I shall flee the Florentine lion from one place to another (just as David fled Absalom). If I find favor in the eyes of the Lord, he shall bring me back again and protect me [2 Sam 15:8]. But if he should say, "You do not please me," I am aware that it must happen in that way since he wills my good, even though it may appear to me like bitter and acrid gall and pus. It would be a thousand times more beneficial to take up the cross and suffer shameful and painful death than for me to abjure God's word and deny Christ [Mt 10:33]. For I know that if I allow my soul to perish and die on account of the word of Christ our Lord and God, I shall preserve it for eternity. But if I find my soul here, i.e., if I love it so as to flee suffering and misery and falsify or negate God's word, I shall corrupt my soul.

Hear then and note, dear friends, if I yield myself on account of God's honor, why then should I not leave you and deny you when you seek to turn me away from God's word [Lk 14:26ff]? I know that I cannot be a disciple and follower of Christ unless I leave father and mother, brother and sister, all my friends, my own nature, and everything else [*Haut und Haar*]. Everything within and around me must be yielded—everything that prevents body and soul to attain to the kingdom of heaven [//]. May the gracious God grant that. Amen.

[mar: Gelassenhait] I know that there is no greater virtue on earth and in heaven than detachment, when a person leaves behind all possessions, honor, friends, body, and soul. Even if I should burn in the midst of the flames, but if I have no detachment, my suffering would be of no merit to me, i.e., if I did not love God and place my trust, comfort, faith, and hope in him, I would be like a sounding bell [1 Cor 13:1].

Christ says, "No one has greater love than to give his life for his friends" [Jn 3:1].[28]

I have friends in Christ (whom the precious blood of Christ fashioned); on their account I am to suffer (so that they might not decrease in God's word). No evil, fire, or death can happen beneficially without divine love. The reason: Anyone who loves God aright seeks nothing other than God's honor in suffering and works, in sweetness and bitterness. But the one who places himself before his eyes and pursues his own glory, loves himself and not God, and does not serve God in any of his suffering, or else merely through works. For this reason Paul says [1 Cor 13:2], "Although I believe in miracles so that mountains should move themselves into the sea on my word, but if I have no divine love, and if I do not hate, my faith would be of no avail."

Therefore, Christ diligently admonishes us, saying, "Whoever wants to follow me, must deny himself, carry his cross daily, and follow me" [Lk 9:23].

[mar: Gelassenhait in suffering and works] Is it not a painful matter that I cannot accept any suffering as if it were my own doing? If I desire to suffer something or carry a cross for God's sake, I must first deny and forsake myself. I must totally submerge my own will in God's will and drown self-will in all things. Hence, I must will as God wills.

[mar: Gelassenhait of all persons] Therefore he places detachment ahead of works and suffering, even people themselves, saying, Whoever wants to come after me, must deny himself. See and hear how works fall away from self-will. If you want to hear of suffering, note what he says about the cross [B iij].

[mar: Lk 9:26 *Qui erubuerit sermones meos*—whoever is ashamed of my words]

He must deny himself and take up his cross. Whoever is ashamed of me and my words, of him I will also be ashamed. How hard this is to nature. Nature likes to think highly of itself and is naturally ashamed of God's honor. Therefore, Christ says, "He must deny himself," i.e., he must be ashamed and seek to praise me. For anyone who seeks his own honor in works or suffering seeks self-interest and is not totally yielded. One must never testify to oneself in one's cross, but to God alone through Christ. "You must deny yourself and not boast" [Lk 9], for the apostles rejoiced in suffering on account of the name of Christ. Nonetheless, Paul reproaches himself for having clung too firmly to glorying in his suffering, saying, "I was foolish in being too joyous and in glorying too greatly in my suffering" [2 Cor 12:11]. All nature—be it sweet or sour, sharp or mild—must be drawn out of my eyes. I must have no standing in my own eyes, but Christ alone. He alone is to be in my thoughts and before my eyes. In him and in nothing else, I must stand.

Now that I must deny all works, my suffering and death, yes, even myself, and must alienate myself from myself, neither mother nor friend, pope or the pope's mother must dare make me put him or them before my eyes and cause me to depart from God's word. I would rather suffer tongs, torture, and most gruesome death. Christ our Lord clearly expressed how detachment ought to be [Lk 14:33]. He said, "Whoever does not hate his soul, cannot be my disciple."

I must develop a tough, serious, and rigorous hatred and envy against myself when I hear the voice of my Lord and note how my soul draws me away and blocks me. No, dear soul and dear body, though you dislike to die and though you want me not to follow the word of God, I shall nonetheless follow Christ cheerfully unto death.

[mar: *Diabolus et suus papa*—Satan and his father] I know beforehand that both of you shall fight with me and that I must let you. And I also know that if I myself do not harm myself, the devil and the pope are also unable to harm me.

If you, my flesh and blood and you, old Adam, would die gladly, what could and would death concern me? [//]

I know that I shall not be spared the daily trials I endure, such as.[29] Yes, God's verities and promises are indeed just and do not deceive anyone, but I am not one who is equipped for them. "You evil flesh, you vile enemy concupiscence, how often you lead me astray." [mar: Mk 11:24 *Orantes credite quia accipietis*][30] God is merciful and mighty to give, and he will give to everyone who asks in faith and who does not doubt that he shall grant it. Therefore, (wicked Adam), I shall believe in God to spite you; I shall avoid[31] you and all my friends and I shall defend myself against you as against my enemies.

My sins too (of which I have many), ought to cause me readily to accept with greater patience and more readily to suffer sneers and scoffing. Death shall be to me as a healthy medicine, for I also know that Scripturest does not lie which says [Jn 12:25], "Whoever hates his life in this world, shall keep it unto eternal life." Likewise, "Christ came to save sinners."[32] Likewise, "this is the lamb which carries the sin of the world."[33] Likewise, "recall your sins and I shall forget them" [Isaiah].[34] And finally this promise [Jn 15:16], "If you remain in me and my words in you, then everything you ask shall be given you."

On these and other comforting promises, I shall stand as upon a rock. As much as is granted me, I shall remain firmly in Christ; in faith, hope, and love; and I shall flee no tumult. I shall be in God, in full confidence that he will maintain me in his word and equip me with eternal life after I suffered death. May the gracious God help me and all of us to this.

AMEN

I have this to bring to you regarding carnal love and fear, written as best I could, so that you may escape God's wrath. And I humbly beg of you not to allow any slander to distress you, and I commend the matter to God in sincere prayer. This would be my greatest reward. With this, God be with you.

2

Regarding the Worship and Homage of the Signs of the New Testament

Andreas Bodenstein from
Karlstadt Wittenberg

[1521]

Published in 1521, this booklet addresses the issue of the right interpretation of communion in and with Christ. Carlstadt obviously no longer held the scholastic understanding of transubstantiation. He was not, however, in agreement with Luther's "in, with, and under" description of the divine presence and did not as yet share the notion of spiritual presence, as Zwingli was to develop it.

On the basis of his reading of key biblical texts, Carlstadt does grope for an understanding of the breaking of bread and the drinking from the cup by both clergy and laity that would more closely resemble what Carlstadt believed the practice of Jesus and his disciples to have been. As in his other writings on the Lord's Supper, the simplicity of the biblical meal is the key to "purging" the use of signs in Christian worship from obtrusive additions and falsifications.

The tract is not without seeming contradictions. At times, Carlstadt's meaning is unclear and difficult to grasp. Fortunately, he limits himself to twenty short sections and leaves it to Albrecht Dürer,[1] the intended recipient of the booklet, to fill in the necessary "evangelical" details.

To number this prominent painter among Carlstadt's patrons may seem surprising. Although Dürer's work as graphic artist, painter, and writer found extensive expression in religious works such as altar pieces, ornamentation of the New Testament in German, and other religious works, he seems to have been committed to Christian humanism more than to the Protestant Reformation. Carlstadt would have known him through the circle around the humanist Willibald Pirckheimer and such radical Reformerss as Hans Denck and Sebastian Franck, who would have met Dürer in his native Nuremberg. By what means Carlstadt assumed Dürer to have been informed of evangelical teachings is not clear.

Freys/Barge have identified three extant printings of this tract, published in Wittenberg, Augsburg, and Strasbourg respectively. Our translation is based on a copy of the Augsburg edition, located in the UB, Basel, signature F.L. viii.16. Cf. Freys/Barge, Verzeichnis der Schriften, no. 69.

To the honorable and renowned Albrecht Dürer of Nuremberg, my dear patron, I, Andreas Bodenstein, extend God's grace and peace.

Gracious patron, since hatred and envy have given rise to many lies and libellous sayings perpetrated behind the backs of us Wittenbergers; and since wickedness always seeks out hiding places from which to bark, cajole, and chatter; and since some inventors of dreams allege that hereabouts we preach and dispute but do not accord any honor, praise, and dignity to the most blessed sacrament, I wish to dedicate to you a short booklet regarding the worship and homage of the above-named sacrament. Through this I hope to render due service to all of Christendom, and fulfill my obligation to you for your kindnesses toward me by serving you to the best of my ability. God be with you.

Dated, Wittenberg, All Saints Day in the twenty-first year of fifteen hundred.

1. First of all, it should be noted that worship is a fruit of faith, for true worshipers must worship in spirit and in truth, Jn 4:23. Faith makes spiritual; it unites believers with Christ in whom all creatures are made new and spiritual. Just as a person becomes a Christian through faith, so one also becomes spiritual, as is written, "He gave them power to become sons of God, as many believed in his name," Jn 1:12. Without this faith all prayer is blasphemy, contempt of God, lies, and deceit. God cannot be moved in this way. It were better by far if a person did not pray at all than to pray without faith. *Peccatori dixit*

deus—"God says to the sinners, 'Why do you take my testament in your mouth?' " Ps 50:16 and Is 1:15. "I will avert my eyes from you when you pray." Without faith it is impossible for anyone to please God, Heb 10.[2] Such faith has its own truth and word, as we read, "Faith comes through hearing the word of Christ," Rom 10:17.[3]

"My sheep hear my voice," Jn 10:3ff. I shall lead them to pasture and feed them in the mountains of Israel, Ezek 34:13. Similarly, "whoever does not hear him shall be removed from the people," Acts 3:23.[4] Just as faith fastens its eyes on Christ, so does it also on the word of Christ, and of all the prophets. Anyone who does not have the divine promises in his heart when he prays, does not truly pray; rather, he prays in the visions and machinations of the heart. It follows from this that no one prays correctly in seeking salvation, unless he worships God in faith. This leads him to Christ and through Christ to God. It follows further that Christ does not become for him the way, the truth, and the life if he does not continue to dwell in the words of Christ. It is written, "My disciples remain in my word," Jn 8:51. In short, it is impossible for you to believe aright when you are not in the truth of the divine promises. As unlikely as it is for faith to spring up and be sustained without the word, so unlikely is it that you can truly pray outside of [A ij] God's word. These two aspects of prayer Christ sums up as follows, "When you pray, believe that you receive it and you will."[5] In these words you find both spirit and truth. The spirit is in the term "believe"; the truth in "that you receive." Everything we desire in prayer, we must believe that it will be given us. God has given us his promises which indicate what he will give and what we ought to ask; without that we do not know what is good and beneficial for us. Note, it is here that we learn to expect something through prayer to the one whom we worship.[6] From this derives the premise that I ought not worship that from which I cannot receive and which cannot give me anything. One who pleads with and begs for something from someone he knows cannot give it is a fool.

In this connection I could appropriately speak of bread and wine in the sacrament. I could examine what the bread and wine give us, and how we are to worship them; but I shall hold back until a more suitable time.

• In Hebrew "to worship" often means "to bend one's knees and to fall down and pay homage." It is often used that way, as for example in Gen 49:8, "The children of your father shall pay homage to you."

• Though such worship is insignificant and common, God prohibited, nonetheless, that we should render such honor to creatures and worship them as gods. Thus God forbade us to worship either sun or moon.

2. Let me now speak of bread and wine. I wish to say that I do not like to use the human, popish, and deceptive term "form of bread and form of wine." I have amply written of this in my booklet *On Both Forms* which I dedicated to George Reich. God willing, I will soon have it printed.[7]

3. Accordingly, I ask whether the bread over which the priest thanked God or spoke a blessing [A ij] is to be worshiped, though it is said that the bread is the body of Christ?

4. First of all, I believe that the bread and wine (which the papists call "the form of bread and wine") have not been instituted so that we should honor them on bended knee or accord them such ceremony.

• The Gospel describes clearly how bread and wine are to be used. There is nothing secret when he [Christ] presents the bread to be eaten and the wine to be drunk, saying, "Eat the bread which is my body and drink the wine which is my blood."[8] Had Christ desired and intended us to honor bread and wine with our eyes, on bent knees, with kisses and remonstrances, he would have been wise and vocal enough not to have kept that fact hidden from us.

I therefore do not lavish particular praise on the Mass for Innocents[9] (which was designed and endowed to have the Blessed Sacrament carried about). For I know that in trying to please and serve God with external things, I am setting aside his law and the way he wants me to live in imitation of Christ. I am also aware that I am not to use ceremomies in any way other than that which God is prepared to accept. Now, Christ has said that we are to eat his flesh and drink his blood. It is for this reason that I believe the Blessed Sacrament is not meant to be honored through adoration.

5. It does not follow, however, that because bread and wine are not intended for our adoration or reverencing, you therefore are not to afford bread and wine any honor at all. For we all know that Christ says, "I did not come that you might serve me, but rather that I might serve you," Jn 13.[10]

Nonetheless, he praises the kindness and care of the woman who washed his feet with her tears, caressed him with her face, and kissed him with her lips, Lk 7:38. And at the same time Christ said that the woman did well and had done a good [A iij] deed when she poured costly ointment on his head, Mt 26:10.[11] Neither did he scold Martha or punish Zachaeus for taking him to their homes in peace, Lk 10:38ff. and 19:6ff. Moses had been given to the children of Israel to lead them out of Egypt, protect them from evil, and even carry them, as a mother carries her children in her arms or on her back, Ex 3:10ff.; Num 11:12. But God did not tolerate anyone showing him disrespect or causing him trouble. This is verified by the story of Mary[12] and Aaron, Num 12:9, and that of Korah, Dathan and Abiram, Num 16, and by many others.

It does not follow therefore that Christ instituted bread and wine—his flesh and blood—that we should honor and adore them. You must therefore not honor, praise and laud them. We are obliged to honor him and must respect what Paul has sufficiently expressed to the Corinthians saying, "When you gather, you quarrel, and there are factions among you. You drink as if you were in a house of drinking and pleasure. Everyone seeks to outdo the other in eating and drinking. Therefore, some are drunk and full and others sober and hungry" [1 Cor 11:18ff.].[13] If you have such intentions, it is not fitting for you to receive the Most Blessed Sacrament.

"Don't you have houses for eating and drinking? Or do you despise the house of God, putting to shame those who have nothing? In this I cannot commend you," Paul says in 1 Cor 11:22. He then teaches about partaking of the sacrament worthily, saying, "Whoever uses the sacrament in an unworthy manner and eats the bread unworthily and drinks from the cup of the Lord unworthily is guilty of the death of the Lord and like one of those who profane the body and blood of Christ" [1 Cor 11:27]. That we are to receive the Blessed Sacrament with respect and discernment, Paul explains [//] by giving the following reason, saying, "You must discern the body of Christ." [14] Paul had earlier spoken of bread and wine, saying that the Corinthians are to receive them with respectful dignity, giving as reason that the recipients are to discern the body of the Lord. With this Paul expresses privately what earlier he had written publicly, namely, that the bread is the body of Christ. And thus we are to honor the bread. Anyone who does not look to the bread in this way, takes it unworthily because he fails to discern the body of the Lord. This is what Paul earlier in 1 Cor 10:16, "The cup which we bless is communion in the blood of Christ and the bread which we break is communion in the body of Christ." Note that this is the reason which Paul, following Christ, often gave for honoring the sacrament—that the bread is the body of Christ and the wine the blood of Christ. Anyone then who dares say that we do not honor bread and wine which have become body and blood of Christ says that we ought not honor the body and blood of Christ. No one other than an opponent of Paul and all the prophets would say that—they are blasphemers who shall not be heard here for all eternity. How well these hypocrites depend on nothing other than invented lies.

6. Now this bloated frog (whose eyes glitter and shine with evil and lies), must hear, nonetheless, what it does not like to hear, and must eat its own words[15] for having said that the Wittenbergers aim to attack Christ in heaven and bring him down even. We do no such thing, you poisonous and miserable dragon. We have a lion from the tribe of Judah who is able to gag your deceitful throat. The laity will believe him if not us. Hear then what I learned from him; he taught me what in this matter I should hold on to.

7. Therefore, I honor the signs (i.e., bread and wine), since I know that the consecrated bread is the body and [//] the wine is the blood of Christ. I have demonstrated this at length, and with reference to Scripture in the booklet *On Both Forms*.[16] Note, in the same way as I believe that Christ is both true God and human being, so I also believe—simply because Scripture says that the bread is body of Christ—that the bread which has been consecrated is body of Christ, yet remains bread which he held in his hands or which the baker baked. I find one as easy to believe as the other, for I believe both. I also know that if laypeople had studied the gospel for a longer time and had repeated the line "bread is body of Christ" as often as they had repeated the line "the human has become God," it would be as easy and right for them to believe the one as the other.

8. I reckon that a person born blind will consider strange a statement like "The wall or the person is white," for he won't have seen either. Similarly, nature cannot believe that a human being should be God and that natural bread should be body of Christ. In faith, however, both concepts seem simple and are easily believed. Just as I know that bread is white and roundish because I can see it, so also do I know that the bread is body of Christ, because I find it written in the gospel. I do not doubt the word of Christ; I believe it even when it appears to be bitter and heavy to me and my Adam.

9. I know, then, without wavering that consecrated bread is body of Christ—and as such Christ, as he said—i.e., the total and living Christ, and that consecrated wine is blood of Christ. Therefore, I have no doubt whatever that I ought to honor the body and blood of Christ and that I may say with Thomas, "My Lord and my God,"[17] or with the centurion, "I am not worthy to have you come under my roof. Rather, say a word and my soul shall be saved."[18] Or else, like Zachaeus, I can receive it with joy, which is more praiseworthy, more comforting, and

to the greater glory of Christ.[19] [//]

10. Thus I can worship the bread which is Christ and ask it to help, though it has been instituted to be eaten and was given as a sign so that I might worship Christ with whom the bread is one thing, just as the divine and the human being is one person.[20]

11. Not that the bread itself gives me grace and succor [hilff]. Nor do I intend to give such exclusive power to natural bread made by a baker, now that it has become body of Christ. Nor do I in the end intend to count on and stand firmly in the bread with love, faith, hope, worship, and respect. For in that way I should be worshiping what a baker produced or a creature brought about. Rather, I stand and grow in Christ and I honor the bread sincerely because it has become body of Christ and the wine, because it has become blood of Christ. If I were to worship the bread because it is bread or simply because it is a sign, then what happened to the Babylonian king Belshazzar of whom Daniel 5 writes might happen to me.

12. Our papists[21] cannot in good conscience honor or worship their form. They lack the basis for right worship, which was given by Christ and, after him by Paul and, now by me. Why? They lack scriptural proof to say that the form of bread is the body of Christ and the form of the wine, the blood of Christ. Thus, they are the ones who are incapable of honoring the sacrament, and all defilement will flow into them. We know through the Gospel that the bread is the body and that the wine is the blood of Christ. Therefore, we discern the body of the Lord which they are incapable of discerning.

13. We, on the other hand, continue through the bread in Christ whose body is bread. Thus, we honor that bread, not for itself but because we know it to be the body of Christ. And we honor it, by not clinging to the bread, but to Christ.[22]

14.[23]·This should not seem strange to the pious Christian, for our faith does not ultimately rest in the humanity [B] of Christ, but works its way past all creatures to God. Therefore, Christ says, "whoever believes in me, believes not in me, but in him who sent me," Jn 12:44. Note how you resent and hate when Christ says, "whoever believes in me, believes not in me." Yet, I say similarly with regard to the bread[24] that whoever believes the bread does not believe the bread. If I am to believe in God, I must first believe in Christ, for in Christ we have access to God. It is for this reason that Christ says, We must not believe in him, but in his Father. Note how faith abandons heaven and all creatures and clings to God alone. What else did Christ mean when he said, "Whoever believes in me, believes not in me"? He meant that whoever believes in Christ does not stop with the human Christ, but transcends to his Father whose commandment and word Christ proclaimed. Christ also said, "Whoever sees me, sees the one who sent me," Jn 12:45. To have seen Christ was of no help to the Jews; but when believers see Christ, it helps them toward their salvation, for they see something which is above every creature. Therefore, Christ says, "Blessed are the eyes which see what you see."[25] Christ always leads his disciples beyond himself to his Father. Similarly, anyone who intends to worship and honor the bread, or anyone who seeks help therein, must go beyond himself to the heavenly bread which is Christ who says, "I am the bread of life which came down from heaven," Jn 6:35. In this manner one may worship, honor, laud, and praise the bread which is body of Christ. However, when I undertake to separate bread and body of Christ, and when I will not or cannot believe (God defend us from that!) that bread is body, and wine, blood of Christ (as Christ stated so clearly), then I must not expect any help from it [the bread]. Neither should I worship and honor it, for in this way I set up a creature as my idol.

Therefore, each person must consider whether or not he believes in Christ. [//] Only after he gives credence to the words of Christ can he truly honor bread and wine, in that they have become body and blood of Christ, as I described above.

15. Bread and wine are not merely signs, such as the rainbow or the cattle of Abraham, Gen 15,[26] or, the woolen coat of Gideon.[27] Rather, they are signs and have come to represent that which suffered and that which was shed for us. In other words, bread and wine have become body of Christ and blood of Christ which we are to worship, as I stated above in the fourteenth article.

16. Some are offended by this and claim that many people are annoyed because we call the sacrament a sign. I respond: those same people call much worse things than we "a sign." We call bread and wine signs, not of the body and blood of Christ or of the bread and wine, but of the word; both these have the promise of Christ. What do we care when some are angered by the word of God. There have been many who took offense at the words of Christ, which he and his disciples confessed. Christ is a stone of stumbling to all unbelievers. They will be vexed and astonished by him, as in 1 Pet 2.[28] Does not Simeon say that Christ has been set to be the ruin of many, Lk. 2:34f.? Should we avoid those who are more likely to receive and praise human findings than divine Scriptures? Must the light and God's word remain hidden under a bushel? No. God's word must be spoken and written

openly. Anyone who conceals it out of fear or for financial gain, Christ will also refuse to acknowledge. Bread and wine are signs of the divine promises; they have been given to silence our doubts. If you are puzzled by this and insist on saying useless or unchristian things about us because we call the above-named things signs, what then are they going to say when they read Christ's words who says, "As Moses lifted up the serpent in the wilderness, so must the Son of Man [Bij] be lifted up, that whoever believes in him should not perish, but have eternal life," Jn 3:14? With these words Christ made known to us that on the cross he would be a sign just as the serpent of Moses in the wilderness had been set up for a sign, Num 21:8ff. What will people say now when they are clearly informed by the word of God that Christ on the cross was a sign just as was the serpent of Moses which had been suspended, so that those who had been bitten [by poisonous snakes] and who then looked upon it were healed. All who look on Christ in faith have eternal life and are assured against damnation. The serpent then was a sign of the promise of physical health, while Christ is a sign to all believers of the promise of spiritual health, of protection from destruction, and of eternal life. Note that Christ is a sign. Note also how Christ transfers all righteousness through himself to his Father who alone is God and not united with any creature, as Christ was united. Note what Paul says, "He himself is righteous and he justifies the one who through faith is Christ's," Rom 3:26.[29]

17. Though this should be sufficient, our enemies must know, nonetheless, that the Lord is called a sign in Isaiah who in the fifty-fifth chapter [Is 55:13] speaks as follows, "The Lord will be a name and eternal sign to him which shall not pass away." Note, the Lord shall be an imperishable sign, as he himself says, "I shall remain with you to the end of the world."[30] So also Christ is an eternal sign for us. To the godless he is a sign of offense which everyone fights and speaks against, as Simeon said in Lk 2:34.

18. Isaiah also said that the Lord shall become for us a new name, i.e., we shall be called by his name; thus, we call ourselves Christians—from Christ. And as we have one name in him, so, too, are we one body in Christ. Accordingly, Paul says [//], "We, too, are all one bread, who eat of one bread."[31] So, in the bearing of the Lord's name we become one bread, one body, one Christian band.[32] It follows then that, since Christ is a sign, therefore bread and wine may well be called two signs, and that those who use or partake of these signs thus obtain their name—they may be called one bread. Therefore, no Christian should be perturbed when bread and wine are called signs.

Anyone who is angry has a quarrel with Scripture.

19. No one, of course, should be bound to bread and wine in worship or in faith—either initially or in the end; for these are mere creatures. The bread remains the bread which the baker baked, although it may have become the body of Christ, just as Christ remains a human being which he became in his mother's womb, even though that same human body is also God. So, when I invoke the sacrament and direct faith, hope, and love to it, I do not cling to what I see, but to that which is invisible, i.e., the body and blood of Christ.

20. Therefore, I do not praise those either, who regard the bread of the sacrament like ordinary bread, as the Piccards allegedly do.[33] For Paul states that all dishonoring of consecrated bread (which is body of Christ), is [a dishonoring of] the body of Christ, as I said earlier. Let each person be guided by this, but not without looking up Scripture, to determine whether my writings are in line with and like God's word.

I did not intend to write here of most recent events (which do not properly belong in this booklet). However, I do praise and glorify God's grace especially now and will not keep from you the fact that my most gracious lord, the Archbishop of Magdeburg and Primate, etc., and His Grace the Elector Prince render honor and glory to God. May [God] splendidly enlighten his princely office that His Grace, the Elector Prince, [Biij] seriously begin reading and contemplating evangelical truth. It is rumored here that His Grace the Elector Prince intends to manage the supreme episcopal office himself (if he is equipped for the task) and to preach the gospel. This delights me greatly. I cannot think what I should like to hear more. May the living God deign so to preserve and increase His Grace that others might follow and without doubt rid themselves of the Roman yoke and prison. It is ever to be pitied when our German prelates (whom God has given a great deal of understanding and who are aware that papal rule rests on clay feet), do not themselves govern the German nation, unperturbed[34] by papal appointment or confirmation, especially in view of the fact that they send a lot of money to Rome for which they bring home nothing more than letters and empty words. The pope is useful for nothing other than to clean out our purses[35] and seduce our Christian souls. I would love to have this type of government come about and, with God's help, it shall. I know that in their hearts the prelates will agree with me. If their mouths and consciences were at one, I would have their ready "yes."

Would to God that they had the will as they have power, authority, and good cause to tear the Roman net asunder. It should soon tear and grind to a halt. (However, it would be good if in the process no priest would have to go begging for bread or be assaulted in his person. Anyone who desires that is not evangelical).[36] They lack nothing but good will; I lack power. If they had my will or I their power, we would this very day expel from German lands all popish and unchristian teaching, virtue, customs, and religion and we would pronounce an anathema on the pope. In his dominion we are captive like the Jews in Babylon; indeed, worse. For not only do we lack divine bread[37] and sacrifices, as did the Jews, but in addition we also lack the word—this is much more harmful, Hos 6 and Dan 9. [//]

The priest who was imprisoned on account of his marriage has been released and is free. He keeps his parish and his wife to boot. I have this from a reliable person. This is visible proof that my gracious lord of Magdeburg will increase in evangelical freedom and truth which befits and is appropriate to His Electoral Grace and the Primate of Germany. May the merciful God strengthen and preserve His Electoral Grace.

FINIS

Title page of Carlstadt's 1524 tract, published at Wittenberg, on "Whether or Not We Can Be Saved Without the Intercession of Mary."

3
Regarding Vows

In the year 1522

The nature of vows, particularly as they affected the lives of young men and women who had made vows of celibacy in their youth, engaged many of the best minds in the early decades of the sixteenth century. Carlstadt's contribution to this debate focuses primarily on the Mosaic Law but draws on other biblical texts as well in his attempt to apply the **ius Biblicum** (the law operative in Scripture), rather than following ecclesiastical laws which were established in the course of the Middle Ages. He works with the biblical law as his hermeneutical principle throughout the tract.

Unlike the earlier Latin version of this tract, which makes some harsh statements on the alleged corruptions in monastic houses, the German tract is more cautious and addresses the issue of vows in a generally conciliatory manner. In 1521 Martin Luther also published a booklet on vows. For an English translation see **Luther's Works**, vol. 44, U.S. ed. (Philadelphia: Fortress Press, 1966).

Freys/Barge list four German editions (50-53) of this important tract. The earliest publications appeared in 1521, the later one in 1522. Our translation is based on a copy of the 1522 Basel edition, located in the Zentralbibliothek Zurich.

Instruction by Dr. Andreas Bodenstein from Karlstadt
Exposition of Numbers 30 which speaks of vows

This booklet concludes, on the basis of biblical, Christian laws, which are Holy Scripture, that priests, monks, and nuns may and ought to marry and enter upon the marital state with a good conscience and [in keeping with] God's will without having to obtain a Roman dispensation or release which is totally unnecessary. It advises above-named persons to cast off their deceitful living habits along with gowns and scowls and to enter upon a true Christian life.

To the honorable and respected Conrad Gutmann, treasurer[1] and criminal judge at Kitzingen,[2] my benefactor and friend, I, Andreas from Karlstadt, desire prosperity and everything that is good.

Since my gracious benefactor has experienced many strange vows which simple folk are inclined to make—though at times ill-advisedly, so that it were better they gave up such irresponsible acts and asked divine Scriptures for advice to prevent harm to themselves in making such vows and thus to show themselves willing to please God—I undertook to write on the subject of vows.

First, I shall make an earnest effort to write a preface or introduction. I will then write a commentary on the thirtieth chapter of Numbers which speaks of vows. Along with this commentary, I will indicate whether nuns, monks, priests, and such who wish to mate and increase the population are allowed to become engaged and be married within the bounds of God's laws, without burdening their consciences or forfeiting their salvation.

I will write in the way I would were I to write or speak in the coming, severe judgment of God. Let no one, on this account, be angered or hurt. Should there be someone to whom this lesson may seem wrong or contrary to the truth, I will respond in keeping with his needs and as occasion warrants.

I have dedicated this booklet to you because of the special love and friendship which I have had—and continue to feel strongly—for the highly learned John Pfeffer,[3] your son and my dear brother, in the hope of securing your favor. I greatly long for this grace, humbly rendering my willing service to you.

Given at Wittenberg, on the feast of John the Baptist in the year of the Lord 1521.

PREFACE

Not in vain is it said that whatever you sacrifice ought to be seasoned or mixed with salt [Lev 11]. Do not remove from your sacrifice the salt of the divine covenant. Have salt in all that you sacrifice. For salt in Holy Scripture means scriptural and divine wisdom or someone who is highly knowledgeable in the laws and sayings of God, as Christ says, "You are the salt of the earth; when the salt loses its savor wherewith shall one salt? And what good is salt then except to be thrown under foot and trampled on" [Mt 5]? God commands us to have salt in all sacrifices, i.e., divine wisdom of which our pastors are obligated to have more and in greater measure than other people. Now since the salt has become foolish, bland, and unsavory, it has happened that many bad sacrifices and useless vows have been presented to God of which not one among thousands has pleased God. Why? We have no salt in our vows and sacrifices. The pope, the bishops, priests, and monks know little or nothing of divine wisdom, and they have kept us in addition from searching Holy Scripture. From this it follows that we are not able to throw any salt into our sacrifices, vows, works, and lives and that we make foolish and bland sacrifices and vows before God. By our folly we move him to anger rather than to mercy and no one ought to be too fast to make vows, for silly vows displease God. The reason is that where there is no wisdom, there is nothing that is good [Eccl 5]. Anyone who runs fast hurts and bangs his feet, Prov 19. Folly ruins a person's way and weighs him down and causes him to rage against God, Prov 19. [a ij]

Now since Scripture says that human folly angers God and causes human beings to rage against God and it obstructs a person's every step, everyone must hold back and not hurry. Above all, one must make sure to have salt in one's vows, sacrifices, ways, and in every step, so that one does not end up confirming oneself in these presumably holy endeavors. If you were merely saving yourself some toil and labor by making silly vows, it would be tolerable. But to move God to disfavor, and to harm yourself and inflict suffering on you through unwise and foolish vows is serious. Look around again and again, and consider well in advance what you will say to God and how you will deal with him. As Scripture says, "Do not speak wantonly in God's sight; do not let your heart be quick and hasty to speak before God. For God is in heaven and you are on earth," Eccl 5. Human thoughts cannot ever be divine, but they may serve God and be pleasing to him,

Isa 55. They are then of such a nature as Scripture indicates. Therefore, the less you can speak before God, the more useful it is to you, Eccl 5. Now divine Scripture further warns us especially of thoughtlessness in praising, so that a person may well reflect and seriously consider whether his thoughts are divine or carnal. As it is written, "Do not believe every spirit, but first ascertain carefully what sort of spirit moves you."[4] For this reason Moses says regarding vows that you are without sin when you do not make vows or when you refuse to make vows. And whatever you have once spoken with your mouth you must fulfill and what you have said to God in your mind or with your mouth you must then do.

With these words Moses warns you not to be too hasty in making vows, and he teaches you that you will remain without sin when you do not make vows. The churches ought to examine this [//] and all who seek holiness should take it in and hold on to it.

But they come with a mere show of Scripture, saying that Scripture admonishes and drives us to vows, wanting us to be inclined to and quick, with vows, as it is written [Ps 76], "Make your vows and render them." You must make vows and render costly vows unto God. Here, they say, we are told to be prepared at all times to make our vows unto God and to render vows unto him.

No, my friend, this passage of Scripture does not order you to stoop or to be agile, quick and anxious to make vows. It does, however, prohibit you from making and rendering vows to anyone other than God. If you must make vows, you ought to vow unto God. And if you cannot be without the delight of vows, you must make all your vows to God alone.

Therefore Scripture says that anyone who makes vows and renders sacrifices unto the gods and not to God alone ought to be killed. At one time the Jews made their vows to alien gods. And now Christians render vows and sacrifices unto the saints. Both of which is wrong. Therefore God has established a law [Jer 7] by which anyone who renders vows or sacrifices unto gods and not unto God alone is to be slain.

Hence, the verse does not order you to be quick and fast in sacrificing or making vows—for then this passage of Scripture would be contrary to many other Scripture passages. Rather, it calls you away from vows which you render to someone other than God. This, too, is what Moses says [Lev 19]. They are no longer to sacrifice unto false gods with whom they were immodest. Nor are all so-called Christians who adore the saints like gods, call on them, and render vows unto them and behave unchastely with gods, thus becoming spiritually dead. For they ought to render vows and sacrifices unto the true God alone. Scripture stresses this also in Isaiah [19], God is to be known by the Egyptians who shall honor him with sacrifices and gifts and shall make and render vows unto him. [a iij]

If these words are interpreted to the effect that we are to render unto God sacrifices, gifts, and vows in order to appease God with such things, you might throw the first and last chapter of Isaiah onto the same pile.

On the contrary, the meaning is that we are not to render vows unto any god, creature, or saint, but to God alone which the cited verse teaches unmistakeably saying, "Render and make your vows unto God" [Ps 22]. Elsewhere David says, "I shall render my vows unto God, before all who fear God." By this he wanted to say, I shall render vows unto God and not unto any creature in heaven or on earth and I shall render my vows in such a way as for the god-fearers to see how I sacrifice to God alone and thus learn from the rendering of my vows. From this verse follows that David speaks of physical vows, otherwise he would merely have said I shall render my sacrifice in the sight of the god-fearers. The above-mentioned verse is against popes, bishops and other unsavory salt who teach people to make vows and promises unto the saints. For Scripture intends us to make vows and sacrifices unto no one but God.

Therefore those mariners err who, when experiencing trouble at sea, call on St. Gertrude for protection and make vows unto her. Such vows are contrary to divine laws. Those also err who make their vows unto St. Liborio that he might protect them from the pain of stones. When they have sore eyes, they talk to St. Othilia; it is St. Apollonius for the teeth, St. Sebastian for the plague, and St. Sigismund when they have the fever. They make promises to St. Valentine that he might protect them from dropsy or rehabilitate them and to St. Anthony that he might avert flash fires. To St. Job some people devote sacrifices against evil pocks. And some promise [//] sacrifices to St. Lawrence that he might protect them from fire. And some Jewish peasant-like people call on the tools (with which the saints were martyred) when they are afflicted; they swear oaths and seal their promises and sacrifices. There are so many and varied cursed vows and sacrifices which spring forth and flow from false faith that one can hardly enumerate them in a single book. I hope that a few will discern, know and remember the immediate and great value of being saved from above errors. Since we ought to praise God alone, it is a wanton and harmful thing for a person to make vows and bring offerings to one of the four-teen deliverers or to St. James or to the holy sepulchre. This is espe-cially true for a person who has a wife, children, and domestics. For one ought not leave the same on account of vows. But one who is fool-ish enough to allow the pope to lure him to St. Peter's at Rome or else-where, away from the care and administration of his own home, must know that he is worse than an unbeliever and that he has betrayed the faith, as Paul teaches in 1 Tim 5. Moreover, it is against God and di-vine Scripture for us to call on someone other than God when in need and tribulation. Scripture speaks as follows: "You are to call on me in your dealings and in your misery [Ps 50] and I shall deliver you." You must call on and render vows unto God and not call on the saints; to him you must make your vows [Ps 20].

Someone might say that a person may and should honor God through the saints, since Scripture says, "Honor God through his saints" [Ps],[5] therefore I, too, can call on, praise, and promise to raise vows unto God through his saints. Jacob did that. In his anguish he said, [Gen 32] "Lord, the God of my fathers Abraham, and Isaac, re-deem me from Esau." Scripture uses this form [//] in several places. In Ex [25] and Deut [5] Moses says, "Lord, remember your servants Abraham, Isaac, and Jacob." And since God is sought out and called upon because of his saints, it follows that we may call on the saints and render vows unto them.

But I say that these [passages of] Scripture are introduced and used improperly. For to praise God through his saints does not mean to render vows unto the saints. Similarly, when we pray to God to be mindful of his saints, it does not mean either to call on the saints or to bind oneself to them through vows.

Whenever you praise God through his saints, you acknowledge God's work, mercy, grace, and benefits which he shows toward his saints. Thus when we pray to God that he might remember his saints and grant his grace, we praise God's benevolence, grace, and mercy which God showed toward his servants. As if I were to say, I beg you on account of your friend whom you benefitted not to forget your goodness and help me, too. This does not mean to call on that same friend, but to call on the one who showed good will toward another person and to remind him of his benevolence, ask for and call on it. Thus let us not think that we are making vows unto saints when we praise God through his saints or when we remind God of his servants.

The saints sing daily, "Not unto us, O Lord, but to your name be glory given." And so we pray, "Hallowed be your name." And the saints tell us that it is not we who help you, but faith in God through the name of Jesus Christ [Acts 3 and 15]. Further, we are your brothers. At this point I have to say more in order to stamp out foolishness. There are some who are not content to call on God only; they render vows unto God and a saint at the same time, such as God and their apostle or patron. I noted this in the testaments of some priests and hated it. They commended and entrusted their soul unto God and their patron, [//] as if God on his own were not able to save them or as if he refused to be gracious and merciful unto them. They are bent on doubting this and thus they do wrong. The reason: You shall not have more than the one God and seek only his help. Of this you have the clear story of Asa, the king [2 Chr 16], when God allowed the enemies to win over them because Asa did not trust in God alone but sought help from physicians, in addition to God. I fear that we shall experience the same when in addition to God we make vows unto or call on saints. If you desire to have saints as intercessors, do not make vows unto them and do not take them to be helpers in need. Just as little as you make vows to a righteous person here when you take him to be an intercessor, so little are you to make vows and offer sacrifices to saints.

From this excursus it follows that the verse [Ps 76; Deut 32] "You ought to make your vows unto God and perform them" is not a commandment to make vows. For Moses places vows under our will saying that we cannot make vows without sin. Rather, the verse is a prohibition and a discounting of vows that might be made to other creatures rather than to God. This psalm is against those who make vows to saints and who call on them to win them through vows and against all who lack the salt of a divine command.

Had God wanted to have pleasure and delight in sacrifices and vows, Christ would not have kept it hidden from us and David would not have said, "Lord, I know that you have no pleasure in sacrifices" [Ps 5; Ps 49] and also, "Do you think that I eat the flesh of oxen or drink the blood of he-goats?" I do not belittle the spiritual and true sacrifices which take place in the spirit. And I do not intend to keep anyone from spiritual vows in any way. Rather, [//] I wish to have reminded everyone with great diligence to observe these. Of such David writes, "I shall make my vows to God daily" [Ps 61].[6] Spiritual vows are the praise of God, prayers, adoration, hope, sighing, and a desire for God. A righteous person is to make such vows at all times; they come from a broken and contrite heart and please God exceedingly. It is written that [Ps 50] a penitent heart is the sacrifice which God wants to have.

And Asaph says, "Render praise unto God and your vows to the Most High. Call on him in the days of your travail and he shall redeem you and you are to glorify him." I do not speak of this kind of vows. Rather, I speak of those that are accomplished through the will and a person's mouth, those that refer to and include something, be it modesty, money, wax, an arm, suffering, a house, one's homestead, land, meadows, clothing, weapons, spears, stones, and such like.

With this I ought to have come to the conclusion of my initial preface. But my conscience forces me to say more on the matter. I am aware that many persons might be offended at this and that some scholars are afraid. But I am courageous and do not allow myself to be intimidated. I state freely whatever God states and speaks through his words.

Regarding sacrifices and vows, our religion reminds me of and looks like that of Indians in their temples. As far as I can see and hear, they compare themselves to heathen and unbelievers. Of these God speaks as follows through Jeremiah [Jer 7; 2 Chr 7], "You come and stand before me in my house in which my name alone ought to be called upon and you say, We have been delivered because we have committed such defilement and have done such horrible things."[7]

You say that you called on St. Sebastian in your distress and that you were able to recover from the plague [2 Chr 6]. Another says that he promised to St. Gertrude or St. Nicholas an image made of silver when he was floating in the water but was rescued. A third one says "I lay in chains and made vows unto St. Linhard, and I saw how the righteous saint broke my chains." A fourth one says, "I placed a linen or silken sash around the chair of St. Peter at Rome which I then wrapped around my wife when she was in labor and the fruit [of her body] came into the world with ease." A fifth person says, "I sprinkled consecrated water into a foul well and the worms died." The sixth speaks of how St. Barbara saved him from the sword, and the seventh, how St. Catherine made him smart.

Not one of them wants to hear that they are worshipers of sun or moon. And now God says, "You state that we have been made well and have been saved or that we have reached this or that for having made such vows to the saints." Hear what God says. "You have turned my house into a den of murderers." God would have said this just the same if the Jews in their anxieties and distress had called on their dead patriarchs and prophets. Scripture canonized and declared to be holy Abraham, Isaac, Jacob, Moses, and David and such like. However, God does not want to prevent us from turning to him with our concerns. *Ad aliquem sanctorum convertere?* [To which of the saints will you turn?][5] says one of those whom Job brands a liar [Job 5:1].

Now since God calls the gathering of those people who claim that they rendered vows unto the saints (whom we do not consider to be God) and were saved and redeemed by them, a disreputable tavern [Spelunke] and a den of murderers, I cannot offer them any comfort either. Rather, I have to say that God will deal with your gathering and company as he did with Shiloh [Jer 7], "He shall raze you to the ground and cast you from his presence, just as he cast away your brothers" [b ii].

After this God says to Jeremiah, "Do not plead for the people, for I shall not hear you" [Jer 7; 11; 15]. That which God spoke to Jeremiah is to apply to all saints. For Scripture also says, "Whether Moses, Samuel, or Daniel were to plead for the people, I would not hear them." Christ says to this [Jn 17], "I do not pray for the world, but for those whom you have given me." Christ points all his lambs to his Father. All the saints do this. And those who do not are not holy in God's sight. They may be popish saints, but not divine and genuine saints.

It is possible, as the pope himself confesses, that his saints sit in hell and curse us when we sing, "Pray for us."

I let that go and state that these words must be looked at carefully and in depth, that God is prepared to cast from his sight such people who disregard his divine words and who sacrifice and render vows to someone who is not God. And that, too, is not to be looked at indolently which God speaks to his saints, "Do not plead for the people."

At this point someone might say, well-intentioned or ill, "Those always return healthy who have rendered vows unto the saints." To wit, if it were not of God and not pleasing to God that human beings should promise and render vows unto the saints, they would remain unaided.

I reply: Dear friend, do you not know that the devil also performs miracles? And I might say, as does Augustine, that God gives also to those who ask it of the devil and who think that such help and gift has come from the devil.

This is intended for those also who call on saints for help and redemption and render vows unto them. At times God helps them and saves them, though they take it to have received help from the saints. Christ's word is appropriate at this point [Mt 9], "My Father lets his sun shine on good and wicked alike." Also what God says, "Stars have been created to serve everyone who lives under the heavens," Deut 4, i.e., the good and the wicked. For Adam in the beginning had his serpent, Abel his Cain, Isaac his Ishmael, Jacob his Esau, and the righteous their persecutors and the stars shone for and served them all together.

Thus God helps the godless and wicked, even though they seek help with creatures contrary to divine counsel and will. He tolerates when you say, Blessed Mary in Grünthal in Franconia restored my sight or, the blessed blood in the marches made me walk straight again, or, St. Anne at Deuten preserved me from poison and death, even though the saints do not hear or know of our pleas and vows. Were they able to hear our folly, they would be displeased by it and they would forbid us to engage in such clamor and rendering of vows. However, out of great goodness, God helps by being silent for a time, even though you rob God of his honor by ascribing it to a creature.

God does this because he knows your heart better than you do; he sees that you have forsaken him and that you have made for yourself new gods of the saints; yes, what is even greater, God sees how you run after the images of saints. For this reason God leaves you to the desires and lust of your heart and allows you to run to your eternal loss, as is written in Rom 1.

It is not without reason that God overlooks your faults and allows that you thus go astray [Rom 1]. For you first left God and carried his glory in and to a creature. This is for one. For the other, it is written that God imposes times when deceiving gods such as [B iii] lying prophets and preachers will arise, and he does not prevent false prophets, such as popes, bishops, and monks, from preaching to us. Why does God do this? Because he tests us by this to see whether we desire to cling to and stay with him [Deut 13]. So that it may become apparent to everyone whether we love God with all our heart and whether we follow him alone, Deut 13. This is what Paul says also that there must be quarrels and divisions so that true believers might become known, 1 Cor 11.

Not only does God allow new preachers to arise and prophets to run about whom he did not send, but God sees to it that they do signs which he veils with the miracles of the saints. In this manner the sorcerers of Pharaoh also performed their signs, Ex 7. But their end will be ignominious, which can be readily learned from the history of the prophet Ananias.

We wrote that true prophets, whom God has sent, perform miracles and that what they proclaim will take place. Again, that the proclamation of false prophets shall not come to pass, Deut 18. This is the sign by which to distinguish true prophets from false ones.

To this someone might say, this is a sign and token by which the distinction between righteous and unrighteous saints might be noted. Further, that we ought to take the saints who help us to be true saints. Yes, this is a seemingly good argument.

But listen to the history I began regarding the prophet Ananias. One may conclude that God allows sorcerers to do wonders for a time, but not for long. Soon their skill and power subsides, Ex 8. Ananias says to the prophet Jeremiah, "Thus says God, I shall break the bond, yoke, and chain by which the king of Babylon [//] holds you captive." To which Jeremiah replied among other things, as follows, "A prophet who proclaims peace is known as a true prophet when what he said also takes place." Thereupon Ananias took the chain from the neck of Jeremiah and broke it. This was to have been the sign of a genuine prophet. But God said to Jeremiah, "Go to Ananias and say to him, you broke a chain made of linen; in its place you must make an iron chain." After this and on account of it, Ananias had to die. Note that this is what happens to false prophets and their signs. Even if they manage to do signs, these do not last long and they receive their reward and penalty for them.

From this we learn two things. Firstly, how dangerous and harmful it is when a person speaks contrary to God's word or says something on behalf of God which God did not command him to say.

Secondly, that God allows us to be led astray through miracles (on account of former sin). As the prophet says, God forsook you because you first forsook him. Likewise, that God punishes body and soul more harshly on account of the signs we accepted, be it now or later. Ananias freed Jeremiah from a linen bond; for this God bound him with chains of iron.

This is what will happen to those who do not improve their ways and wish to remain in their old trot and error, who render vows unto saints as they did hitherto, and who allow themselves to be deceived by signs. Should they become physically healthy, regain their hearing and sight, become clean and quickened, God shall afflict them in spirit and soul, making them ill, blind, deaf, leprous, and dead, thus binding them with iron chains and consigning them to the inextinguishable flames. Saints do not help; only God does. Saints are too far from us; God is everywhere. You may more surely call for help on a living person [//] who is near you and can see and hear you and lend you a hand, than render vows unto a saint.

And the great multitudes will not excuse or discharge you before God nor will the preaching of mendicants set you free, for the entire lot can err and act contrary to God's commandments. Lev.

Listen, God says, "The children gather wood, their fathers kindle the fire, and the women pour fat onto the fire to bake small cakes for alien gods thus to provoke me to anger" [Jer 7:18].[9] We fools collect money, cheese, oxen, clothes, and such like, and cart them off to Rome and other places to what we think to be our spiritual fathers; they merely kindle the fire and fan it with womanish preaching. What does God say to all that? This is the people that pays no attention to my words and refuses to accept any admonition. Their faith is corrupted and has been removed from their mouth and heart.

Where there is no faith, there is no life, for the righteous person lives by faith [Rom 1].

Lord, it is not in our power to overcome this enemy or this temptation and we have nothing in store or left to us than to lift up our eyes to you. Note that righteous Jehoshaphat [2 Chr 20] does not have any creature in his sight to whom he might flee at times of war to seek help.

Our knights and soldiers call on St. George and St. Sebastian and render vows unto them. They do this to dishonor God, to be sure, and at the loss of their soul's salvation, sinning against the first commandment, "You shall have no foreign gods before me." [//]

They should now learn from the example of Jehoshaphat, the king of Judah, a genuine warrior, that they must call for help on God alone at times of war, leaving St. George and St. Sebastian at rest in the bosom of Abraham.

Had it seemed right to Jehoshaphat to call on warrior-like saints, he undoubtedly would have had such saints as Moses, Joshua, Gideon, David, and others like them. But as a believer, Jehoshaphat knew well that he ought not call on a creature when in anguish and tribulation, but only on God. Therefore Jehoshaphat says [2 Chr 20:12], "We know no one but you, O God, to whom we will turn our eyes."

I don't say this with the intention of praising wars and battles, but only to say that if by chance wars should beset us, we are to call on God. And if we want to rid ourselves of our desire and affection for vows, or break with vows altogether, we must render our vows to God alone and not to saints.

This is what Esther did, saying, "Lord, deliver me into your hand; help me. Without you I have no helper or help," Esth 14.[10]

Neither should you say, "In the name of St. N. I will set out," or "I sail through wind and waves in the name of holy St. Gertrude" or courting some such dangers. Rather, do everything you do or endure

—be they words or deeds—in the name of God, as Paul teaches. "For there is no name by which we may be saved except the name of Jesus Christ" [Col 5]. And Peter says, "His voice and word are feared by wind and wave, storm winds and devil."

In that name David cuts down Goliath [1 Kings 17]; in that name Asa stands, saying, Lord, with you it makes no [2 Chr 14] [c] difference whether you do it with much or little help; help us. In you and in your name we take comfort and strength and go against our enemy. You are our God—a strong God—no human being can withstand you. Note, the Jews put all their comfort in God and his name and not in saints. We do likewise, 2 Chr 16; 1 Kings 4; Ex 23.

I said this to unburden my conscience and free my soul. Ezek 3. This is no laughing matter to me, and I am not at all comfortable with it. Therefore I say that no oath which you render to saints is good—be it spiritual or carnal, external or internal. For I must ask you whether St. Clare, Benedict, Dominicus, Francis, Augustine, and Bernhard and such like are truly God? I fancy that you will have to confess that there is only one true God if you wish to be taken for a Christian [Deut 5]. I believe in one God, Creator of heaven and earth, etc. I know that you will have to confess one God with heart and mouth and that you will have to say that St. Clare is not God and Francis is not God, etc. For I believe in one God only and recall Scripture which says, "Hear, O Israel, your God is one and God alone. You shall love God with all your heart and all your soul and with all your might," [Deut 6:4].[11] Note later, when Moses said, "Israel, your God has established his honor and has commanded how you are to love God."

I must take some time now to deal with this passage of Scripture. For this commandment belongs to the very first commandment when God says, "You shall have no foreign gods, for God is zealous who does not tolerate you to love him with divided or shared love" [Ex 20; Deut 19]. No one loves God unless he loves him alone. Therefore, Scripture says, "You shall love God with all [//] your heart, soul, and strength," as if to say, God alone must occupy your heart as Creator, Redeemer, and Helper in need. God alone is to be your father. To him alone you should entrust all concern, burden, anguish, delight, suffering, hope, comfort, love, and faith. He alone wants to nurture, guard, and protect you and lead you out of your anguish. You must have a circumcised heart; God commands and demands this of you, saying through Moses, "You are to circumcise the skin of your heart and rid yourself of the stiffness of your neck [Deut 10]. For God is the God above all gods and lord of all lords." Now observe, if God is God of all saints and of all living creatures in heaven and on earth, then I ought to call on him alone in all godly matters and an no one else.

[mar: Circumcised hearts]

Note here that we are to have circumcised hearts and soft necks. A circumcised heart has removed from itself all other saints, all angels, and all creatures (and all those pieces that are God's prerogative alone).

It cannot love or believe in any saint or angel besides God. We also know from Scripture that neither angels nor saints accept it as something good when we bestow on them divine honor and praise them as gods. Indeed, they fend these off as too close, blasphemous and detestable when we approach them with divine honors. They therefore reject such rendering of honor. God too is displeased when someone besides him places himself into human hearts, for God is zealous and jealous, as mentioned above.

Since this is so, it follows that all vows, glory, and praise rendered unto the saints in godly matters is useless and impotent, yes, even subject to punishment, for God is an avenging lord and he destroys all who attach themselves to someone else with vows, oaths, promises, and alliances. All creatures must have circum [c ii]cised hearts. In other words, we are to love God with all our heart and our heart must not partly cling to angels or saints and for the other part subject itself to God. God desires to be praised, called on, feared, and loved in divine matters singularly, alone and perfectly. This is what it means to be spiritually circumcised, when a person solely loves God with all his heart, as Scripture teaches, saying, "The Lord will circumcise your heart so that you may love him with all your heart and soul" [Deut 30]. In other words, God will cut out of your heart all creatures and alien gods so that you may love him alone with your total heart. On this account God says [Ex 20; Deut 5], "You shall make no likeness for yourself of things in heaven, on earth, or in the water." All external images are prohibited because of the internal images. For Christ says [Mt], that external works and deeds do not soil a person, but what comes out of human hearts, does. Similarly, it must follow that external images do not harm as much as the images of the heart.

Now external images are prohibited; that is clear. It follows then that you are not to make any images in your heart of things which are in heaven, on earth, and in the water. Therefore he also says, you shall not worship or honor them. For I am the Lord, a strong God who is suspicious and jealous and seeks revenge unto the third and fourth generation [Ex 20]. By this we learn how God cuts out from the heart the image of every creature in heaven and on earth. In like manner, God circumcises your heart firstly with prohibitions, laws, and demands, saying [Deut 30], "You shall neither worship nor honor them." After that he sends his spirit to break the hearts of stone and gives a new spirit and a new heart and circumcises your heart, so that you may love God with all your heart and all your soul. He brings about that you form no image of a creature. Yes, when God circumcises your heart, your heart must [//] find all creatures to be spiritually and physically unsweet, bitter, and sour. So much so that you should feel pained if you had to honor something as God which God created for common use.

Now you might say, but I do not know what your words are aiming at; therefore I ask how I have to behave toward parents and neighbors. For you insist that in spiritual circumcision all creatures are cut out of one's heart.

By way of a reply let me resolve this as follows: the one acts contrary to the first commandment of God who in divine works and matters seeks out a saint or angel besides God. Monks and nuns do this. They not only join themselves to God, but besides God to a saint through oaths and vows; because of this they have an uncircumcised and divided heart. By this everyone can readily conclude that their worship, honoring, vows, and covenants are displeasing to God and harmful to them.

The first and greatest commandment is "You shall love God with all your heart, with all your soul and with all your mind" [Mt 22; Ex 20].

The second commandment is "You shall love your neighbor as yourself." It follows then that we ought to love father and mother. Likewise, that we are obligated to honor our elders.

These Scriptures have to have rhyme and reason; it is therefore impossible for a person to love God with all his heart if he has not been well circumcised spiritually, as was said. For Christ says that this commandment is the first and greatest, "You shall have no alien gods." And again thus, "Your hearts shall be circumcised that you might love God with all your heart, soul, and strength" [Ex 20; Deut 30]. All images must of necessity be removed from sight, and all creatures in heaven, in the air, on earth, and in the water must become unsavory to us, otherwise it is [c iii] impossible for us to love God fully and perfectly with a circumcised heart. God must be singularly loved, otherwise we court alien gods.

It is also good to know that these words (regarding love toward

God and creatures), provide a rule, form, direction, and instruction in which manner and form love of God and love of creatures is to be undertaken. I confess that I ought to honor and love God's angels, saints, righteous, yes, even evil persons. But I also know well that I must not place and love them beside God. For God ended the first commandment and after that the second which Christ speaks, "You shall love God with all your heart and your neighbor as yourself." Hence, I must not love myself with all my heart.

Neither must I honor and love any creature, angel, or saint for their gifts, things, or works, all of which they—like me—received from God through grace. I should instruct you from within your faith which articles are God's and his prerogative alone. Listen. You say, I believe in one God, Creator of heaven and earth.

With these words you demonstrate that you believe in God alone by which you deny all foreign gods, saying in secret, I thank God for having a circumcised heart. By words such as these you have shown in what things you confess God alone. For when someone says, I believe in God, the one Creator of heaven and earth, he says that in divine works and matters I intend to confess no one other than God.

[mar. Divine matters and works]

But what are divine things? Note, he says, "I believe God to be the only Creator, etc." Now if he believes that God alone has created heaven and earth, he cannot include either angels or saints in the creation of heaven and earth. For he confesses that angels and saints, heaven and earth have all been made by God. On this point all Christians have been taught. Now [//] everyone respects therefore that when someone honors or praises God and an angel, or saint at the same time and for this reasons says that they created heaven and earth, he does not serve God, the angel or the saint. Rather, he robs God of his honor and creates strange gods. I also know that if a believer is aware of someone who in the creation of heaven and earth seeks to place a spiritual being with or alongside God, he would look on it askance, object to it strenuously, and say, What do you intend to do? Do you not know that there is only one God? Are you unaware of the creation of heaven and earth? What do you pray in your faith? Are you crazy or demented in esteeming angels and saints as creators of heaven and earth? Stop it, for you will provoke God and the saints to anger. You must confess God as the sole maker of the world, believe, honor, praise, call on him, and render vows unto him. Note that on this point all Christians—be they uncouth or subtle, alleged or genuine—are of one mind, for they read this at the beginning of the confession of faith: "In the beginning God created heaven and earth."

But even though many things and works are attributed in Scripture to God alone, they are not known to everyone just because they are not written on the first page and because some demand a diligent and sharp reader. For uncouth heads and stubborn people may well believe that they were originally created by God. But they earnestly deny that God (without their aid) created them righteous, holy, and good. They are able to darken otherwise clear Scriptures with their invented faith.[12] In this way they ascribe their holiness in part to themselves and not as an excuse when they confess God in such works with a divided heart and with uncircumcised lips. But their additions and frivolous undertaking will in the end be to their eternal harm.

For the sake of the simple and so that I may remain with this matter, I will now present a work and piece (which befits God alone as Creator and maker). By this I will make known to everyone that from now on no one be upset by this (at the risk of harming his salvation), and that those who sinned foolishly against God's prohibition think carefully and let go of their insidious folly [Lev 4].

Chastity is a divine thing or work; no one except God can create it [Mt]. For this reason Christ says, Not everyone is able to feel and sense that it is as good as impossible for him not to touch a woman. No one can fathom this unless it is granted him by God.

Hear now for whom it is good not to touch a woman. Paul says [1 Cor 7] that whoever is able to control himself should do so, for it is good for a person not to touch a woman. But one who feels unchastity and feels inclined to marital activities ought to take a wife in marriage. On account of unchastity everyone ought to take a woman in marriage and every woman ought to have her husband. Here learn through the words of Christ [Mt 14] for whom it is helpful not to marry and that such a one has this gift from God. It follows from this that chastity is a divine thing and work—one which God alone creates. Wisdom 8 has it in like manner. I know that no one has been able to be pure and chaste except when God granted and gave him chastity. You could have discovered this from Paul's words too who writes of all good works as follows, God works in us good will and good works. Chastity is not a good work unless God alone creates it. However, chastity [//] is a divine work. Hence, God alone creates it. Therefore, I must not attribute purity to any saint, just as I cannot attribute the creation of heaven and earth to any saint. And since I cannot place a saint or angel alongside God in the creation of the world, but rather must confess God with all my heart, therefore I cannot say that a saint has created chastity along with God. From this follows that I cannot promise chastity to a saint.

As little as one can say casually, I confess that Adam was created by God and an angel, so little can one say, chastity derives from God and from an angel or saint.

Paul compares creation of persons to the creation of divine works, speaking thus [Eph 5], God created us unto good works which God prepared that we might walk in them. We have been born anew and spiritually in Christ; God has given us a new spirit and a new heart. Just as this birth and creation of spiritual persons does not belong either with angels or saints, but is God's alone, so do good works belong to God alone. God prepares good works and pours them into us so that we may walk in these works. This is what Ezekiel says also [Ezek 36], God has wrought within us to walk and work in divine works. All this is included in spiritual circumcision, Deut 30. It follows from this that chastity is created, implanted, and made by God alone and that one wrongs God when placing, calling on, or confessing another master or creator next to God. Chastity is a good work or thing.

At this point I must say once again that the believer, too, must have the same circumcised heart in this thing or work, as he does in the Creation of heaven and earth. For both works have one creator, namely God [d] alone. And if I must confess God alone in the Creation of heaven and earth and deny all creatures, I must then be circumcised as well in confessing chastity, saying, No creature, angel, or saint can make me pure and chaste; God alone is the master craftsman. Chastity is a divine thing and work.

After this I ask monks and nuns (who vow chastity to God and a patron such as St. Clare or Benedict) what they are doing. With my limited understanding, I reckon they should do one of two things. They must ask God and their patron to bestow all chastity or that they might keep them in the purity that was bestowed. But they must attribute their chastity to God and the saint.

I gather this from what David says [2 Chr 19], "Lord and God, all things are yours; whatever we have received from you, we offer and give to you." By this I take it that they have the third link in mind and thought whenever they vow purity to God and their chosen saint. For they will ever have to say that the external vow which is visible has been bestowed and made accessible to them by God and that they give to God that which they have received by grace. Now, if they do this in carnal matters, how much more ought they do that with spiritual gifts. If they promise chastity in this form both to God and their chosen saint, indicating thereby that chastity is granted by both out of compassion, they sin and promise what is evil. They ought to bemoan their vows and let go of them, as we may read in Lev. 4 and 5. The pope himself says, *In malis promissis rescinde fidem*—Through false promises faith is abolished. For they were unbelieving and had an uncircumcised heart. They did not love with all their heart, but sought out alien gods because they attributed to a saint divine honor (in divine works). [//]

I say nothing of the fact that even without this they were wanton. For they promised to give what they were not able to see in the box yet. It would be the same for us to vow chastity unto God as it would be if we were to speak to God of running waters which are to run forever when we do not know how the water will run tomorrow. I am quite sure that all of us agree that a person is wanton and mad who promises an eternally running water unto God. By the same token, chastity and eternal chastity are no more in our power than such external waters or other things.

And if now they venture to say that God creates chastity and the saint protects it, they go contrary to Scripture. Chastity is protected by God alone, for it is written, "Unless God protects a city, all other administration is useless and to no avail," [Ps 127:1].[13] In this work, too, they have to confess God alone. But they are like a horse without sense and they forgot the salt by which they were to have seasoned their vows. It would have been more useful to them had they for the time of their vows tilled the field, built a house or farm, or spun a distaff. For they made vows contrary and in opposition to the divine will in that they vowed to God and the saints at the same time. In their ignorance they reached for alien gods, angering the saints and God. For those who are genuine saints desire that we worship, honor and make vows to the one whom they honored, praised, and made vows to and whom with one accord they honor, praise, and to whom they render their spiritual vows. And they do not want to hear that they are such unbelieving people and that they are like those of whom Isaiah says, "The people praise me with their lips, but their heart is far from me," [Isa 29:13]. Their lips say that they praise God and the saints besides God and that they do this with the best intention. But God's word convicts them and shows that [Dii] they act contrary to God's will and that their heart is full of creatures and that their own thoughts appear to them no less good than divine teaching.

In short, from the word "you shall love your neighbor as yourself," it follows that I ought not love more intensely than myself any saint, angel, or human person. Hatred and envy might well be allied to such love. Christ says, "Whoever does not hate father and mother, yes, his own soul, etc." and Moses in the last chapter of Deut [33:9], "who said we know neither father nor mother . . . have fulfilled your commandment."[14] What if an angel should come from heaven, Gal 1? Angels and saints are God's servants. Therefore it is inappropriate for us to set them next to God or in the place which is exclusively God's. It also follows that we ought to become no less disconsolate with them than with ourselves. *Maledictus homo qui ponit spem in homine*—Cursed is the person who puts his hope in human beings, [Jer 17:5].

Conclusion of This Preface

From this a person might take to heart how to guard against and abstain from vows. For trouble, anxiety, and impediments overtake you; not because you promised and presented God with bodily vows, but (for God is pleased with nothing) because you rendered vows to angels and saints.

Of necessity it ought to be indicated that unseasoned and foolish vows displease and alienate God, so that you must not only break and suppress the bond of some vows, but you must, in addition, also bemoan them with tears and anguish. And that chastity too is not to be promised to God and the saints; just as no other vow is to be made to a saint in particular and is inappropriately rendered to saints and God together. I ought through other perils make such vows detestable or somehow unpallatable to the human heart and instead implant the honor and teaching of God, but that is inappropriate at the moment. However, I believe that the common [//] man, moved by abovementioned passages of Scripture will be more cautious in his vows.

I do not mention that nuns and monks who vow chastity follow heathen more than they do divine Scripture. And I should gladly like to see one who could show with solid Scripture the difference between the vows of chastity which young women rendered to the false goddess Vesta and which our nuns now render to St. Clare or Benedicta.

In my opinion they would do well to avoid these and give attention to what Paul writes in 1 Cor 5 and 6.[15] For the sake of brevity, I will quietly disregard this now. But I hope that other reasons are given in the subsequent 30th chapter of Deuteronomy. These should lead an erring conscience back to what is right. For this reason I have translated the text to the best of my ability and in keeping with Hebrew ways of speaking—within the limitations of our German tongue.

Text: Numbers, Chapter 30
Moses told the children of Israel all the things which God had ordered and commanded.

This beginning belongs to the previous chapter. But since it is attached to the 30th chapter in the Latin version and since it informs the commanders how they are to carry out their orders, I simply wish to include it here.

Holy Scripture often uses words like this so that God's representatives[16] never say anything other than what God commanded, set down, and ordered them to say. The pope adheres to this so strictly with all his lieutenants that he treats all things and matters outside his orders to be null and void. However, he himself does not live by the commands of the one whose vicar and viceroy he wants to be. But [D iii] in order for us to become wise and not to believe any priest or monk unless he is able to show us divine orders, Scripture says, Moses reported that which God ordered and commanded him to say.

Moses was a faithful servant of God and taught believers nothing other than divine commandments. For this reason Moses says to the Jews [Num 11], You shall experience a new and unusual thing and you shall know that the Lord sent me that I might do everything that you see and nothing of my own accord [Num 16]. Note how firmly Moses states not to have spoken anything of his own accord, but only what God ordered him to say. Christ frequently qualifies similarly that he did not say anything of his own accord, but only as God commanded him to do. But our popes are so wanton and willful that they not only say something other than what they were commanded, but they create paltry, beggarly laws [*mosigte*] and filthy decretals, contrary to divine commandments. Yet they want us to call them vicars of God and Christ. But we must open our eyes before it is too late and search Scripture to determine whether or not the pope teaches what is in line with divine commandments, instead of following him any longer.

This text reminds us of all that when it states, Moses said and reported what God commanded him to, etc.

Text
Moses spoke to the princes of the tribes of the children of Israel saying, This is the word which God has commanded. The man who makes a vow unto God or who made himself swear an oath to bind his soul with a pledge must not hold back on his words, but everything which he causes his tongue to utter, he must do.[17] [//]

Explanation

This text has been rendered in German in a Hebrew manner. No one must think it strange that I translated it into German as "who made himself swear an oath," or, "everything which he causes his tongue to utter, etc." Although our Bible at times allows such Hebrew manner of speaking to slip through, it would have been more useful had attributes been faithfully rendered in Latin and German. The reason is simply that much depends on the words which are called transitive verbs.

This includes careful consideration of what the text reports. Everything a person causes his tongue to utter, he must do. I consider that a vow (as we now speak of vows) is fulfilled, not only through the will or desire, but also by the mouth adding its words. In other words, no vow is complete unless it is made by an act of the will and through words. This is what Moses teaches. "Whatever proceeds out of your mouth, you must keep," [Deut 23:21f.].[18] And you must do what you said you would with a free will and tongue. Moses teaches that lips and mouth must vow together with the will, if it is to be taken for a vow [Num 23]. For this reason Moses says in this text, "Do not hold back from giving everything you have caused your mouth to utter." From this follows that whatever I do not promise with lips and tongue, I am not bound to pay; the sick and immature ought to note this. Scripture does this for our benefit to prevent vows that may be done hastily and in a hurry.

The will can render vows instantly, but the mouth is not capable of speaking in a moment; it must first move flesh and teeth. That's why many reckon that nature has given a person upper and lower teeth—and quite a number of them—[//] so that wanton and thoughtless speaking may be prevented. Since then not only the will but the mouth also, together with the will, must add its work (if I am to make a binding vow), it follows that thoughts and the desire to render vows do not make a vow. Note this.

Now follows the right plan by which to look upon and distinguish vows; first, I shall look at this rule or general saying: "Whatever a man vows with mouth and will, he must do without delay." Similarly, if a person has sworn an oath or if he imposed a pledge upon his soul, he ought to do it without delay as soon as he has allowed it to come out of his mouth.

Many more passages of Scripture of similar content contain this teaching, as for example, Deut 23, "When you render a vow unto God, do not tarry to fulfill it, for God demands the vow from you." Similarly, if you promised God anything, do not delay, but give everything you promised [Eccl 5].

This means that I have to remain or become a monk since I made a vow to God to become a monk or a nun. To wit, I would have to give unto God what he does not want.

I say that no passage of Scripture can be understood sufficiently without placing it alongside others and comparing them, for the two cherubim look upon the same thing, even though they are divided into two.

Since the true meaning and content of a passage can be noted by the addition of other passages of Scripture, I will now quote Scripture passages that speak of vows.

Firstly, you should know that the vow (by which a person promises his soul to God) is in the hands of the one who renders the vow in order to save his soul and to pay money for the soul. Scripture says in Lev 26,[19] "If a person has made a vow, [//] and committed his soul to God, he must render the equivalent after appropriate valuation." The valuation depends on a person's years and gender. The number of years is the same for men and women. If a man who has promised his soul to God is between twenty and sixty years, he is to give fifty shekels to the temple. But if a woman is twenty and if she is between twenty and sixty years when she makes a vow, she is to give thirty shekels to the church, and she shall be free and unencumbered.

One shekel is about 20 pence [Heller], Ex 30.[20]

I have no idea what, other than their souls, monks, nuns, and priests are able to promise to God. That kind of vow they must keep according to the ordinances of Scripture which empowers them to liberate their souls. For if monks or nuns between the twentieth and sixtieth year promise their souls to God, they are able to set them free by paying fifty or twenty shekels, respectively.

Monks and nuns who promised their souls to God alone, in an appropriate way, can ransom them. How much more so if they rendered wanton vows—which they have generally done. For they were not satisfied with having promised their souls to God. No. They also had to offer and promise them to an invented God such as St. Benedict, Dominic, Francis, Clare, Hedwig, and the like.

The money or shekels should today not be given to stone churches; we have more than enough of those. Within a mile and a half, or in any given city, there should only be one church in which the word of God is preached.[21] Neither should there be any church in which the word of God is not preached. But we observe that there are many chapels, monasteries, cathedrals in any one city, and Satan cannot supply priests or monks. When they want to build churches, they sputter and make us think that there is a change for the better; they lure the poor person's money out of his pocket [mar: Take a look at St. Peter's cathedral in Rome]. They [e] put up sanctuaries and say that they ought to be adorned with silver and golden vessels, and they talk those out of their money to whom the saints would rather give some than take it away from. We see too many and useless churches, and we know that they stand full of silver-embroidered idols. And yet, no monk or priest is prepared to write, Stop your sacrifices and the carrying of money into church. They say, [Ex 13] "You must not come empty-handed and you are to repay your vows with money." And they claim that Moses says so. But unlike Moses—who also did what he said he would—they do not want to forbid the giving of money to dead churches. He said, "Neither man nor woman is to give anything to the tabernacle, for such sacrifices are superfluous and too numerous" [Ex 36]. When do the priests ever say that? More likely than not, they tear down many of the old churches and build new ones. They would probably pass off a goat's beard for a sanctuary before they would shout, Stop, the sacrifices are too numerous.

Now since we have too many churches, the money (which monks and nuns give for the salvation of their souls) should be given to some living, pitiable temple of which Christ generally says, "What you have done to one of mine, you have done unto me." What you give to thirsty, hungry, naked, sick, and imprisoned people, etc., you have given me. These are the true and living temples in which God governs and walks about; to these monks and nuns ought to give their money whenever they render their vows with money. They are not to give money to those raven-black, fat beggars or to other monks and priests, but rather to needy, poor people whether they be laypersons or spirituals.

This is a comforting, godly teaching which God himself gave through his infallible word. Monks and nuns are to rejoice in this, and not be led astray by papal laws, for the pope is just as foolish and [//] mad as others. We are not to concern ourselves with his commandments or his prohibitions. Neither is it necessary to ask the pope, bishops, or anyone else for advice or to request absolution, since Scripture gives you advice and absolution in clear and understandable words. You must not run out of your house to seek advice when you are able on your own to discern divine counsel. *Si stetissent in consilio meo dicit*—But if they had stood in my council, [Jer, chapter 23:22].

The pope taught contrary to this advice when he said, that when girls of twelve or boys of fourteen promise their souls to God upon entering a cloister, their vow is so firm and strong after a year of probation, that no one can release them from it.[22] This is untrue, with all due respect to the pope. Why do you contradict Scripture, more even than your father, the devil! You say that someone who is over fifteen years of age and remains in a cloister after the probationary year, or one who binds himself hand and mouth to an order through a vow, ought to remain for ever in a cloister.

I ask firstly, where do you get such teaching from? You should then note that Scripture commands that we are to dedicate all firstborn children to God. You find it written a little later in the same chapter, Ex 13, that you are to redeem with money all firstborn human beings. What more can a monk or nun do when he or she enters a cloister than to dedicate themselves unto God? Nonetheless, God says, you are to free the same with compensation [*vergleychung*].

We also have another estimation of years from that established by papal brains; the age between five and twenty is considered of less value than the age between twenty and sixty. Scripture says in Leviticus 27, that a young man between five and twenty years of age is to give twenty shekels for the soul which he vowed unto God while a young woman is to give ten.

God granted such freedom in appropriate promises. [e ii] The pope must not coerce people to keep inappropriate vows, and he must not invent his own times by which to bind monks for ever. Scripture in Leviticus 27 recounts all ages and time spans of humankind from the twentieth to the sixtieth year and from the fifth to the twentieth and from one month to the fifth year. It considers the poverty of people sixty years and over and grants to everyone who vowed or committed himself or his soul to God the power and freedom to cut loose and make himself free.

Yet the pope's small decrees—in violation of Moses (whom Christ fulfilled)—solidifies the vows of monks and nuns so that he removes from them the power to redeem themselves and he arbitrarily establishes that no one can liberate his soul after the fifteenth year.

God says that he or she at twenty years of age may free themselves with a certain sum of money. The pope states that one cannot free oneself any more. The pope contradicts not only Moses, but Paul as well. Paul teaches and orders every pastor and bishop to encourage young girls to marry, telling them to take men. The pope has filled all monasteries with small children. Paul says to Timothy that he ought not allow any woman who is younger than sixty to profess widowhood if she did not earlier have a man and, as a result of the marriage act, children. The pope pays heed to none of that and gathers everything that he can grab into his net. Paul says that those who are younger than sixty should be stopped from profiting from, or from promising widowhood. The pope says (contrary to Paul), that a woman who has remained in a cloister for more than fourteen years, must remain there forever, even when she is younger than sixty. Note how the pope agrees with Paul. A papist might say that Paul speaks of widowhood. My dear [//] father, give attention to the reasons for Paul's prohibition and you will discover that he meant virgins, as well. Paul included all young women who desired marriage.

Paul says, You must not allow any of them to reach the profession of widowhood, unless she had a man before. And what is the situation now with beghins and nuns?[23] Paul did not want to have anything to do with nuns, for the estate of a nun is a heathen, not a Christian estate. The pope is not concerned about whether a woman had a husband before or not. But Paul wants the young to take men, to give birth to heirs, and to take care of their homes in service. The pope says, "I want all who have been in cloisters for more than fourteen years not to take a husband."

Paul considered rankness and incontinence small sins and, as a result, he dissuaded all young women and widows who were under sixty from their intention of professing widowhood [1 Tim 5].[24]

The pope allows great vices, sin, and shame to happen and take root before he will admit that one might leave one's bondage and enslavement after having rendered vows, even though no profession is binding that has been made under the age of sixty. Thus the pope acts and teaches contrary to the apostles and Moses. I will not mention that he acts in opposition to Christian liberties, divine honor, and common love.

But this is not yet sufficient and enough; he must also strive and rant against what Christ has shown openly. St. Peter and other apostles were considerate and courageous men who said, it is good not to court a woman. Whereupon Christ said that not many can accept this, but only those to whom it has been granted [Mt 19]. Anyone who can sense that may abstain from marrying. Note that Christ says that chastity is a divine gift and that no [e iii] one should refrain from marrying unless he senses this gift of God. Christ intends that those who wish to enter the married state not feel the gift of chastity. The pope does not give much attention to whether people feel that gift, and he allows them to fall into making vows of chastity, as pigs might fall into husks. No one can learn in sixty years whether or not God has granted the grace of chastity; no one under fifteen years is able to learn that, either. One may well live chastely for twenty years, but in the thirtieth year become unchaste.

I presume that the pope ate the meat of a rabid cow when he set the maximum age of temptation in the fifteenth year; I know many a young boy and young girl who in their sixteenth year do not feel what their Adam drives them to. The inclinations of the flesh lie quiet and dormant for that period of their lives.

The crucial year [*Annus probationis*], according to Scripture [1 Tim 5], is the sixtieth. Paul says that no one under sixty years of age is to be admitted to widowhood.

The pope himself says that vows made by girls under twelve and by boys under fourteen do not bind them to any order, and that it is within their power, and they are free to leave their cloisters and go into the world. And popes penalize abbots, priors, and guardians by imposing the ban and anathemas when they elicit vows from such young folks.[25] Why then should I not advise monks and nuns to leave their cloisters when they are ready to pay such an exacting toll? Why should I not tell them that vows of chastity, made under sixty years of age, are not binding when St. Paul says that no woman should be chosen to profess widowhood, unless she has reached the sixtieth year? The sixty-year limit is appropriate for men also. If Moses considers the age of men and women always to [//] be equal, can the pope then say that no vow is in effect before one has passed the fourteenth year? He says this without the backing of Scripture and applies it to a time of life which is insufficient to determine one's inclination. Why should I not say, supported by the writings of Paul, that vows of chastity made under the age of sixty are not binding? For no one can say how long one can remain chaste, though it may be possible for a time. The pope penalizes those by anathemas who disobey his commandments. Why then should I not explain to an obstinate pope who acts contrary to divine teaching that, for more than four hundred years, he and all his forebears would have come under the ban, the anathemas, and curses of God, lain dead and buried by Pontius Pilate, unless they would have repented of their teaching.[26] For they taught other than and contrary to divine teaching. They ought to keep boys and girls away from such evil and pestilential vows and undo vows that have been made, without money.

What wrong is there in breaking vows? Paul says [1 Tim 5], "They have been judged for breaking faith." Nonetheless, it is a small wrong and much less important to break a vow of chastity in order to be married to a woman than for us to lead impure lives. Had Paul not said that those sin who leave the first faith, I would conclude that nuns, monks, and priests may set aside, without sin, the vows they made through some agreement. At the moment, and in view of Paul's prohibitions, I consider all vows which have been imposed on men and women as not binding until a well-informed pastor or bishop who is as learned as Timothy or Titus knows them [to be genuine] and confirms them publicly or privately by his silence.

Although our bishops may have become foolish and incapable of advising, we still have Scripture [//] which gives advice and rejects and annuls all vows of those monks, nuns, and priests who have not yet reached their sixtieth year.

We take comfort in the fact that we may clear and shed these vows with the help we give people in need, as Moses allows, Lev 27. It follows from this that the chapter before us must not be read according to the letter, but according to the import of its content. It must not be understood to say that, everything a person vows, he must also do. For I may absolve myself of all vows in which I promised my soul to God, as we saw.

At this point I must say one more thing regarding monks and nuns, [Lev 27]. I will accept that parents dedicate their children to God when they are still in the cradle. Nonetheless, they are free to redeem their infants by giving help to the poor. Moses says, "If someone dedicates a son or daughter of between one month and five years to God, he is to give five shekels for the son and three for the daughter. But if he is poor, he ought to give according to ability; if he has no money, he may help the poor through service and assistance."[27]

This is the first article on vows which affect souls. Our monks, nuns, and priests render this type of vow, though with a difference.

Monks and nuns vow chastity without qualification, directly and freely, [Gen 6; Rom 7; James 1]. Priests, on the other hand, vow as follows, "I promise chastity as far as human frailty permits." This is not a vow of chastity. No. It says rather, "I promise that I will not be chaste or righteous [frumm]." Human frailty never rests; it is always ready to do evil and does so against our will and always gives birth to sin. Therefore, a person [//] who promises to be as righteous as his sickness allows him to be never intends to be righteous.[28] In one thing, however, I consider monks, priests and nuns to be alike, namely, that their vows remain without force until they are over sixty years of age.

Regarding the second article, you must note that no one is obligated to do or give all that was promised. Scripture speaks as follows
[Lev 5], "A person who swore with his lips to do good or evil, come
what may, and then fails to do it, and who recognizes his error later,
must do penance by sacrificing a sheep or lamb. The priest will then
pray for him, and his sins will be forgiven him. And if he is poor, he
must give a pair of doves."[29]

The passage provides a beautiful explanation of the text. We
learn here that a person who vows to do something good, which he
considers to be good—such as monks and nuns do—and persons who
vow unto saints fancy that they do what is right. But when they are instructed in the faith and learn that their vows are inappropriate, what
then shall the one do who has vowed something in this manner, which
at the time he considered to be right and good, but which later he
found not to be good? Should he continue? No. He must think on it
and learn, and he must be repulsed for having vowed something in ignorance which is evil and wrong. He must offer assistance to the living temples in the form of money, goods, or counsel or assist others
and do penance in this manner.

Observe here that Jephthah also made a vow which he considered to be good, but which in reality was an evil vow and against God,
[Judg 11]. Scripture says, "You shall not kill," [Ex 20]. Against this
prohibition Jephthah made his vow, saying, "If you surrender the sons
of Ammon into my hands, I will offer up as a burnt offer and sacrifice
unto you the first who comes running [f] toward me out of my house."
Jephthah should not have done this, for it was against God's will and
counsel; St. Augustine sees this the way I do.[30]

Do not be disturbed by Scripture saying that the Holy Spirit was
with Jephthah [Judg 11]. In half an hour or much less, one may lose
the Holy Spirit by doing what is wrong.

We see this clearly in the case of Peter who in the very hour in
which Christ said to him, "You are holy" was told by Christ, "Get behind me, Satan; you are an offense to me" [Mt 16]. A great change
may take place in a very short time, as was the case with Jephthah. His
vow, therefore, is not worth noting, though he had the Spirit of God.

By this you may perceive that no one is to fulfill one's vow after
having learned that it is evil. Rather, one is to show regret and endure
pain and penalties, as stated.

All monks and nuns, who vowed something in ignorance which
later they discovered to be evil and harmful, should heed this. They
must cling to what is best, and regret their foolish vows and their igno-

rance, and help the poor people by way of compensation.

Since it is much better, and more pleasing to God, that nuns and monks take husbands and wives, and raise children in God's teaching and love, and that they are pleasant rather than that they mumble in churches and pray without any understanding, neither teaching children nor anyone else the word of God, and being envious of each other and not graciously inclined toward anyone, they ought, above all else, choose, seek, and do what is best.

To wit, because nuns and monks commit such beastly sins which are best left untold because they are worse even than common unchastity and adultery, and happen because of their strong nature and their tendency to uncleanness, it would be a thousand times better [//] for them to change than to be driven to such beastly sins. Marriages are to be instituted in order to avoid unchastity, as Paul teaches [1 Cor 7], "On account of fornication, each man should have his wife."[31]

I say that there are some young nuns and monks who commit sins (I lay them upon their conscience and into their hearts and shall keep silent on account of my shame) which are weightier than bestiality.[32] Yet they might be saved if they would enter upon the married state, even though they made vows and gave their oaths.

Since they may then learn through daily experience that their irrational and stupid vows contribute to their destruction and to loss of their salvation, they are, as we said, to make retribution for their vows and enter into a safe state. Because of sins like these, they are not chaste anyhow; in God's sight they are whores and knaves who do not live up to their vows. And even if they refrain from committing such despicable vices, they sin in their passionate thoughts and designs. Therefore, let go of your risky state,[33] take hold of the marriage bed which God permits, and which in addition is wholesome medicine.

Anyone who is inclined to chastity ought to remain chaste, but without making any vows until after the sixtieth year; for under that age he does what is wrong and the pastor must declare his vow inadmissible. Refuse those who are younger than sixty, 1 Tim 5:9ff.

Whenever we vow to do something that is wrong, we must not fulfill that vow. Rather, we must rethink it properly and declare to God that we vowed wantonly.

This is the second addition to our text from which we may deduce how a vow is to be fulfilled. Nor will I conceal that Moses in the same chapter in which he says, "What you have promised someone with heart and mouth, you are to fulfill without delay," Deut 23, also says shortly before that, "You are not to offer any income [f ii] earned in a house of harlotry and not bring any carnal money into the house of God, though you promised them to God; for both these are an abomination and curse in God's sight."

Note that Moses does not allow us to give everything we promised to God. He says that if we promised God carnal money and money earned through unchastity, we are not to give him any of it; for God will not look upon or accept any such. Therefore we are not to understand "what you promised, you must give" in this manner. If we promised something that God hates or which displeases him, we must not give it. Rather, we must bemoan our foolish vow and pay the penalty, as was said above in the context of the fourth chapter.

Now if I were to look at and evaluate the office, work, and life of so-called spirituals (I mean those who walk impeccably and appear in a good light with people and are taken to be righteous), I find nothing more outstanding than long prayers, eternal churchiness, the hearing and reading of masses. Yet, none of these is good in the sight of God. Christ forbids long prayers saying, "You are not to talk like the Gentiles (when you pray)," Mt 6:7. Yet priests, monks, and nuns babble day and night, chattering like magpies. They do not know what they pray, and they pray more and other than what God desires.

I know that if they include such prayers in their solemn vows, they promise something to God which he does not desire. For Christ says, "Do not talk much." Since Christ forbids such long prayers, one ought to desist and hold to the one who is the truth and the right way. God says through David, "Why does the sinner take my word and testament into his mouth?" God commands that no sinner is to carry God's word in his big trap. A sinner is the one who does not believe the word, "Therefore I swore in my anger that they should not enter into my rest."[34] How can [//] nuns and monks believe when they neither hear nor read God's word? How is it possible for them to speak such long prayers in faith? They bring little faith and many words, none of which pleases God, or has ever suited him.

Christ says, "Do not pray in public, as the hypocrites do, but in secret, for God sees what is hidden and secret," Mt 6:5. "God judges the heart, not outward appearances," Jn 8:15f.[35] "God is spirit and is to be honored in spirit," Jn 4. We silly fools have allowed ourselves to be convinced that it is sufficient to sing, shout, write, or pray publicly in front of all the people and in broad daylight. We like what Christ prohibits. And whatever Christ does not want, monks and nuns offer up to him. Moses applies here. If you promise something that is evil, repent of it and cut it out.

Monks and nuns are to let go of such caterwauling and no longer offer it unto God who does not want it. I say nothing about the uselessness of all visible and external worship and that God values highly the spirit alone, as Christ says, Jn 6:63, "The flesh is of no avail." And 1 Peter 3:4 says that the hidden self in the heart is precious and dear in the eyes of God. External works God deems to be useless, for he sees into that which is inward, secret, and hidden. Thus all visible, public prayer is like the howling of wolves. God prohibits it. How then can you serve God with a good conscience and how can you continue in such vows?

I will accept it when monks and nuns first openly show their prayers to be in the Bible and then teach the content of their prayers to those who stand about—as long as they do so briefly. Paul says, "I would rather [f iii] say five words that can be understood and heard, when I pray in church, so that I might teach other people, than speak five-thousand words in tongues which those who stand about cannot comprehend," 1 Cor 14:19. Our priests, monks, and nuns themselves do not understand their prayers. How can they expect to be understood? I let go of this, having shown that God is displeased and annoyed by such buzzing of flies, and I will now turn to the saying of Christ which I had started earlier [Jn 3]. Christ says, "God is spirit, and all who are true, must worship him in spirit and in truth," Jn 4:24.[36] From this it follows firstly that those carnal worshipers who pray externally are deceitful worshipers and their prayers are untruthful. We must not bring any lies before God, neither are we to pray carnally and in body only. And if we have promised to offer such prayers, we are not to fulfill bad promises.

Moreover, since God is spirit we are to serve him in spirit, as Paul says, "Whom I serve in the spirit," Rom 1:9.[37] Poor laborers do this much better than idle monks and nuns.

Thirdly, true worshipers are to pray in spiritual freedom. For this reason Christ says that true worshipers will worship God neither in Jerusalem nor upon a mountain, but only in spirit and in truth.

[mar: Truth and Spirit] Spirit is tied to no single place, but is in more than one place. Truth is not tied to any corporeal or visible thing; it is fastened on God alone. It does not stand in anything other than faith in God. Thus a true worshiper—the one God desires—is free and unencumbered by places and external things. He is lord or willing servant of all creation. Against these two virtues, those monks and nuns render their vows who in their promises and plans think [//] of ways in which they might serve God in this or that cloister with singing, shouting, droning, and babbling. If the vow is sound, it is to be fulfilled. But must you keep what you foolishly vow and foolishly give? Allow yourself to be informed by Christ, Paul, and Moses. Christ says, "If you remain in my word, you are my disciples and the truth shall set you free," Jn 8:31. Observe how closely linked the two articles are: to be a disciple of Jesus and to be free. Anyone who is not free, is not a disciple of Christ. And one who is not a disciple of Christ is not free either. If you are a disciple, you are free. Free of what? Remember what I said earlier from the words of Christ. You are free of places and of all external things. Take, for example, the handwashing of the disciples and Christ saying that true worshipers worship neither on a mountain nor in a specific place.[38] This freedom and discipleship we learn from the sayings of Christ who says, "If you remain in my words, you are my disciples and the truth shall set you free."

Here monks, nuns, and priests might well say, we are servants of God and free, and yet we depart from the teaching of Christ. In addition, they attach themselves to their poor, miserable cloisters, and to stone and wood. They claim to be doing a good thing when they seize and hold spiritual freedom captive, turning it into carnal freedom, contrary to the word of God and Christ, according to which true worshipers worship neither on a mountain nor in Jerusalem.

It is also contrary to Paul. For although Paul at times becomes the servant and companion of all people and their affairs, he says, nonetheless, that he retained his freedom, "so that I will not be enslaved by anything," 1 Cor 6:12.[39] And again, "Where the spirit of the Lord is, there is freedom," 2 Cor 3:17. He does not bind himself with any vow. [//]

Paul retains his spiritual freedom in all servitude. And although he allows himself and Titus to be cleansed and circumcised, in keeping with the law, he does so to benefit the imprisoned people so that he might redeem them from Jewish ceremonies and circumcision. Therefore he preaches directly, with power and unceasingly, that carnal circumcision and Jewish ceremonies are useless. Note how he is thus free in spirit and in the truth of faith, and he holds in scorn what he does for the deliverance of the sick.

If monks and nuns would bind themselves in this way to places and external things so that they consider them to be as nothing, and if they thought others who are unlike them in works and in the saying of long prayers, to be good and righteous and higher than they, one might have patience with them, if they admit publicly that their lives are useless and of no worth. But we can see how monks, nuns, and priests place all their diligence, their salvation, and all their loss on their caterwauling and heavenly ceremonies; in fact, they bank so much on these that they consign the negligent to the devil and before that despise those who make fun of their orders and religion, their cloaks and beads. But those who make their prayers come true, or who praise them, they commend to God.

In this way they eliminate Christian freedom and divine truth. Such manner of life cannot lead to their salvation; I vouch for that. As I have shown, they do not serve God and do not believe in God. For this reason they shall not attain to salvation. Scripture says, "Anyone who does not believe is lost."[40] And again, "if you wish to enter into life, keep God's commandments" [Jn 3:36].[41] God expressed the form and nature of the works that are pleasing to him, as I said above. Contrary to these very characteristics they render their vows and they continue in that which is forever against God and which he prohibits and damns.

After all this they ought to understand Moses. God says [//], "You shall sanctify unto God all firstborn human beings," [Ex 13:2; Num 8:16]—I touched on this earlier. Nonetheless, he wills them to untie and free themselves. God demands of us more freedom than servitude. God delights in a free spirit considerably more than in an imprisoned servant. Though a free person in God is God's servant, he, nonetheless, dominates all creatures in the air, in the water, and on earth. He is not bound to a place, nor to time, nor to food or works. He does everything freely, willingly, and without conditions. Therefore, even though the Jews were to offer and sanctify their firstborn children unto God as a sign of their servitude and imprisonment in Egypt, from which they were graciously liberated, they still had to redeem their children. This indicates to me the wonderful evangelical light of Christian freedom.

How then shall I advise monks and nuns? I should carry their yoke along with them if they were prepared to know themselves. I sense, however, that they would then conclude that I approve of their foolish imprisonment. They should set themselves free and serve God in truth and spirit, i.e., serve the neighbor in faith, hope, and love and by giving assistance in true love. This would be more useful and more desirable for them, for thus they would walk without perverting divine works and laws. *Oportet misericordiam fide et iudicium primum facere* [One should, above all, show mercy, faith, and judgment].

Accordingly, I should like to copy and repeat above-mentioned texts, Lev 5 and Deut 23, in order to show that God so hates certain things that he refuses to accept them either as sacrifices or as vows. But I shall introduce new texts and examples such as Lev 22:20 where it is written, "You shall not sacrifice a blemished offering, whether it is a freewill offering or in payment of a vow. Anything blemished you shall not sacrifice, for it is displeasing to God." Note how Moses speaks of freewill and required offerings as when he says, "You [g] shall not offer to God anything that is blemished. You shall not render to God a blemished vow." Visible spots indicate spiritual and hidden spots which arise from lack and use of faith. For this reason Paul says that the conscience of unbelievers is impure and that they have been rejected for any good works, [Tit 1:16]. Without faith nothing pleases God, Heb.[42] There is no doubt that long and public prayers, uttered from necessity, are contrary to Christian freedom and that the following are contrary to faith. It is fully apparent that Christ uncovered and revealed the tattle, wrinkles, and spots of such long-winded public prayer. Isaiah also did this, saying, "If you lengthen and increase your prayers, I will not listen to you. If you stretch out your hands, I shall avert my eyes from you. Your hands are full of blood" [Isa 1:15].[43] [mar: Bloody hands]

Note there that long prayers are perceived to be defiled and blood-stained. Observe how many spots and wrinkles are in long prayers.

In the first place, spiritual truth, which is faith, goes by the boards. Much damage, many lies, and prayers spring up along with vexation and false judgment, fictitious appearance, and splendor.

Secondly, Christ teaches that long prayers are blemished and that they contain Gentile unbelief. For this reason he says, "Do not make long prayers like the Gentiles."

Thirdly, Christ says elsewhere that hypocrites cheat or talk widows and orphans out of goods and possessions through long prayers. This is the blood that Isaiah thinks of and of which hypocrites, priests, monks, and nuns are full. Is it not blood when one does not mean well toward others, seduces everyone, and envies and hates everyone? Fraternal enmity, spewing, and derision arise from such. There are many who would rather endure pain and sharp knives than envious tongues. What do spirituals mean [//] when they say that we ought to love one another? What is more alien to us? We must always be intent on, and committed to, the increase and growth of the neighbor. What seems more foolish to us? We ought not demand any temporal goods from lay persons. What is more worthy of scorn?

All courts, monasteries, and collegiate churches wait for the testaments and possessions of their neighbors. If you had the bag and money, you brothers, what would you care for souls?

For this reason Isaiah says that your hands are full of blood. Are envy, hatred, and derision not blood? Are cheating and robbery not blood? Is forgetting the neighbor not blood? Is neglect of the righteous and saving of the evildoer not blood? Are your prayers not blood, when you show off your reading which you call prayer, allowing widows, orphans, and the poor to be oppressed, whom you could have saved? Is such prayer not the blemished animal which God refuses to take, either as a sacrifice, or in place of vows? I cannot understand Isaiah in any other way when he says, "Your hands are full of blood" and who shortly after explains the meaning of blood, saying, [Isa 1:16] "Remove your evil thoughts from before my eyes." You must be clean and pure, abstain from doing evil, learn to do good, come to the aid of the oppressed, and defend widows and orphans before the law; as if he wanted to say, you do not do this, therefore you have bloodstained hands, and blemished and impure prayers which you are not to pray or vow, nor are you to render such prayers. The reason is in what Moses says, "You are not to sacrifice blemished and sick animals to God, nor are you to bring them to God in payment for your vows."

Monks, priests, and nuns ought to learn from this that their prayer is not respected and that it is worthless before God and that they have no basis for rendering such [g ii] prayer (though they may have vowed to do it), unless they first cleanse themselves of blood and blemishes. Since then they take such life to be the highest, and since they boast of it mightily, and dare to transmit their holiness to others, rather inappropriately as far as God and prohibitions are concerned, they would be well advised on this account alone to leave beads and cloisters and live unto spiritual truth and endeavor, above all else, to serve everyone. If there were still some free time—of which I am not aware—they might present their fiddle-faddle as the freedom of the flesh. This I had no intention of praising here. What do we do when we wish to sacrifice and give to God that which God heartily dislikes? We will never fulfill our vow, even if we were to give the very thing we promised. We would merely move God from being annoyed to being greatly enraged.

It should be quite clear from this that a single text cannot be sufficiently understood without setting it alongside and comparing it to others that speak of the same matter. Several of above-quoted texts state that a person may cancel and free himself from his vows. Take for example Lev 27. Yet others teach that we are to confirm our vows, as for example, Lev 5. And some forbid that we bring to God what we have promised God, as Deut 23 and Lev 22. Should we not accept the text, "What a man vows he must also give," straightforward and unchanged, somewhat as follows, "What a person sacrifices to God in keeping with the content of Holy Scripture, must be done without delay?" God is not pleased by any vow and sacrifice which is not seasoned with the wisdom of divine Scripture. To sum up: divine, scriptural, upright, and orderly vows alone, known in Latin as *vota legitima* [legitimate offerings] and which are authorized and expressed correctly according to the statutes and the commandments of Holy Scripture, are to be given and sacrificed to God without delay. [//]

Any others must not be given because God hates and despises them. These vows must be given not as vows but by way of some compensation and conciliation—as stated above. Anyone who desires additional information should read all of chapter 22 of Leviticus alongside the thirtieth chapter [of Numbers].

Text: [Numbers 30:3-5]

When a woman makes a vow to God and binds herself by a pledge in her youth while she is in the house of her father, and her father hears of her vow and of the pledge by which she has bound her soul, and the father says nothing; then all her vows are confirmed. And she must honor the pledge which she laid upon her soul. But if her father objects on the day he hears of her vows or rejects them, she must not honor any of the vows and pledges which she bound upon her soul. And God shall be gracious unto her because her father opposed her or rejected her vow.

In other words, if a young woman or girl is under the authority of her father when making a vow to God, she must not honor her vow until the father has directed her to do so. Until then she is to hold off and delay her vow until the father is fully cognizant of her vow. After that, once the father has heard of his daughter's vow, he has no more than a day to consider whether through his consent he will confirm or prevent the vows that have been made. If he is silent for the entire day and does not speak against it, he validates the vow of his daughter by his silence; the daughter then must honor her vow and obligation.

But if the father should say on the day on which he heard of his daughter's vow, I do not in the least stand by your vow or I do not want you to honor your vow, the daughter then must not honor it. Rather, she is to pull back and let go [g iii], and God will be gracious unto her.

Monks and nuns ought to heed this and not tempt or lead astray any of the children to make vows unto God for as long as they are under the authority of their father. Instead, they preach, "Of course, it is quite true that one is not to honor a vow against a father's will. But since vows are to the honor and glory of God and in support of a sacred cause, you may fulfill your vow without the knowledge of your father." Dear children, beware of such wheedlers. They cheat you, empty your purses, and fill their own houses. What can be more gracious and godly than when a person approaches God without any mediation?

Yet, Scripture says, "As long as a young girl is under her father's authority when she makes a vow, she must not honor her vow before her father has heard of it without objecting. And if the father opposes her, the child is not to honor her vow, and God will be gracious unto her."

Note that God wants to forgive whatever you vowed foolishly, as long as you do not fulfill your vow, if it goes against your father. But should you honor the vow against your father's will, you must know that God will not be gracious to you and that he will punish you.

Neither should one coerce parents or move them by bending their ears[44] until they approve the vows of their children, privately or publicly. Scripture does none of these things, and we are to follow Scripture implicitly. Therefore, elders must be more alert in future. Above all else, they must look to what their children, servants, and maids need. And after that they must look out for their neighbors and for all who are in need, by helping them with the very money which their children would likely have given to well-fed monks or priests. Parents have one day from the hour in which the father hears of the vow; in other words, when he is aware of his child's vow, to consider [//] and to counter the vow. I reckon that Scripture intends this to be a full day of twenty-four hours, "And morning and night made it one day" [Gen 1:5].

The children, too, should not take too long in letting their parents know of the vows they made, for Scripture says not, in vain, "If the father remains silent on the day on which he becomes aware of the vow," [Deut 30:4]. By this we are informed that the children must be well aware of their father's silence and secret compliance. But if a child rushes speedily and is not fully aware of the father's awareness, she does not render any service to God by honoring the vow that was made. What the text said concerning girls, applies, in my estimation, to all children who are still under the authority and control of their parents. It is also true of orphans who are under twenty and live under tutors and trustees. For the term here given as father, in Hebrew means one who, on account of age, honor, care, and authority, deserves to be a father. We know, for example, what Paul says of young heirs, "An heir, as long as he is small, does not differ from a slave. Though he is a lord, he lives nonetheless under tutors and guardians," [Gal 4:1]. But we also know that no servant has the right to promise something to God which belongs to his master. By the same token, young children have no right to do anything without their guardian, nor do they have permission to vow or give something.

I ask at this point how I am to behave when my father is a nut, i.e., a foolish and uncomprehending man who probably allows me to make a vow which would be displeasing to God and might be to my hurt, as [//] when I vow to lead a small girl on the eighth, or a little boy on the ninth day, through fire, thus to purify them, which Deut 18:10 forbids? And what if I want to make a vow unto a saint or keep something else which, however, is wrong? Must I honor that vow, if my foolish father, who is ill-informed in Scripture, has given his approval? No. If you have God's counsel, you do not need human counsel. "In the council of my people, those should not be represented (says God), who speak the truth from their own heart," Ezek 13:2f.

I desire the kind of father who has understanding, like the one who says [1 Cor 4:15], "I have born you in Christ Jesus through the gospel." I wish to have such a father when it comes to vows, who gives birth to me through the word of God, and who sets up no other foundation than that of Jesus Christ, [1 Cor 3:14].

Text [Num 30:6] [45]

If a woman becomes a man's while under her vows, or has bound herself by some thoughtless utterance of her lips, and her husband hears of it, but says nothing to her on the day he hears of it, she is to honor her vows, and the pledges by which she bound herself shall stand. But if her husband disapproves on the same day on which he hears of it, he nullifies all the vows his wife spoke or pledged herself to. And the Lord will be gracious unto her.

This text clearly speaks of vows made by women who have husbands. It demonstrates that the vows of such women stand fully in the will of their husbands. A woman's vows are static and imperfect until the moment when her husbands know of them. Before a husband hears of his wife having made a vow, a woman should not honor any vow—be it great or small. But as soon as the husband is [//] cognizant of his wife's vow, he has no more than a day to object. If he objects and does not allow his wife to honor her vows, she must abstain and not attempt to honor her vows. God will then be gracious unto her and will forgive her wantonness in making vows. But if the wife attempts to honor a vow against her husband's will, she angers God and falls from sin into sin. And if the husband remains silent and does not contradict her vows on the day he hears of them, the woman must honor her vows.

Thus the husband's silence is taken to mean approval, as we said above with regard to daughters.

This clause covers simple and unadorned vows which are not endorsed by oaths. Vows that are affirmed by oaths will be dealt with in what follows.

I should repeat here what was noted above, namely, that earthly vows which pertain to things of the spirit are not complete without a verbal expression. Scripture says for this reason, "If a woman has a husband and makes her vows" or "if the utterance of her lips has bound her." No vow reaches its full inner promise unless it is verbalized. And even if it is perfect in mind and expression, a woman must not honor it by the work of her hands or through other works without her husband's knowledge. In other words, there are two ways of completing a vow: one with heart and mouth, the other through works and deeds. The first happens often; but the other does not always follow.

Wives are to report to their husbands the vows they made and ask them how they react to them. Husbands, too, must be able to instruct their wives, children, and servants, as Moses taught, [h] Deut 6, 11 and 32. Paul does likewise, "Wives ought to ask their husbands at home and learn there [1 Cor 14:35]. How can they do that, however, if their husbands know nothing about divine Scripture, like the pope and his ilk, and if they do not understand which is a divine or scriptural vow and which is not? I know that there are quite a few womanish men who are as the woman to whom Christ said, "Go and call your husband," [Jn 4:16]. They do not know what God says to them, nor do they know whether they are manly or not. How many still cling to the pope who is himself a womanish wench. There is nothing more effeminate than his teaching; it is unable to hear Christ's word, nor does it know that it ought to have a husband. Not only is the pope an effeminate wench, but so are all priests and monks and all laypersons in general who lack such a man. To them Christ says, "Go and call your husband."

Who is that man? He is one who works day and night and who

works and rests in the law of God [Ps 1; Deut 6; 11; 31]. He sets his mind on the word of God. He fills his soul with the word and teaching of God. He is capable of admonishing through Holy Scripture, and he can put down his enemies through the divine word. He carries the teaching and truth in the ephod, and the judgment of the children of Israel on his breast. This is the man whom we should ask and from whom we ought to learn. We know that popes and priests today are not quite that skilled.

The pope made his own laws and invented dreams and lies; there is not a single divine teaching in his head or heart. Why then do we run to Rome for advice and dispensation, for teaching, truth, and judgment? He has neither advice, nor dispensation, neither teaching nor the truth of God. Therefore I humbly suggest that if someone needs a man, he had better seek out one who is learned in Scripture. But one ought to believe him only [//] what he is able to show with the Bible. The Thessalonians did this; they checked out Paul and enquired whether the Scriptures did indeed contain what he preached.[46] If you say that this is extremely difficult, I reply once more, that it is more difficult and more harmful if one is too quick to make vows, and to pay for promises which God hates.

In this matter we are all women who are affianced to one spouse, Christ. Therefore, we all must listen to the voice of Christ, whether we be man, woman, servant or maid, pope, bishop, priest, monk, or nun, especially before we make a vow or honor our promises.

Yes, you will say, how do I get to Christ? I say to you, his voice is near you in your heart; it is heard in all the world. How then can you ask so derisively, "Read or hear his teaching and consider it seriously"? You will then undoubtedly learn whether you are permitted to carry through on a vow. If Christ is silent, go and honor your vows. But if Scripture says something other or better than that which you promised, take it as if your husband did not permit you to honor your vows. Everyone knows that the voices of every prophet, and the voice of Moses, are attuned to the voice of Christ and how often Christ has said to the hypocrites, "You do not know that it was said, 'I desire mercy, not sacrifice,' " [Mt 9:13]. Sacrifice includes vows, for no earthly vow can be fulfilled without sacrifice. Scripture clearly states that some people sacrifice of their own free will, while others do so because of a covenant, as do those who pay for their vows. Notice, vows pay the sacrifices. Yet Christ says frequently that God demands mercy, not vows [Mt 23:18f]. And David, "I know that you have no delight in sacrifices," [Ps 51:16]. Isaiah states, "You offer your sacrifices in vain," [Isa 1:13 and 66:3f.]. They say this when our and the neighbor's benefit and salvation are obstructed through sacrifices and vows. [h ii]

It follows then that I must refrain from making vows whenever I note that God inclines me toward something which contributes to my salvation or, when I discover that I cannot fulfil my vow through deeds, without harming or neglecting my neighbor. I then hear that my head, i.e., my husband, does not consent to my sacrifice and vow. When one sees that through payment of one's vow one harms wife, children, or servants, one must refrain from making vows. For Paul says that the one who leaves her house is worse than an unbelieving woman, [1 Tim 5:13]. As soon as you get away from understanding your neighbor because of vows, you must set aside your vow.

Similarly, when I see that a human being (be it a believer or an unbeliever) is in distress and anguish and I am able to help or lead him out, except that the fulfilling of a vow prevents me from doing so, I am to put it on hold and assist this person, for my husband[47] desires order in the works I do. For he says, "I desire mercy, not sacrifices," [Hos 6; Mt; Isa 1; Deut 15]. You must help orphans, widows, and the poor. There must not be a beggar or anyone suffering want among you. Therefore you must open your hand and assist the poor among you. You are to turn your eyes intentionally toward those who are in need. "Blessed is the one who gives attention to and cares for the poor" [Prov 28:27]. Your diligence and attention must not be obstructed by any vow. Therefore, let everyone examine himself and look to all the people in the city in which he lives whether there be someone whom he might be able to help through assistance, advice, or in any other manner. Let him set aside any vow which may draw him away from showing such mercy, for our husband Jesus Christ has clearly and openly spoken his word to us. [//]

Listen now, you pilgrims. You run to Rome, Jacob, and Jerusalem, but you give no attention to the word of Christ, your head, of which all of Scripture speaks. He says, "I desire mercy rather than sacrifices," [Hos 6:6]. You, on the other hand, often allow land and people, wife and children, neighbors and others to end up in disarray. Yes, at times, you allow them to languish in anguish and distress, although you could help them with that which you carry off to above-named places. How do you expect to stand in the presence of your head (who calls you to other kinds of work)? And why do you kindle divine wrath so wantonly?

And even if none of this happens, you are still duty bound to look after your own. I will not even mention that vows offered to St. Peter,

St. James, or to the Holy Sepulchre are unchristian and idolatrous and good for nothing. The reason is this: St. Peter, St. James, and the Holy Sepulchre are not God. Although they may be holy, you must make your vows and sacrifices to God alone. St. Peter himself teaches that. And even if such vows were fitting, they would still be useless, for the flesh of Christ is of no use. Christ says so [Jn 6]. How then can his grave, cross, and the like be of any use? How are you to stand (if ever anything depended on your defense), since Christ says to you what he said to St. Thomas, the doubter [Jn 20:29], "Because you saw me and placed your fingers on my wounds, you believe me. Blessed are those who do not see, yet believe." If Scripture is not sufficient for you to believe, the grave will not be sufficient either. The grave, cross, nails, gallows, and death of Christ are all there so that Scripture may be fulfilled. Christ says [Lk 24:25], "O you foolish and slow of heart, to believe all the things the prophets have spoken. Do you not know that Christ had to suffer? And he began with Moses and all the prophets and interpreted the Scriptures (which [h iii] spoke of Christ)." If you wish to know the suffering of Christ and what good his birth, suffering, and death have wrought, then read or listen to Scripture. Out of the sepulchre you will not pluck anything special. Pope Innocent III should be severely punished for having forced the son of the king of Hungary to move toward Jerusalem and to leave his land and people, by threatening with the ban and with the loss of royal inheritance.[48] God desires rather that the lords govern their land and people than for them to make pilgrimages. Paul says, "One who does not preside over his household is worse than an unbeliever," [1 Tim 3:4-5].

Other popes, too, deserve punishment for turning one pilgrimage into another—such as the one to the Holy Sepulchre into one to Rome.[49] They do this not to obtain Christian blessedness, but on account of the almighty Mammon whose frailty they know better than God's will and righteousness.

Text [Num 30:9]

But if a widow, or a woman who has been cast out or repudiated makes a vow, everything she bound upon her soul must be carried out by her.[50]

Compare this text with what I said above, namely, that all the vows which you intend to honor must be appropiate[51] and scriptural. In that way the widows will retain their goods and houses. Further, that widows who are less than sixty can claim widowhood. Thirdly, that although they may have sworn widowhood with an oath, they could still free themselves from it. Fourthly, that it is always better for them to marry [again] than for them to be burdened with the fire and heat of carnal turmoil. Fifthly, since Christ has wedded them and given them in marriage, they are not be be prevented by vows from doing their Christian duty. A true spouse of Christ has Christ always in her arms; what Christ desires, she desires, and where he is, there she is. This text gives widows such power be [//] cause they are not under the jurisdiction of husbands. Add to this what Paul says, Rom 7.

Text [Num 30:10-12]

When a woman binds herself by a pledge with an oath and her husband hears of it and keeps silent toward her, i.e., he does not disapprove, they then have approved her vows. The woman then must honor or carry out all the pledges she made. But when the husband nullifies the vows of the woman on the day on which he hears of them, the woman must not honor the vows or pledges (which she laid upon her soul), because the husband has nullified her vows. And God will be gracious unto her.

Explanation

This text clearly states that husbands have the power to break the pledges or vows of their wives, and that women are to rely on this confidently, for God will be gracious unto them. More still, wives are not to make pledges or vows when they know of their husband's disapproval or disfavor. Therefore, Scripture places the approval and canceling of vows under the will of men, having them say yes or no.

This is said of all vows, especially of sacred and appropriate ones. Vows that have been rejected, no wife ought to undertake, even though favor and approval of them might have been given. One who approves of inappropriate vows would not be a man, but rather a pope or Nabal.[52] O women, do not let any creature, angel, or priest draw you away from this teaching of Moses. Your husbands are your glory and crown; you have been made of their flesh and bone. You will never be able to serve God and be agreeable to him except it be according to what [//] Holy Scripture indicates. Any other kind of service displeases God, as both Isaiah and Christ state, *Mandatus hominum me colunt*—Human laws displease me.

It will be useful to you and detrimental to the pope if you know that the authority of your husbands extends, not merely to promises and vows, but also to oaths.

Had a widow promised something in the house of her husband and solidified it with an oath and had her husband shown disapproval, she would not have been obliged to keep it.

Note also, you wives, that there are some things you are not to do. Note that your husbands are able to counsel you more surely—provided they are even slightly educated—than the pope, a bishop, priest, or monk.

Observe how one of the main reasons for your going to confession—to seek the advice of priests—and which compels many people to go, is set aside by this. Wives should seek their husband's counsel in the first instance. If the husband is able to give divine counsel, they ought to be content and not look further. If he is a *nabal*, they are to ask their pastor or preacher (provided they are learned in Scripture). Such problems are not part of confessions which are useless anyhow.

Text [Num 30:13-15]

Any vow or any oath by which a woman binds herself to castigate her soul, her husband may either approve or annul.

However, if the husband is silent until the next day, or if he pretends to be deaf or mute, he confirms all vows. The wife must then honor in deed all the bonds which she established through an act of will and with her lips. This is so because her husband remained silent on the day when he became aware of her vows. And even if the husband had been aware of his wife's vow, but did not speak against it, he has solidified it by his silence. But if he undertakes later [//] to resist the vows made by his wife, to stop or annul them, he himself must accept any castigation or pain.

This says, in other words, that the husband must himself pay for and endure the constraints of the flesh or the pain and castigation of the body, the toil and work to which his wife committed herself through vows and oaths, if he keeps his wife from honoring the vows and oaths which earlier he had approved and confirmed by his silence.

Take the following example: assume a brash, proud, or joyfully undisciplined and willful nature in a woman. When she feels this naughtiness and evil inclination, she wants to castigate herself so as to make her flesh obedient and submissive. For this reason she vows to God to fast for a few days, and she places an oath on it so that she should have several cords and bonds on her conscience. She tells this to her husband, but the husband remains silent for twenty-four hours and does nothing. By his silence he thus solidifies the vows and oaths of his wife.

When he later discovers that his wife becomes sick and weak or

helpless and unpleasant, he wants to stop her and achieves by his prohibition that she begins to neglect her vow and oath. He must now
suffer her castigations and honor them, for a wife ought always to
obey her husband's orders and please him.

This too must be specifically learned from this text, namely, that,
on their husband's orders, wives must relinquish their vows and oaths
(even those which their husbands approved). But husbands must accept their weight and burden. Husbands ought to be watchful therefore and forestall their wives' vows and oaths, if they wish to have
peace and quiet.

I do not want to hide the fact that the Latin Bible uses the term
statim at this point which in Hebrew [i] means *day*. Also, that it is
written here, "then he shall bear her iniquity,[53] which basically is the
term which the translator puts into Latin as *afflixit*. I therefore stayed
with the Hebrew truth. Likewise, the term for *ieiunium* is not found in
the Hebrew [text]. I reckon that our text mixed a gloss in with the
text—which happens often, though it is not praiseworthy.

It is true that castigation, pain, or tribulation include fasting,
work, and constraint. If a woman vows that she will flagellate herself
with switches and strips in order to tame and subdue her flesh, and if
she tells her husband that she made a vow and swore an oath to flagellate herself once or twice a week (which wives ought to tell their husbands), and if the husband agrees to this in private or publicly, but later wishes to prevent his wife from bloodying herself in this way, the
woman ought to obey, but the husband must flagellate himself in her
stead. This is the meaning of "the husband must endure his wife's pain
and castigation." If husbands want to save their skin and have unhurt
wives, they ought to prevent their wives from making vows and swearing oaths on the very day on which they become aware of their wives'
vows by saying to them, "By virtue of the authority bestowed, given
and commanded me as husband by God, I lift your vow and oath and
declare your vow and oath null and void, and I forbid you to do anything further in the matter." The wife must believe this word and give
way to it. She must be peaceable and sure in her conscience, for God
who taught, bestowed, and commanded such great dignity and authority to men [husbands], does not deceive.

At this point I must insert a small speech for my gracious brother
and friend George Reich, citizen of and merchant at Leipzig. He is a
passionate searcher of Holy Scripture, who does what is proper and
fitting for a righteous Christian.[54]

The chapter, gracious brother, [//] after having dealt with and explained [matters], concludes as follows, "This is the law between a man and his wife, between father and daughter, [Num 30:16]. It frequently elevates and enlarges on the man's authority, giving men greater power than any pope or bishop ever had. Although the pope has robbed men of such authority and power, it is still vested in you men, with all the freedoms and authorities. And you are no less than men used to be at the time of Moses. Since above-mentioned authority of men is praiseworthy and is to be appropriately respected by women and children, I should like to deal, very briefly, with the following Scripture passage. "It is not good for a man to be alone; let us give him a helpmeet which is his equal. Woman was thus created in the beginning. God fashioned the rib (which he had taken from Adam) into a woman and led her to Adam who said, 'This is bone from my bone and flesh from my flesh; she shall be called he-man, for she was taken from her man.' "[55] All things look to their beginning and origin and honor it. Rightly then do women look to and respect their men. Paul says therefore [1 Cor 11:7], "Woman was created to be the glory of man, just as man was made to be the glory of God. For man is not from woman, but woman is from man. The woman is there because of the man, but the man is not there on account of woman." Women ought to note and learn from their beginnings that they must direct their hearts and eyes to their husbands. In the creation of both sexes, authority, representation, honor and advice, maintenance and rule were assigned to men. Women were given submission, discipleship, and servitude. For this reason Adam calls his wife a *she-woman*, in Hebrew, *ischa*. Thus Eve came from Adam. [I, ii]

More could be said regarding equality, for God our Lord says, "Let us make him a helpmeet who is his equal," [Gen 2:18]. There is an old proverb that says that two equal and common companions rarely govern well or are able to live in peace.[56] From equality in honor and authority, inequality and disagreement in will and heart often come about. Accordingly, God created a helpmeet for Adam who was his equal, yet different. He therefore created Adam first and Eve afterward and gave the man authority and the woman submissiveness. Just as he created Adam to the glory of God so that he might fully cling to God's will, praise, counsel, and help. Spouses retain their equality if they remain in the instituted unity, with the woman being obedient and submissive to her husband, holding him in honor and treating him well, always mindful that she has been taken from the man and is called *she-man*. A husband, on the other hand, must not forget that woman is his bone, flesh, and blood. He ought always to

love her and never hate or envy her. He ought to refrain from anything that might separate him from his wife, as Adam says [Gen 2:24],
"On this account a man shall leave his father and mother and cling to
his wife." When married people pervert the instituted order so that
she becomes man and he she-man, it is inevitable that conflicts and
tensions arise. For wherever God does not govern, there unrest and
the devil's play take over. Man is the head on the basis of the divine
order. This order is perverted when the woman rules and the man is
being ruled. I do not here speak of the ordering of the kitchen, the
barn, or such like. I speak of the governing of the will and of advice, of
which this chapter speaks.

Just as equality is found in the unity of both wills, so it is with giving assistance in physical service. The helper is less than the one who
is being helped. The helper looks to his [//] master and tries his utmost to serve the master and to be pleasing to him. This is the meaning of the term *adiutorium* which in German means *help* and in
Hebrew, a *helpful person*. Female help in Hebrew is a person who
stands in the presence of her husband and who goes to and fro according to the good pleasure of the husband. Thus God taught wives
through the term *adiutorium* that a wife should stand willingly and
ready in the presence and at the bidding of her husband, and be at his
beck and call, with ease. In sum, a wife should see by the commands
and prohibitions of her husband what the man wants and then want
the same thing, too. In short, whatever pleases the man should be her
heart's desire. From his eyes she ought to learn what he wills and desires, thus drawing out of him joy and sadness, derision and seriousness. That's why it says, "the man's helpmeet." For this reason God
made women (who are normally soft and gentle) especially tough. He
hardened them so that they may serve their husbands. I doubt it not
that many men would become tired of a woman's work. Note then
how the woman was made a helpmeet of the man. God also gave a
commandment to human beings, saying, "You are to grow and multiply," [Gen 1:28]. God commanded coupling in the marriage bed and
the increase of children. Not in the manner which is told of the immoral Grubenheimer,[57] but rather, that each man diligently apply
himself with his wife to bring forth children. For this reason Paul
writes [1 Cor 7:4], "A wife does not have control over her own body,"
and again, "The husband is not his own master," [1 Cor 7:4]. They are
to render respective obligation to the other and not to cheat on the
other. From this commandment of divine order and assistance, monks
and nuns strongly distance themselves. They have greater regard for

anti-Christian [*endchristische*] institutions and prohibitions than for divine order. And they even think that the pope is wiser than God. Shame on them. And they dare commit abominable sins which God hates more than adultery and sodomy and yet they want [I,iii] to present themselves as monks and nuns and chaste persons. Christ says, "Whoever vies with unchastity has departed from chastity."[58] Not only do they desire, but they also commit the sin of impurity. It is no wonder therefore that God destroys and crushes monasteries and their people.

What the holy fathers fled, our monks seek out; what holy women bemoaned pleases our nuns. They hear and read of how much such women as Sarah, Rebekkah, Rachel, Lea, and Hanna would have liked to give birth to children and what pain and suffering they endured to prevent the label of unfruitfulness. Our nuns, however, forget the assistance for which they were created. They despise the commandment to multiply. They laugh at the raising of children and reject that which is divine and, what is more, they do what is of the devil, popish, and inferior. I would very much like to see the pope showing me a spiritual order of believers who have avoided the marriage bed. Priests and all the spirituals before him had wives according to the law. Aaron, the Levites, the prophets, and the apostles of Christ were married. The antichrist's rule alone is extramarital and of satanic standing. If the pope ever wants monks and nuns, he ought to give wives and husbands respectively to those who are inclined toward the marriage bed. I should have liked to explain further what is meant by "woman being a helpmeet" and what marriage is, but I have run out of paper.

Read the Bible and take your children out of cloisters, you lay folks—the sooner, the better—and give them in marriage. You will thus serve God, be good parents, and assist your children in gaining their salvation. Amen.

Printed in the fifteen hundred and twenty-second year after Christ's birth.

4

On the Removal of Images and

That There Should Be No Beggars Among Christians

Carlstadt in the Christian city of Wittenberg
[1522]

The place of images in chapels and churches as the so-called picture books of the uneducated and their widespread veneration was a crucial issue in the early sixteenth century. While scholars and preachers spoke against the continued use of images in worship, images had economic as well as religious implications for many artisans who produced them. Since Reformers seemed to see only their negative impact, they sought to halt their use by calling them unbiblical. Conflicts often had far-reaching effects in the communities which tackled the problem. The removal of images generally led to violence or vandalism.

During Luther's temporary absence from Wittenberg, riots erupted which Luther blamed unfairly on Carlstadt and his followers. In Zurich the problem was less acute, since Zwingli had prepared the City Council and a large number of citizens through sermons and tracts.

In Anabaptist circles, Ludwig Hätzer's stand against images is noteworthy. Carlstadt entered the fray with the following tract which was to embroil him in a published controversy with H. Emser and John Eck. Both decided, in opposition to his views, to defend the use of images in their respective tracts. Carlstadt, on the other hand, urges the removal of images, since reliance on them is harmful to "weak consciences." He bases his argument on selected biblical texts, drawing heavily on the Hebrew Scriptures.

*References to the two known publications of this tract may be found in Freys/Barge, 88 and 89. The rather striking variations in spelling suggest that the printers sought to appeal to the people of a specific area whose dialect they employed. A modern German edition was produced in 1911 by Hans Lietzmann in his series **Kleine Texte für Theologische und Philologische Vorlesungen und Uebungen**; this translation is based on that edition. For another recent English translation, see Bryan Mangrum and Guiseppe Scavizzi, ed. and tr., **A Reformation Debate: Karlstadt, Emser and Eck on Sacred Images**. (Toronto: CRRS Translation Series 5, 1991).*

To the noble, gentle-born, Wolf Schlick, Count of Passau, Lord of Weissenkirch, Elnbogen and Falkenau, my gracious lord and patron, I extend God's grace, peace, and joy before I offer my willing, obedient, and untiring services.[1]

Noble, gentle-born, gracious lord, may I inform Your Grace that the almighty, living, and powerful God has softened the hearts of our rulers and wrought his work within them. As a result they undertook some necessary reform and restored an ancient and praiseworthy Christian custom: Friday after St. Sebastian's[2] they ordered the mass to be celebrated uniformly in their entire parish. They also intend to remove and do away with all the deceitful images and idols which have been standing on their altars for such a long time, frivolously occupying space on walls and ceilings, in the air, and all sorts of other places in churches.[3]

They decided further (all this in the presence and with the consent of several of us) that henceforth no one should have to run after bread and that no beggar is to be maintained here. While they are quite ready to feed poor people, they are no longer willing to tolerate beggars. They hope that after above three articles have been carried out, other Christian practices will be undertaken and that the best will be advanced. Among these it is highly desirable for a Christian magistrate earnestly and diligently to concern itself—motivated by its own Christian duty—with widows, orphans, and other oppressed people, to protect them from violence and injustice and to punish severely anyone who might have harmed them or their possessions, or who might have inflicted injury on the oppressed.

This article, too, will (God willing) be taken up [3] as one which preserves true Christian order without which no prayer or alleged good work has ever pleased God.

In the meanwhile, gracious lord, the eyes of all the world are upon us, observing our deeds and life. Some look for a good example, but others think up vile allegations—as sacred matters have always prompted gossip mongering.

Allow me then, Your Grace, to present Christian reasons (which I have culled from divine and infallible Scripture) for these two articles. I wish to show that the Council's honorable and noteworthy undertaking is upright and godly and one which all Christians should emulate, honor, and praise.

The first article of which I approve was in part dealt with in the booklet on the Holy Supper of the Lord.[4] I will not, therefore, write on the evangelical mass at this point. I hope that Christians will draw some considerable benefit from these two articles and that Your Grace will see by this missive my ready and willing inclination to serve Your Grace to the utmost of my potential. To this end I am at your beck and call and herewith declare my submission.

To my gracious Lord, Christoph, I extend all that is good through Christ. Amen.

Dated, Wittenberg, on the Monday after Paul's conversion[5] in the twenty second year.

Your Grace's servant,
Andreas Bodenstein from Karlstadt.

On the Removal of Images

1. To have images in churches and houses of God is wrong and contrary to the first commandment, "You shall have no other gods before me" [Ex 20:3].

2. To have carved or painted idols upon altars is more harmful and devilish still.

3. It is good, necessary, laudable, and godly to do away with them and to give the reasons found in Scripture for their removal.

Houses of God are buildings in which God alone is to be honored, called upon, and worshiped. Christ says, "My house is a house of prayer and you have turned it into a den of murderers" [Mt 21:13]. Deceitful images destroy all who worship and offer praise to them, as is written, "They are not known to God and covered with shame and they have become detestable like the things they loved," Hos 9.[6] We could never deny that we placed these images of saints in our churches out of love. Had we not loved them, we would not have put them where God alone should dwell and rule. Had we hated them, we would have fled rather than accepted them. Our deed convicts us of having loved images. Have we not [4] shown them the honor which we show for and expend only on great lords? Why have we allowed them to be painted and adorned with velvet, damask, silver, and gold clothing? Why do we decorate them with golden crowns and precious stones and do for them, out of honor and love, what we would not gladly do for our children, women, parents, and supreme princes and lords? Who will believe us when we say that we do not love these stuffed dummies—carved or painted images—when our deeds convict us? God hates and despises images, as I shall show. He considers them an abomination and says that all human beings are in his eyes as the things they love. Images are an abomination; it follows therefore that we too shall become abominable, if we love them.

They thus destroy their worshipers and those who honor them. That's why our temples may readily be called dens of murderers, for in them our spirit is put to death and destroyed. May the devil reward those papists who thus kill and destroy us. It would be far better for them to stand in hell, or in a fiery furnace, rather than in the houses of God.

Now hear further regarding the purpose and origin of the houses built for God. Solomon speaks as follows, "Your house, O God, has been built solely so that you may look upon the prayer of your servant and receive the request which he pours out before you and that you may keep your eye on the house in which your name shall be called upon, day and night," 2 Chr 6:19f.; 1 Kings 8:28. Of similar things which ought to be reserved for God alone, Solomon speaks frequently—so much so that I often wonder how God has tolerated and suffered until now our great wickedness.

Note that God's house has been built so that he alone will rule in it and so that he may cast his eye upon us needy people to aid us. In other words, God alone is to be worshiped, and he alone is to be called upon. I would dearly like to know what we should say to the true Christians or Jews who understand the Bible or to God who has given us his teaching through the Holy Spirit, should they or he ask us, "How is it that you are so bold as to permit images and idols to stand in my house?" "How dare you be so bold and forward as to bow and genuflect in my house before images which were created by human hand? Such honor is to be reserved for me. You light candles before them which you should do for me, if you wish to burn a light at all. You bring waxen offerings to them in the shape of your diseased legs, arms, eyes, head, feet, hands, cows, calves, oxen, sheep, house, property, fields, meadows, and the like, as if such images would give you healthy legs, [5] arms, eyes, head, etc., or would provide you with fields, meadows, houses, honor, goods, and possessions."

Thus you acknowledge foreign gods. I restore your health and you. "I nurtured them and carried them on my hands and they did not know that I restored their health and bore their burden," Hos 11:3. I saved them and they spread lies about me. "I taught them and strengthened their arms and they thought up evil against me," Hos 7:15, "I nurtured them and made them great, yet they despise me."

"The ox knows its owner and the slow donkey the manger of its master. But Israel—my people—does not know me and my people do not know the good I have shown them. Woe to this sinful people, etc.," Isa 1:3.

I cannot deny and must confess that God rightly says to our alleged Christians what he here says to the Jews. For they also run to idols as a crow or raven goes after a cadaver or a dead body. They look for them in special places such as in the Mark, in Grimmentahl, at Rome, or in similar places.[7] They bring them their tools, silver, gold, wax, and goods, as to their gods who saved and protected them, even though these idols are blinder than the ox at Leipzig or the donkey at N.N.;[8] these two at least recognize what good is done them and by whom. Thus they call on idols in the house of God, seeking health, help, and counsel with such senseless fools. In this manner they blaspheme God in his own house. This in itself is burdensome and is sufficient reason for chucking them out of churches. I must concede though that some of them remove their cap at least, which they would keep on if this handmade God were not present. I think it not a small matter that many bend their knees before the saints and I will speak of this in what follows.

That it is against the first commandment to hold images in honor, you need not learn from me but from Scripture. Exodus 20:3 reads as follows, "You shall have no other gods before me." This means that you must not ascribe God's goodness, help, grace, mercy, and preservation to anyone else but God who is just. You may learn this from an example: God led the Jews out of Egypt, liberating them from the prison of servitude. This goodness ought not to have been ascribed to any strange god. However, they made a calf for themselves and said, "These are your gods, O Israel, who led you out of Egypt," Ex 32:[4]. [6]

The calf was a strange god which had not saved the Jews. Nonetheless, they said that it had led them out of Egypt. In this way people create foreign gods when they attribute to others, rather than to the true God, the benefits they have received. As I said earlier, God often bemoans this in Holy Scripture. This is why God reproached Israel when they chose a king for themselves, 1 Kings 8; Hos 13.

One might even turn a person into a foreign god or set oneself up as a foreign god, as is written, "Cursed is the one who sets his hope in a human being and makes his own arm strong," [Jer 17:5]. And again, "blessed is the one who places his hope in God, whose hope is the Lord" [Jer 17:7].[9] For this reason the prophets frequently stipulate, saying, "I shall not put my trust in my bow. My sword will not save me" [Ps 44:7]. "You ought not rely on princes" [Ps 118:9]. They do this in order to avoid creating foreign gods and because they do not intend to have an image in their heart. They want to confess only the one of whom there can be no image. For God does not tolerate it.

For this reason God said soon after he had given the commandment, "You shall have no other gods. You are not to make carved or hewn images. You shall make no likeness of anything that is in heaven above or in the earth beneath or in the water. You shall not worship these; you shall not honor them. I am your God, a strong and jealous God, a zealous God who punishes the wickedness of the fathers in their sons" [Ex 20:4].

Note how God prohibits all kinds of images. Because human beings are fickle and might worship them, God states that you shall not worship them or give them honor. Thus God prohibits all homage and destroys the hiding places of the papists who by their slippery ways always violate Scripture, making black what is actually white and evil what is actually good. And if one should say, "I do not worship images and show them no honor on their own account but only because of the saints whom they represent," God answers in short and clear words, "You shall not worship them. You shall not honor them."

Interpreted any way you like, you simply must not worship them or bend your knee or kindle a light before them. "Should I desire," God says, "that you honor me or my saints in the form of images, I would not prohibit you from making any image or likeness."

I will now show you that Christians have to admit that they honor their idols. Proof: they wend and bend before them (on account of departed saints). From this I can clearly deduce that they show honor to images. For when I honor a marshal [7] on account of his prince, I honor both him and the prince; the servant because he is the servant of a prince and the prince for himself. Neither would anyone want to deny that as servant he is being honored in his own right. Hence, when I honor an image because of God, I nonetheless honor it fully— which God has prohibited.

Now let me ask further: Is it a small honor when we call images saints? If we were to think on this properly, we would find that we denigrate the honor of genuine saints and transfer it onto their deceitful images. Therefore, by calling them saints, we attribute holiness to images.

Further, no one can deny that it is a great honor indeed to be placed upon an altar. Indeed, the pope considers it such an honor that he does not permit any pious lay person to lie or stand upon an altar. It is a great and high honor, indeed, when you put someone in the place on which the body of Christ is handled and where God alone is to be called upon and which has been erected for the special praise and exclusive honor of God.

Altars have been invented that one may use them to call on God's name, there to bring sacrifice and honor to him alone. Thus Noah built his altar, Gen 8:20. And so did Abraham, Gen 12:12, and Moses, Ex 17:15. Because of this, God gave reasons for altars, Ex 20:24. There his name was to be praised, and sacrifices were to be made to him by anyone who wanted to do so. This is the honor we render to idols when we place them upon altars and light candles before them and when we call upon them because of the saints they represent. Whatever we transact upon altars we ought to render to God, Deut 27:6ff. It is never possible, therefore, to have images on altars and to deny that we are thus honoring them.

Since altars have been especially erected for the purpose of calling on the name of God, it is more devilish to place the images of saints upon altars than to nail them on walls, as the following article shall demonstrate.

Pope Gregory did not forget his papal nature.[10] He gave to images the honor which God had given to his own word, saying that images are the books of lay persons. Is not this a truly papal teaching and a devilish addition, to let the little sheep of Christ use deceptive books or examples?

Christ says, "My little sheep hear my voice" [Jn 10:27]. He does not say, "They see images of me or my saints."

God says, "My little sheep are the little sheep of my pasture" [Ps 79:13], i.e., of my teaching—not of my images. [8]

Moses says, "Teach your children the word of God from their youth onward" [Deut 4:10]. Gregory, however, says, "Let lay persons use images instead of books." Tell me, dear Gregory, or have someone tell me, what good might lay persons learn from these images? You will have to admit that one learns mere carnal living and much suffering from them and that they cannot lead beyond the flesh. They are incapable of getting beyond that. Take an example: From an image of the crucified Christ you learn no more than the physical suffering of Christ—how Christ bowed his head and such like. But Christ says that his flesh is of no avail but that the spirit is of much value and gives life. Peter, too, says that Christ has words of eternal life and spirit. Since images are mute and deaf—incapable of seeing, hearing, learning, or teaching—and point to nothing other than to mere flesh which is of no benefit, it follows inevitably that they are useless. But the word of God is spiritual. It alone is useful to believers.

It cannot be true therefore that images are the textbooks of lay persons. For they are unable to learn their salvation from them. They can draw nothing from images which serves unto salvation or which is necessary for Christian living. I do not wish to magnify them and ascribe to pictures the great honor which Gregory attributes to his idols. But I do understand why the popes laid such books before lay persons. They noted that when they led the little sheep to books, their junk market did not prosper and people wanted to know what is godly or ungodly, right or wrong. Paul says that we are to remain in the teaching of Christ; and Christ claims that he taught his disciples the word of his Father, Jn 17:26. Never did either talk of images!

Christ also says that the truth sets people free and makes them his disciples, Jn 8:32. No image can do that! Therefore, to say that images are the books of lay persons is also to claim that lay persons ought not become disciples of Christ or that they can never be free from the bondage of the devil or take on a Christian nature. Paul also teaches that we are not to have anything in common with those who honor images, 1 Cor 5:9ff. He says, "You shall not honor images; shun the worship of idols," 1 Cor 10:14. Note how Paul hates such respect given to images and says that we must have nothing in common with those who honor images, even though we do not worship them.

Yes, they agree, Paul does state that images are nothing, 1 Cor 8:4, and we know that they are not gods, and that there is only one

God. I answer, "Would to God that those who claim images are the picture books [9] of lay persons did know this; but I don't think they do." You must also remember that Paul says we are to avoid any respect rendered to images.

Don't you know that Paul says that anyone who does these things will not be saved, for how can you save lay persons when you ascribe to images the power which God gave to his word alone and when you keep them in the place in which God alone is to be honored and called upon? I shall soon touch your heart, O priestling and monk, by demonstrating that you cling to images and have made a veritable idol of an image made by human hands.

You must finally take this to heart, as well.[11] I cannot advise anyone who is sick unto death to cling to a carved or painted crucifix, for the simple reason that these are good for nothing, as I said, and incapable of getting the sick any further than the physical suffering of Christ which is of no avail. Christ himself says, "The flesh avails nothing," Jn 6:27.[12] It does not please Paul when you know Christ in the flesh only. He therefore says, "We do not know Christ after the flesh" [2 Cor 5:16]. But those who worship images intend to make the human Christ known to lay persons. This is not good. They prefer to teach how Christ was hanging rather than why he was hanged. They teach of his body, beard, and wounds; but regarding the power of Christ, they do not teach anything. Without the power of Christ, no one will be saved; but without the physical form of Christ, many thousands shall be saved in days to come.

Secondly, I say that images generally have been prohibited and that the prophets have preached against them. God says, "Woe to the one who says to a piece of wood, "Awake" and to the silent stone, "Arise," Hab 2:18f. And this is soon said when one worships a piece of wood. God further says, "Woe to the one who says to a stone, 'Get up' which means 'Come to my aid' " [Hab 2:19]. Those fools say to people who are sick unto death and who dangle on death's hook, "Look here, the Lord Jesus is in your hands."

Habakkuk says that there is no spirit in an image. When God arises all images tumble. And where images are placed, there God cannot be, as it is written in Mic 5:13, "I shall destroy the images in your midst and you shall no longer worship the work of your hands."

Thirdly, even if I were to confess that images are permitted (which no Christian can confess), there is still no comfort other than the word of God in which the just is justified, quickened, made whole, and saved. It is immeasurably more therefore when you recite for someone the two gospels which the Lord gave toward the end, shortly before his death. In other words, recite for the sick person the essence and meaning of the comfort: "My body is given for [10] you; my blood is shed for you unto the forgiveness of your sins" [Lk 22:17ff.]. These gospels have a quickening spirit. The image of Christ, though, is nothing but wood, stone, silver, gold, or the like.

Fourthly, I must uphold to the Gregorists the deed of Bishop Epiphanius[13] who before Jerome's time had removed a cloth from the church because an image either of a saint, or of the crucified Christ, was painted on it—against the prohibition of Scripture. This illustrates well how pious Christians in former times hated images and removed them from houses of God. Epiphanius came to Anablatha and there went into the church in which he saw a curtain colored and painted. It had an image like that of Christ or of a saint. He says that he actually did not know whose image it was. Nonetheless, he did not tolerate it in the church because it was hanging there contrary to Scripture. For this reason he cut the curtain in pieces. This is written in the books of Jerome, tome 3, fol 75, lra c.[14] Remember that even if I were to admit that lay persons might learn something useful and redemptive from images, I could not allow them against Scripture's prohibition and the divine will. The Scriptures state clearly that God hates and despises images, yet the papists call them books. Now I ask you, if you were to really hate and dislike a picture with all your heart, so that you could not bear to see or hear of it, how would you like it if someone insisted on getting to know and honor you through such a hated, horrible book? You would without doubt hate and flee me, along with the book or picture, should I try to honor you through the very thing which you forbid, which you hate, and which you flee. And God says that he does not like any image which we make, and, as mentioned above, that he hates and despises all who love images. In the forty-second chapter Isaiah writes, "They are to be put to shame who trust in images," [Isa 42:17].

But God had an image made of a firebrand or a serpent which was not in his likeness; nor had it been erected for any purpose other than for those who had been stung or wounded by a serpent to look up to it in order to be healed, Num 21:8f. God himself gave this image; it had not been devised by a human brain. Nonetheless, Scripture praises King Hezekiah in 2 Kings 18:3f. for doing away with said serpent because the Jews were sacrificing before it.

Our images do not originate with God. Indeed, they have been prohibited by God. We would not defend them even if many poor people were not harmed or hurt when they donate lights and money, [11] when they bow before and bare their heads before them. Neither ought we to defend idols and keep them in our churches, allowing the poor simple sheep of God to go to hell because of the abominable abuse of honoring them as if they were books.

I must, therefore, say more about the uselessness of images—in line with what is in Scripture, since I do not want anyone to depend on, or to believe me alone. Let the devil thank you if you believe me or rely on me. Direct your eyes and ears to Scripture which speaks as follows, "Makers of images are nothing and the most precious and dearest of them is for nought, Isa 44:9. They themselves testify that their images cannot see or understand.[15]

Take note, you idolatrous non-Christian, that the creator of an image is nothing and that the very best image is good for nothing. They are certainly no good unto salvation. You yourself must confess that you would not ask the maker of an image what would serve towards your salvation, because he is a maker of images. How then does Pope Gregory dare to be so bold as to say that images are the books of lay persons if even their makers cannot teach us what is beneficial unto salvation? Observe how these masters see, hear, understand, and bear witness that their images can neither see, nor hear, nor have understanding. You do not wish to, nor should you, take the makers of images for books. How then can you take images for books?

What use could images have as books?

Who would deny that books are useful? No one. Let me now briefly demonstrate that even pictures in themselves are useful and all this through Isaiah—an evangelical prophet—in chapter 44.

Isaiah speaks as follows, "Who formed or made God and carved an image which is good for nothing? Note how all who are involved and associated with images are put to shame. They shall all come together, be afraid and put to shame, etc.," [Isa 44:10f]. He goes on to report, almost derisively and acidly, how idols are made and how they are good for nothing.

Further, I cannot remain silent about how God does not tolerate the bending of knees, the bowing and genuflecting which we carry on in front of idols. God says through Isaiah, "The maker of images makes an image and bows before it. He bends down before it, worships it, and says, Set me free, save me, for you are my god" [Isa 44:15ff].

They have forgotten then that the eyes of images cannot see and that they have no understanding in their heart, and they cannot recall that they said earlier, "I used the one half of the wood for firewood and made this god from the other half. [12] With the one half of the tree, I heated the furnace and boiled the meat. And from the other part, I made this false god. In front of this piece of log, I will now fall down."[16] At the end of that chapter God says, "I am the Lord who does all things and there is none beside me," Isa 44:24.

Had I leisure and space, I would gladly deal with Isaiah. For the sake of brevity I shall begin at the end and get from there to the beginning, thus returning to the matter with which I started. Note well that images in churches contravene the first commandment. In no way can God tolerate our placing of a created object beside him. For this reason he ends with the words, "I am the Lord who created all things and there is none beside me."[17]

You holy gluttons must note that God alone gives aid and comfort and no one is with or beside him. This must ever be true (if the truth is to be believed) that no creature besides God can assist us. Tell me now, you idolatrous worshiper and giver of honor, if the saints were unable to help you, what help could their deceitful images give? Through an image you want to pay homage to the saints, giving them the very same honor which during their lifetimes they shunned and prohibited. During their lives they could not bear you sacrificing to them or calling on them. As Peter says, "Among humankind there is one name only by which you are to be saved," Acts 4:12. And if there is only one name, why then, you idolater, do you create many names through which you promise salvation?

Do you not know that they looked at Peter and were shocked when Peter said, "Why are you men surprised, and why do you look at us as if we had made the lame to walk by our own strength and power? We made him well through trust in the Lord Jesus whom the God of Abraham, Isaac, and Jacob sent," Acts 3:12. Note, you well-fed, rotund maker of images that what Peter prohibited while he was alive, you cannot attribute to him after his death. Do you fancy that he would now teach something contrary to what he taught during his lifetime? You admit that he spoke in the power of the Holy Spirit while he was on earth. What power do you think he works with in his death? Peter says, "Do not look at us." Yes, you might say here, we are not to look at images as if they themselves could do something in their own strength.

But listen. Would to God that you might speak the truth and that you might have no idols which have great power over you. What are you going to say to the bacchanalian song "St. Christopher,[18] your virtues are so great that whoever gazes on you in the morning will laugh or live at night"?[19] Tell me, how many thousands of people have gazed at the image of St. Christopher for a time in order to be saved from death or in order to have a happy eventide? [13] Did they not put great hope and comfort into their gazing upon a painted picture?

On account of their offensiveness to faith, you should advise that all images be carted to the devil. Examine whether these people take the image of St. Christopher to be a god.

You will have to concede to me that many lay persons cling to other images in a similar way for hope and comfort.

Does not such pleading as the following indicate worship? "Dear Lord, hear, hear." Is not this like saying, "Dear image, quicken me or set me free or save me from sudden death"?

Note how you tolerate it when lay persons light candles and make sacrifices before the images of Saints Paul, Peter, and Barnabas, who shunned such things like the plague while they were living. You are so super smart. If you are really such a learned chap, I ask you sincerely to tell me whether Peter, Paul, and Barnabas would themselves have tolerated to be placed upon altars. You would have to say, again and again, "No." Why then do you place their forbidden images upon altars—images which they themselves would not have accepted? And take note, dear friend, that genuflecting and bending of knees are honors which you render to any image against the will of God, as I have suggested above on the basis of the forty-fourth chapter of Isaiah.

Note also how mad, foolish, and stupid are all those who honor images. For Isaiah says, "They bend down before their gods, genuflecting and forgetting or not understanding that these images cannot see or hear." They do not understand that they cut shavings and sticks from the log (which they take to be a saint), with [the other half of] which they boiled their meat and warmed their chamber and living room. They refuse to look at that. Therefore, they shall come to grief. They will be afraid and will tremble and shake. O how those who thus cling to idols, bending and bowing before them, will suffer in their moment of death. They will not be exonerated by the fact that they do this for the saints. God knows their hearts better than they do themselves. Through his word he will convict them for having honored images, namely through this, "You shall not honor them," Ex 20:5.

I now return to the beginning and to Isaiah who says, "They are good for nothing," Isa 44:10.

Books are useful to the reader. It follows then that images are no books of lay persons—despite what Gregory and all his cronies say.

You Gregorists and papists, listen to what Ezekiel relates, "When someone turns away from me, places idols in his heart and then comes to a prophet and asks me through him, I shall answer him myself [14], making an example and a proverb of him and I will banish him from amidst my people," Ezek 14:9.

Note, you extoller of idols, what Ezekiel says about images and don't ever forget when you take an idol or image into your heart (as many do and as I have shown with regard to the image of St. Christopher), that God will answer you by destroying and damning you. God still answers us through his own word. You ought not visit prophets. But if anyone in our day and age insists on approaching doctors, masters, and bachelors on these matters and refuses to believe the voice of God without wavering, then let him hear what follows in the fourteenth chapter of Ezekiel [14:9], "The prophet who leads them into error, I, God the Lord, have made to err and I will banish him from amidst my people." Note how God destroys both the prophet who errs and leads into error and the one who asks such a prophet for advice. Be guided by this.

One who knows God's prohibition and will must follow the same without fail. He must not listen to angels or saints, or prophets who seek to draw him away from divine commandments, even though they may appear to have sound opinions. 1 Kings 13:18ff. spells this out clearly.

Ordering him neither to eat nor to drink, God sends one of his servants to King Jeroboam. This prophet or man of God, Shemaiah, although aware of the command, allowed himself to be seduced by another prophet who said, "I am a prophet like you." The angel of God has spoken to me, saying, "Lead him to your house that he might eat and drink." Shemaiah went with him and thus became disobedient to the voice of God. For this reason God had him torn apart by a lion."

Note, when we have words of the Lord but are disobedient to the voice of God, allowing another to persuade and deceive us, we have to die. Though the persuader or deceiver has the appearance of a prophet, an angel, a teacher, or a Christian who extends Christian benevolence and provides food and drink, if such benevolence prevents you from obeying God's commandment and word, you must not follow him, though he be a big, strong, and opulent monk or doctor. But if you should follow someone on account of his status, appearance, pleasant words, and friendly disposition, thus coming in conflict with a divine prohibition, you will surely die (as did Shemaiah), through the lion who stalks the world, seeking out the ones he might devour.

Thus God killed the sons of Aaron, Nadab, and Abihu, because they sacrificed unholy fires[20] before God, which they had not been ordered to do, Lev 10:1.

Note, anyone who kindles an unholy fire which is like the fire of the Lord in essence and intensity will be punished by God for having sacrificed on such a fire. [15]

I say, therefore, that we should not tolerate images in churches or among believers, even though they indicate a good thing. Just as Baalam had to confess, saying, "There is no image in Jacob and no idol in Israel." Num 23:21 and Ex 20:4 openly express this. Therefore, no Christian or believer must accept images, for he has clearly heard, "You shall have no images." A believer must live by these words and heed no appearance, whatever form or name it might have.

If someone should come along and say that images teach and instruct lay persons,[21] just as books do scholars, you must answer, "God prohibited images, therefore I intend to learn nothing from them." If someone should come along and say that images remind us of, and recall for us, the suffering of the Lord and often cause someone to pray an "Our Father" and think of God when otherwise he would not pray or think on God, you should reply, "God has prohibited images." Similarly, Christ says that God is spirit. Everyone who truly worships God, prays to God in spirit, Jn 4:24.

All who worship God through images worship falsehood. They are focusing on the appearance and external signs of God. Yet, their heart is far from God, creating its own idol in the heart and being full of lies, as Isa 44:10 says, "In their foolishness and ignorance [nerrisch und tolh hertze] they worship them [images], neglecting to say, "I have falsehood in my right hand."

No Christian can deny that spiritual prayer is a divine work which God alone effects. It is written in Jer 33:6, "I will show them the prayer and adoration of peace and truth." That which God alone effects, no image ever can. You also must not say that an image of Christ brings you to Christ. For it is eternally true that "no one comes to me unless my Father draw him." All who come to Christ must have learned from God,[22] Jn 6:44. They cannot have been admonished or taught by images to come to Christ. Even if all images on earth were to stand together, they would still not be able to elicit from you as much as a small sigh toward God.

If I should ever want to have external admonitions or reminders, I would seek out those which Scripture suggests and not those which it hates and forbids. Thus I should much rather be subject to trial and anguish with horse and wagon than to come to an image and draw from it a blessed admonition, for Isaiah does not hide the fact that images are useless, Isa 44. They would be of some use if they were able to admonish us and lead us to God in the spirit of truth. Scripture, however, teaches us that tribulation does teach and admonish externally, causing us to know, call on, and worship God. [16] It says, "Affliction and vexation give understanding," Isa 28.[23] "You punished me and I was taught," Jer 31:18. "God beats us and teaches us as a father his sons," Prov 3:12; Heb 12:5f.[24] God wants us to cry to him in the day of our distress, Ps [86:7].

But God does not want us to call on him by looking at images; those he wants us to hate and run away from.

On the day when the Lord shall be lifted up, people will cast away and flee their images, Isa 2:17; 31:7; Micah 5:12. From this we conclude that images are not ever books from which we are to learn.

Scripture likens images and idols to knaves, saying in several places that the godless court images as whores court knaves. I am forced to sound coarse and uncouth, but I am not ashamed to speak unabashedly as Scripture speaks. "I broke their hearts which had turned away from me and rubbed out their eyes with which they courted and philandered with images," Ezek 6:9.[25] Likewise, "you made yourself images in human form and committed adultery with them. Gold and silver which I gave you for an ornamentation, you gave to have images made and then you carried on an affair with them. You took your clothes and clothed and covered them," Ezek 16:11-17.[26] We do this to idiots whom we do not intend to treat as foreign gods. We would not want to be told that these idiots are our gods. How easily we are led astray by our own words and deeds, when we name them gods and honor them. The image of the crucified we call "Lord God." At times we say that it is the Lord Jesus, and give it such respect as if Christ himself were present. Our wicked popes and foolish monks brought us to that. We also say that this is St. Sebastian, that St. Nicholas, and such like. Thus we treat them like objects which God loves and we convince ourselves through word and deed that images are our gods and [17] our eyes make love to them and court them. The truth is that all who honor images, seek their help, and worship them, are whores and adulterers, Hos 2; Ezek 16 (Here I wanted to sleep with a wife of the devil and pay her well, but I was hoping that she might follow the guidance of the Holy Spirit. This is an aside with which I want to have warned her for the next time.). These whores of the devil who give their silver and gold for images (so that they might turn that which God gave them for their own adornment into church images) are like the whores of which Ezekiel writes in chapter 16—mentioned above. They make life-sized reproductions and sleep with them; they cover them with their clothes and bring them a rich aroma of bread, wine, beer, along with chicken, goose, and horse.[27] Indeed, they also bring their children and their sick friends. God says to them, "Do you think this knavery to be small and insignificant?" There are many more than a few writings along this line which call such idol worshipers whores and adulterers. They come to the conclusion that churches in which images are placed and honored might readily be considered brothels.

All images are alike—male ones like St. Sebald's and female ones, like St. Ursula and Othilia, or such like. And as it is written in Deut 4:16ff, all are prohibited and are not allowed in. For Scripture calls those who honor such images whores and adulterers; and it calls the fraudulent images "men," that we might become aware of how significant and respected such idols are in the hearts of those who honor and worship them.

This is the reason why God said in the first commandment, "I am jealous," Ex 20:5. He desires to be our only dear husband and, as Hos 2:24 and 7:13ff, and other prophets teach, Isa 1:29 and 44:1ff, to be the only one on whom we call and whom we ask for help.

God knows very well how dangerous and harmful images are and how in an instant we might desecrate them. Therefore he has repeatedly prohibited images through Moses, and had them cursed often through his other prophets.

No excuse and pretext will help you, even though you repeat a thousand times, "I do not honor these saints on their own behalf, but on behalf of that which they represent." O you hopeless adulteress. Do you fancy that God does not know your heart better and more profoundly than you? Had God not known that someone might create an idol in his heart so easily as not even to notice it, God would have allowed us to honor images in someone else's name. Find escapes, cover yourself, and explain whichever way you want and are capable of, but you will, nonetheless, be unable to escape divine sentence and judgment [18] which simply prohibits images and curses all those who carve or praise images or protect and honor them, Deut 27:15.

I now wish and am compelled to tell all Christians that they have idols in their hearts if they reverence images. With a sigh I must confess my secret thoughts before all the world. I admit that I am fainthearted. Though I know I ought not fear any image, and I am certain that God demands of his own not to fear idols, as is written, "You shall not fear other gods, neither shall you worship or honor them, and you shall not sacrifice to them, but to God alone, etc.," Judges 6:10; 2 Kings 17:35, I also know that God is as small in me as my reverence of idols is great. For God desires to indwell my whole and total heart and cannot in any way tolerate my having an image in my mind's eye. And when I trust God with all my heart, I need never fear his enemies.

Therefore God, or his Holy Spirit, says in Holy Scripture, "You ought not to fear other gods. Do not worship them. Do not honor them." And he instructs us that it matters to him when we honor and fear images. Therefore, I ought not fear any image just as I ought not honor any. But (heaven help me!), my heart has been trained since my youth to give honor and respect to images and such a dreadful fear has been instilled in me of which I would gladly rid myself, but cannot. Thus I am afraid to burn a single idol. I fear that the devil's fool might insult me. Though I have Scripture (on the one hand), and know that images are incapable of anything and that they lack life, blood, or spirit, fear (on the other hand) holds me back and causes me to fear a painted devil, a shadow, and the slightest noise of a rustling leaf, and to flee that which I should seek out bravely.

Thus I can say that one finds out how solid one's scalp is when one pulls him by the ears. Had I not read God's Word and heard the spirit of God denouncing idols, I would have thought that I loved and feared no image. But now I know how, on this matter, I stand toward God and images, and how firmly and deeply images are rooted in my heart.

May God grant me his grace that I will fear the heads of devils (as saints in churches are commonly referred to) no more than I fear stone and wood. And may God grant that I never honor stone and wood in the appearance and name of a saint. Amen. Read Jer 10:2-5 on this.

From the above passages we see that Christians must strictly follow divine counsel, will, and commandment and must no longer tolerate images, [19] regardless of the old, evil custom and pestilential teaching of priests, according to which they are supposed to be the books of lay persons. For God has prohibited the making and keeping of images.

And God bemoans intensely and deeply when we visit images with small or with great hope. He says that they defile and stain his house, Jer 32:34. We have trustworthy documentation and infallible proof of the first two articles, namely, the testimony of the Holy Spirit.

The third article does flow from the above-mentioned passages and does stand on that foundation and rock, but I wish, in addition, to bring special proof from Scripture to bear on the third Article.

"You are to do thus to them," says God, Deut 7:5, "you are to throw over and destroy their altars. You are to smash their images. You are to cut down their linden trees and you are to burn their carved images." These are no divine altars, but only pagan or human ones, as is noted in Ex 20:4. Thus, in keeping with Scripture, Christians are to do away with them. They are external things. Whenever you intend to honor God in external things, or seek him through ceremonies, you are to follow his ceremonies and his law. The authorities, too, are to put away images and judge or sentence them to the penalty, which Scripture requires.

I had also hoped that the almighty God would have brought to fruition the seed he had sown—a predisposition toward removal of images which would have led to the external work. But so far, no execution thereof has taken place—probably because God allows his anger to trickle down on us with the intent of pouring out his full wrath when we become so blind as to fear that which cannot harm us at all.

I know that the authorities are punished on that account. Scripture never lies.

Now, if our authorities had accomplished the divine counsel and resolution by ordering the wicked and deceitful wooden blocks from our churches and consigning them to their deserved punishment, we would have to praise them, as the Holy Spirit praised Hezekiah. He reduced images to powder, cut down linden trees and broke the image which God had given, as recorded in 2 Kings 18:3f. Would to God that our lords were as the worldly, righteous kings and lords of Jewry, whom the Holy Spirit praised. According to Holy Scripture, they always have the power to take action in their churches and to put away everything that might annoy and hinder believers. They are also able to teach and lead priests to the laws of God and stop deceptive and harmful practices. Everyone can see this from 2 Kings 23:4ff. King Josiah ordered the supreme high priest and other priests to throw out all vessels, linden trees, and such-like Baals. These he then [20] burned outside of the city of Jerusalem. We see from this that priests are subject to kings by divine right. On this account our magistrates should not wait until priests begin to carry out Baals and their wooden vessels and obstructions. For they may never begin. The supreme temporal power must order and undertake action. If they tolerate images, they must hear it said that they cause Judah to err and sin, much as, in a similar instance, Manasseh had to hear it, 2 Kings 21:11ff. And if they should say that our forebears instituted them and we will follow in their way, Scripture says, "Ammon did evil like his father Manasseh and walked in the way his father walked"; see also in Kings [2 Kings 21:20]. Like mother, like daughter. "Your mother is a Hittite and your father an Amorite," Ezek 16:45. God will not have you make the excuse that as our parents have gone, so we intend to go.

Several admirers of images will say, "The old law prohibits images, but the new one does not. We follow the new and not the old law."

Dear brothers, may God preserve you from such heretical adage [sermon] and word and may you never say, "We do not follow the old law, nor do we accept it," since it belongs to non-Christians and breaks and diminishes the teaching of Christ. For Christ verifies his teaching through Moses and the prophets. He says that he did not come to break the law, but to fulfill it, [Mt 5:17]. He also taught his disciples how he had to live and suffer that Scripture might be fulfilled. Christ did not trespass on the smallest letter in Moses' law. Neither did he add or subtract anything from Moses. In short, Christ did not set aside anything which pleased God in the old law. Christ stood by the old law both in intent and in content. Anyone who can reconcile the two sayings, namely, *Fide legem antiquamus* and *Fide vel gratia legem stabilimus*—"Faith supersedes the law" and "Faith and grace strengthen the law," understands Moses, the prophets, Christ, and Paul. In that article the old law is no longer binding. At this point it would take me too far to explain that. But I know that the enemies of the law will not understand me. So, I shall answer my objectors as follows: Dear chaps, you claim that the old law prohibits images. For this reason you will allow them in houses of God, considering such prohibition to be insignificant. Why then do you not also say that we are not obligated to honor father and mother, because the old law commands it? Further, murder, unchastity, stealing, and suchlike evil deeds which are prohibited in the same tablets of the law which prohibit images—with the prohibition of images being the first and foremost law, while prohibition of unchastity, stealing, etc., are placed at the bottom as the lesser and smaller. Why do you not say that we shall indulge in adultery, stealing, murder, and suchlike? Why not tolerate them in our churches because they have been prohibited in the old law?

Christ showed what the law demanded to the person who asked him, "What must I do to inherit eternal life?" Why, in this case, should

I not also lead you to the law of Moses? You say that Isaiah and Jeremiah are evangelical prophets. Yet they prohibit images. So why do you dislike it when they prohibit images?

I tell you that God prohibited images no less and with no less fervor than murder, robbery, adultery, and suchlike.

Lastly, you will have to admit that Paul is a fulsome preacher of the gospel and the new law. He reached the depth of Moses' meaning and brought it to light. He proclaimed Christian promise in an abundantly comforting fashion. You must then also say that when Paul prohibits images, I will also shun them. Now hear this. Paul says, "They exchanged the glory of the immortal God for an image not only of a dead human being, but also of birds, four-legged and crawling animals," Rom 1:23. Can you perceive how evil and harmful Paul considers images to be? He says that those who honor images rob God of his glory and equate him with creatures. In this way they diminish and blaspheme God. Moses also says repeatedly that God cannot tolerate our images and likenesses. Thus Moses and Paul agree. And I have shown from the epistles of Paul that no one who honors images, comes to God. [22]

The Second Article: Concerning Beggars[28]

I have written too much, yet not enough regarding idols. As a result, what follows has to be much shorter. In short, then, let me say that I receive certain clues when I enter a city from seeing people running about for bread. It suggests that there are no Christians or else very few, dispirited ones. A change is needed, therefore, so that we do not act like those (hapless sophists), who open their hands when a needy person is in extreme need or on his last breath and is no longer aware of their help, when nothing can nourish or refresh him. These detestable people say that the Scripture passage "blessed is he who considers the weak and the poor" [Ps 41:1] is to be understood as meaning, "blessed is the one who gives heed to the poor in his extreme and last hunger," i.e., when he no longer suffers pangs of hunger. As if we were not obligated to prevent begging by gracious assistance and by forestalling the pangs of hunger.

I have said, and will continue to say without ceasing, that beggars are a sure indicator that there are no Christians, or else very few dispirited ones, in any town in which beggars are seen. In short, you may understand this as follows: beggars are those who must run from place to place looking for bread or who sit in the streets, in front of houses or churches, asking for bread. We should not tolerate having such people, but should rid ourselves of them—not in an unreasonable or despotic way, but by the giving of well-intentioned help. As Christians we are not to let anyone descend to such poverty and need that they are driven and forced to cry and search for bread. However, I am aware that we shall always have poor brothers and sisters, Mt 26,[29] who require help and support. We must eagerly look to our neighbors and fellow Christians and together help them in their need before they cry to us for help. If we fail to do this, we are simply not being Christian.

For Christ says to those at his left hand [Mt 25:41ff.], "Get away from me, you cursed, into the eternal fire. I was hungry and you fed me not; I was thirsty and you gave me no drink; I was without clothes and naked and you did not clothe me. I was a sojourner and you did not take me home or shelter me, etc." He concludes that it is he who endures and suffers these bodily afflictions in his own. This text consigns to the devil everyone who does not [23] feed the hungry and who refuses to give the thirsty to drink, etc. He declares that these are strangers and unrelated to Christ. From this and other writings I am able to conjecture and conclude that Christians should not tolerate beggars, but must help the hungry, the thirsty, and other needy persons before these are forced to run for help or go a-begging from door to door.

For the Truth[30] does not fail or deceive us. It says, "I was hungry and you did not feed me" or else, "My relatives suffered hunger and you gave them no food. Go then to the eternal fire which has been prepared for the devil and his associates."

And if they are to go to the devil and into his fire, they are unknown to Christ and are no Christians.

It follows, therefore, that those are no Christians at all who allow the hungry to chase after their bread, for they must apply such diligence to the hungry that they are fed before their hunger drives them to cry for bread.

For the sake of brevity, I wish to cite a beautiful text which makes the point clearly, Deut 15:4. It reads as follows: "There ought to be no beggar among you so that the Lord your God may bless you in the land which he shall give you as an inheritance." The text goes on to say, "If one of your brothers who dwells within the gates of your city becomes impoverished, you are not to close or harden your heart toward him. Neither are you to close your hand, but rather to open it toward the poor and lend him that which he needs," [Deut 15:7f.].

This passage is crystal clear. It informs us that every city must care for its own inhabitants. Thus, where someone might have fallen into poverty, the others must take pity on him—superiors above all others—must open their hearts and hands and lend the poor brother that of which he is in need. Hence, Christian magistrates must be especially diligent in helping the poor who dwell in their cities. For, as Paul teaches, we must first help our own people and take utmost care how we feed them. Not that we ourselves should suffer affliction and want while the others live in opulence. Rather, that when we have sufficient to eat and drink, and when our wives and children, our servants and relatives are also provided for, then we ought to be content and satisfied and wanting to help our fellow citizens and neighbors. Each city must look after its own citizens; each village, after its own farmers, and lend to their poor brothers that which they need. In addition, princes, officials, mayors, judges, village mayors, and other magistrates ought to find appropriate ways and means by which to maintain poor brothers and sisters, each according to their standing in the community, so that no one has to go after bread. [24]

It is proper also to send students back to their parents; for through begging they learn much more knavery and unseemly behavior than virtue and sound teaching. How much better by far, that they learn the trade of their parents instead of begging for bread which makes them good for nothing other than to become papistical, uncouth, and untruthful priests.[31]

It is also proper when superiors look for beggars who are strong and capable of working, and when they force them to work so that they might feed themselves. This should take place in a way which will give them direction and help in beginning a trade or job. If a person wishes to learn how to be a printer, a goldsmith, a baker, tailor, cobbler, or some such craftsman, or if he begins to practice and carry out such a trade, he should be helped to secure what he needs. For they [Christians] are to lend to their brothers that which they require.

Should one of these former beggars reach a position where he is able to repay for received help, this should be accepted and used in helping others.

But if someone is hard-pressed to return that which was lent him, the benefactors are not to demand it back or expect [repayment] from the person they benefited.

For the text reads as follows, Deut 15:9: "Take heed that this unwholesome thought does not enter your mind; that you not say, 'The year of release of all debts is now near.' And that you therefore avert your eyes from your poor brother, refusing on that account, to lend him that which he needs." Take care not to entertain such an unwholesome thought, giving the poor person cause to cry out to the Lord against you.

To us Christians all days are the same, for Christ made no distinction between one day and another. Thus all years are also the same. We thus have the perfection of time and the seventh year is eternal. This is the year of remission and release of all debts, wherein all debtors are set free and relieving them of all their debts. We are responsible, therefore, to lend our poor brothers whatever they need, without demanding or hoping that the good deed rendered will be reciprocated. Neither are we to sue them or charge them before a judge. This Christ taught us. Therefore, the seventh year is with us always, and we have no rightful claim on the poor.

It is true, of course, that they are obligated to help us when we are in need and to help out in other ways, if they are able to do so. But we live in the seventh year and can demand nothing.

Neither are we to avert our eyes from the poor brothers and sisters, but we must lend them whatever they need.

In short, we must single-heartedly come to the aid of the poor without any threat or cunning, Deut 15:10. With this word, Scripture disallows any great argument [25] as to whether or not a person is deserving of help. It is true that all of us ought to work and earn our daily bread by the sweat of our brow, and we should not let others see our poverty. But when God makes a person poor, the rich need to know that they must feed and maintain the poor person.

For this reason God, at times, snatches a person's bread from his mouth and allows him to suffer want, so that the rich person might help the poor, out of the knowledge that he ought to. Therefore, God commands that no one is to harvest his cornfield to the ground, thus giving an opportunity for poor people and strangers to glean the fields, Lev 23:22.

The text (Deut 15:9) goes on to say, "You will always have poor people in the land of your possessions. I command you, therefore, to open your hand toward your poor and needy brother." Notice that God says we will always have poor brothers among us. Yet, we are not to have any beggars. This is the text with the divine commandment—stated above—which Christ renewed. We are not to have any beggars, though we shall always have poor brothers. And God shall always, and in all things, bless us when we serve the poor with a willing heart. This is why it is said that alms cancel sins.

The text further states, "If a believer has been sold to you and when the seventh year has arrived, you must set him free and release him. In addition, you are to give him food for the journey from the abundance which God has granted you because of the hard work you did and from the storeroom where you keep your grain and from your winepress or from the cellar where you store wine and drink," Deut 15:12-14.

This text teaches us that we are not to let our man[servants] or maidservants, or any other laborers, leave us empty-handed. We are to give them assistance.

It is true, of course, that the Hebrew speaks of a Hebrew being sold, but I have translated it "if a believer is sold to you." For Scripture calls all those believing or Hebrew who live in the midst of believers. On occasion it has happened that in order to protect his name or glory God destroyed those enemies who threatened the alleged people of God even though in God's sight these were not a believing people. He did this to preserve his glory, as you may read in several of the prophets, for example, that God arose and avenged his alleged people because he found it offensive and onerous to have his enemies say, "See, the people of Israel are the people of God, yet we pursue and murder them." Such words God could not tolerate for long. For even though these alleged people of God did not obey God, he nonetheless sought to defend the glory of his name and did not permit his divinity to be touched and besmirched. Therefore Moses, or God through Moses, says, "You must not say in your [26] heart, 'God destroyed our enemies because of our, or my, righteousness and led us to the good Promised Land.' Rather, you must know that your enemies flee on account of their own wickedness. You must know, therefore (says Moses) that God has given you this rich and fertile land not on account of your righteousness, for you are a most stubborn people," Deut 9:13. Nonetheless, I call only those "Hebrew" or "believing" who walk on the side of believers. Like Moses I say, "If a believer is sold to you, etc."

Listen now to how this sale takes place. In former times people were able to sell themselves to others and to become the purchaser's chattel. Purchasers were allowed to sell their purchased servants to others—just as if one were selling an ox, thus making it the purchaser's chattel. To this day such practice is not uncommon or strange in Naples and Rome. The sold people, along with their children, are called servants; it is these servants of which our text speaks.

If a Hebrew sold himself to you, and when the seventh year—the year of release and liberation, cancellation and absolving of all debts

—arrived, an *exceptio peremptoria*—an incontrovertible exemption for debtors was created.[32] It enabled debtors to silence and subdue their creditors who could not sue them further. As is written in Deut 15:12, "In that same seventh year all Hebrew men[servants] and maidservants were entitled to their freedom; their masters had to let them go free." In other words, when a Hebrew servant or maid was sold to someone and had worked for six years, then the Hebrew master had to set him free in the seventh year and aid and assist him in this, as mentioned above.

This should also be done by all slave traders in Rome and elsewhere in the world. They should set the slaves free, without later enslaving them by force. For they anger God and besmirch the covenant and the name of God when they keep Hebrew slaves so deceitfully and cunningly, or when they recall them after their release, or when they allow them to depart without any help. For to God it is the same whether people despise and tarnish his name, glory and commandment or whether they handle them with cunning. You find this in Jeremiah 34:8ff. Read Jeremiah's entire chapter and find this matter referred to.

Accordingly, abbots, vicars, provincials, clergy, and monks should set their sold brothers free—and not only when they express a desire to be free. In addition, they are to give them money and other aid and help them toward the trade [27] they might enjoy doing. Thus they will be able to feed and maintain themselves in a Christian manner. And (if they have no money), it would be better for them to sell chalices and vestments in order to set their Hebrew, i.e., Christian, servants free. For to live in a monkish fashion, as (in our estimation) the most sanctimonious are now living, does not lead to salvation. It does not please God. Indeed, he hates it because their greatest pieces of art, to which they cling and with which they stand and work, displease God, as Isaiah, other prophets and Christ have clearly stated. These poor monks would be much better served were they working for wicked men instead of feeding and delighting themselves in monasteries.

What I have said of monks applies to nuns as well. I feel a great deal of pity for these poor children. They might and, without doubt, would serve God much better out in the world than away in their poisoned cloisters. I describe them thus, because all of the cloisters are wicked and harmful. They are full of superstition, of idolatry, of blasphemy, uncleanness, and evil, though this poison is so well covered over with honey that the occupants are unable to recognize the evil.

But it is the fault of the endtime Christ,[33] and the devil's will and intent for them to live in such total blindness.

Superiors should now, it being the [perpetual] seventh year, release and set free such monks and nuns. They should also give them guidance and help them, as they are able, with their daily living and daily food needs. For they have been kept and treated like servants and maids and it is now their seventh year every day.

Especially are the mendicant cloisters prohibited. They ought to exist no longer, for begging is forbidden.

It does not even help if they are willing beggars. Their will as well as their activities are unchristian, deceitful, and harmful, for there is not the least reference to their begging in Scripture. They often cheat the poor and rich alike of their possessions. They harm the poor person with their demands of cheese, grain, bread, beer, wine, their last wills, and much more. They tear out of poor children's mouths what they themselves need. Servants who walk about with a beggar's staff in this way are to be let go immediately by their superiors and are to be helped to a better life.

Hereabouts praiseworthy ways and means have been suggested, which would be accomplished with God's blessing. The following was undertaken. A common bag or box was to be set up in which to gather what would be collected from all the congregations,[34] in view of the fact that these congregations are against divine honor and glory and fragment Christian unity. They delight in eating and [28] excessive drinking, and are like fish in the water and like a wall upon a rock. They despise all others, are full of slander and pursue useless hopes which are of the devil.

Furthermore, the interest on loans, made by the local Council (after they have been cleared by the departure of priests), should be deposited in this proposed box.

It must be remembered that many a fee is dedicated and given here for masses [to be read]. This is a devilish thing and contrary to the character of the blessed sacrament. It must also be remembered that we have too many priests who refuse to serve either God or their neighbor and who do not wish to learn anything.

Priests who are still alive should not be cut off from any moneys. They know full well that it is unchristian to fight mendicancy while creating new beggars.

I should also have liked to see the yearly income from the church tax directed into said box and contributing toward brotherly assistance.

But, alas—I address my plea to God with deep sighs—I fear and observe that the devil does not rest and does not diminish his efforts to cause us to fear when there is nothing to fear and to accomplish through priests what he could not accomplish otherwise.

And I am afraid that this fundamental Christian mandate which has been issued and which should be carried out—if indeed we are and wish to be known as Christians—will not, in fact, be done. I have done my share. They shall, doubtless, receive their reward and experience it bitterly if they oppose these two articles by blocking the advice and will of our living, strong, true, and avenging God. May almighty God soften their hearts of stone so that his divine name and glory may be magnified within us. And may the same living and merciful God infuse his grace, and the knowledge of his divine will, into abbots and monks and all alleged spiritual persons, both male and female. Would that they might come to their senses and exchange their tainted lives for true and better ones which includes the release of their poor, duped, misguided, and corrupt prisoners so that out of their wolf-like and foolish life might spring a brotherly, Christian, affable, wise, and sensible life.

In short, God willing, I shall offer my services to the abbots at Cze. and Czy,[35] and of other Far monasteries,[36] and plead with them on behalf of their enslaved servants, asking for their release or else that they change their hypocritical and unchristian lives to ones which are more pleasing to God, and which more closely resemble a Christian community and are more useful and beneficial to the friends of God. I will explain to them the [29] text, "Do you not know that mercy is better than sacrifice, etc." [Mt 12:7]? You do not know (you brothers) that it means "I like mercy much better than sacrifice and the knowledge of God suits me better than burnt offerings. God rates your lamps and lights, your howling and prayers rather low. His teaching and the knowledge of God, on the other hand, he extols greatly. Your sitting down, your rude tricks, your silence, your furrowed and downcast brows and your narrow, ingrown life, God despises and derides. God desires, instead, that you look to the trials, needs, and anguish of your brothers—indeed, of all people. And you are to forestall all mendicancy by gracious benevolence. You help no one more than your own bag.

I am also informed that you do not allow preaching in your cloisters. This indicates to us that you serve neither God nor the world. I will point out this and many other things to you in breadth and depth, unless you promise me that from now on you will give permission and make arrangements for the word of God to be preached among you pure and clear.

The uncouth Klotzerschlepper at Lausigh,[37] whose teeth rattle from all their poisonous breath, and fall out because of their great barking in opposition to evangelical truth, I will in due course sprinkle with holy water by which several evil, paltry worms will be driven out of the drinking water.

For the ignorant barkers and oiled bearers of tonsures at Hain,[38] should they continue to rant and rage against divine teaching with their whims and their bluster, I will have a tassel made with which they may brush the fleas off their dogs.

Printed at Wittenberg by Nicholas Schirlentz in the fifteen hundred and twenty-second year after the birth of Christ.

Title page of an alternate edition of Carlstadt's popular tract, "On Receiving the Holy Sacrament."

5

Circular Letter by Dr. Andreas Bodenstein from Karlstadt Regarding His Household Recently Sent Out from Wittenberg About Priests and Monks

Wittenberg
[1522]

Among the twenty-odd tracts and booklets which Carlstadt circulated between July 1521 and August 1522—during one of the most productive periods of his reform activities—this small tract addresses the issue of married versus unmarried clergy. The pamphlet may have served as an announcement of his own decision to marry. Similar arguments, often on the basis of suitable biblical texts, were advanced by other reformers—Huldrych Zwingli among them. By at least 1520, Zwingli had come to recognize that the long-standing tradition in the Western church to enforce clerical celibacy had no biblical foundation. Some time in 1522, he secretly married Anna Reinhart.

On 13 July 1522, Zwingli and ten other priests signed a petition to have clerical marriages legalized.[1] Whether Carlstadt was familiar with some of these activities is not evident. Carlstadt's own point is to stress the freedom of the gospel for all who are in bondage to human institutions pertaining to those who serve Christ. In passing he refers to his engagement to Anna Mochau and to their intended marriage on January 20.

Six editions appeared in Erfurt, Augsburg, Strasbourg, Speyer, and Colmar. While the dedicatory letter is dated January 5, 1522, the first edition did not appear until later in the month. Freys/Barge list all six known versions of the pamphlet, without always identifying the printer (cf. 81-86). The following translation was made from a copy of the 1522 Erfurt publication, located in the Zentralbibliothek, Zurich.

The six points that follow the greeting are drawn up in a form that would suggest that they may have served as a basis for discussion at the chapter meeting of Augustinian Friars, held on January 6, 1522, and were adopted at that meeting. The address and greeting is polite to the point of being subservient.

Noble, honorable, gracious, worthy, highly learned, respectable and firm, my most submissive, unwearied service be always at Your Grace's disposal, my gracious, kind, imperious, beloved lords.

I noticed in Holy Scripture that no estate is more pleasing to God than the marital estate and that no life is more useful and serviceable to Christian freedom than married life which is further graced with numerous and great blessings when that same life is lived in the godlike manner for which God instituted it. I have further considered that God calls his priests to the marital estate and has proscribed for them a righteous, married life by which they are to live. And so I observe, as I look at it, that many poor, miserable priests are now in the devil's prison and dungeon who, without doubt might be helped and counseled by a good model and example.

For this reason I have become formally engaged to Anna Mochau in the presence of several of my lords and friends. God willing, I am prepared to begin the wedding ceremonies on the evening of the forthcoming St. Sebastian's[2] and to bring it to a conclusion the next day, in the presence of my dear lords, patrons, and friends.

Your Grace, at whose most humble service I am, is asked to be good and gracious enough to appear here on the evening of St. Sebastian and show his grace and favor by honoring this union through merriment and pleasure. I would greatly cherish being found worthy of Your Grace's presence and render my most humble obedience beforehand.

Given at Wittenberg, the Sunday of the circumcision of our Lord[3] in the twenty-second year.

Your Grace's most obedient servant, Andreas Bodenstein from Karlstadt[4] [A ii]

In the name of the Lord

We, the vicars, doctors, and priors of the Eremite order of St. Augustine of the congregation in Germany, all together gathered in the Holy Spirit at Wittenberg find, in light of the gospel of our Lord Jesus Christ and the truth, that many people are exposed to danger and many who are weak in faith are offended and that many obstacles to a right Christian faith have been set up. In order to avert such harm and danger, we agreed unanimously on the following points. Without prejudice to counsel and consideration not alone of ourselves but of other righteous Christians and in such a way that our fathers are free to address these at the next chapter and all others who love God's law, enjoy God's peace and fear God.

First

As far as we are able we grant the freedom of the gospel and of Christ to all our brothers, so that those who want to leave the pretense of our hitherto unbecoming life may do so and live with us according to evangelical teaching. And if a person wishes to serve Christ the Lord in a perfect manner, he should be free and permitted to do so. We do not, however, intend to give cause to anyone to embark on carnal liberty.

Second

Since our clothing, or any other external form, is neither beneficial nor inconvenient, we are well satisfied to retain our clothing until the spirit of our Lord Jesus Christ instructs us differently.

Third

We cast off the many servitudes of envy and sin, to the extent that human affliction can bear it, especially such things as begging and the many circus-like activities such as votives and masses for the soul and other matters.

Fourth

Whoever has been granted grace by God to instruct people in Holy Scripture in a congregation ought to do so. For this is the only work by which one may serve God in spirit and in truth. The others, on the other hand, are to apply themselves diligently to external labor and exercise, so that they have sufficient to live on and to aid other needy persons.

Fifth

But anyone who wishes to live for the flesh (which God avert from all righteous persons), we leave to divine judgment. And a person who wants to seek the truth and God, we faithfully advise as a brother and admonish him besides not to complain about being obedient to the superior[5] when he orders something according to the law or according to true love. [A iij]

Sixth

In keeping with St. Paul we are to be Jews to the Jews, Greek to the Greeks, and suchlike, so that we assess the matter correctly and in no way depart from the love of the faith, for the sake of ceremonies or external things such as clothing, or aggrieve or destroy Christian peace.

- *Invictas Martini laudes intonent Christiani.*
- *Sparsis[6] reduxit oves ad Christum aberrantes reconciliavit peccatores.*
- *Fortis viri libellos oppressere tyranni dux vite Martinus regnat vivus.*
- *Dic nobis Martine verax iuste et pie doctrinam. Christi viventis et gloriam passim resurgentis.*
- *Angelicos testes Paulum Evangelistas surrexit Christus spes mea Romam aversans ut Gomorream.*
- *Credendum est magis soli Martino veraci quam papistarum turbe fallaci.*
- *Scimus Christum revixisse per Martinum vere tu nobis illum deus tuere*
- *Sequentia in laudem resurgentis Christi per Lutheranos.*[7]

6

The Meaning of the Term Gelassen and Where in Holy Scripture It Is Found[1]

Andreas Bodenstein from Karlstadt
A New Layperson
[1523]

In a period of about six months, from approximately December 1522 until the beginning of May 1523, Carlstadt produced only five booklets. Among these were two significant tracts, **The Manifold Singular Will of God, The Nature of Sin** *(see document 8 below) and* **The Meaning of the term "Gelassen."** *The latter appeared in April/May 1523 in two editions, both in Augsburg. Although Carlstadt identified himself on the title page as "a new layperson" the booklet did not attract as many readers as some of his less significant tracts.*

More than in the 1520 tract, **On the Supreme Virtue of** *"Gelassenhait" (document 1 above), Carlstadt here provides a detailed analysis of the kind of disposition a genuine Christian ought to develop. The ethical implications of taking seriously total surrender to God's will are developed by him through an interesting use of relevant Scripture passages. While he reads these under the influence of late me-*

133

dieval mysticism, he does not shy away from developing his own specific understanding by which he, in turn, seems to have influenced Anabaptists and other radical Reformers. Notable is his own detachment from former academic honors and accomplishments while intentionally living as a "new layperson" and for a while working the land and earning his livelihood by the sweat of his brow.

Freys/Barge, numbers 104, 105, list the two sixteenth-century editions. For this translation we used a copy of 104, located in the Zentralbibliothek, Zurich.

I, Andreas Bodenstein from Karlstadt, extend the peace and grace of God to the honorable, God-fearing Jörg Schenck, citizen of Schlesingen.[2]

Since you, gracious and dear brother, wish to know and have asked me to explain for you the terms *Gelassen* and *Gelassenhait*[3] and to trace their origin, I readily oblige out of Christian love. More so because my ready response and explanation might, I presume, be of use to other Christians as well. Since you understand the booklet *A German Theology*,[4] yet wish to know what meaning and origin these words have, there is no doubt that more people wish to see and know what these words mean and where they originate.

You obviously connect two petitions of the *Our Father* and read them as contradictory sentences. You state that when I pray, "Your will be done" I have to be detached in order to pray aright; but when I say, "And lead us not into temptation," then (say you)," I am unyielded and wish to anticipate God's will. You think these two petitions to be opposites and contradictory. You ask me therefore to help you out of this snare. Dear brother, I am willing and able to serve you in this particular matter with great diligence and to the best of my ability. However, do not hold it against me—since I have to be brief and tentative at this point—should these two petitions cast wider circles than was anticipated.

With this I commend you to God, the living Lord. Given at Wittenberg on April 22, in the year of the Lord, 1523. [//]

Whether the terms Gelassen, yielded; and Gelassenheit, yieldedness, originated here in Saxony or in another area I cannot say. But I know that peasants in the March of Brandenburg[5] use them. And I gather that they are more common and more widely used among them than elsewhere. Perhaps they are peculiar to them, as *vehlich* [seemly] and *unvehlich* [unseemly] are peculiar to the people of Mecklenburg, and as *schlewnig* [speedy, quick] is peculiar to the

Thuringians. Among Bavarians *verheyern* [disgraceful] and among Franks *myslich* [precarious] and *gelungen* [felicitous] and among Swabians *iehen* [to speak, declare] and *necken* [to tease] are common terms.[6] I speak of peasants and common people and not of those who talk the Queen's English [*aus der Tabulatur*]. I suspect that each area has certain proper words, peculiar to that area. But as to the origin of the terms *gelassen* and *gelassenheit,* I have to plead ignorance. I have used both terms and observed them in other writers.

The meaning of detachment

Gelassen means about the same as *verlassen*—abandoned, forsaken. When I want to write or say, "We ought to abandon foreign money," I might substitute the term Gelass for abandon and say, "We ought to detach ourselves from foreign money." And when we say, "I am assured safe conduct," a Mecklenburger might instead say, "I am given seemly conduct." You have two words, but one meaning. There is no difference except in the letters and syllables and in that one of the words may sound more pleasant or appear stranger than the other. To German Franks *vehlig*—seemly—sounds odd and strange. For this reason chancery officials use it. Yet common folk—peasants, children, and women—in the Rhineland or in the low lands have the term "seemly" on their lips daily. It is somewhat like that with the term "detached" which is not used in every area by the common people—peasants, children, and women. But in some villages it is as common as bread and cheese. Where it is foreign, it is more likely written than spoken, but is used orally by those who aspire to be public speakers. [a ii]

There is no difference whether we use "detached," or "forsaken," "detachment," or "abandonment." Let it not worry you then when, on occasion, I spell Gelassen with one *l* and then again, with two, for I noted that those who like to be considered expert writers do it too.

The nature of a detached person

One who lets go of or leaves something is a detached person. And although one who has been abandoned may be called a detached person, what is important in this usage is the fact that one has to leave and turn away from what one wishes to be detached from. Hence, in the statement "a detached person," the term is active, i.e., it is real and in the doing mode. In that context it means something other than "abandoned." Let me explain: When I write that one is an abandoned person, you would assume that someone has been forsaken; it is passive, means suffering, and is in a suffering mode. Of course, I do not deny that the term "detached" also means "abandoned," i.e., it is passive and means that one who is forsaken has been left. If you wish a Latin term for this, I can think of no better one to give you than the word of Christ, who said, "Whoever leaves father and mother, etc."[7] The Latins use *relinquo* and we laypeople say, I give up or abandon. As we wrote, "A man shall leave father and mother on account of his wife and cling to his wife."[8]

However, we may also circumscribe the term "detached" or "abandoned" by numerous Latin words such as *deserere, renunciare, dimittere*, and the like.[9] Note at once how the love of a wife surpasses and cuts out the love of father and mother. Likewise, the love of God ought to supersede all love and delight (which we have toward creatures). Nowhere other than in God ought a person be content. Yes, we must leave all creatures if we want to have God as our protector and indweller or Lord.

Spiritual marriage between God and the created soul [//]

This then is the reason why a genuine marriage and matrimony takes place between God and the believing soul. Because of this Christ calls himself a bridegroom and, at times, God our husband, Hos 2:7; Jer 3:1, and, at other times, our wife, Isa 46:3. From the marital union and duty, we may understand how we must let go of all things and cling to God alone, learning from this that we are flesh and bone of Christ and that we are two in one spirit, Eph 5:23f. Thus we must lift our eyes to God and see in his eyes what God loves and do that, or what displeases him, which we must avoid. By so dying to self-will, we come to live in his divine will and become one with God, just as Christ and God were of one eternal will and shall remain so—unchangeably. All this takes place when we cling to God as Paul says, "Whoever clings to God is one spirit with God." [10] Or as Moses says, "God is dwelling among you," Deut 10:15ff.

Why God unites himself with our soul

God enters into marriage with human beings so that we may discern and know how we are united with God, and that we must leave father, mother, house, and possessions for the sake of God's will and follow God our husband faithfully in all things, works, and ways. But when the soul breaks her marriage vows or bond, she becomes a whore of heaven and a disgraceful sack and a malodorous adulteress in God's eyes. Therefore, God calls all people whores and adulteresses who break the commandment, "You shall have no strange gods,"[11] or, "Israel, know that your God is one God."[12] All of us must fear that very same God in such a way as to fear no other power, Deut 3:22; Isa 51:7. We are to serve that same God at the exclusion of everyone else; we must not even serve ourselves if we engage in God's works. For this reason Moses says, "You shall serve God with all your heart and with all your soul," Deut 10 and 11. [a iij]

God is to be our delight; he alone is to be universal. But if we seek our own or derive pleasure from God's gifts, appropriating them to ourselves, we forsake God whom we ought not to forsake, and we break the marriage vow, thus becoming foul whores and unyielded bags. We must also love God with all our soul, with a full heart and with all our strength, Deut 6:4 and 30:20. But if we love ourselves and what is ours, we have not yielded everything, and we will not be of one spirit or will with God our husband from whom all matrimony is derived in heaven and on earth. To God alone we must cling if we wish to be upright brides and righteous wives of God. And for God's sake we must leave our parents, children, and all possessions and no longer cling to them. But this is so odious that rarely anyone clings to God sufficiently. Therefore, evil and sin which dwell in our flesh must be confessed. It is very much easier for our nature to cling to a created wife than to cling to its Creator. Therefore, the yieldedness of married folk in sensual ways is better known and more tested than is the abandonment which we owe God. But from the yieldedness of married people, we might learn how for God's sake we are to divest ourselves of all things and rise above all created beings—always to look into God's eyes in the way in which a maid focuses on the eyes of her lady. Yes, better and nobler than any created thing can ever point to uncreated and higher things.

I hope that you understand better now than before what the term "Gelassenhait" means and to what extent I have done justice to my task. Nonetheless, I should like to deal with one or two sayings of Christ, so that the evil vice unyieldedness may be recognized and fled.

What we must let go

Note, then, that I am not in any way to seek my own or to think that I can please God. The word "mine" includes my honor, my advantage, [//] my hurt, my desire, my displeasure, my reward, suffering, life, death, sadness, joy, and everything that might affect a person—be it in external goods, or in things that affect the body or the inner being, such as intellect, willpower, and desires. Everything to which ego and I-ness [*icheit*] may cling must leave me and fall off, if I am to be detached. For detachment penetrates and flows over every created thing and comes into its uncreated nothing—for it is uncreated and has no being. In other words, it returns to its origin and creator. Wherefore, when you were nothing, you stood wholly in the knowledge and will of God, and there was nothing at all in heaven and on earth which you could rightfully have adopted as your own.

We must all continue in these to this day. I must not want to know or find out anything about myself and my own, which I might then hanker after, and I must be so fully immersed in God's will as to have truly died to self. It would be worse still to have sensed and experienced severe bitterness yet carry about my desires which I know within me.

I should wish therefore to be nailed to a cruel, shameful cross and to have a holy dread of myself and to become wholly ashamed of my thoughts, desires, and works as of a horrible vice which I would avoid as one avoids a yellow, pussy boil. To see nothing else in my soul and powers but my inability to do the good and, on the other hand, my capacity for and inclination toward everything evil, punishable, dissolute, and shameful. None of this I would want to accept, but much rather deny as an evil misdeed. Yet, whatever is good and praiseworthy, I ought to carry to its origin, attributing it freely and wholly to the one alone who created and gave it.

To seek mere necessity

Nor should I seek anything else in any other creature but pure and simple necessity—not just superficially, but with great fear. For just as I have to work on my holiness with [//] great fear and trembling, as both Paul and David indicate, saying, "Serve God with fear and jump about with trembling," Ps 2,[13] so I should enjoy or use all creatures for mere necessity. We must serve God; this is risky. But we must not seek after anything, except to serve, which is a necessity. And this necessity must be sought with great fear and terror, just as a sick person eats his food with great trepidation, from sheer necessity or as medicine toward survival, but without pleasure. For this reason David prayed to the Lord, saying, "Hold my flesh in fear of you" or, as the Hebrew has it, "My flesh was so afraid that my hair stood on edge," Ps,[14] as if David wanted to say, My flesh experienced horrendous fear in your fear, such a gruesome trembling that it could not ever accept what is good. Yes, eating and drinking is the body's necessity. Nonetheless, a God-fearing person does so with great fear, being ever mindful not to forget that the one who gave him food and drink is God alone, Deut 8 & 6.

All pleasure without God is sin

All pleasure is sin. Soon a person violates this and burns himself with eating and drinking. It would be better for us were we to sprinkle food and drink with ashes than to have our food praised in song; for the nature of our pleasure prevents us from knowing God and his divine works. Therefore, Isaiah says, "You have harp, lyre, timbrel, and flute and wine at your feasts, but you do not regard the work of his hands," Isa 5:12.

It is dangerous to use even the smallest thing with pleasure. For, as Christ says, everything one hankers after becomes one's heart and treasure. It turns us into servants and takes possession as a lord possesses his cattle. Therefore, we ought to ask for, seek, take, and enjoy every necessity with fear for the simple reason that we are unworthy of anything good. [//]

For when I look at and know myself, I will discover that I, my strength, and anything I have coming to me, are of no worth; there is nothing good in me and mine and I am ashamed of what is mine. How then can I accept and love anything? I find evil within me and a poisonous inclination toward what is evil. It follows, as God says, that human thoughts are inclined to what is evil.[15] There are many weaknesses and vices I discover within me which I would rather flee than seek out. Therefore, Gelassenhait, detachment, pervades everything that is mine and judges me and whatever is mine as being unworthy of the good, saying, By right I deserve nothing good that God or a creature might give me, and for all that is mine I should be penalized and deserve imprisonment. In this way detachment takes to flight and casts a person into severe disdain and dread of self, causing us to think it right and proper when God and all his creation are set against us. As is written, "Cursed is the man who says, why have you created me thus?"[16]

Unyieldedness

Again, the devilish vice of agreeableness or unyieldedness grasps after foreign honor and possessions (as Lucifer grasps God's glory). It is blind and unable to discern a person's obvious uncouthness and the infirmity or wickedness that clings to him. It looks at itself, but cannot find any unworthiness. Thus it falsifies God's judgment and righteousness. This poisonous evil regards itself worthy of every good. It seeks pleasure and its own doings in everything God provides. It is angered when it is deprived of some good; its own is always considered to be the best and when someone other than its own is praised, it turns up its nose. If another receives something good when it does not, it is greatly angered, claiming that God is unjust. It seeks to be proven right in everything, and in all necessities it looks to delight and sensual pleasure. It is to be deprived of nothing and is always to be well. And if it has been convicted of being in the wrong, it musters a great many excuses [b] and covers (with excuses) whatever it can. It is rightly called "unyieldedness" because it is unwilling to leave what is good, or "agreeableness" because it quickly appropriates all virtues and draws them in with great pleasure, taking them to be its own.

The difference between detachment and unyieldedness

Detachment loves and desires God purely without any mediation. It does not love God as this or that, but as an essential good. Unyieldedness loves and desires that which has been created; it loves this or that good as its own. And though it may speak or preach of God a thousand times, its pleasure is nonetheless in that which it says, or else, in its own wisdom, or in the letter which it composed and drew unto itself for its own glory, praise, desire, and treasure, rather than being purely in God.

Example: I fancied myself a Christian when I picked profound and beautiful sayings out of Jeremiah's writing, for a disputation, lecture, or sermon, or for other speeches and writings, and I thought that this ought to please God extremely well. But when I began to think and reflect properly, I discovered that I had neither come to know God nor to love the highest good as a good. I saw that the created letter was what I had come to know and love; in that I rested; it had become my God and I did not notice that God said through Jeremiah, "Those who kept my commandments, knew me not and did not ask for me, Jer 2.[17] Note this, how can one handle and keep God's law when one does not know God or ask for him? Though one knows and delights in the letter, one does not really know God as long as one's love and desire are in the letter. For those who are sons of God are impelled by God, not by the letter. Yes, such wisdom is cursed and deemed to be human, not divine wisdom. God says regarding it, "Woe to you who are wise in your own eyes and who look out for themselves," Isa 5.[18] What is this wisdom other than a wisdom in human eyes [//] when we bring in Scripture and other created things (through which we ought to know and love God), for our own pleasure, wanting to know something ahead of others? There are regrettably many laypersons these days who grasp and learn Scripture so that they are well-versed in signs and can say something before another knows. Is not this called "wisdom" in our eyes? Search your heart and answer me. Is it not a cursed wisdom? Read Isaiah, Paul, and Christ and observe that you are not seeking God, but yourself, for you are bound to hear in your heart what Christ spoke to a similar situation, "You seek me, not because you have seen signs, but because you ate and had your fill," Jn 6:26. We do likewise and seek God in the manner I indicated, not because he is God or because he has given us his word, but rather because we can speak well of Scripture and are seen and praised. Note how wantonly this vice behaves which I call agreeableness and unyieldedness, and how directly it seeks itself. But if I could let go of my ego and I-ness [*ichts* und *etwas*] and bear not to be or become anything in human eyes, I would then come into the right knowledge and love of God and become a detached person. When this happens, I will undoubtedly neither write nor preach, admonish or obstruct, praise or cajole and say, "I washed my feet, took off my clothes and I sleep, although my heart is awake. Should I rise again? I rejoice in the inner hearing. Should I teach or preach and defile myself?" Song 5:3.[19] I would refrain from all forms of speaking and teach nothing unless I were compelled to do so out of godly obedience, brotherly love, and Christian loyalty. I would have to do all of that with great fear, for the sake of God's will and honor, and would do as little of it as possible. For in all of it there is great danger, since unyieldedness assails us mightily.

Christ says, "Everyone of you who does not let go of all he possesses cannot be my disciple," Lk 14:26ff. [b ij]

Detachment prepares the soul for the study of divine matters

There is no lesser preparation than this if someone wants to be an apprentice or disciple. And when a person intends to learn a trade, he is not in need of one whose master engages a thousand. Of all the skills, this is the least apprentices must have—even though it is great and something, it is rated lower than the skill of the master. Now Christ demands of his apprentices such skill as transcends all natural resources. He wants us to leave everything we possess and not to permit any creaturely thing to enter our soul and that our soul overcome all things. But this is not reasonable at all, as Christ confesses when he says, "Whatever is impossible with human beings, is possible with

God."[20] It is not possible for a person to leave his possessions for God's sake unless God especially and wonderfully bestows such yielding [Gelass]. Socrates and other ancient fellows considered riches and money of little value. But the riches of wisdom were so valuable and highly rated by them that they did not abandon temporal goods, but merely exchanged or sold them for higher goods. Therefore, they did not abandon any goods for God's sake, but for the sake of wisdom—which in God's eyes is nothing but folly, as is written, "The wisdom of this world is folly before God."[21] Therefore, all human beings must also abandon worldly care and become fool's in the world's eyes if they desire to be counted clever and wise before God, 1 Cor 3:18ff. Accordingly, it is apparent that the ancient philosophers did not totally abandon goods, but instead gave up lead for gold. Such yielding ought not be the skill of Christ's disciples, for they are not to let go for gain, but must become atrophied for God's sake [verzeyhen]. For it is one thing to exchange or become atrophied and another to remove or to abandon and to wait [beytten].

I say, therefore, that the preparation (a student of Christ must have) is more important than any preparations an apprentice of worldly arts or trades is expected to take. [//]

The first demand of a master
Above all else, a master demands that his pupil show love and desire for his trade. Where such hearty desire of an apprenticeship is not present, there everything is lost. But if he shows pleasure in and love of the skill of his master, no one will doubt that the young chap is an easy learner. Furthermore, the apprentice must be free of all hatred and envy of the master and his craft. This follows inevitably from the first.

The skill of a disciple of Christ is the highest
Yet, Christ places before his apprentices a skill which is far more than merely to be free and unencumbered of all desires and comfort when he says forthrightly, "Whoever does not forsake all cannot be my disciple or apprentice," Lk 14:26ff. This means as much as It is impossible for anyone who still possesses a small thing, i.e., one who hopes, is comforted, desires or loves, in small or large measure, to be my apprentice.

To have possessions is to put trust in goods. Christ himself explains that to have money is to trust and take comfort in money and goods, Mk 11:16f. Therefore, to abandon money means as much as not to desire or love, hope in, or derive comfort from money. This is better than to let go of money literally, or to let go of it in deed, but retain it in one's desires.

Now, just as Christ explains this yieldedness with regard to money, so it must be understood with regard to other matters as well. This is the goal to which Moses, the prophets, Christ, and his apostles point, that those who have something ought to be as if they had nothing and, in turn, those who have nothing and are poor ought to be as those who have and are rich. The poor must not fret over what they will eat tomorrow or who will feed them, and those who have are not to take comfort in their money. Even if they are robbed of all their possessions, they must say, "God has given, God has taken away; as it pleases God, so be it; [b iij] the name of God be praised and blessed," Job 1:21. They must remember that God is able to nourish them until they die, just as he brought them into the world, as Job says, "Naked I was born and naked or bare I shall return to the ground." This is truly so, even when God does not nourish and feed us. Although we eat or drink, we shall not be satisfied, as is written in Hos 4:10. Therefore, let us work heartily, but without a care and we will, in this case, become God's apprentices. Otherwise, it is impossible for us to learn and take in something from God, in spirit and in truth.

You see then that yieldedness is the beginning of the Christian life and must maintain all divine virtue. Wherever it is not vigilant, the apprentice drops out of the school of Christ. For Christ says, *Non potest meus discipulus*—"It is impossible for an unyielded person, who looks to the smallest thing and is not detached from everything, to become my disciple." Accordingly, all things must be abandoned and our agreeableness must come to nought and be dissipated, as the wind blows away a speck of dust.

Yieldedness in detachment[22]

You must give attention to yieldedness in detachment, i.e., you must not concern yourself with your detachment and not delight in and love the highest virtue, and you must not stand still when you ought to flee.

If you were yielded in an active manner, you would not desire and love either your suffering or your works, so that nothing might be seen or noted in your mind, and you would not think to yourself, I must not, by rights, demand from God even the smallest bread or grain. You would know that you deserve it, if God were not to give you food or life or heaven, and that it would serve you right were you to perish. You would then wait for this noble virtue in a yielded and serious manner so that your yieldedness would not be marked by grace, love, desire, and selfhood [*eigenschaft*]. [//]

Christ says in clear words, "Unless a person leaves all he possesses, he cannot be my disciple." Note how bitter and harsh the school of Christ is, and what a frightful, pitiable thing it is to our intellect, will, and nature. Note also that Christ was right in saying, "Whoever does not carry his cross and follow me cannot be my disciple," Lk 14:27. Christ said this before he began his general farewell speech which I dealt with. There Christ teaches that yieldedness which surrenders everything is a daily cross that we must carry without standing still. Rather, we must follow Christ and be where Christ is in will, thought, love, desire, suffering at the right hand of God. And all that is ours must be fused in God's eternal will and become nothing.

Suggestion or reckoning of one's skill

Nor did Christ speak of this virtue once only or in one farewell speech. Rather, he said many times and in one epilogue frequently that an apprentice had to do what one who thought of building a house or tower would have to do: he would have to check his pouch or bag and count his wealth to see whether he could finish such a building. When he finds himself sufficiently capable, he begins building. All Christians must do likewise. Those who intend to become students of Christ must first consider and pass over everything. Yes, in the end they must bid them farewell and yield them in a way and with the intention of one who finally lets go of something he hates and no longer wants to take to himself. This is called *renunciare*—finally to give leave to, and drive away from oneself.

Anyone who thus surrenders all things can become a disciple and apprentice of Christ. The soul must to this day be without form, i.e., naked and deserted of all creatures, if it is to receive God and let God possess, rule, and adorn it, [//] as it was in the first creation (of heaven and earth). When we discover that we are unable to divest ourselves of all creatures—be they holy or unholy, spiritual or corporeal, heavenly or earthly—we should not dream of becoming an apprentice of Christ. Let no one think that God enters, as long as creatures fill, comfort, or please the soul, Jer 7:7. "They departed from me in the desires and the wickedness of their hearts and refused to hear me," Jer 7:24. If we turn our backs on such a Lord and repudiate him, should he then turn his face toward us and be well-disposed? No, these two-timers (several of those cheese hunters) have turned his forgiveness into a lottery.[23] They mean by *renunciare* to have nothing in public, but to be laden with riches inside the monastery. They do nothing good externally, but inside they are full of blood (i.e., envy and hatred). They renounce and resist the world, but at the same time they are ensnared by the devil and the world. "I let go of this," but what they say is a lie and sheer knavery. It is part of being a monk to take leave of everything. For Christ says that a disciple must let go of all things and in the end to bid them adieu, renouncing all hope of ever possessing them again. Whoever does not do so will be ridiculed as one who has started a building which he did not complete.

What is to be renounced

Someone might ask at this point what am I to abandon if I wish to become a disciple of Christ? And what are the goods called which one must renounce when one becomes a disciple of Christ? To this the prophets answer as follows, "You must renounce all things in heaven and on earth and sincerely and permanently divest yourself of them, never again to possess them with longing or in hope."[24] For as much as God wants and demands, Christ details those possessions more clearly than most prophets, since he is a shining light. Were I to recount the sayings of the prophets, I would have to write an entire booklet which [//] is not possible. I will therefore take a solid saying of the most yielded servant of God, Moses, who speaks as follows, "You shall love God with all your heart, with all your soul, and with all your strength," Deut 6:4; 10:12f.; 30:2f. Note there that I must love God alone. If this is so then I am not allowed to accept anything with love and joy which is not God—this is the case with faith which is like a mustard seed. Were I to love something besides God, I should not love God with my whole heart. For that place in my heart which loves something else is taken away from God; hence, I cannot love God with all my heart. This love is the spiritual circumcision, i.e., a cutting away from the heart of all creatures, Deut 30:6; Jer 3:22. As long as not all of the creatures are separated from the heart, the heart is not able to love God fully. When help, comfort, and trust are sought in a thing which is not God, the heart is uncircumcised.

Faith circumcises the heart

For this reason it is said that faith circumcises the heart, because it lifts up the heart to trust in God, robbing it of comfort in everything else.

Uncircumcised ears

Note what Jeremiah says, "Uncircumcised ears cannot hear what God teaches," Jer 6:10. This is the same as when Christ says, "Whoever does not forsake everything, cannot be my disciple," Lk 14:33. I note clearly then, that an unyielded ear is an uncircumcised ear. And it cannot hear for the reason that it is preoccupied with desire and trust in other teachings and creatures. This is what God says through Jeremiah. "I said, hear my voice, then I will be your God and you my people. But they did not hear and did not incline their ears, but went away in their lusts, etc.," Jer 7:23. Is it now clear that an uncircumcised heart or ear is a heart or ear which delights in other teachings that were not given by God or [c] one which otherwise delights in, loves, finds comfort in, or fears and worries about other things. Not all of its love or pain is in God or for God's sake. Therefore, we must know that a circumcised heart first divests itself of all creatures and lets go of everything that is not God. Further, that no heart can love God totally with a full embrace and fully when it unites itself or mingles with external creatures. The reason: one who fully clings to God cannot cling to something else, too. Now, since we must always wholly cling to God alone (Deut 10:20; Josh 23:8), it follows that our heart must not cling partly to God and partly to angels or saints; for then it would not just cling to God, but to other things as well.

The yieldedness of the saints

In the same way in which all nations are God's, even though God attached himself in a special and unique way to his chosen nation and not to others, Deut 10:15, the heart, too, must bind and attach itself to God alone, even though it might have before its eyes or in its thought numerous saints, angels, and people. This is what God says, "I attached the house of Israel and Judah to myself that they might become my nation and my name's glory and praise," Jer 13:11 and 30:3. We must not cry or run to the saints, but to God who attached us to himself in order that we might go after him. And we must abandon angels and saints for whose salvation I would have to write that love is the glue.

It must be noted moreover that God attaches and affixes us with that glue which Moses calls love. You may read this in Josh 23. And what he calls "attach" or "affix" is found in 1 Kings 18a and 19a. Now, since a truly believing heart clings to nothing other than God and since the love of God is the glue which binds us to God, it follows that a circumcised and loving heart has abandoned all creatures and in love clings to nothing other than God. Further, it is impossible for God's love to enter a heart unless love, desire, comfort, and trust in creatures have gone from the heart. [//]

For this reason Moses says that God circumcises the heart first, which means that he drives all creatures out of the heart. Such circumcision and expulsion of creatures happens so that we might love God with all our hearts, saying, God shall circumcise your heart that you might love him with all your heart, Deut 30:6.

No one can circumcise himself

Such love does not grow out of our own strength. No. God must apply the glue himself, for God says, Yes, I would add him to or appropriate him for myself and he would then come to me. Why? Because how else would anyone willingly incline himself toward me, to be near me? Jer 30:10f.; 17; 22.

No single heart can of its own strength empty and rid itself of creatures; God alone circumcises. For this reason children are circumcised by others. By this we indicate that no creature is able heartily and eternally to lift himself up [*erwegen*] and withdraw [*verzeyhen*]. Neither is any heart able of its own to incline itself toward or attach itself to God. Rather, God himself has to create and order all things which he wants to have in his own house or temple.

Prepucium/Hardening

The Jews translate "prepucium" by a pleasant term which means "obstruction." Now circumcision is the prevention of obstruction. Actually, the heart that is uncircumcised is clogged or hardened, and it is certain that creaturely things obstruct human hearts so that God refuses to enter and possess his house until these creatures have been dropped off and the soul is empty and free.

To be yielded and to have a circumcised heart is one and the same.

Look for yourself whether or not it is the same to say, "No one can love God unless his heart is circumcised of all desires, [c ij] trust, comfort, and fear of creatures" and what Moses and Christ say, "Unless we let go of all we have (i.e., the things in which we find comfort, pleasure, and trust or which we fear), we cannot be his disciple." We read that Christ called numerous people to his supper, none of whom came, since each of them had an excuse. One had bought a village, another had bought some oxen, the third had entered into marriage, etc., Lk 14:18-21. All of them discovered their clogged and unyielded hearts in that all could not or would not hear God's voice and accept the invitation to a good meal.

Christ gave this example especially so that we might learn how the host invited them to be his guests and to enjoy themselves, and not to judgment or a reckoning. But they refused to come. As a result, the truth became known that no heart which delights in, worries about, and fears creatures is able to hear God's voice. For if [the heart] cannot accept a friendly invitation, how can it suffer a hostile and angry demand? For this reason Christ says, "Unless a person lets go of everything, etc."[25]

In this parable Christ also names the creatures we must abandon if we wish to hear and obey his voice and teaching and truly know and love God. Christ names a village, oxen, and a wife. Though these creatures point to all other creatures which we are to abandon, I wish, nonetheless, to name a few others which Christ also mentioned. Christ named houses and fields, Mt 19:21; Mk 10:21; brothers, sisters, fathers and mothers, children, and wife, Mt 19:24 and Mk 10:25, just cited, and Lk 18:22; further, our own soul, Lk 14:26; 17:33; Mk 8:35; Jn 18.

Degrees of self-ness [sicheit] and I-ness [icheit]

Through these creatures we are to understand others as well. And even if no creature is named, it should be sufficient to know that a person must yield the self; for humankind is the whole, and the lower creatures are the parts. Thus humankind is sometimes called "all creation" and by some, a microcosm, in as much [//] as human nature contains the nature or essence of all earthly creatures. For example, humankind contains the nature which all elements such as wood or stone have, which is a common, essential self-sufficiency. Further, humankind has a mode of existence which it shares with grass, foliage, trees, and such. These are alive and growing. So much on the second point.

Thirdly, humankind has a sensitive nature which is capable of sensing and feeling. It shares this with animals and cattle such as cows, oxen, sheep, goats, he-goats, deer, etc.

Fourthly, humankind has special reasoning powers; it can reason, plan ahead, be wise, will, desire, discern, and choose. In this humankind surpasses all of the lower creation. As a result, it would have been and remained lord over creation, had it known God, the Lord of lords, and rendered him eternal obedience. But when man fell from the order, the other animals also lost their obedience and developed fear. Still, anyone who is prepared to know and love God in total obedience will also be lord over all creation. Neither poison nor snakes nor basilisks can harm this person, Isa 11:8. We lack faith and God's grace, Heb 11. Enough on this.

In the fifth place, human beings differ from all other human beings, with each having talents and gifts from God—in keeping with what God gives and bestows, Mt.[26]

Each stage has its own I-ness and self-ness

If we wish to be yielded persons and to become disciples of Christ, we must let go of everything and surrender all that might affect us in any way. For example, nothing good must be appropriated to ourselves. Neither must we covet any nature, life, growth, understanding, wisdom, or even our own soul. It is certainly true that if you reach the point at which you have divested yourself of your own person, you are then free of everything. Then everyone gives skin for skin, cloak for cloak. [C iij] But allow the soul and your own flesh to meet and see whether you will be able to stand. I do not think it necessary to say again that such Gelassenheit is not grounded in a person letting go of everything as one lets go of a nickel. Who is able to let go in such a way? But we must not, of course, kill either father or mother, or commit suicide. Hence, this Gelassenheit is a cutting off of love, pleasure, worry, trust and fear, which we may have in and for ourselves and the things that are ours. In short, such letting go is to destroy all we are and a turning away from everything that we might covet, so that God [alone] is our love, pleasure, worry, trust, help, fear, and everything; to him we must cling. We must, then, understand this yieldedness not in a worldly, but in a godly manner, in such a way that the truth is in our heart. We must honestly leave it to God to maintain one entity, without worry or fear, for better or for worse, in pleasure or displeasure.

As to how and in which way we are to grow up, we must also commend to God, for who can add an inch to his height through anxious thoughts, Mt 6:27? Likewise, we must remain without concern regarding the growth of grain, fruit, and grass. For our worries do not bring about the growth of a single blade of grass. Sow, plant, water, etc. All your doing is for nothing and will remain unfruitful if God does not grant the growth. The bearing of fruit is God's doing and derives from God's grace and not from our strength.

God makes things dry and green and dries up the grass. God turns wetness into drought. He creates everything according to his pleasure. Therefore, cast all your cares on God; let the old master of the house worry and govern, for his care is good and his rule just. Apply yourself in God's name and thank him for having graciously granted you to work. Commend unto him your work, the growth, and all honor.

In common with animals and cattle, you go after food and drink and you know your parents and your children. But you do not have in common with them to be full of care. We must be free of care, like the animals, and enjoy our food only as a necessity—as cattle do. Yet, we are worse than horses and [//] mules. We prove the saying true which states that a wise man never commences a small folly, for we eat and drink more than is necessary and our health can take. Furthermore, our fullness blinds us; we anger God by setting up our belly as our God. Further, we are more anxious than sparrows. They do not worry about what they shall eat on the morrow. In addition to the pressing anxieties of the current day, we burden ourselves with the cares and concerns of the coming day and think about how, what, and with what we are to eat, drink, or clothe ourselves. We do not learn from God's works that God knows and understands what we need and that he clothes and feeds lilies and birds, which are so much less than a human being.

We ought to open our eyes and look to the lilies and trees and to the birds and learn from theses creatures who clothes and feeds them and observe whether or not they worry. If we did that, we would undoubtedly find that they have no care for clothing or food. Yet, God clothes and feeds them, nonetheless. But because we worry about clothing, a place to rest, food and drink, we must needs cling to these creatures and serve in comfort and confidence. This is what Christ has to say, "O you of little faith and confidence in God," Mt 6:34. Add to this what Christ says in reprimanding his disciples, "O you of little trust. Why do you worry within yourselves for not having taken bread with you?" Mt 16:8. Read and weigh this story and observe whether this Gelassenheit is insignificant.

Unbelief gives birth to unyieldedness about earthly food

Anyone who is burdened by confidence, comfort, desire, care, and fear with regard to money or food sins against faith by as much as he has cares about money or food. Reason: Christ says that we always show little trust and confidence in his heavenly Father when we worry excessively about food, drink, or clothing, Mt 6:34. [//]

On serving two masters

God gives sound reasons there. No one can serve two masters. No one can serve God and riches.[27] For the least that will happen is that one will cling to the one and neglect the other, since it is ever true that where your treasure is, there your eye or heart is also; anyone who looks diligently to the one forsakes the other, Mt 6:24-33. But when we serve God and cling to him with all our heart, it must needs follow, Deut 10:20, that we would have to neglect or forsake God, the moment we set eyes on food with care and concern.

Learn from this that we commit a mortal sin whenever we are afraid, worried, or preoccupied on account of food, or when we trust in, desire, and hope for money and possessions. Such sin comes from unbelief, even when it is daily in us. Note this well.

Note also that this sin (or unyieldedness) indicates or reveals an uncircumcised heart, and that with such a sin a person must hate or at least neglect God and count him for nought or for little, Mt 6. You may conclude from this what I stated above, that we must cling to God with a total love, and that no one can cling to two things at once, Mt 6:24. Note in this connection that Moses says, "You must fear God or cling to God," which means as much as you must fear God alone. *Noli timere eos qui occidunt corpus*—Do not fear those who kill the body."[28] You must be attached to, or cling to God alone—*aut uni adherebit et alterum negliget*—for either you adhere to one, or you neglect the other, Mt 6:24. *Sicut servorum in manibus dominorum suorum. Ita oculi nostri, etc.*—Therefore, we must seek God's kingdom alone in sure confidence, with fervent love, and in certain fear, and all necessities will be added unto us, Mt 6:33.

Yieldedness tolerates no looking back

Yes, we must firmly and with steadfast eyes seek God alone so that we would rather die than look back. Similarly, we should prefer to die a thousand times rather than willingly step away from God even once. Whenever we fix our eyes on temporal goods, it means stepping away from God. Christ says so, "No one who puts his hand to the plow and looks back is fit for the kingdom of God," Lk 9:62.

Hear then, my brothers, that we are unfit to enter the school of Christ when we look back. And understand how you must cut away everything or sever everything from your heart and you must sweep your house clean, if you wish to be an apprentice of Christ. Place the two chapters, Lk 9 and 14, alongside each other and compare them by combining their meaning and understanding, and you will undoubtedly get a shock and cry out, What poor people we are. O how we are in need of the suffering of Christ at all times.

And that you may further note that God does not tolerate our looking back and our fear and concern (that something might be lacking if we believe in God), I will put before you yet another saying of Christ. It is this: "When the Son of Man is announced and a person who left something below finds himself atop his house, let him not come down to fetch any of the furnishings. One who is in the field should not return for the goods he left at home," Lk 17:31. Note what Christ prohibits and how he wants those whom he intends to visit and to whom he appears, to leave their own happily and not to go after their things or to be allowed to go after their things. This will do.

Concerning the subduing of the wickedness of our Adam, I say with Christ, remember Lot's wife who looked back and was turned into a pillar of salt, Gen 19:26. Lot's wife was probably looking back on her goods, income, or friends when God had sulphur and fire rain down upon Sodom and Gomorrah, destroying everything that was blooming. Now, what will happen externally when Christ shall appear must also take place within a person when Christ secretly lets his light shine in. Thus it is that all wranglers[29] sin [d] who quarrel over money or possessions, as Christ indicates in Lk 12:13ff. and Paul in 1 Cor 3:3ff. Further, the circus of the lawyers is troublesome. In short, money and possessions cannot either give or take away life. There are thousands that live quite well who carry their possessions with them, while other thousands who have many possessions live poorly and miserably. The moment they have filled up their cellars and barns, they die, Lk 12:16-21. Therefore, if we wish to be yielded Christians, we must not be anxious to acquire goods and preserve wagon-loads full of food. Neither must we be shocked when the goods we have already acquired vanish in an instant. Neither should the goods we now have either comfort or console us; nor should we fear or worry if we lose them. Instead, we ought to accept the kingdom of God, i.e., his eternal will, with love and delight.

But if we focus our eyes on or turn to silver, gold, and possessions, God will leave us and say, I forsook you because your ground or land is filled with silver and gold, Isa 2:6f.[30] We must therefore either leave God or cast aside care about food. In such unyieldedness we are more wicked than unreasoning animals, for horses or mules know that God or their masters feed them and they let their master worry. If he wishes them to look nice and smooth and strong, he must provide food and adornment accordingly.

If we had the right faith in God and trusted God with all our hearts and knew God to be our Father who cares more diligently about us than we ourselves and never feeds us less than the unreasoning animals, we would be without care and yielding with regard to food. And God would sufficiently provide for us what is best for us and in keeping with his glory and honor. If he wants us fattened and big, he would have to fill the crib, since God would undoubtedly place a lot before us if it were to our benefit. But it happens occasionally that someone serves God and his belly; therefore, God feeds his own on bread and water and provides the bare necessities so that we will always cry for help, and he remains the rich God who likes to help us to attain whatever benefits us. [//]

The yieldedness of intellect

Human beings have intellect which enables them to be wise and to plan ahead. It allows them to build cities and houses, to make weapons and all kinds of protection. This leads people to become rather unyielded when they ought to leave shelter and protection to God and not to seek more. I could demonstrate this by reference to several prophets, but I won't for the sake of brevity, and merely refer to what God says, "You put your trust in your own defenses which you made for yourselves," Jer 48:7; Isa 2:11, 17; 9:5; 16:8; 31:3. Therefore God will forsake you and surrender you to your enemies. Thus many princes and warriors were destroyed who might otherwise have survived and recovered before God.

I should also mention at this point that David took no comfort in a bow or sword, but killed Goliath with a slingshot. That is a simple matter and not worth writing about. But the sick should take notice who put a deceptive trust in doctors and herbal medicine, 2 Chr 16:12.

Hence, all external things are to be clearly avoided and yielded, so that they might not deceive us as the Jews were deceived who said, "The temple of the Lord, the temple of the Lord"—*templum domini, templum domini,* Jer 7:4 or who fled to the ark, Jer 3:16.

Letting go [Gelass] of Scripture[31]

Here I must also state how a truly yielded person must let go of Holy Scripture and not know its letters, but enter into the might of the Lord (as David has it), and ceaselessly pray to God the Lord for true understanding. Then when a person fails to understand something or would like to hear a judgment, he ought to stand in full surrender, i.e., he must divest himself of self, hold back with his reasoning, and earnestly ask for God's favor and hear what God has to say to him. He would soon recall and then verify and justify it with Holy Scripture. I should develop this further, but that is not fitting at this point. Read the *German Theology* if you are not satisfied. Should you not be satisfied yet, wait until I publish my booklet about the school of God. [d ij]

With these stages I did not intend to set out a goal or establish rules. Let everyone speak or write God's truth in keeping with his imprinted admonition.[32] I should also say that above-mentioned stages are carnal and adhere to carnal persons; but I am not sure that I can sustain that.[33] This, however, is true: you must apply great care when you yield something and not make much of your yieldedness.

Note that when you recognize, confess, and shun above-named afflictions [*gebresten*][34] of unbelief—which may also happen through detachment—you must then wait to see that your knowledge, confession, and flight do not become your love and joy, lest you perish in your detachment.[35] It often happens that a person is slapped in the face for God's sake, who then decides not to think of it so harshly as to revenge himself or to take offense. Yet he would very much like to have his patience praised or to be taken for a Christian on account of his patience. Then again, he might be secretly irked for having allowed himself to be hit without hitting back although he was strong enough, and for allowing himself to be mocked or called a donkey, reveller, blusterer, and peasant without retorting that he suffered all this for God's sake. Nonetheless, he has an eye on his suffering and stands there, enjoying and loving it when he should have fled this, too, for God's sake, to serve God alone and focus his eyes on God only.

Serving God

Take this as follows: All who wish to serve God ought not serve him halfheartedly, but with all their soul and will, Deut 10:12, i.e., they ought to and must cling to God alone and not serve another besides or alongside of God. For you heard Christ's word that one who intends to serve two masters will deprive one of them of that which the other should receive. If he loves the one, he is bound to hate the other, and if he clings to the one, he must needs part from the other. Thus, if he clings to a creature with love, joy, fear, concern, and trust or the like, he must at the same time lack these toward God. [//] So in all he does or fails to do, in his work or suffering, he will cling by that much less to God with love, joy, fear, care, suffering, trust, and the like.

Where your treasure is, thereon your eyes dwell

The heart follows the eyes. Where your eyes are, there is the treasure of your heart, there are your desires and feelings. Therefore, you must serve that on which you look and that upon which you are firmly planted in love or pain, joy or sorrow, pleasure or displeasure, dread or trust or disbelief. This is so even if you do not stand for long since such small spiritual services happen fast and instantaneously.

Therefore, whenever you look to your activities or suffering and whenever you hanker after your service, you do not serve God but yourself and your works with which you wanted to serve God. Note at this point how a person can mean himself; and when he does so or when he finds his soul, he does not serve God, but himself to whom he clings, thus forsaking God.

Self

From this you may learn the meaning of self and also how a true and detached service of God uplifts the eyes of the soul to the un-fathomable will of God, creeping into the fathomless good which is God himself, where there can be no ego [*ich*] or self [*sich*]. For as long as the soul looks upon nothing other than God's will and the eternally good which is God, the heart, too, will not be grounded in any crea-ture. Yet, through its uplifting it breaks through and is immersed in God's will; there it falls, dies to self, and wholly loses itself and its self-absorption [*sicheit*]. This is how it must be and happen. Therefore, I should like to say with others that anyone who rightly yields ego and I-ness or self and self-absorption is well-surrendered.

Humankind originally was not; since he yielded and properly surrendered his ego and his somebody [*Etwas*], or his self and self-absorption, he had to surrender it to the one who made somebody of him—an ego or self; i.e., he had to surrender to God himself [d iij] and everything that is anything within him, along with his ego and I-ness. He had to be immersed in God's will. Anyone who does so will be yielded in suffering and in works.[36] Yet, here, friend, you must again take heed not to hanker after your yielding and not to pay attention to your ego in your yielding. If you stand in God in your detachment and surrender (and if you daily train in this yielding), I guarantee that you will be afraid of and flee yourself and be better able to know human malady and call increasingly on God's grace.

In short, anyone who wishes to be totally yielded and be the one who detaches himself must irrevocably divest himself of self and free-ly give up his I-ness or self-centeredness. Then the yielded self will be a Christlike ego of which Christ says briefly, Anyone who desires to be wholly yielded and in truth must irrevocably deny and divest himself (and all that is his and which means anything to him). He must become one with the divine will, so that he does not see, hear, taste, desire, understand, and will anything other than what God wills. Whatever prevents or diverts him from accepting God's will must become his martyrdom. This is the cross which we must carry daily, Lk 9:23.

The new life in Christ

Then the surrendered ego or the despised and forsaken ego, selfhood or I-ness becomes a Christlike ego or self and a new, Christian life when one discovers and admits one's life not to be a human but a divine life and that it is not I who lives, but Christ in me, Gal 2:20. Don't let the terms self, ego, self-absorption, and I-ness grieve you, for you know that they are frequently found in the *German Theology*. To say that self or self-absorption is yielded is to state that a person has surrendered and yielded the self and all that is his. Anyone who denies himself as one who is ashamed is yielded, Lk 9:23. To yield ego or I-ness is to despise myself and surrender and grant that everything good belongs to the one who gave it to me. For all rivulets [//] must flow and return to their source if they intend to return properly. This ego or self is usefully yielded when self-will is surrendered and when self-will melts away and when God's will does its work in the creature and nothing else is willed except that which and how God wills. At that moment ego and self-will surrender, and everything that follows the created will, or springs forth from it, is altogether truly yielded.

Whether or not we have thus yielded ego or self can be determined and decided when nothing pleases us except what pleases God and when we desire nothing of any creature except what God wills. Then we are detached because we no longer love what we will but only that which God wills, and we desire all creatures to will what God wills. In this, i.e., in God's will, our love, desire, joy, glory, life, and salvation are rooted. We therefore pray sincerely, Lord, your will be done on earth as in heaven. Let your will work mightily in all earthly creatures.

By contrast to the love of God, we must not be sorry for or regret anything other than what is contrary to God if we have truly surrendered our ego or self. If we observe a creature willing or acting against God's will, we experience severe pain, anguish, displeasure, sorrowfulness, anxiety, death, hell, and eternal fire over such a contrary creature. But note that when everything that can affect us comes to be

God's and is surrendered because of his will or displeasure or is placed upon us by God, yieldedness has reached its fullness. However, we must be on guard constantly that this same yielded egoism or self-absorption is seriously judged and surrendered, for the devil sits in wait of unsurrendered yieldedness[37] as a fox looks out for chickens which he plans to devour.

Christ is the way, the truth and the life

God sent us Christ his Son (who led such a yielded life in the highest and best manner), to be the way, the truth, and the life, especially on account of the virtue yieldedness, so that we may have a true and living way whom we might more certainly follow and know so that we will not be deceived as long as we follow in his steps and walk as he walked. Hence, we must see what Christ and the immovable truth teach.

I said (and there were not a few others who said it, too), that a person who has given leave to his ego and self is well-yielded. Christ teaches this, too.

Two kinds of seed, Jn 12:24-26

Christ compares two things, namely, grain that falls into the ground, dies, and then bears fruit, and a person who hates his soul and saves it for eternal life.

Christ told another parable as well, namely, that seed which has not died, bears no fruit, and remains alone. To such seed Christ compares the person who loves his soul and destroys it, Jn 12:24a. In this way Christ compares a soul which loves itself to grain which stays alive and therefore remains alone and without fruit. According to this, we cannot have new life or any good works as long as we love ourselves. Everything then is lost and for nought and not of God, however much we may tear ourselves root and branch, coat and shirt, as long as we remain in self-love. We and all that is ours will perish. God curses such a tree and its leaves, and consigns it to the fire because it bears no fruit. We may run, work, sing, fast, pray, suffer tribulation—all in vain God's eyes—if we continue to love our soul. Just as seed which remains alone and unfruitful is in our eyes, so are we in the eyes of God if we love our soul. We will go down to the devil though we may speak like angels and have the skills of all the prophets, in addition; because we are like seed or trees without fruit, we will [//] surely be consigned to hellfire. And if we have false fruit, the fruit would be considered evil in God's sight and the tree made ready for the fire, Mt

7:19.

It follows from this and is firmly supported that if we love our soul, we will destroy it; we are like seed that has not died and therefore yields no fruit.

The second reason follows on this. It is that we must despise ourselves and what is ours if we are to stand in the sight of God and be accepted. From this you know what it means to be yielded.

Why we should love the good

One must not seek all that is good and think it to be of benefit to the soul. Rather, one should love and do what is good because it is God and not because it is good for oneself and one's own. For the truth is that anyone who loves his soul destroys it, for he remains a seed of the old life—without fruit.

God does not care whether the seed was thrown, sown, or beaten if it does not die, but remains alive. From this you may learn, dear brother, how we must divest ourselves of our soul and not do anything good to it. And if we do something or yield something for the sake of our soul, we remain alive in our self and in our self-absorption or egoism and destroy our soul.

We must be without reward

Note with dismay, then, how those will stand who torture their soul with fasting and prayer in order to save their soul and bring it into the kingdom of heaven. God's will alone, and not partiality toward and love of our soul, ought to be held before us all our lives. We must also be free of any fear of punishment for not loving our soul. For those who do something, or leave it undone, for fear of being punished or condemned, fear for their skin or the punishment. But they do not fear God for his justice. What harm do you think could concern, fear, pain, death, and hell inflict on us, if we were hostile to self-love? [e]

Hence, love, partiality, and inclination toward our own soul must die and be blown away, as dust is blown away by a storm wind if we place our soul in God's grace and hope to keep it there.

Note once again how much we need Christ to carry us and do penance for all our sin and weaknesses [*gepresten*], which means to break the law and dominion of sin and death. I would know of no comfort if I did not know of God's mercy. For it is true that everyone who loves his soul destroys it. He is like living seed which remains unfruitful, for the Truth which cannot say anything but what is true, says so; it must be so, therefore, and cannot be otherwise.

Hatred of the soul

However, it is not sufficient simply not to love one's soul. A strong salt must be added; a supernatural hatred and envy must replace our natural love.

How desires decline

There the grain must die and yield fruit. There love, desire, partiality, the life of our soul and all lusts die. There the soul irrevocably divests itself of its nature. This is baptism in the death of Christ—the old, natural life is being attached to the cross of Christ, pierced, killed, and buried with Christ in baptism, to rise again, not in the old, natural life, but in the new, unnatural life, Rom 6:4-11. One is then able to say truthfully, "It is not I who lives but Christ in me," Gal 2:20. You must feel and confess this as the apostle did if you wish to be a yielded person as the apostle was. I suspect you will send me more.

The old and the new life

There are two lives which are opposed to each other and in tension: the old or natural and the new or supernatural; the life of the old Adam and that of the new Christ; the earthly and the heavenly life. The love of and inclination to the old life comes from below, [//] from the earth and the flesh, and it is earthly and carnal. For that which is born of flesh is flesh, Jn 3:6. But the new life, the new love, the new inclination, and the new fear come from above, from heaven where rebirth takes place, Jn 3:6bff.

The nature of the old life

The old life is sheer disobedience and self-will and loves its soul in all it does; it grunts and groans when one gets too close.

The new life

The new life is the pure will and obedience of God and hates the soul of a person in all its active and affective aspects; it kisses the father's rod, however hard and long he may hit.

You should now hear of the way we must be yielded and how we must irrevocably divest ourselves of the self. Then we must forever hate our soul, (as we must) if we wish to be sure that we have irrevocably divested ourselves of our soul. How better can one divest oneself more fully than by becoming divested through envy and hatred? Envy and hatred separate more forcefully than do walls and places.

The Truth stands before us and says, Whoever does nothing or whoever forsakes what delights the soul shall be saved, and whoever does not give his soul what it wants preserves it.

And whoever gives the soul what it flees, and removes from it what it wants, preserves it unto the kingdom of heaven. And whoever apportions to the soul what belongs to it, i.e., wickedness, vice, shame, and sin, of which it is the cause, hates it and wages war with it. Whoever takes from the soul all that is good and gives it to God the Creator, fights with it. And whoever seeks God's will alone deprives the soul of its food. Again, it is the seed that has died and is dead to all its own desires, pleasures, will, and life and boastings which alone brings forth God's will. In such a one God says, "You have [e ij] been bid to do my will," Isa 5; 8 and 62.

The soul appears as if it is easy and dear to nature and as if it always wishes and desires God's will. But if one could know oneself properly and sincerely for an hour even, one would sense in oneself the cross and a thousand mortal sins, and hate, avoid, and flee oneself as one flees a hostile person and look upon oneself as one looks upon one's worst enemy.

Note that if you were to help a poor brother by lending him money, you would have to fear that you cannot ever demand it back (because the seventh year is an eternal day among Christians). Yet, the rich person's thoughts are cursed if he divests himself and lets go of his own flesh before he is willing to yield filthy lucre, Deut 15:1ff.; Mt 5:21ff. He will not, or ever did, pay attention to his devilish thoughts, Deut 15. How then might or could we give serious attention to our evil thoughts which we have toward God in spiritual matters, when we do not understand our evil thoughts in corporeal [*leyplich*] matters? Each thought and all self-will is deserving of hell, however small it might be when it happens for the sake of one's soul in the various services to God. For Christ does not lie when he says that whoever loves his soul, ruins it.

Mortal sin

Learn from this that agreeableness and unyieldedness are mortal sins and devilish vices of Lucifer, Isa 13.

The perils of our life

From this you may learn in what horrendous peril our life is and how quickly an unyielded person destroys his soul. For as soon as we love ourselves and not purely for the sake of God's will, we are corrupted. I reckon that the yieldedness (when we divest ourselves of everything that is something and good) may be observed in the words of Moses, "You must not till or plow the land with firstborn oxen. You must not [//] shear firstborn sheep. They are holy to God," Deut 15:19. What else is the tilling and plowing to indicate to us than that we must not serve ourselves with God's gifts. Firstborn oxen belong to God. Therefore, no one was allowed to till with firstborn oxen.

All good gifts and everything God wants, God creates in his servants and all that is good belongs to God, not to us. For this reason we must not serve ourselves but God with good things. And what does "You must not shear firstborn sheep" mean other than that you must not seek your own advantage, honor, glory, or any other thing for your own benefit, in all the things God consecrated unto himself, which is everything God created.

Is not this what Christ teaches, "You shall not love your soul, for if you love yourself as you love your soul, you corrupt it."[38] It is a mortal sin and contrary to God's will to love and not hate oneself. Neither could we trust, believe, or love God if we thought and asserted our own, i.e., everyone his own and his self. Christ says, "How can you believe if you honor one another and do not seek the honor which comes from God alone?" Jn 5:44. Earlier Christ says, "I have known you and that you do not have God's love in you" (see the same chapter).[39] If we were God-fearing people, our ears would undoubtedly ring and tremble at these words of Christ which he spoke not only to the Jews, but to all those who are like the Jews.

Truly, truly, all God-fearing people's hearts are moved and water or faith has its billows[40] and waves or floods when we receive these words of Christ with a fearful and trembling heart. For Christ says in clear words, "How can you believe, as long as you receive glory from one another?" As if to say, "It is impossible for you to believe God as long as you give honor to one another."

We must take this to heart and see whether we want to be everyone's foot bandage or shoe rag—especially those who have some of the hypocrisy of this world. We must examine ourselves, whether [e iij] we can seriously endure to be laughed at, scorned, and taken for total fools and demented persons.

Higher education[41]
What does one seek in the higher schools than to be honored by others? Therefore, one aspires to be a master, another, a doctor and then a doctor of sacred Scripture. They give up goods and chattel for the

honor which Christ did not accord his apprentices. Yet they wish to be the ones who teach and maintain Christian faith and to be called masters and doctors, even though they seek doctoral honors with such avarice and greed that they envy and persecute all other equal teaching when they have acquired their honor. They allow no one who does not have the same title to come up and sit with them. And if I or someone else wants to deny this, God's penetrating eyes will find us out and convict us that on account of academic glory we kneel down, give money and set up festivities and costly meals to gain some clout with and earn respect from people. And we refuse to admit that we are unbelievers. Yet, it cannot be that we believe and trust God while we receive such honors. Christ says, "Not the one who seeks honor." He narrows the scope and says, "Whoever receives honor from another cannot believe God."

Do you see now what sort of a worm agreeableness or unyieldedness is and how it eats away and gnaws at faith and how God harshly judges and sentences us so that everyone would have to say, "O Lord, do not sit in judgment with your servant, for no one living is righteous in your sight."

What I said of universities also applies to bishops and priests. How can we stand before God at the judgment when he will say, "All of you together forsook me. You had trust in God, but then you received honor from another, [//] although you still pretended to be believers." Think about it and see whether you do not show love, pleasure, and delight when you or your work is praised, and again whether your noses are not put out of joint when someone says, "He is a dumb mule; whatever he has someone else has given him, etc." The word, "How can you believe when you honor one another?" remains ever so true. It is impossible for you to believe, inasmuch as such honor pleases you. Your honor and your desiring of honor must die and must drop off like a pus-filled boil which has been cauterized, i.e., you must yield yourself and the faith which has been compared to a small bitter and sour mustard seed, Mt 13:31ff. Christ does not conceal who is able to believe. "Seek God's honor which comes from God alone" (says Christ), "if you wish to believe." When God's glory, honor, praise, will, and love rule in us with might, then ego, I-ness and everyone's self or self-absorption must wither and become nothing. This is the very characteristic and nature of faith—to see God's glory and our shame, God's virtue and strength and our wickedness and weakness [*gebresten*], God's something and being [*icht*]. And, on the other side, to know our nothingness. Therefore, it is impossible for us to believe God and remain unyielded; of necessity, then, God's honor must be directed to God, and not to ourselves.

Christ also says privately, "I know that you do not have God's love in you, for you seek your own honor," Jn 5:44. Christ saw this because they had self-love from which came the evil that prevented them from having God's love. God's love and love of our soul cannot stand together. Yet, God's love and the hating of our soul stand firmly together as these two things: to love God and preserve our soul and to hate and envy one's own soul and thus preserve it unto eternal life. And when hate and envy of one's soul are able to quench and destroy the self or self-centredness of everyone, and Christ teaches and wills that everyone hate his soul, Christ also wills that we yield ourselves irrevocably. When we have seriously forsaken ourselves, we have surrendered and wholly yielded all things. [//]

Now it might happen that we abandon fields, meadows, parents, children, and wife, yet be unyielded in our soul. This happens when we love and enjoy such surrender and yielding, for we would then love our soul and are not truly surrendered. Our self and ego and something are before our eyes like a treasure after which the heart pines. The cursed devils and souls are in hell—free of both creatures and desires—yet they retain, nonetheless, desire of creatures and hanker after them, as the prophets Isaiah and Jeremiah and others write. Nothing therefore is achieved by such a yielding.

We ought to love father and mother, wife, and children and everyone who is neighbor to us for God's sake and not for ourselves. If our self-will were to stand over against a person, such love would be wrong and against God. Therefore, Christ says, "Whoever would come after me, but does not hate father and mother, wife and children, brother and sister and his own soul, too, cannot be my disciple," Lk 14:33. I said this earlier, that it is impossible to become an apprentice of Christ without surrendering all things, (see Luke, as cited above). For when I have self-will and not God's will, I am unyielded and against God in unbelief and I lack love.

Whatever I am to love, I must love for God's sake and because it pleases God. If I do love for God's sake, love remains firm, even though people move and change. If I love a person for the joy of it or for my sake, I must relinquish love whenever such a person is against God. This is so with regard to love and hatred of neighbor of which I shall write some other time.

Those wishing to discern God's will must read Holy Scripture and if my work can be of assistance in the matter (which is granted by

God if it happens), they should read my booklet on sin and God's manifold will.[42] It will be a better reminder than I can give at this point.

My dear brother, you know that I called yieldedness the most supreme virtue in my previous booklet[43] and you now wanted to have some reasons. I am at this point letting you [//] discern whether I was wrong, and I hope that you will come to know and say what the yieldedness of which I spoke is, namely, that it is faith, hope, and love of God. And where there is unyieldedness, there is sheer unbelief, self-love, and nothing but corruption. And if there is time and space, you can learn from the sections pertaining to God that all gain and loss are determined by detachment and agreeableness respectively. The sections are as follows:

to love		with one's whole heart
to fear		and nothing else
to trust	**GOD**	and no other
to cling to		and to no one else
to serve		with all one's soul

To seek God's glory and honor and to proclaim his word, and the like. In works of neighborliness, unyieldedness gnaws away at bone and marrow and renders all of them rotten.

I should now like to conclude since you must know by now what detachment and unyieldedness mean. But since the poisonous snake unyieldedness or agreeableness entangles itself secretly and lustily along with self-absorption and something in things which she has no right to draw to or appropriate for itself, I must give one more example. Perchance you will recall through the one, if not the other, what and how much diligence a God-fearing person must have every moment and every hour to acknowledge and confess the damage done by unyieldedness toward God, and to long for the satisfaction rendered by Christ, believing that Christ is the one who took our sin upon himself and remedied it. Inasmuch as it often happens that we learn to know a virtue by its opposite, such as righteousness and grace through anger, or honey through gall. We must learn in whatever way we can, as long as we learn the right thing.

Our intellect and will, in fact, all our powers have not the minutest right to appropriate and claim good works or suffering for themselves. For all that is good is created by God alone within us, and without [f] our aid. We contribute no more to this than we did when God created us. We contributed nothing to our creation, therefore we are not entitled to it. And since we have no rights or encouragement, we cannot rightly have or seek what is ours, the ego, mine, selfness.

It follows without fail that seeking my own in my creation is against what is reasonable. I am cursed and damned when I say to my Creator and Father, "Why did you create me?" Isa 45:9 or, "You did not create me," Isa 29:16. Now he is a Creator who made desert and barren land and gave them their beauty and embellishment, Gen 1. Therefore, God compares whatever is good in a person to the first Creation, saying, God made us for good works which God created so that we may walk in them, Eph. If there is a good thought, a good will, a good existence or a good work in us, it is God's alone who is the Creator. We have no right to these, however often we may think or fancy ourselves to be involved in thought or will.

I, we, etc. In this way we attribute something to ourselves to which we have no right or claim—we steal and rob God of what is his.

Learn one more thing from this: we must be detached, for unyieldedness is a thieving robber. But if God moves a person to do good, it is like moving a stick to assist us. We cannot appropriate to ourselves that which happens through us, any more than we can attribute something to an assisting stick.

Example: King Assur[44] was a rod of God's wrath. Through him God poured out his wrath and punished evil. God could not bear it therefore when Assur said, I marched against and defeated [them], for his ego and I-ness, his my and mineness brought great trouble and anxiety to Assur and caused irreparable damage. Though it was true that Assur had punished the disobedient Jews with great strength and might, he nonetheless ruined his case when he claimed to have done it with the might of his hand. Note that Assur was strong when he waged war and won. This strength, however, was his in the manner in which a rod handled by a weak little child has strength. [//] Thus, Assur robbed and stole this strength when he stated, "In my strength or in the strength of my hand I fought." Had he said, "God is my strength, my wisdom, my protection, my shelter and stronghold," he would have spoken the truth. But when he said right out, "I beat my enemies because of my strength and might," he sinned.

Note from this example how our own thoughts corrupt us and turn everything which was right into a wrong. What Assur did with strength was right and true. But to wage war in his own strength was wrong and untrue. You can learn from this that Assur ruined himself in his selfhood [*seinheit*] or through his unyielded selfness. It is all too true then when Christ teaches that anyone who loves his soul ruins it, Jn 12:25.

Further, warriors must have wisdom and foresight like Assur; but it must be from God, not from themselves. Assur sinned, therefore, when he said, "In my wisdom I understood it," for he ascribed the wisdom and understanding which he received from God to himself. When God intends to use someone, he gives wisdom, speech, and strength.

Therefore, Assur could not truthfully and rightfully say, "In my wisdom, etc." However, had he said, In God's wisdom, he would have spoken correctly.

Do you now wish to hear how God rates such thinking and speaking? Listen to what God says. God says, "For a person to say, I did this in my own strength or I understood that in my wisdom, is as much as for a person to pick up a rod which then turns on the one who picked it up, saying, I raised myself up. Is not the rod a piece of wood which can neither move nor raise itself?" Isa 10:15.

These words suggest that it is the same in God's eyes to raise oneself up and to rise up against God. For Scripture reports, as Assur said, In my strength and in my wisdom, etc. But we find rather that Assur spoke against God in words other than the above. Therefore God gives the example of an ax or a hatchet and a saw, a rod and a stick which appropriated their own significance and boasted against their mover by the simple fact that the saw says, I sawed and the hatchet, I split, and the rod I hit, and the stick, I beat.

God sees the heart and thoughts and it is one and the same in God's sight whether I think [f ij] wrongly about what God thinks or does through me or whether I think that God did not do it at all. This would apply to creatures as well. I made or did it, hence, no one else did it. It is said at times as a result, How can he boast of the work or deed when he did not do it alone or did not do it at all. Thus it is the same not to be with God or to be against God, as Christ says, "Anyone who is not with me is against me." Therefore, whoever says, I understood, thought of, invented, worked, or suffered this is not with God. For he boasts and vaunts himself in his flesh and not in God. And such boasting is against God. It follows then that agreeableness or unyieldedness are always against God, however undemonstrative and secretive it may be. Note this and think on it and consider whether our daily sin is not a mortal sin and whether we can remove it with holy water.

Unyieldedness is vainglory

Read Isaiah chapter 10:5-19 on Assur and observe what God punishes in him and you will soon understand that Assur sinned in saying, "In my strength I toppled the princes and nations." To wit, "My hand found the might of the nations as one finds a nest." To wit, "I gathered them in as one gathers in eggs." To wit, "In wisdom I reflected, etc." These are the thoughts and words of Assur which were against God and for which God punished Assur, saying that honor and glory are the prerogative of lofty eyes and supercilious hearts.

We find similar material in Isaiah which says that words such as I, my, and the like derive from vainglory, Isa 2, 5 and 13; Ezek 28 and 29. And since everyone says that vainglory is a mortal sin and unyieldedness a common occurrence, it has to be admitted that our daily sin is a mortal [//] sin and that unyieldedness is not an unimportant pock or sin.

I say this so that we look the more seriously to our daily, yes, sinful[45] and momentary life and know that our life is full of mortal sin. For all unyieldedness merits hell fire, Isa 14:24ff. Your vainglory pulled you down to hell, etc. Tell me now whether Christ's teaching which he addressed to everyone does not serve as well as this, namely, "Anyone who intends to follow me must deny himself and daily carry his cross and follow me," Lk 9:23. If we wish to be Christians who follow the Lord Christ Jesus, we must deny ourselves, i.e., surrender and lose or reject our ego or self, otherwise we cannot follow Christ or be Christians, since we can neither love nor believe God.

Such self-denial cannot be tepid or distant, but must be sincere and red-hot. It must not last for a day, but forever. In addition, we must daily watch for unyieldedness and agreeableness and wait, just as an angry bear or fierce lion might wait for their prey which their young will eat and devour. We must daily bear the cross of wrath, hatred, and envy against our soul and never lay it down if we are to follow Christ and intend to become apprentices of God and Christ.

God help us to this through our Lord Jesus Christ, Amen.

On heavenly yieldedness

In conclusion we should know: when the spirit of restfulness takes hold of us and fills the house or temple of God, which is the soul, with its splendor, yieldedness comes to an end and turns into unyieldedness. For nothing in the soul is empty and free [f iij] inasmuch as the Spirit of God leaves it undeified, moves through, fills and remains eternally in the soul, leading it to a divine life. Then creatures, desires, and lusts no longer have access to the soul when the human is in the whole soul and leads the soul to total peace and obedience. In this way, creaturely detachment becomes divine unyieldedness. God help us to this, Amen.

My answer to the other question: When we truthfully pray, "And lead me not into temptation," we ask God to protect us from evil, but not from tribulation and castigations, in line with what Christ says, "I do not ask that you take my disciples from the world, but that you protect them from all evil or from the evil one," Jn 17:15. So you, too, pray that God may work his eternal will in you and that you be fully yielded. In short, you pray that God may protect you from a wrong judgment and not surrender you to the world which perverts all of God's things and speaks what is wrong.

I will soon write more on this. Be virile and strong in your desire toward God. Amen.

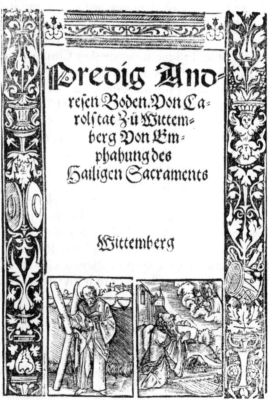

Title page of Carlstadt's 1522 tract, "On Receiving the Holy Sacrament."

7

Reasons Why Andreas Carlstadt Remained Silent for a Time and On the True, Unfailing Calling

**Printed at Jena in Thuringia
by Michael Buchfürer, 1523**

With this tract Carlstadt seeks to explain a seven-to-eight-months period of self-imposed silence. It is impossible to determine whether he failed to publish on account of the turbulent events in Electoral Saxony focused in Wittenberg or because of Luther's efforts to silence Carlstadt—whom Luther perceived as a threat to effective reforms because of alleged iconoclastic activities.

*Carlstadt's last major publication prior to **Reasons** had been the publication in April/May 1523 of his tract "The Meaning of the Term* **Gelassen.** *" Unlike some of the earlier tracts, this booklet was printed in Jena, as were at least four others which followed in quick succession from the end of December 1523 to early 1524. The apologetic tone of the tract reflects Carlstadt's discomfort because some of his friends interpreted his silence as a sign of cowardice. He is obviously torn between the desire to "make God's name known" and the need to hold back for fear of being misunderstood by his detractors.*

Freys/Barge, numbers 110 and 111, list two printings of this Carlstadt tract of 1523. See also A Zorzin, Karlstadt als Flugschrifte-nautor, Göttingen: Vandenhoeck & Ruprecht, 1990, pp. 98-100. Erich Hertzsch reprinted the tract in Karlstadts Schriften aus den Jahren 1523-25. While we followed the text as printed by Hertzsch, we compared it with a copy of the original in the Zentralbibliothek, Zurich, signature No. V. 160.24 and 18-271.9.

> Peace and the knowledge of God's unfailing[1] righteousness from God the living Father of Christ Jesus our Lord be to you, the brothers who have called me. Amen.

Brothers, you wonder why I am silent and do not write. You attribute this to my laziness and behave like some of those who daily clamor against me, saying that I have left the better task of teaching and have engaged in the external labor of a layperson. You dare force me to write as if I am obligated to be at your disposal by writing, almost as if such service could happen without risk and to the detriment of the spirit. I hope to give you sufficient reasons and convince you through testimony from Scripture, and lead you to admit that no external testimony (such as writing and preaching the truth) can take place without some risk and without gravely tempting the Spirit of God. It would be better for me, too, if I were to stand still and listen to the voice of the bridegroom only, rather than run from the bedroom and outside the range of his voice.

You know, above all else, of the boundless evil of these days in which love has cooled and has been extinguished and that the world spares no effort and is ashamed of no blasphemy which it hurls against the Word of God. To hear the fierce grinding of teeth and look into the gaping jaws of lions and bears has, in turn, caused the evangelical preachers to scold and deride too much. They forget, of course, that they are not to speak, but merely to hear evil. And they are not ashamed to fill their booklets with rebukes rather than with divine words and scriptural testimonies of what they think and know. From this (I reckon) common people derive their sharp and prickly tongues. Few of them, as a result, wish to speak of valorous and serious matters, for the simple reason that they have drunk [3] both good and evil with equal diligence. Because of this, brotherly love has in part been nipped in the bud,[2] and all writing is inclined more to ridicule and derision than to instruction and teaching.

In this matter I blame the reader more than the writer, because the reader gobbles up into mouth and belly whatever is presented in books, without discernment and knowledge, mistaking evil for good. And those who did write were forced by their vehement and wanton opponents to practice works of evil and to subdue evil desires through lack of desire.[3] To this day there is no end to this lack of desire. As a result, the elect have not been brought together from the four corners of the world. And the evil ones have not been sifted out from among the good. Indeed, the world demonstrates its wickedness daily to the highest degree, erecting mountains of wickedness where before it had erected small hills only; and all wantonness and longing is at fever pitch. No one looks to what ought to be done, but everyone does as much evil as possible. They deride Israel as if it had been found among thieves and pick it apart as a hawk tears apart young chickens [Jer 48], and they jump about like exuberant calves in a fresh pasture of new and succulent grass. They do not act toward Israel according to their ability, but beyond their ability and more than they are able to do, with their tongues, in words and deeds, just like the children of Moab.

Dear brothers, if a Moabite or Babylonian servant has you by the throat, it is difficult to show moderation toward such a one and to refrain from excessive curses and maledictions.

You are aware that jeering Philistines[4] have surrounded us and that they come toward us out of their tents, just as in former days they came out of their dwellings against the people of God with threats and insults, shouting as if the God of Israel were deaf and could not hear, blind and could not see, or else so weak as to be unable to protect and save his people or else, as if the living God were without love and so fierce that he would forsake his people and bear a grudge toward them forever.

You are also aware that we are surrounded, as in a state of war, by Moabites, Ammonites, Babylonians, and many other enemies of God. [4] Nothing is more certain than that we will have to listen to their derision and taunts.

It is also not hidden from you that I can hardly hide from them and that I am often unable to retort to their useless invective without rankness. In this I might ensnare those who have little understanding (as some have done) and so cause the decline of divine love and [the increase of] invective which fools gather in along with the good [Hos 4]. This would bring dishonor and harm on God and his people.

Here then you have a reason why I have hitherto been peaceful and quiet and why I want to continue in that manner. For I cannot write without mocking by which I would then offend my brothers through harsh words. This would not benefit them at all and might bring me under severe sentence of judgment in which many will have to give account of themselves for useless words. I would have to suffer the unbearable heat of the fire for the small word *raca* or fool.[5]

The other reason why I do not like to write is that I have noted, not with a little dismay, the lack of enthusiasm in the printing of my books. You well know that some [printers] not only changed my words, but in addition have obscured entire sentences and covered them with the mists of blindness. Worse still, in some of my books they have rearranged entire columns, thus totally distorting the meaning and content of those books.[6]

Now I know that such indifference brought me much slander and did not advance or serve the neighbor in any way. I therefore wanted to restrain myself and not write anymore.

But since you have said and promised that you yourselves would spare no effort and see to it that everything should go forth with sufficient care, I shall drop this reason. More so since you turn my argument against me, saying that I should write all the more, and that your great diligence will correct and eradicate the neglect, indolence, and defect. So much for my second reason.

But what would you say to this, that no one should write or preach or render any public service to God [5] except when God has chosen him to do so! That you and others of my brothers called me and sent me forth is a human and external sending forth which may well be worthless in God's sight; indeed, it may even be opposed to God.

In truth, such a human call is a dangerous and deceptive pledge and to depend on human calling is presumptuous and wanton if God's inner call is not added to assure inwardly the one who is called with this imprinted seal and sure pledge. For discipleship which is creaturely only, without any foundation, is fabricated and hypocritical, full of the sourdough of the Pharisees.

And even if it were not arrogant and wanton, dangerous or deceptive, nonetheless, the ability to glory in God is lost and the one called could not (as Paul did) boast and rejoice in God. Therefore Paul says unabashedly, "I have not been called by human beings or by a single person, but I have been placed by Jesus Christ and by God the Father, etc. [Gal 1:1].

Paul makes this splendid and wonderful claim at the beginning of all his epistles, that he was not chosen to be an apostle by human beings or by any single person. This assures him and he boasts of it in both epistles to the Corinthians where Paul says at the outset, "I am an apostle, called by the will of God" [1 Cor 1:1; 2 Cor 1:1]. In Ephesians, Colossians and in 1 Timothy, he says, "An apostle according to the commandment of God" [Eph 1:1; Col 1:1; 1 Tim 1:1] and in 2 Timothy, "An apostle according to the will of God" [2 Tim 1:1].

Do you think that Paul claimed in vain to be an apostle of Christ by God's will and command? What can or may those boast about who cut off and deride God's living call? How will they carry out the servanthood of Christ and their apostolic office confidently and freely in God's sight when they know neither of God's will nor of his command? They can only boast of that which Paul is ashamed of, namely, their human calling. If I had no more than your summons, what would God have to say to me? Undoubtedly the following: "He runs and I did not send him; he talks and prophesies in my name and I did not encourage him." Just as God spoke to the prophets who allowed their own thoughts and dreams to call and drive them, saying, [6] "They run, yet I did not send them; they prophesy, yet I did not encourage them, etc." [Jer 23:21].

Even if I wanted to preach and write God's word, I would have no power to do so publicly without God's commandment, for God might say to me what he says to all who are not called, "They go or run, etc."

Assume that I preach God's word without change and straight, but that my proclamation is without God's bidding and will. Would I not have to fear that God might say to me, "Did I command you to take my word into your mouth on your own initiative and preach it to the people?" I know for a fact that I would be a transgressor and punishable should I preach or write publicly without knowing God's will and commandment.

Paul himself says, "How can they preach before they are sent?" [Rom 10:15]. It follows then, "How can one write profitably for the people when God did not ordain[7] one to the task?"

The apostles were never so arrogant as to choose another in place of Judas Iscariot to witness to and proclaim Christ, before they had discerned God's will by casting lots [Acts 1:26]. Do you dare to be so smart and bold that you would urge me to write without knowing God's will?

It makes no difference whether we witness, write, or preach Christ, for the Spirit grants all these testimonies. No one can bear witness of Christ unless the spirit first bears witness to him of Christ. As Christ says, "He shall bear witness of me and you too shall bear witness of me.'"[8] No one can truly write or preach about God, unless the spirit of God has first led him into the truth and has compelled him to write, speak or testify.

We also know that the apostles ascribe their testimony and teaching to God. They say unabashedly that God's Spirit drove them to testify, as Christ says, "You shall receive the power of the Holy Spirit and shall be my witnesses." Acts 1:8[9] That God's Spirit drives and urges them to testify to Christ is also pointed out in the story of Paul whom God's Spirit compelled to proclaim Jesus to the Jews at Corinth.[10] In another place, however, God gagged Paul so that he was unable to speak of Christ.[11] [7]

Now Paul was led and overcome by the spirit of God to bear witness to Christ; and where the Spirit did not drive him, Paul could not testify. Should I not learn from this story that I too ought not to testify of Christ unless I am driven by the powers of the Spirit of God and not by human beings?

And what pertains to testifying applies to the proclamation of the word of God, for the apostles only then spoke God's word with joy when they were full of the Holy Spirit.

To conclude: if we are to preach or write of God and Christ with benefit and without blame, God's spirit will have to prepare and call us to the task, encourage and drive us, and we must receive the command from God through Christ.

Without a commandment from God and without knowing God's will, it is sheer insolence when a person allows himself to be placed in such high office. Unless, of course, God has become mute, unable to teach or draw anyone, and Christ no longer desires to be with us to the end of the world. Even if angels and human beings were inciting us to preach or write, it would be worthless before God and unprofitable to human beings.

God alone bestirs his servants and places them on their feet, and urges them to reveal God's glory, and sends successful laborers or harvesters into his harvest. No other power, gathering, congregation, or single person is indicated by the Truth who says, "Ask the Lord of the harvest to send workers or servants into his harvest" [Mt 9:38]. If it were within human power to order servants to work in the harvest, it would be their harvest and not God's. Human beings and not God would then be masters over it. Christ's teaching would then also be in vain which says, "Ask the Lord of the harvest, etc." The one who asks does not have power over that which he is to achieve through prayer. And since God alone is God and Lord of his people and of his harvest, it is not fitting for human beings to send servants into someone else's harvest. Rather, they are to ask God to put shepherds in charge of his sheepfold, but they are not to take control of God's flock.

For this reason no one ought to consider himself a pastor, church leader, or bishop unless he was chosen by God to be responsible for those people. I know that no one is entitled to boast of [8] being the pastor of a group of people unless he is quite sure that he has been appointed by God whose harvest it is and who alone provides laborers for the harvest. Just so, no one is a shepherd unless God has assigned him to his little sheep. And no one can know for sure that God has placed him to be a shepherd when he has not specifically learned to know God's will and mind and that God has chosen him.

The work of laborers and shepherds reminds me to hold back, for true shepherds and harvesters among the people have authority over those to whom God sends them (not that they are to rule people for the sake of wicked gain). Rather, they have been placed over the people that they might carry out God's word mightily and with great joy, to pluck up and destroy and scatter and grind down every heart with God's word, as with a sharp sword and heavy hammer, for which it has been sent. Then again, true shepherds are to gather in what has been scattered, make whole what has been broken, and return what is fugitive and has gone astray. They are to heal what is diseased and straighten out everything through God's word, as is called for by its nature. Never are they to return without fruit, and they are to work a thousand similar things, none of which I am capable of.

Since I do not find such fruit within me, it is better for me not to try to be tree or root, but rather to wait until I am wonderfully kindled and uplifted by the Spirit that works within unto such public proclamation—the Spirit which holds all hearts in hand and moves every shepherd to speak or be silent, as he wills. Scripture indicates that no one must think himself a shepherd or pastor unless he discerns such power of the word of God within himself, Ezek 3; Jer 1:33; Jn 10. Paul's saying should also be added here, that the spirit of prophecy is subject to the prophets, although it is hidden from carnal eyes [1 Cor 14:32].

The inner calling is precious, sure and essential, for it gives truthful testimony that the one who is called is a servant of the Lord God whose little sheep they are. Whoever has found this to be true and rightly understands it enters by the door. But the one who cannot discern the calling enters by climbing the wall—[9] and comes on the path which thieves and murderers use.

But we are rash people (I along with everyone else) who move fast in godly matters, allowing ourselves to be picked up as straws are picked up by a small gust. We allow ourselves to be servants of God and then go to bigger, older, jollier tyrants or even all at once to Pharaoh, Zedekiah, and Nebuchadnezzar, unwilling to recall how awkward it was for Moses, Jeremiah and Ezekiel, and in a similar case Gideon, when God called them and sent them to the people. These should be good examples for us that we might carry out God's work [Amt] and sword with greater circumspection than I for my part have done thus far.

Now flesh and blood do understand what the spirituals refuse to understand and are more deeply ashamed of wanton deeds than the spirituals. Observe that no one should think of himself as the servant of a prince or king unless he knows that the prince or king has hired him. If one has not been summoned orally or has in some other way discerned the will of the master, one would not consider oneself a servant of the prince. And if he enters royal service, he will forever be fearful. His conscience will not be at peace. And he will fidget until he understands the nature of his service. The children of this world work it that way, and they are wiser than the children of the light. But among us there are thousands who respond to a certain noise. We place ourselves in the service of God without any external sign that God has called us to it. Nor do we know anything of the inner call and we are not ashamed to do in God's sight what we would be ashamed of in the sight of people. It agitates and frightens me to note how alien and strange this is, for God's will ought to be readily understood.

Rejoinder
You say, I understand God's will. Whether I write or not, whether I preach or not, I know it to be God's will, since without God's will I am unable to do anything. If God did not want me to preach or write, I would have to be silent.

Response: [10]
Anyone who undertakes to write on such fatalistic understanding of God's will can do so at his own expense; I won't. The devil, the damned, thieves and murderers, false sheep, and ravening wolves bank on such divine will; they do what God does not tolerate. Even the devil could not have lied had not God tolerated it. By the same token, Judas the betrayer would not have betrayed Christ without God's

permission. Yet, they sinned and became guilty of God's judgment. I shall ask God to give me his spirit of mercy who informs me of his gracious will. To his will I shall gladly submit, for it makes me pleasing in his sight. All shepherds who pasture their sheep well and properly are in need of this, and they must discern this spirit if they are true shepherds. The reason: they must first experience the fatherly pull which draws them to Christ the shepherd of souls, and understand the work of the spirit of Christ. Without that they would be neither spiritual nor true shepherds.

You, brothers, appeal to Paul's command who says to Titus, "Fill the towns here and there with priests." You want to arouse and prod me with Paul's teaching so that I might step forward without fear and boldly in response to your calling and that of others. You undertake to convince me by saying that, though Titus was alone, he nonetheless received the command and the power to provide the people of God with servants for the harvest. The whole congregation is much more likely commanded or permitted to hire a person to carry out the public office of God.

I concede nothing to you. You are doing violence to Paul, for if this were indeed the meaning and intent of Paul, many another Pauline text and several writings would be rendered worthless and void. Let me name one: "Do not be hasty in the laying on of hands." The power of Titus is restricted by Paul's command, "Do not be hasty in the laying on of hands" [1 Tim 5:22].[12] This is Paul's reasoning. A Christian congregation or individual persons, be they high or low, must be prudent in the laying on of hands. What is this other than that you must know people above all else and inquire about the inner call and the secret will of God and discern God's grace in the one on whom you would lay your hands. [11]

The ability to recognize God's grace in another person is not strange to anyone other than the one who does not know God's Spirit or Scripture, for a Pharaoh recognized God's grace in Abraham and another in Joseph, Nebuchadnezzar in Daniel and, to mention one of the saints, too, Jacob in Ephraim. Take a look also at the stories in the Acts of the Apostles, chapter 6.

A Christian congregation is not to proceed with too much haste and should not trust in its own will and intention, but should first know the persons and discern and understand God's inner call, along with his divine will, before choosing a shepherd or pastor. This is Paul's intention when he forbids the laying on of hands. This is what the apostles did in choosing Matthias, Acts 21:23ff. and what Samuel did before anointing David [1 Sam 16]. One must rigorously and seriously enquire about the divine secret calling with great diligence and serious prayer and sincere sighs. Then God will inform his people inwardly and outwardly to know whom he has given to them and sent into his harvest.

Only then are they to lay on their hands to indicate thereby that the one on whom their hands have been placed has divine wisdom and good will in sufficient measure and is prepared and graced by God to lead God's sheep faithfully. Of that we have evidence and example. The Spirit of God spoke to the apostles, "Select for me Barnabas and Paul for the work to which I called them." The apostles fasted and prayed and laid their hands on them and sent them forth; and when they entered the city of Salamis, they proclaimed God's word, Acts 13:2ff. The work for which God had set apart Barnabas and Paul is the proclamation of God's word; and the Spirit called and set; them apart before the apostles did. Apostolic commissioning followed divine commissioning; and the apostles first recognized God's will before they sent out above-named two apostles. That they were serious about this is shown by their fasting, prayer, and laying on of hands. It must be noted that it is not written that the Spirit spoke through visions, in their sleep, or through dreams. Rather, without any addition, the Spirit spoke. It is likely, therefore, [12] that the Spirit of God addressed and taught the apostles inwardly that they were to set apart Barnabas and Paul.

It follows clearly that those who appoint or place shepherds and desire to call someone to proclaim God's word must first know God's pleasure before they choose, lest they choose, contrary to God's will, one whom God has rejected.

Those who are carnal cannot understand God's will and grace as do those who are spiritual. Therefore, only those are to choose, call, and appoint whom God's Spirit compels to do so and who have the spirit of Christ the supreme Shepherd.

You have an excellent example of this in the case of the apostles who asked the other disciples to choose men to serve at the table who were known for being full of the Holy Spirit and of wisdom.

You did not cite Paul correctly nor did you use him according to what he intended [Acts 6]. Furthermore, you approached me unwisely in urging me to write as before in response to human demand. Paul gave Titus a model and directive for choosing preachers and other proclaimers of God and how he was to perceive the inner call and suitability. To this end he outlined for Titus articles and points by which a person to be appointed shepherd ought to be judged—what gifts he is to have received from God, what vices and handicaps he must be free of.

Accordingly, you must not be too hasty in the laying on of hands regardless of who it is—learned or not, high or low, young or old. You must first see whether he has God's gifts or whether he relies on human wisdom. Don't be too hasty; it is difficult to probe the depth of another person. Allow works and fruits to mature. Some there are who pursue the office of apostle by soliciting letters of commendation or prayer; some do so for the sake of money, others for the sake of honor. Some, however, are driven by God's word which compels them and leaves them no rest until they confess it openly. On that we have many written stories. But human knowledge can be false and deceptive, for there are many raving wolves who come dressed in sheep's clothing. And some bear fruit as if they were sound trees. All of these will be revealed [13] at the completion of their work which an experienced spiritual person, who discerns and judges all things, can understand.

My brothers want to overcome my dread and fear by asserting that those might be heard who sit on the chair of Moses. Yet, they work against Moses. It won't help them nor will I be moved, for the little sheep hear them to their great detriment, and they will hear something unworthy as readily as they hear something worthy of the chair of Moses. Besides, I do not find that God ever led or directed a single little lamb (which thirsted after the righteousness of God) to such a voracious churchman or greedy bishop as are those who lead an anti-Christian life.

Christ points Cornelius to Peter that he might hear him. And just as God points Cornelius to Peter [Acts 10], so God points all his little lambs to the shepherds who have suffered or tasted the spirit of Christ. For this reason God says, I shall rescue my little lambs from the hands of false shepherds and will have my servant David pasture them [Ezek 34:10].[13] This is Christ, born of David. For the same reason, Christ also says, "Beware of false prophets [Mt 7:15]. Beware of the sourdough of the hypocrites [Mt 16:6]. My little lambs do not heed a stranger [Jn 10:8]. Therefore, be wise as serpents" [Mt 10:16] says Christ.[14] Since God demands such elect people to proclaim his word, you can understand without effort that I have good reason to be silent and wait until God—whom no power can resist—prods me.

To above-mentioned reasons for my silence, I will now add another. It is this: God's word is pure and upright and only those who are upright and pure—not the unclean—are to handle it. For the Spirit of God says, "God's word is pure as silver that has been purified seven times in a chamber of the earth," Ps 11 [12:6]. God did not say that in vain, but for our sake, so that we might understand how God's word is to be handled, who is to handle it, and who is to leave it alone.

Not without reasons was it said to the sinner, "Why do you take my word into your mouth and why do you recite my covenant?" [Ps 50:16]. For who can say before God, I am pure? And who would say, My heart is pure? Assuming there is one who has not been reproved by his conscience, would he therefore [14] be righteous? Paul never was that presumptuous, though he was a chosen vessel and did not have a bad conscience. Is not the heart evil and unfathomable? Are not our thoughts and will inclined to evil from our youth [Gen 8:21]? Yet, we parade those thoughts every time we speak or write God's word. How then is it possible for us to handle God's pure and upright word in a blameless manner? If God's word were not of the highest degree of purity, it might perchance be possible for a person to handle it without blame. But it is the most upright. As the Spirit of God says through David, God's word is pure like purified silver which has been refined seven times [Ps 12:6]. To handle holy things blamelessly, we must be pure and holy just like the things which we touch and handle.

Accordingly, everyone who undertakes to handle God's word through speaking, preaching, or disputing ought to be swept clean seven times. The reason: It was not said in vain that silver which is compared to the word of God was purified seven times. Just so the figure of Moses regarding the sevenfold sprinkling was not offered in vain [Lev 4:6].

I know that the priest did not dip his finger in the blood without reason and then sprinkled the curtain seven times. We, too, must understand and undergo the sprinkling of the blood of Christ seven times before all our curtains will fall off, and ere we become pure and white, well-purified silver. For God leads his people through fire [Jer 6:27ff.]. Anyone who is not improved in the first or third fire is like cast-off silver [Zech 13:9]. But one who lets go of his wickedness or who burns his impurity in the fire, becomes pure. However, he is not sufficiently clean and pure until he has gone through seven fires and until he has become better and pure through a sevenfold purgatory [Lk 9].[15] For God's word calls for the perfect purity which it has.

You know that we must daily bear our cross of hatred and envy of our own soul, and those who lay it aside for a moment destroy themselves. For Christ [15] says, "Whoever finds his soul in this world loses it. And whoever does not carry his cross and follow me is not my disciple."[16] Accordingly, I ought to hate my soul unceasingly and carry my cross continuously and follow Christ, especially when I want to proclaim God's spotless word. I have nothing myself, and it is God's doing and not mine.

But the soul gloats whenever the word is praised as if it were its own and thinks of itself as better. For this I ought to hate it profoundly. But I feel nothing within me except for will and desire. Would that the love of my soul had become ice-cold and that it were scattered like ashes. Would that envy and fierce hatred had taken its place. Would that I could handle God's word as I should—without finding my soul.

Yet, how far from me is the power and resolve to do what God demands and what I like to do. That which I do not want to do is often closer so that I have to do it, and I know that I cannot do what I want to do.[17]

Note how dangerous this situation is and explain it to me.

Even though I might greatly and extensively enjoy the proclamation of God's word, nonetheless the inner joy exceeds the external in inexpressible ways and means. And it is always better to be leaping inwardly in spirit than externally with one's feet. And it is by far safer to lift drooping members and bones that are crushed and to strengthen what has become limp (when God speaks) than when human beings go forth with divine Scripture or with preaching.[18] To remain within is always less dangerous than to go forth. Nonetheless, there is grave danger in the internal handling of God's word when the soul first hears of God. Should there not be even greater danger when a person breaks out with God's word and penetrates the armies of the enemy which are marching to meet him—a feat which I cannot ever claim for myself?

Be that as it may, I can see a remedy. God's will be done and I will obey. The evil lusts and the lack of surrender [*ungelassenheyt*] or love of my soul will be masterfully consumed or else quenched and contained by the insults of the godless Philistines and Moabites [16] and be swept away as through hot purgatory. For I know that I shall not be more free than my master Jesus Christ was who even let me know beforehand that I must be prepared to endure laughter and derision, just as he did. It is not surprising at all that they call the servant Beelzebub when they derided the righteous lord in like manner. And I earnestly desire that my harmful wantonness be burnt up through aversion [unlust] and the finding of my soul, through the taunts and envy of those who hate me and that the shortcomings of my lack of hatred of my own soul, which I have in small and insufficient measure, be made up and fulfilled through their plentiful hatred and envy. Thus, (I hope) that my dangerous going forth can almost be set alongside the fact of my remaining within. For my suffering may restore what I spoiled by my willful [ungelassen] going forth. Therefore, let it be known that I desire neither the devil's peace or company nor peaceful and friendly words.

We all must ever be Christlike and follow Christ and eager to praise the honor and holiness of our Father, as Christ did—each according to his talent.

Accordingly, we must reveal God's name to each other and proclaim the name of God to our brothers—not in some corner but in the midst of the congregation so that they may be enticed to accept and praise God's clear words. For it is the gracious will of God that everyone ought to trade with and humor others with his talent. For the Lord's sake I should handle his goods faithfully not only toward myself by returning a profit on the main gift, but also toward my fellow brothers whom I ought to love as myself. Everyone needs the other, especially since God's gifts are diverse and since no one has them all. But one who has something ought to share with the one who needs it, so to win him over and render him along with the talent. I fear the sentence of Christ toward the unprofitable servant who buried his talent because he feared the very thing in which he should have been bold [Lk 19:24]. I hear how Christ calls him a knave and how he condemns him. No doubt this is to serve me and all God's servants as a striking example of how all [17] of us are to work earnestly and willingly with the given talents for ourselves and our brothers.

Obedience is better than sacrifice [1 Sam 15:22], and it is always better to do what God's will intends and to confess the flaws in our works than to relax God's commandments on account of such flaws. Saul did this and forfeited and lost his kingdom for it. God's commandment to all heads of households to teach their children and servants remains in force, and everyone is obligated to preach God's word in his house, at table—be it morning or evening—in the field, or in the barn. Whether one is idle or at work, one ought to contemplate God's word and step forward and proclaim it to one's companions. We ought to sharpen God's word which is to bring its masterful content to the neighbor. This is a common commandment, addressed to all who are able to understand God's word, for through this commandment

God has appointed all to be priests (all people in general) to whom he has revealed himself. Here no one is excluded, since God's commandment concerns everyone and deals with the love and honor of God and the neighbor. Whoever relaxes the commandment for the sake of a better intention is disobedient and can anticipate nothing more surely than that God will strip him of Christian honor, just as he stripped Saul of royal honor because of his disobedience. We must surrender or set aside our thoughts, our cares and fears, along with all better intentions, to realize God's will.

It is better therefore that I feed my hungry brethren with God's blessing and that I do all I can to confess Christ and his spirit and God his Father, and as far as possible preach it, than to be cast from God's face or to be denied by Christ without whom no one can come into God's presence. Were I to conceal God's word for fear of the sins—which I cannot escape or flee—that would be like fleeing a puddle of water only to fall into the sea. It would be like deliberately committing a sin because of the sin which I must commit unwittingly whenever I intend to do well. But it is better for me to do what I do not want to do than not to want that which I am able to. And it is less harmful and more pardonable to confess God before my brethren and so to sin unintentionally and against my will than to conceal God's name in silence [18] and intentionally commit sin. Also it is more Christian to know and bemoan the harm caused by good works than willingly and violently to break God's commandments because of fear and through a wicked deed. I am certain and sure that God does not allow the smallest spark of faith to be lost. I see that Christ would not hinder the one who has the smallest spark of the confession of Christ, [Mk 9:39f.]. There was the one who cast out devils but did not follow the apostles, even though the apostles grumbled and complained to Christ that he did not follow them. Christ assured those with the smallest faith that it shall not be destroyed or lost. Neither can it be true that God would allow good intentions to perish (though it is also true that those with the smallest faith cannot enter the kingdom of God unless the heart has first been brought to its greatest lowliness and childlikeness). A good intention toward God does no evil, even if it commits evil [Mt 18:26ff.], just as a small, immature child cannot sin though he commits a sin. The fear of God does no evil. Rather, it is a font of life and preserves from the fall of death. It effects a horror of and flight from that which is evil, causing the heart to understand its wickedness and to confess what it does.

I am content then that God demands turning toward him [Isa 43] and that he is willing and gracious to forget all sin and not to remember it any longer, provided we poor sinners know ourselves and are mindful of sin. I also know that if I handle God's word with good intentions this will purify me no less than faith. Christ purified his disciples through his word [Jn 15:20]. What then should God's word be lacking which purifies those who handle it in the fear of God? For God's word is like a fire which burns and sweeps out. Therefore, I go forth in God's name, fully trusting God. Anyone who wishes to correct me may do so. Pray God for me.

Dated Orlamünde in December in the year of the Lord 1523.

FINIS

8

The Manifold, Singular Will of God, The Nature of Sin

Andreas Bodenstein from Karlstadt, A new layperson

Anno 1523

Among Carlstadt's major tracts written in German is this booklet, published in March 1523 by Arnd von Aich, a Cologne publisher. Within a year a second edition appeared in Augsburg, but there were no further prints or reprints. For the first time in his publishing ventures, Carlstadt identified himself as a new layperson on the rather ornate title page.

The author touches on complex theological matters such as the perceived distinctions in the divine will, the nature of sin and grace, and faith or belief which leads to new life. While he is aware of great interpreters of the faith such as Augustine, his main support comes from both the Old and New Testament.

Freys/Barge list this tract as numbers 102, 103. Pater, "Karlstadt as the Father of the Baptist Movements" (p. 308), established the 1523 print as a production of the Cologne printing house of Arndt von Aich. The following translation was made from the copy in the Zentralbibliothek, Zurich.

The nature of sin

People ask from time to time what sin is, and there is a great deal to be said on the matter. In this booklet I intend to relate and lay out the best and most excellent teachers' responses and through testimony of the Holy Spirit give visible indication that we should not speak of sin superficially nor treat it as insignificant. Hence, I will first give the opinion of several God-fearing persons who describe sin as follows: "Sin is nothing other than disobedience [*wyderwil*], being of another will or of a parallel will which wills contrary to or other than God wills." Understand this as follows: Whoever desires to be a friend of God and to stand in the sight of God must do God's will and live in keeping with the divine will; must will, do, or neglect to do, work; rest, labor, or keep the Sabbath. If we do not follow God's will directly and do not will as God wills, or omit that which God does not will, we must not think ourselves God's friend or capable of thinking, committing, or omitting anything that pleases God.

Christ says, therefore, "You are my friends if you do what I command you," and, "I do not now call you servants, but friends and beloved, because I have revealed and made known to you everything I heard from my Father," John 15:14f. Note that anyone who does what Christ commands or wills is his friend and beloved. And again, whoever learns the hidden will of God and does what God wants done is a friend of God. And whoever does not immerse his will in God's will or does not lose his own will in God's must not ever think himself a friend of God. Example: It is said [A ij], They are not in the same sheepfold, for they are not of one will. Any two who have one will are at one; they are at peace and they are friends. But when they are of two minds, they are said to behave badly, and to be disunited and unfriendly. Whoever lives according to your will is your friend and whatever he does or leaves undone pleases you, provided he remains of the same mind with you. But when his will is turned away from you, though he may bow and scrape, suffer or work, weep or laugh, jump and dance, sit and lie, be well or sickly, help you or do anything of that nature before your very eyes, it would not be to your taste or pleasing to you.

This is also what Christ says, "Whoever is not with me is against me," Lk 11:23, and "Whoever is not against you is for us," Mk 9:40. By this Christ meant to say that whoever lives, wills, does, or omits doing something against my will is against me. Everything he wills, does, or omits doing is against me. In all his commissions and omissions, he sins against me.

Now Christ is a beloved son of God who has come not to do his own will, but that of his dear father, Jn 5 and 6. Anyone then who is of one will with Christ must accept God's will, for he says, "I have not come to do my will, but the will of my Father." He means the Father who is in heaven and not the one who is said to be the father, namely Joseph, who is on earth. Christ indicated this during his last suffering, saying, "Father, not my will, but your will be done."[1] Since Christ was of one will with God and had consented at the highest level with his Father, no one can be a friend of Christ unless he is first of one will with God and wills, desires, does, and omits nothing except what God wills and desires him to do or omit doing. Whoever does so is a friend of Christ, yes, an innate friend of Christ who is not [//] related to Christ through a carnal birth and blood relationship, but who is inborn of God. He cannot sin, as John says in 1 Jn 3:9, "Such a person is not born of flesh and blood, but of grace and the will of God."

Everyone who does the will of God is a mother, brother, or sister of Christ, as he himself says, "My mother, brother, and sister are those who do the will of my Father," Mk 3:34f.; Mt 12:48-50. By this is shown that I become an inborn friend of God and follower of Christ when I truly accept God's will without looking back or looking to this and that, and without accepting something else. I am thus united with God and become one spirit and one thing, as I shall further show. And if I am a friend of God, then everything will delight me which God does, works, or leaves undone with me and all who are mine, yes, with all creatures.

By the same token, everything that I work, commit or omit, suffer and exercise in will please God. I do not sin as long as I remain and stand in God's will, as is written in 1 Jn 3. "All things work for good for those who love God," Rom 8:28. "To believers all things are pure, good, and of service," Titus 1:15. "If you hear the voice of your Lord, you and all that is yours are blessed," Deut 28:1f.

Abhorrent infirmities which Christ makes good

Behold, Christ and his Father stand there and purify all uncleanness of everyone who is of one will with them. If it happens that you are in Christ and of one will with Christ, as a grapevine is of one nature with the stem of the vine, you will bear fruit and God will cleanse you so that you will bear more fruit and that your fruit might remain eternally in the eyes of God, Jn [A iij] 15. But should you be self-willed and have a will other than God's, nothing in you is pleasing to God, even though you were to pray yourself to death, hunger and castigate yourself, and have a voice like that of an angel, give alms, be naked, and give your body into the fire to be burned. Even if you had the visions and proclamation of all the prophets and a faith capable of moving mountains to go with it, it would all be of no avail to you and displeasing to God. You would not be a friend but an enemy of God who, although externally praising in such words, would internally be far from God. You would be one who praises God externally with your lips, but scorns him internally in your heart. This is what Paul says, "If I had the speech of angels and a faith that is able to remove mountains, but had not God's love, I would not be useful at all," 1 Cor 13:2f. Inasmuch as those who love God remain in the love of God, they must also remain in his will, since God is love, 1 Jn 4. In short, you must remain in God's will if your life, your commissions and omissions are to be eternally pleasing. As often as I stand outside God's will, nothing that pleases God is in me and my life. If we are eternally outside God's will, we are eternally corrupt. Anyone against or outside God's will for one hour is lost for that long. For all times and all life, work, rest, commission, and omission are lost when they are not begun, continue to stand, and come to their end in God's will. That seed remains alone which does not fall into God's will, die, and sprout anew. Although we were to stretch and tear our veins, we would accomplish nothing, however much we were to run, work, sweat, as long as we sense self-will in us without attacking, repenting of, and overcoming it with hatred and envy. As Christ says, "Whoever finds his soul ruins it; but one who envies and hates his soul, [//] preserves it unto eternal life."[2] Learn from this.

Examples from Scripture to show that neither life nor works which do not spring up from, are lived, and done in God's will can please God

There are not a few priests, laypersons, and especially monks who daily run to church in the opinion that they are seeking God. They want to know God's ways as for example a nation that has done what is right and has not departed from God's sentence and judgment. They approach God in manifold ways. And after they have fasted or celebrated or prayed and lit their little candles and burned incense or stretched out their hands which lay folded for a long time, or if they have sung for a while or built sanctuaries or donated and sacrificed cattle, chickens, calves, bulls, silver and gold to God's honor and have done similar things, they think that their good works have been well-deserved in God's sight. But after having done many works, celebrated, and fasted, they think in their hearts and say privately, why did we fast and you, O God, did not look on us? Why do we castigate our soul and you do not want to know of our torment and suffering?

God answers and gives the reason that all their works did not please him, however beautiful and holy they may appear, saying, "On the day of your fasting, your self-will has been found out and noted," Isa 5.[3] This is why God rejects the work of certain people, for they remain in their self-will. God says in clear words, "I do not look on your fasting because your self-will has been found in it." This reason God gives in the chapter on the matter of festival days saying, "When your foot is diverted from doing your own will on the day of celebration, your Sabbath shall be pure and tender." The festival day is good, holy, and dear to God because we do not do our will, but fulfill God's. [//]

It follows, then, that our self-will makes unclean and defiles all holy days, soiling all works with sin. Further, God desires a man who is of his divine mind, Isa 46. Therefore God says, "You shall be called [by a new name],[4] Isa 62:2. Anyone then who has his own will is not a man of God. And if he is not a man of God, he cannot do any work that pleases God, as has been intimated by "he is not a friend of God." It follows further that God has a terrible hatred and envy toward all our works which spring forth from self-will. Further on God our Lord says, "I hate your festival days. Your sacrifices are an abomination or horror to me," Isa 1:13. He also says, "You shall make no more sacrifices," Isa 1:11ff. "Do not fast as you have fasted to this day, though you may groan from your fasting and though your voice be heard on the heights," Isa 58:4-5. Though the crying and fasting of Nineveh was accepted by God, God nonetheless does not want to accept or praise anything that happens from self-will.

God the Lord says, "Did I choose such a fast and do I desire [*geliest*] that you torment and torture your soul through the day?" You see there that some people call it a fast and name it a day pleasing to God when a person moves about head over heels like a potter's wheel or a ring, Isa 58, yet remains, nonetheless, in his self-will. If we are not blind and look on these words of God, fully made known, Isa 5, and assess fasting by way of an example, we will readily note that no suffering or torture, no life or work is pleasing to God which has not flowed forth purely from God's will. Further, that everyone who directs his eyes and desires toward something other than divine pleasure is corrupt. And further, that a tree with all its fruits which does not grow and flourish within God's will is evil and sinful. Since this is so and since the life and death, gain and loss, salvation and condemnation of the Christian stands solely in fulfillment of and surrender to [//] the divine will, all Christian disciples, old and young, great and small, are diligently and earnestly to apply themselves above all else to knowing God's will. They must then be of a good and free will, and they will know that same divine will which is God himself, in line with the prayer, "Your will be done." For this reason it occurred to me to be a good thing if I further uncover and reveal this matter, so that common people might be encouraged to look into this great art more deeply and thoughtfully so that they might live their Christian lives in a Christian, godly, and salvation-bringing manner.

Several descriptions of sin

Before I do that, let me set out several sayings that are widespread.[5] "Self-will causes sin." "Sin is nothing other than not to will as God wills." The phrase "not to will" I understand to contain the clause "to will contrary to God." Inasmuch as "everyone who wills other than or not as God wills is also contrary to God's will," it may also be expounded through another word, as when we say, "It is sin when the creature turns away from the Creator" or, "sin is a turning away from the whole to the parts." Sin is the disobedience which we show toward God. Such teaching is given strong support in Holy Scripture by the Holy Spirit, as in Hosea 10:6. There the Holy Spirit says, "Israel, you shall be scorned in your will." Similarly, Hos 13, "Israel, your destruction comes from you."[6] God does not shame or scorn anyone; but the sins which we commit, do so. Thus, Israel and we in our self-will shall be put to shame. Hence, self-will gives rise to sin. [B]

A person who does not do God's will sins

That a person sins who does not obediently fulfill God's will, Christ teaches, saying, "A servant who knows his master's will but does not act in line with it ought to be beaten with numerous strikes. But one who did not understand the will of his master and acts unwittingly against the will of his master is to receive fewer strikes," Lk 7:41f.[7] Note how two servants are struck and beaten for not living by, committing, and omitting the will of their master. One is struck harder than the other. One who knows the will of his master shall be greatly trashed simply for not doing, working, or resting according to his master's will. In a similar way, the one is also to be beaten who might well know, but does not want to know the will of his master. But the one who is unable to know what pleases his master, yet does something that deserves punishment shall be penalized less harshly. Why are both these servants beaten? Is it not for not living, working, or resting according to their master's will? But now they are castigated only because they have not lived in keeping with their master's will.

It follows then that all the works (which we are obligated to do toward God) are against God and sinful if they are not done according to his will. It is clear therefore that sin is to will other than or not to will as God wills.

The will separates our works

Again, to do well or to omit something means to do God's will and to avoid his displeasure. Hence, the will alone separates good and evil works. [//]

Evil works arise from our will; good works, from God's will. Works of our will lead to hell, even though they may sparkle and shine most beautifully. Works of the divine will lead to salvation, as is written, "Not everyone who says Lord, Lord, shall enter the kingdom of heaven, but the one who does the will of my Father who is in heaven," Mt 7:21. Not those who say, Lord, Lord, or those who do externally beautiful works shall enter into God's kingdom, but those who do the will of my Father. Not those shall attain heaven who bring many sacrifices or build huge churches, but those who live strictly according to God's will. The more one walks in line with God's will, the closer one is to God and the more promptly shall one get into the kingdom of heaven. The farther one is from God's will, the more sin does one have.

Samuel says that all works which are done contrary to God's will, are mortal sin. Samuel teaches this exceptionally well when he chastizes Saul for resisting God's will. Saul was commanded by God; and he knew that God had commanded him to kill and destroy men, women, sons and daughters, great and small, bulls and camels, and everything belonging to Amalek. But Saul spared the best cattle and intended to sacrifice it to God. Yet, although Saul did so with good intention, wanting to make a burnt offering to God of the best cattle, he sinned, nonetheless, by not strictly living out and being obedient to God's will. Therefore, Samuel spoke to Saul, "Does not God desire more that one follow his voice obediently than that one make offerings unto him? Obedience is much better than sacrificing the fattest and best animals." Since a deed done against God's will is, like sorcery and like the vice of idolatry, an abominable sin, so also is disobedience or not wanting to obey God's will a devilish vice, 1 Sam 15:22f. [B ij]

Everyone ought to accept, fear, and never forget these words, i.e., that Samuel compares disobedience (which is perpetrated toward God) to two vices which God hates fiercely and passionately and which he severely punishes, namely, sorcery and idolatry. Since it is fully apparent that sorcery and idolatry are two abominable vices, so disobedience, too, is a grave and abominable vice.

The nature of disobedience

Now, disobedience is nothing other than not to will as God wills. And from that same unwillingness follows the external deed which also does not go according to God's will, as the story here mentioned indicates. God revealed his divine will to King Saul through his prophet Samuel. He was to kill all living cattle of Amalek. Saul should have followed this will straightway and should not have transgressed it by a hair's breadth, nor should he have presumed to do something better—which, however, Saul did. Therefore, though he meant well and intended to do better, he nonetheless came under God's wrath because of his disobedience, for not obeying and following the voice of God. As Adam also sinned through his disobedience when he followed the voice of his wife more than the voice of God. And to this day all sin happens because of the disobedience by which a person does his own will more than that of God—preferring to go after the will of one's flesh and blood rather than obeying God's will and following him in full obedience. From these writings we have inevitably shown that [//] the explanation that sin is nothing other than to will contrary to God's will, is contained and well-grounded in Holy Scripture.

Of the manifoldness of the singular will of God

Here I should point out that at times those who do not strictly do God's will do not sin. In this way I will write of the manifold will of God so that a simple person might properly discern from this article in what life and death, gain and loss are grounded. I should also indicate how God's will is revealed to us, as for example through Scripture, through the impression or advice of God-fearing persons and the like, and how two wills may be experienced in God. Further, that God has an unfathomable and wondrous will which no one is able to fathom but which is nonetheless always just and good, although poor human beings cannot fathom it.

But first of all I want to report how a person becomes alienated and distanced from God through disobedience and how human beings seek and do their own will. And although the just-mentioned articles call for a booklet of their own, I shall briefly indicate them, none-theless, and cause the reader to reflect on them.

Why disobedience and sin separate us from God

With respect to this article, we find many people who show them-selves unthinking and who dare trifle with things toward God which ought to be considered great and important. They presume that what a person commits or omits against God's will to be a small matter, and they are surprised [B iij] to find that on that account someone might be separated from God and stand far removed from his divine face be-cause he sinned. Yet they cannot see anything funny when someone acts willfully or forgetfully or out of sheer simplicity against their will. Soon their head swells[s] and the little worm eats away at their noses when someone speaks, commits or omits something which displeases them. And they avoid people who do not live in line with their will. They scold and swear and refuse to be in their company. They consid-er such contrary persons to be enemies, avoid their eyes and face, and look upon such persons with disdain when they say, commit, omit, have, keep, or practice something in opposition to God.

And although they commonly say, "That person and I are far apart because he does not will as I will," they, nonetheless, wish to be close to God when they live, act, or rest in opposition to God. There is not one among the subjects of a prince who would not confess to hav-ing sinned and become unworthy to be in the master's presence for having disobeyed his prince's commandments. Yet they do not want to be deprived of God's benevolences, grace, or face, even when they act a thousand times a day contrary to God. They admit that a son who speaks ill of his parents, or is otherwise disobedient, should not live long on earth but ought to die soon. And although they are constantly disobedient to their heavenly Father from whom flows forth all fa-therhood as from the depth, they deny it and want to live long and well, nonetheless. They say that whoever does not do what the king desires deserves his disfavor and ought to be thrown out of the royal court. But when they are obstinate and in opposition to their most high king, they wish to remain on this earth [//] which he himself cre-ated and continue to dwell in his royal court. Royal dignity and stature weigh heavily when misdemeanors are committed against a king, yet are deemed to be of no significance with regard to God. But to treat the matter lightly shall not excuse them. They ought to know that they have been removed and ejected from God's presence simply because of their disobedience from which all sins have sprung, just as Adam was ejected from paradise on account of his disobedience.

For this reason Isaiah says, "The hand or power of the Lord is not weakened or has become less strong; nor has it been severed so that he might not want to help you. Neither have his divine ears been plugged or become dull so that he cannot answer you. He can help you even today and he hears you well. But your sins have caused a division between you and your God. And your sins have obscured God's face; therefore, God does not answer you," Isa 59:1ff.

Now someone may think or say that God in times past was powerful. He created heaven and earth and did great and wonderful works. He redeemed the oppressed, he dried up the great sea, talked with humankind and wrought wondrous signs. But now he does none of these. Christ says even today in Scripture, "If you love me, God will love you and we shall prepare a dwelling for you. Whoever believes in me or whoever has faith as large as a mustard seed, which is so small, will effect even greater things."[9] In other words, he will say to this mountain go into the sea and the mountain shall arise and go into the sea. All who believe in me shall do the signs I have done and the Holy Spirit shall give them all things. In like manner also, God speaks through the prophets as follows, [//] "Where did the letter of divorce, or of your separation from me, come from with which I dismissed your mother? Whom did I owe anything when I sold you? It is not I who cast you from me, but rather your sin. In your evil doings you were sold and in your vices I let your mother leave me."

Note and see that vice and sin separate from God and cause God not to help us nor to do any wondrous signs. For God speaks as follows, "Has my hand been shortened or become too small so that I cannot help you? Has my strength been weakened so that I can no longer redeem you? Note that I am still the same mighty and strong God. Note that through my firm word I cause the sea to become desolate and the flowing waters to dry up. Without water the fish rot and die of thirst," Isa 50:1ff. God lost none of his presence, power, and goodness. He is the same God from of old who is one God in the heavens above and on the earth beneath. But it is our sins that turn God from us, just as they turn us away from God. This day he is ready to unite us with him, provided you are of good will, a believer, and open and free of all creatures in all your powers and have been pardoned for and discharged of all your works and potential. He is still waiting for all who, in their distress, call on him with all their heart, that he might help them and do all sorts of wondrous works for them. But your self-will, your desires for creatures, and your love of your own soul—in sum, your sin and wickedness—have drawn you away from God's sight, cast you out of his divine hall, and caused God not to answer you when you cry out. Neither will he help you when you are in distress. In all you say and do, your self-will and not my will is heeded, says God. Therefore, you are my enemy and do not stand by me. I therefore stand against you and I am to you as you regard me, as is written, "To the perverse I am perverse."[10]

How self-will gives birth to sin

After these sayings someone might say, I note that self-will gives birth to sin and casts one away from God's presence. I therefore ask how that happens. Answer: Because we accept and love our own more than God's, as Christ says, "Whoever loves his father or mother more than me is not worthy of me."[11] This is so also with our own soul and person. Whoever loves himself more than God is unworthy of God and as a result is alien to and far from God. This happens as soon as we think of ourselves in all we do or when we find our soul there. Therefore, Christ said, "Whoever wants to come after me and does not hate father, mother, brother and sister and his own soul, too, which means himself, cannot be my disciple," Lk 14:26. But one who engages in such self-hate is a disciple of Christ. This hatred is a total dying to our self-will. Since Christ compares such hatred of self to a kernel that falls into the ground and dies and then bears fruit, Jn. 12:24, then, if the soul falls and dies to itself completely, it will yield divine fruit which shall remain for ever. This is the ingrafting into the good vine which is Christ. Anyone whom the heavenly Father implants into his beloved Son lets go of his self-will completely and takes unto himself the full life, growth, and fruit bearing, in line with the nature and quality of Christ whom no creature in heaven or on earth equal and who had thoroughly died to his own will, seeking God's will alone in all his life, teaching, preaching, doing of wonders, eating, drinking, [C] working, and resting. Therefore, Christ said to his elders, "Why do you look for me? Do you not know that I must be in the things that are my Father's?" Lk 2:49. And elsewhere, "These are my relatives, my mother, brother, and sister who do my will," Mt 12:49. As if Christ wanted to say, I am a vine and all who remain in me, i.e., who totally die to self-will as I died, and seek and intend God's will alone, are my disciples and my friends and the kernel which not only fell into the ground, but also died. Those whose total life is tribulation and a cross, and who hate their soul and themselves, are my disciples.

But where love, desire, devotion, or attachment to one's own person or soul remain, there no fruit can grow, even if the grain should fall down and be persecuted a thousand times per day. There everything is hopelessly lost; and whatever we do is all for naught and lost when we do not strongly hate our soul and person and do not disdain and flee our self-will. God said this to the Jews through Isaiah when they cleansed themselves through fasting, castigated themselves, and twisted their necks like rings or tubes, with pain and tortures—all of which amounted to nothing because they were seeking their own will. As Christ says, they fasted and carried on so that they might be seen and praised for it; and they sought to be better because of these works than those who did not engage in such works. But in Isaiah God attacks such fasters with carnal infirmities and says, You want to fast for me, but it is your will that is in such fasting and not mine. You should not seek your own, but hate yourself. You want to take something off, but you are actually keeping what you should earnestly remove. Thus, you seek your own advantage and love yourselves. If you want [//] to fast for me, see to it that you give your debtors their promissory note[12] and return the bonds and the sharp practices with unjust goods. Make friends with the bread and riches of wickedness. Discharge the hands that are full of those letters that oppress your debtors and set scot-free all who are sad and shattered because of their servitude or indebtedness, and tear up all promissory notes, Isa 58. Do my will, then, you and your fasting shall please me, Deut 15; Lev 25; 27. I plead with all Christians to read diligently and understand Isaiah in the chapter just cited, to note how we must die to our own soul and person in both will and works. If we do not, we are like a kernel of grain which falls, but remains alone and shall remain alone in its life and fruit and be consigned to hell.

Self-will in other things must also be overcome

Someone may say, "Methinks it sufficient to die to self-will in those things that pertain to everything we do, especially as this relates and applies to fasting, so that we should seek neither praise nor glory in our fasting, which ought to be to us as if we had never fasted. But now I note that we must disregard our own even in those things that do not affect fasting." You see now that God rebuked and rejected the fasting of the Jews because they did not forgive and cancel the debts of poor Jews. Rather, they kept their promissory notes on the loaned money. This is alien to fasting and a deed which does not go with fasting. However, God wants the rich to help the poor. This is God's will. God wills that a person fast, celebrate, or castigate himself. For God makes [C ij] people rich so that they might come to the aid of their poor brothers. If they fail to do this, but keep the bond and pledge on the borrowed money, they realize their own will, do what God does not want, and will never, in all eternity, please God. Even if they were to stretch their own skin like a drum and turn themselves about like a wicked bullet [they would please as little] as a terrible enemy would please an opponent when he does something contrary to his will. Christ also says this, "You want to serve me, yet you allow me to walk naked before you. I was hungry and you did not feed me; thirsty, but was given no drink by you. I was naked and you did not clothe me."[13] You should have done my will and helped my own people. But because you did not do my will, you are like the virgins without oil, life, without spirit, and you suffer without justification—which God refuses to know, Mt 24. Therefore you are told, "Go to the eternal fire which has been made ready for you and the devil," Mt 25:46. So also Isaiah speaks to those twisted heroes of the fast. "Break your bread for the hungry, the poor, and the pilgrims in your house. If you see a naked person, clothe him and do not destroy your flesh. Then call on God and he shall answer you," Isa 63.

Note how close this is to God and that he has open eyes to hear and that he wants to help like a strong lord when you do his will. But if you were not honestly doing God's will in these works which God also wills, you and all your doings will be ready for the devil, if you refuse to admit your own will and repent. Hence I can readily say, "Whoever is guilty in one thing is guilty of all God's prohibitions" [sic], as James the apostle says, "For there is an eternal, immovable will in all of God's commandments and prohibitions. Therefore, whoever [//] transgresses God's will in one thing is a transgressor and has become guilty of all of God's commandments." It must never be forgotten that a person must not only fear the opposite of divine gifts, but, above all else, everything God prohibited, though these may not be in tune with the work someone else does other than the one who fasts and celebrates.

We must do God's will in all that he commands and prohibits. We must not only look to the acceptability of our fasting. Nor must we simply avoid excessive eating,[14] but strive for sobriety which is appropriate to fasting. We must also give heed to our flesh, i.e., our brother, covering the one who is naked and setting free the one who is indebted, and do the things God desires. Yet, at the same time, we must not unduly cling to fasting. We must consider and place such works (which Isa 63 and Mt 25 speak of) along with fasting, so that we might let go of something through fasting, as do those also who feed the hungry. I don't argue that at all. But this much is true: all fasting and holy days are useless if they happen outside of God's will and if they are kept without a firm faith or do not arise from divine love and knowledge [*kunst*] of God, and which, to sum it all up, do not spring forth from the hatred of our soul.

In short, you must feel a cross in your life, work, labor, and resting if you intend to be in Christ. And you must die to self-will, as was said earlier. But if your will is still within you, says Christ, and as long as you have not died, you will remain alone. You have nothing but foliage like the fig tree whom Christ cursed and caused to wither, Mt. 21. Therefore, the Father of Christ says, "My soul hates your person, work, commissions and omissions, sacrifice and prayer, for your will and not mine is in you and yours." Your hands are full of blood which is hatred and envy. You love yourself and seek your own and you desire and take delight in, [C iij] seek and concern yourself with yourself. And you hate not, as I will, but as you will. Therefore, you are full of blood. "For the one who hates his brother is a killer and a blood hound," 1 Jn 3:15. But the one who loves his brother, my father loves too and this is the will of my Father, that you love one another. This love must not be carnal or natural, but divine and heavenly, otherwise the outflow would be unlike its source.

Therefore, if you intend to love your brother, do not love him according to your will (says God), but according to mine, in keeping with the prayer, "Your will be done."

A person is renewed in God's will

Our spiritual birth takes place through the thorough dying of self-will, for we must, in thought and will, die with Christ and be where Christ is seated. This is also signified by the baptism with which the apostles used to sprinkle and which we now practice through immersing, in order that the heat, desires, and lusts be eradicated as one dampens or extinguishes a fire with water; it is a burial in and with Christ. For just as Christ rose in a renewed life, transforming mortal life into immortal life, so also the old Adam in us with all his desires, lust, self-will, and disobedience, ought to die and lie in the grave; our life must be new in obedience and in God's will. This is to be in such a way that our will goes unnoticed in worldly and physical, as well as in divine and spiritual, things. For the truth does not lie when it compares a person who [//] loves himself or his soul more and does not spoil to grain which falls into the ground but does not die, or when it compares a person who hates himself and thus forfeits [*verhutten*] the right to eternal life to grain which falls into the earth and dies. The truth says further that grain which does not die remains alone, while grain that has died yields fruit. From this follows that self-will and love (which seek their own in every way) are like grain that has not died and therefore corrupts a person. While, on the other hand, the envy and hatred of one's soul is like grain that has died and yields fruit. Hence, our holiness, newness, and rebirth here is the dying of self-will. For where love of ourselves and ourness [*Unserheit*] is to me and mineness [*Meinheit*] and where I am and where my will stands, there is and stands my destruction and hell, unholiness, oldness and carnal birth and life, which cannot think on anything other than the flesh.

Answer to the objection

I would truly have to despair then. For if I were to look at my life, my work, and my rest properly, I would find only my own will and lust and it would pain me not to have done something. I also observe that St. Paul did not die to his own will. For whence comes this voice that the flesh wills and works against the spirit, Gal 5:1-10? I further observe in my members a law and bond which resists the law of my spirit and holds me captive to sin which lodges in my members. And I myself (says Paul) serve the law of God in my mind, but in my flesh I serve sin, 27.[15] God's chosen vessel confesses to be carnal and to have in his body the inclination to evil and sin which [//] lead and drive him by force and hold him captive, so that in his flesh he is bound to serve sin and not only does he do what he does not want to, but moreover that which he wills, he cannot do. His flesh, too, wills what the spirit does not will, for to be flesh is to desire contrary to the spirit. Accordingly, there were not only two kinds of commission and omission in the holy vessel,[16] but also two wills; yes, two persons, a carnal and a spiritual, an old and a new, an external and an internal, Christ and Adam. One was the life and work of Christ; the other, the work of Adam. Now you might say, I must fully die to self-will, but I see that Paul who had been wonderfully converted had failures and weaknesses. What then will happen to me, poor soul? Don't you make me doubtful? Are you not destroying and crushing a sick little lamb which you ought to make strong and well?

Despair of a person

I would very much like you to despair in all creatures and in yourself so that your life be to you as it is to a bedridden sick person whose life is boring and irksome and who is grieved by it. He actually feels the cross. When I look at a person and see him despair of his own strength, I want him to say, Who shall protect me from myself? Who will redeem me from this body of death and sin? No one will, except the favor and grace of God through our Lord Jesus Christ, 27.[17] This cry to the one who is strong, makes strong and healthy, for God never deserts anyone who calls on him in truth with all his heart, so that through him we might obtain and have peace. As often as we [//] discover our sin and are willing to repent, we see that our strength is always too small and that we need a Redeemer who is Jesus Christ, Son of God, the fulfillment of the law, a repayer and vindicator of all deficiencies. If we believe in him and that he was sent for us, we are certain and sure that he places our sin upon himself and pays the ransom for which he was sent by the Father.

Rebirth here is a beginning

Therefore this falling into the ground and dying of self-will is here in its beginning and not yet accomplished or perfected. Rather, for as much as a person surrenders his will and gladly and willingly accepts God's will, for that much he is new, spiritual, and Christian. He has dropped off oldness, carnality, and the life of Adam. Here on earth we must hate our flesh and show no mercy toward its desires, and we must diligently take care not to make an agreement with our will or under any circumstance wed ourselves to it. God empowered all believers, i.e., Israel, and commanded them to subdue and distance themselves from their flesh. But this happens perceptibly and in a long process, so that the poor, unclean human person remains aware of his ineptitude and not presume too much in this awful life. This can be shown by God ordering the Jews to kill all their enemies and not to enter into any covenant with them nor to take pity on them or enter into marriage with any of them, when they entered the land which God had promised to their fathers. All this, so that the unbelievers might not lead Israel astray. But Moses said, You cannot bring this about at once or with one blow, lest the wild beasts [D] of the earth become too numerous for Israel, Deut 7.

The old Adam dies day by day, but not altogether and not all at once

The first is what God commands and himself does, as is found in the same seventh day [sic]. God shall devour and destroy the unbelieving heathen, but only bit by bit, gradually and slowly, Deut 7; 2 Cor 4. The external nature is crushed from day to day.

Acceptance, an abominable beast, stalks us

The other is that these wild beasts and worms of the earth rant and rave and seek to increase against Israel. What are these beasts in our flesh other than pride, acceptance, and other perils? If we did [not][18] subdue our flesh here on earth, we would become proud, insolent, and conceited. If a peacock would not have ill-shaped feet, how could it strut and show off? If we did not have clinging to us our evil, contrary, and displeasing flesh, how often might we exalt ourselves and become haughty? Its uncouth legs remind the peacock that it is a bird. The sick, wicked flesh reminds all saints that they are frail human beings who could step away from God's works into their own works. Therefore, God destroys the flesh, not all at once, but more and more each day, so that the savage beasts cannot gang up on the spirit and attack and tear asunder the soul.

The flesh harms

Note how the flesh gnaws at us with its desires. It does not celebrate to bring the spirit into its domain. [//] If we develop pleasure and love of our own flesh and desires and establish friendship with our nature, our hostile flesh is like a beam in our eyes, a pit and a rope in which we get entangled until God destroys body and soul, Joshua 23.

The flesh does no harm

But if the spirit and new being flee the companionship and peace of the flesh with the intention of subduing it and do not take pity on carnal desires and will, the flesh renders its due, as the gentiles also paid their dues to the Jews and served them, thus keeping the spirit from pride and false security. In this way we learn why God did not totally destroy the enemies that had been allowed in, so that they might [come to] understand how God trains and tests the spirit and teaches it how to fight, Judg 3a; 2d. Anyone able to fight valiantly against his own flesh, i.e., against his own nature and self-will, is well able to fight against all temptation.

God permits good and evil to remain in us

For this reason God does not intend to make us completely new. He'd rather leave some of the old in us, allowing the evil to remain with the good, so that we struggle eternally with evil, humble ourselves, and crucify the old Adam with all his desires, will, and voluptuousness.

How to let go of self-will [D ij]

From this we might note how here on earth a person dies to self-will, namely, in the inner being, and how self-will remains in the flesh. The spirit is ready, but the flesh is weak, Mt. 26:41. And the flesh always blends and mixes in its weeds. Self-will, however, is harmful to nature, though not unto its death, as long as the spirit recognizes the same and is opposed to it, does not take pity on it, but hates and flees it, and cries to God for help on this account and longs for Christ our Redeemer, wanting truly and earnestly to have totally escaped and died to its own will, lusts, and desires.

How to discern God's will

You will probably ask and say at this point, by what and in which thing or sign can I learn God's will? Is not God up in the highest heavens while human beings are down here on earth? If God were to teach me his will and show me what he wants, I would gladly do his will in all of life and live by it. If God were to reveal his will to me, as a person makes known his pleasure or desire through speech, sign, or deed, I would live in obedience to him.

Answer: God's will may be learned in a variety of ways

Should I not answer that the word which all believers ought to obey is near to you, in your heart? You must not either ascend to heaven or travel far below. God has made known his will [//] to the prophets through admonition, visions and through mysteries. In the Holy Scriptures his eternal, steadfast, and unchanging will has been proclaimed and promised in such unanimity through prophets, Christ, and the apostles that we might sufficiently study God's will in Holy Scripture. We may also learn through impression and swift thought, by God's grace, what God demands of us and what pleases and suits God. Further, God addressed his people from Mount Horeb in fire and darkness and smoke and with a living and wonderful voice. He taught his people what a person is to do if he intends to do well before his divine eyes and desires a long life here on earth, Deut 4; 5; 6. God's speech is contained in the ten words and articles, Deut 4.

Whomever God draws to and ingrafts in his Son Jesus Christ and whom through the Spirit he grants his divine knowledge so that he is able to see those ten words in the true light and accept them in living love, knows[19] what is pleasing to God and what God hates. Note how a king expresses his will through commands and prohibitions or laws. So also God reveals his will through his law. For the will is the spirit or soul and life of the law. Whenever the will is given satisfaction, the law has been satisfied. But the one who fullfills the bulk, externals, or letter of the law, but disregards its sense and intention, does not serve the law. The law complies with the will of the lawgiver and is like a messenger who conveys the intention of the master to a given person.

Sins do not happen without God's will [D iij]

"I observe," a reader of this booklet might say, "that God's will is made known through comforting promises and frightening prodding, through blessings and curses, through visions and the like and that his divine disposition is contained in Holy Scripture as a kernel in its husk. To get to the kernel one must crack and discard the shell; one must look for the husk of the kernel or mark and in no way break this order. But whatever might happen, the divine will is more clearly discernible in Holy Scripture than in dreams, visions, and complex parables. This is attested to by Jeremiah, Ezekiel, Daniel, Zechariah, and other prophets who often asked God what their visions meant. Therefore, I will use clear Scripture to state that sinners have realized God's will and still realize it today through their sinful works. The reason is that not a single leaf moves without God's will. A person is unable to think or move hand or foot if God does not will it. It is commonly said that the lowest things do not function when the highest master worker withdraws and withholds his power. Since it is apparent then that we can neither think nor will if God does not want it, it follows that we cannot think anything wicked or will or do any evil except God decrees or wills it.

I am not dissuaded in this by those who make a clear distinction between God's eternal and temporal will or between God's constant [*bestendigem*] and his permissive will [*verhencklichem*] inasmuch as the permissive will is a will, nonetheless.[20] Whatever I cause, order, or permit is not contrary to my will.

Though the yielding or permissive will is mild and compliant, it is, nonetheless, [//] a will, especially in God whose permissive will is a strong and a real power whom no might can withstand. Therefore, it breaks forth into works and being so that we might know that God's permissive will is an active force. But should we obediently accept God's will, it would follow that we sin whenever we do not will what and how God wills. For it is said that Pilate received his authority from above, yet he sinned in killing Christ. The reason: Although Pilate did not sin as severely as Judas and the Jews, and although such power was given him by God and although divine counsel had determined that Christ should die, he sinned, nonetheless, in killing Christ, Jn 19, Acts 4. How then can above-quoted saying be that sin is not to will as God wills?

We have another example in the antichrist [*Endchrist*] who will act according to his will. He will rise up and become great and strong against God until God's wrath is realized, Dan 11. Note what horrendous sins happen because God destined them and how the antichrist shall be puffed up against God who is a God above all gods—all this is happening in line with the permissive will of God.

The third example is clearer, for God says publicly that he will raise up a wicked shepherd who will not seek out the lost and will not gather the scattered and will not heal those who are weighed down, and those who groan he will not feed and keep. He will tear the flesh of the fattened bulls and break their hoofs. Scripture says of them that such shepherds are idols, Zech 11. God also says that such shepherds are beset by woe upon woe, Ezek 34.

This example is clear. It shows sufficiently that God pronounces a woe upon such shepherds. However, God intends to arouse such a harmful wolf who leaves his little lambs in the wilderness and devours the sheep that are present, and he will prompt it.[21] From this we may deduce once again that [//] sins happen with God's approval, as Ezek 16 further demonstrates with reference to a lying prophet.

The fourth example is from Christ who came so that the seeing might be blinded, Jn 9. Christ also uses the saying from Isa 6:10, "They were unable to believe because God blinded their eyes and hardened their hearts," Jn 7; Acts 28. Whoever reads all of Holy Scripture and understands it can see everywhere that God asks no more and nothing more urgently of people than a believing heart toward him; hence, unbelief has to be a grievous and severe sin—which it truly is, as Christ teaches. "Whoever does not believe has been judged now and is condemned," Jn 3:18. And Paul, "To an unbeliever nothing is good and clean," Titus 1:15. And Moses, "God shall punish every work willed by those who do not hear his word," Deut 28:15. Now, although unbelief is such a severe sin, and although God causes several persons not to be able to believe, it is therefore God's will that they are incapable of believing. For God creates all that he wills, Psalm [115:3]. It follows then that sin is not just to will other than God wills. A person who wills what and how God wills, also sins.

I should like to introduce here what is written in Psalm 124:, "God turned their hearts so that they hate his people."[22] If God turns our heart so that we hate God's people, the blame is with God and we do well to realize God's will.

Whether sin is good in God's sight

I think about all things being good in God's sight, as is written, "God saw everything that he created and it was good," Gen 1:31. This saying concludes that all [//] things are good in the eyes of God, because of the word *vidit* which means *he saw*. Now, God saw all things to be good. Thus, all creatures must be good in God's eyes. It is also written, "You hated none of the things which you created," Wis 11:24 and that all of God's works are perfect, Deut 32. I have to admit then that above-mentioned sins and wickedness are good in God's eyes and that they happen according to his will. It follows from this that such sins and wickedness place us neither far from God nor do they remove us from before his eyes, nor do they happen contrary to God's will, so that all this disputing is useless. I also have sound and convincing testimony from Scripture that sins, wickedness, and injustices are good. Paul tries to say this: God created two kinds of vessels—some as vessels of wrath and others as vessels of glory and of his grace.[23] And that it is good that vessels of glory measure God's riches and goodness, as when they see how God allows his wrath to flow into vessels of wrath and how and in which way God uses and handles them. They are able to understand, by contrast, how God channels his glory, riches and treasures through vessels of mercy which God prepared to his glory, Rom 9. How else would we ever know righteousness when we are unable to see unrighteousness over against it? No one knows bitterness better than the one who has truly tasted sweetness.

Again, once we thoroughly understand God's goodness, we will curse lost time and confound our life. Hence, sin is never altogether evil when it serves toward something good.

Answer: God did not create sin. [E] You have not yet demonstrated that God created sin in the beginning when he created all things. Since there was no flaw when God finished heaven and earth in all their adornments and when he ceased from all the work of Creation, these verses are therefore of no use to you. On the contrary, God saw that everything was good. God hated nothing. Further, what you have drawn out of Paul has not been opportune and faithful. Paul never said that God in the beginning, when he created all things in their glory and adornment, created the vessel of wrath, but, rather, that he bore and tolerated them, Rom 1 and 9.

Everything becomes more pronounced by its opposite

It is true that righteousness is more clearly known in its opposite, such as unrighteousness; grace in disfavor; partiality in wrath; sweetness in bitterness. God allowed Adam's Fall for this very reason. But that does not yet prove that evil is good in God's sight and that it is permitted to happen according to his eternal will or, whether it is good for us as well as for God so that God's glory may the better be recognized. It is not good as it is or as it happens, but for a different reason. Hence, I will continue to insist on saying and maintaining that those are correct who say that sin is not to will as God wills. Everything that arises and springs forth from this willing (other than God wills) is sin—be it life or death, heaven or hell, rest or labor, days of celebration or days of work, happiness or sadness, days of eating or days of fasting.

God's will transforms hell to heaven

Indeed, no hell is so abominable that God's will—which is eternal—cannot transform it into heaven and eternal life. Although I might go to hell, when I fully surrender my will to God's, appropriating the eternal will of God, hell will become for me the kingdom of God and death will be unto eternal life.

How God's will breaks the power, kingdom, and righteousness of sin

Hence, by immersing our self-will in the depth from which all things take their being and by thoroughly considering the dying of our will, we are able to become masters of all the powers of devil, death, sin, and hell and we can dare every devil to harm or destroy a single hair even.

The permissive will is a driving force

I readily concede power to you and that God permits sin and that this very same permissive will is a highly effective power, as Paul says, "Therefore God gave them up to the desires of their hearts and to impurity, giving them a perverse heart," Rom 1:26. And through Isaiah God says, "I am the God who gives light its form and creates darkness, I make peace and create evil. I am the Lord who does all these things," Isa 45:6f. A power or might who creates something also effects the same. Someone who gives or drives another to do certain things must also do them. Since God creates evil and gives sinners up to their evil desires, doing all this through his permissive will, I cannot deny that the will of God which imposes and complies is an effective power, indeed. I know well that one who wields a rod [E ii] or stick and beats someone is effective. This is what God's permissive will does who through Assyria beats us as with a rod or stick, Isa 10.

The works of God's permissive will are against the works of God's eternal will

Yet everything that creatures do or leave undone through this permissive will is contrary to the eternal, divine will. "Woe to Assyria, my rod," Isa 10:5. Note that to benefit my brother is God's eternal will and to harm him is God's permissive will. My harming is contrary to God so that God is angry with me.

Take another example. It is God's eternal will that we benefit relatives and love them dearly. Accordingly, Christ says, "This is the will of my father that you love one another."[24] Similarly, "what you do to the least of my own, you do unto me."[25] This may be seen in Isa 1 and 49, as well as in all of the letters of the apostles.

Nonetheless, God permits evil people to persecute God's members and it is nearly impossible to be a son of the promise without having a fierce Esau who persecutes. To be a young Christian without being hard pressed, as Christ our master was, is rare.

Do not let it bother you not to have Annas and Caiaphas, Pilate and Herod on your side if you are a true Christian. Christ says, "If they called the head of the house Beelzebub, what then will they call his servants?" Mt 10:25. To sum up: All who seek to live amicably in Christ will suffer persecution, 2 Tim 3. God decrees all of this and allows it to happen. Nonetheless, it is opposed to and repulsive to God when human beings persecute a deified servant of God. [//]

Another example of God's permissive and eternal wills having limited work

Christ says that the Son of man goes as it is written, but woe to those through whom it happens. Similarly, "as it was written, so Christ had to suffer and rise again," Lk 24:46. Although Christ had to suffer and die, those who caused Christ to suffer and die did what was evil. For this reason he says, "Woe to them." Note here that this will (which is called *permissivam*, i.e., *verhencklich*) must be fulfilled. Otherwise Christ would not have said, "Woe to those at whose hands the Son goes." Hence, Christ says, "There has to be offense, but woe to those who give offense." Similarly, anyone who offends one of the little ones of those who believe in me would be better off if he were cast into the depth of the ocean with a millstone around his neck." Christ does not penalize the works which are done according to God's eternal or immovable will, since he teaches us, "Thy will be done." Rather, he penalizes the works which are wrought against God's eternal will, yet must take place because God's granting [*zugebender*] will must bring his will into being. As Christ says, "It is necessary that offenses and hurt take place." Yet God hates such works and penalizes the perpetrator. This will may be called the hardening will of God, as Moses and Paul call it, or else, a permissive, yielding, granting, or angry will, while the eternal, enduring will of God may be called a merciful will. Accordingly, as Moses and Paul have it, God hardens whom he wills and has mercy on whom he wills.

Differences between the two wills [E iii]

These two wills which we know by their effects and which are seen as two (although nothing in God is divided or split) have two types of effect. The merciful, gracious, eternal, and enduring will softens and removes the heart of stone. It illumines and draws to Christ and brings about good will and good works. By contrast, the permissive will hardens, fossilizes, blinds, deafens, disables, and produces works of error, as is written, "He gave them works of error." Similarly, he blinded the hearts and eyes of these people so that they would not change their ways, Isaiah and Christ in Jn 10.

The merciful will changes evil into good, as when Joseph said to his brothers: You plotted evil against me, but God turned that very evil into a good, Gen. 50. That the evil intent of Joseph's brothers was from God, Joseph teaches when he says, "I have been sent to Egypt, not by an eternal counsel, but because of God's will," Gen 45:8.

Note how in this one sale and in one deed two kinds of willing are apparent. He instilled an evil will in Joseph's brothers, yet turned the evil into what was best, as he eternally intended it. If you want testimony of these two wills (which are one in God), you should give attention to Moses, the prophets, Christ, and the apostles. But how it is possible that one will has two contradictory effects I will leave to God. I have no problem with it because I believe whatever I cannot grasp through reason. Should you be the kind of person that is full of worldly wisdom and wishes to judge and assess divine power through human powers, I don't want to keep from you that heaven is too high for you.

May God grant that I have faith in his divine and merciful will and that for all eternity. Nor must I conceal that the eternal will is a will [//] contrary to ours, or at least above our own will and nature.

The wrathful and permissive will

[It] inclines the human heart to its own affairs. And this temporal or permissive will is after our own heart and adapts to the desires of our nature. For this reason Paul says, "God has given them to immorality through the desires of their hearts," Rom 1:24. He thus teaches that the permissive will agrees with the lusts and desires of our hearts and of our self-will. Just so, the brothers of Joseph desired and inclined to selling Joseph and the priests to killing Christ, although it is written that the devil put such intention into the heart of Judas, etc. The evil spirit of God at times plays to our lusts and debauchery, 1 Kings 22.

How to discern the merciful and constant will of God

It is an indication and sign of God's eternal and constant will to appear painful and bitter to our will. A Christian can understand by this which of God's wills comes to him. If it appears sweet and mild when united with our will, it is harmful to us. We must then earnestly pray, "O Lord, my God, your gracious will be done that I may become your kingdom and you my king; that I may be your clay and you my creator who brings about justice and mercy through his clay," Jer 9^{26} "that I may become small and as nothing within me and that you may be great and all things in me. Hallowed be your name and always spoken of as great. Bring about that everyone will say, 'Behold, this is a poor, miserable and despicable person, yet God made him affable and in keeping with his good pleasure.' Bring about (my God) that I and all humankind [//] praise your name and say, 'What a great and mighty Lord is our God. Yet he accepts little worms and shows his grace toward them by making them great.' Bring about that I do not find pleasure in myself but in you alone and that without you I am afraid and feel ill, with a hellish pain driving me to live, work, rest, sleep, and die for you alone. And that all which is mine—my wisdom, riches, and power—be to me like green poison and yellow pus and that I may become to myself like a bitter boil, so abominable in my own eyes as to desire to flee myself."

If we do not thus become our own cross we have not really experienced God's will. But if we are intent on our own lusts and desires dropping off and becoming unto us as a fierce enemy, we have good intentions. We must not cease to pray to God with eternal sighs and to yield our "self" and all the desires that cling to us as things which we greatly dread and which we would dearly love to spit out. All that is ours must perish and disappear, if God's will is to take hold, come forth, and rule in us.

Therefore, Christ said, "Not as I will, but as you will," teaching us to pray, "Our Father, let our will perish, wilt and die like a wild ox. Father, make your will real within us—the eternal and merciful will which is contrary to our will and which drives out the lusts of our own will. We pray that our will with all its remaining characteristics perish, so that we do not intend, desire, or seek what is ours. Bring about, O God, that I happily and wholly surrender to you (O Lord) all that is me and mine, never to take it back or wanting to take it back and that I am prepared to be maligned and scorned."

All this is against our will and the desires of our own nature. By this we may know whether we have God's will or find our own and whether we follow God's eternal [//] or permissive will. When we feel God's eternal will (when God's will dwells in us and is mighty), we must surely feel that we are without will and dead to self-will.

The baptism of Christians

We are baptized Christians when we have come to the life of Christ and have died in the death of Christ and when our sins are dead and extinguished and when we walk in a new life, in faith, righteousness, and truth and say, "It is not I who lives, but Christ who lives within me," Rom 6.[27] We cannot discern the eternal will through reason, but through our senses, and we must taste, discover, and confess that God's eternal will does not happen within us without bitterness and the agony of the cross. Thus it is not possible for us to retain our natural desires and will and to receive God's eternal will.

The obstacles of a wrathful will

God's wrathful and permissive will incriminates us. For as the merciful will creates another and a new being, so God's wrathful and permissive will keeps us in the former disobedience and hardens even more what is hard already. This is easily apparent in Pharaoh, the king of Egypt, and Shimei, King of the Amorites, Deut 2.[28] The story of Shimei (son of Gera) is clear and transparent. He harassed King David with many slanderous words, calling him a son of Belial—the worst of devils. This was the delight and life of [Shimei] [f] by which he cooled his burning heart. For Shimei was from the tribe and family of Saul. Hence, he was pleased to see one of Saul's family retain the kingdom. Because of this, the heart of Shimei was inflamed against David. His heart burned with anger, brimming over with the desires and concerns of his natural will. However, David claimed that it was God who caused Shimei to use such mockery, which David was in a better position to note than Shimei who was enraged. Hence, David said, "Who dares to say, 'Why does God do this?' " 2 Sam 16:10. I have to admit and freely confess therefore that an evil person may at times scold and curse a righteous one.

This, however, is not the eternal will for which we pray. The eternal will achieves that we attack only what is necessary which we must attack in fear and trembling, refraining from admonition, teaching, and punishment of people except when the love of God and Christian faithfulness move us to do so. I say nothing of one person strongly attacking another.

It follows then that the mocking of Shimei did not come from the eternal and gracious will of God which removes all natural desires from us.

Response to the story of Ahab

Now to respond to the story of Ahab, I ask myself whether works do not indicate the will of the ruler. You will have to reply "yes." And so it is, for God's spirit said, "I will deceive King Ahab and there will be a deceptive spirit on the lips of every prophet." Then God commanded saying, "Go and do so." Note here how God [//] ordered his deceiving spirit and commanded it to deceive Ahab and to be in all his prophets. This was God's angry and permissive will, for Scripture clearly states, "Observe that God put a spirit of deceit in the mouth of every prophet," 1 Kings 22.

How the angry will corresponds to the human will

That the permissive will corresponds to the understanding, natural will can be discerned when God says, "Human beings are deceitful," Ps 62:4. Similarly, "everyone is a liar," Ps 116.[29] The spirit, too, has this characteristic; for it is lying and the father of lies, Jn 8; 1 Kings 22. And it is uncertain whether one acts on one's own or in the name of the devil; whether Eve or the serpent gave the apple. This evil spirit is a spirit of wrath, as is written. The wicked spirit shook Saul, 1 Samuel 16. We are naturally or by nature sons of wrath, as Paul and God say, "All human thoughts and inclinations tend toward evil," Gen. 6 and 5. For this reason God did not want to leave his good spirit in the flesh (i.e., in human beings), Gen 6. Now, since our youth, hence, by nature, we are sons of wrath. And the evil spirit is a spirit of wrath. Since the spirit of wrath is cunning, so all sons of wrath are cunning. From this we have to learn, unfortunately, that our will is not absorbed in God's wrathful and permissive will, but becomes stronger, more evil, more enraged and furious. [f ii]

The eternal and merciful will of God opposes the self-will of the creatures

Accordingly, we do not pray that God's angry and permissive will be done in us, but that God's eternal and obliging will be created. Thus we pray, "Your will be done," Mt 6:10. This means as much as to say, Make us without a will and dead to all conceit.[30] For God's will resides in heaven in this mortifying manner. There God is all things to all the saints and where God is not present, there is neither thinking nor willing. It is impossible for a saint to feel good without God, Ps.[31] The elect and godly love God alone, and nothing besides God. When God wants us to love him alone, anyone who loves something more than God does not love God at all. Christ underscores this for us when he replies to the one who asks, "What must I do to be saved?" by saying, "What is written in Moses?" He goes on to say, "You must love with all your heart." When a heart wholly loves something, no other thing can be loved more than or besides God. For this reason God cuts away from the heart all creatures, ridding and emptying the heart of all and turning it into a dark abyss or into the clarity of the soul. When this has taken place, God's spirit blows over the face of the desert and the barren earth, and showers the soul with divine favor and light, Gen 1. This light and grace points to and unites the heart to the only true good (which is God himself), Ps 5. Then the Holy Spirit pours divine love into the heart, turning a right and whole heart to God, unites it with God and deifies it. Thus it is impossible to love God with a whole heart while we still love something else besides or along with God. This is what Christ means when he says, "Whoever loves father or mother more [//] than me is not worthy of me. And whoever loves his children ahead of me is not worthy of me. One ahead of the other. [*sic*]

Finding one's soul

Now to the third: "Whoever loses his soul finds it," Mt 10:39. There is no one on earth whom we should cause less grief than our parents. And we have no one on earth to whom we owe greater love than our children and parents. Yet, this love must be extinguished and it must dissolve in the love of God. Whoever loves father and mother, his wife, children, or anything else more than God does not love God and is unworthy of the son of God—neither in life nor in teaching is he like Christ. For this reason divine and true love toward God excludes the love of every creature, of all angels and saints and puts all such love second. No creature is so spiritual and great that we should love it with all our heart more than or besides God. And it is impossible that we should love a creature alongside God while our heart has its will and total love focused on God at the same time. It is equally impossible for me to give you a whole loaf of bread while giving the same loaf or a part of it to someone else. Whatever is divided does not remain whole. It is just as impossible for you to give your total love and your whole heart to God while giving the same love to someone else ahead of God, or giving it wholly to both at the same time. You find a wonderful example of this in 2 Chr 16, concerning King Asaph. Read it and do not forget it. Reread also Isa 32; Jer 2 and 7 and several other places, and 2 Chr 32. Take the words of Ezekiel to mean that if our heart intends to love God wholly, it must forget every creature and surrender everything in heaven and on earth. God alone must be loved and if we [f iij] love something other than God, we do not love God. We must let go of father and mother, wife and children for God's sake and, according to another sense, we must hate them, even when the church beatifies and canonizes them. To the extent that we have the love of God, we have the will of the eternal God; for what is love other than a gracious or thankful will? If we love God, we have God's will and are free of self-will. Thus, self-will is opposed to God's eternal and merciful will; by this we may test and see whether or not we act in keeping with God's will. But for us to test and know self-will requires great skill and much practice.

If we were to look at self-will for a whole day and if we examined it every moment, we would do well; we would then understand that our will always wills what is evil and that all we say and do is befouled and stained. But it is impossible to empty one's heart even if we had a whole year, and to know what an evil will can accomplish in one day. Do what you may or will on earth, as often as self-will shines through, so often does it seek its own—whether in doing and acting or in enduring and idleness. The eternal will of God, by contrast, seeks what is best, which is God. Thus God's eternal will and our self-will are at odds.

Our nature and God's wrathful and permissive will converge. But the eternal will of God stands over against our will. The reason: God's eternal will, in part, is that we must not fear anything in heaven or on earth, except God alone. If God is for us, what can be against us? For this reason Moses commanded the people of Israel earnestly to fear God and nothing else. Moses also commanded that they were to love [//] God with all their hearts. Anyone who feared something else doubted that God was with him. If we doubt that God is with us, we are not believers. And what we believe, we experience. Therefore, we must set aside all fear when we truly fear God. You must not fear your enemies, you must not fear their nature, but God alone who is mighty enough to destroy you or your enemies; hence, we must fear God alone, not our enemies—the stories of Moses and all the prophets are full of this. But who is so brave as not to fear a thousand armed, angry, and violent enemies, bears, and lions? Or who is so God-fearing as to have God alone before his eyes, forgetting over the eager contemplation of God the power of all his enemies? That's how it should be if we wish to walk according to the eternal benevolent will (which desires us to be free of all cares). But we fear serpents, poison, arrows, penalties, wild beasts, and all kinds of harm, yet are unable to prevent even the smallest harm. Nonetheless, we deliberate and appear clever in the eyes of the world, although we are fools in God's.

See here how God's eternal will is against our will which corresponds with God's permissive will, and note that the wrathful, permissive will dispenses fear, counsel, and comfort on its own authority and creates anxious concern about enemies. When a monster returns, we look for and seek speedy help. To attest to this, many a thousand pieces can be found in Scripture about how not to be anxious and full of care regarding what we shall eat tomorrow. This would be God's eternal will. But how many of you are there who do not save a penny or two for the coming day? It is our self-will and God's permissive will which bring about that we desire to put money and goods in reserve. Tell me, isn't our nature foolish to believe in a God [//] who, carnally speaking, can neither see nor hear? Isn't all divine skill according to which, through faith, we should live in blessedness and eternally, folly to the wise of this world? Reason cannot grasp this, and the created will cannot accept it. Such blindness of understanding and sanctity of self-will is strengthened by God's permissive will. If we love our own nature, understanding, wisdom, and self-will, we cannot believe in God and are unable to accept Christ wholly. Nor can we believe in God or apprehend his word. Indeed, God's word is to us like scorn and derision. Hence, God's wrathful will comes along, causing blind eyes, deaf ears, and hard hearts, so that an impenitent person reads or hears God's word, deals with it in his heart, but does not believe anything. They see and hear signs, wondrous deeds and stories, yet remain blind and hardened in their hearts. You learn from this passage of Scripture how you may test and discern in your heart whether you are living by the eternal and merciful will of God or by the wrathful and permissive will. If we live by the wrathful will, we remain children of wrath and we sin constantly. If we follow God's eternal will, we are renewed persons or newborn children of God, and brothers of Christ, who do well. And whatever we do or leave undone pleases God. For we are friends of God whose self-will is the cross which we must bear and experience. Thus we can know whether we act according to our own will or according to God's.

God's eternal will never changes in Holy Scripture. But the works of the permissive will pass away

There are other signs as well by which we may learn to know God's eternal will as, e.g., that God's will is eternally unchanging and remains constant in its ways. But the permissive will departs from its works. It has its effect for the reason that its works fall and perish.

Example: God strikes his elect with fear when they disobey his eternal will and he instills anxiety in their hearts, so that a falling leaf or rustling foliage will frighten them and cause them to flee. They will flee a leaf as if it were a sword and they cannot withstand their enemies, Lev 26. God's wrathful will inflicts this and brings it about in self-willed persons until they are ashamed of their sin. God opposes them until the uncircumcised heart knows itself, Lev, ibid. Thus God's permissive will fills our self-will with natural desires, satiates, and intoxicates us until we are ridiculed and derided because of our natural desires and by the burden of our self-will stumble like drunkards and thus begin to know ourselves. This is what happened to the son who squandered his inheritance, Lk 15. Christ's saying points to this, "Whores and knaves will outdo you," i.e., they will recognize more quickly than the hypocrites their carnal desires and the fullness of their self-will and disobedience, and will accept the eternal will of God which they abrogated in their self-will, as was the case with Mary Magdalene, Lk 7. But these hypocritical servants do not acknowledge their self-will. They refuse to accept the charge that "they do not serve God." Therefore, they shall not enter (or at least, only very slowly) the kingdom of God. It is a thousand times more likely that a whore will seek and accept God's gracious will than that a polished wooden clog will know and bemoan its state, or [G] that a monk, who all his life did hypocritical works, will give up his ways and turn to God. This shows that God's permissive will serves carnal desires and burdens us with sins and shame and adds to them without letup until the eternal will is so saturated as to be unable to move because of its great wrath. It then begins to run to God's eternal will. At that point the work of the wrathful will ceases and vanishes.

The temporal, permissive, or wrathful will of God are identical

We must note that although God is wholly singular, his manifold works are distinguished in our knowledge, such as we spoke of regarding the eternal and permissive will. Therefore, one might readily distinguish between the wrathful and the temporal or permissive will, as follows: God has one will by which he wills a thing to be used and practiced for a time, after which it is to cease. Of this will I could say a great deal, for in my fulfilling or neglecting the eternal or temporal will, these two sayings of Paul are rooted: "Faith strengthens the law" and faith supercedes the law.[32] For the sake of brevity, I will give examples which forcefully, yet briefly, teach that circumcision did not evolve from the eternal will of God but from the temporal will. The reason: there were many of God's servants before the time of Abraham who lived according to God's eternal will though they were never circumcised in the flesh, such as Noah of whom Scripture says that he was righteous and perfect in his generation, Gen 6. Abraham [//] too was righteous before he was circumcised—probably, I assume for more than ten years, Gen 15; 16, and 17. Believing women and girls, too, were never circumcised, yet they were saved. Moreover, several prophets such as Moses and Jeremiah despise and belittle circumcision of the flesh. And finally, circumcision of the flesh has recently fallen into disuse among believing Christians. During the time of the Law, several Jews remained uncircumcised in the flesh for forty years in the wilderness, Josh 5. Circumcision does not unite with God, just as baptism and water do not unite us with or to God. It does, of course, make the so-called people of God among whom many were uncircumcised who were not disposed toward God. Indeed, God took them to be uncircumcised in his sight and to be strangers, as is indicated in Jer 9:25f[33] as follows, "Gentiles have their impenitence and Jews uncircumcised hearts." Just so are unbelieving Christians. For faith or circumcision of the heart alone brings forth Christians and people of God, Jer 4; Mt 25; Jn 3; Rom 2.

External signs do not unite us with God

Although circumcision and baptism and other external signs make neither righteous nor wicked, and although they do not unite us with God, as does the eternal will of God unite and glue us to God, when received in the heart, believers, nonetheless, have to accept such external signs in their own ways and use them as signs [G ii] of the inner righteousness and oneness. How and what for did they use such signs? Surely, so that they would take the Lord, whose signs they used, for a righteous, truthful, and living God.

Example: those who used circumcision correctly confessed that the Lord who created heaven and earth was their living Lord who could and would give them everything he had promised them, such as increase of their seed and other good things.

Take baptism for an example and note what is promised to a person who is to be baptized. Christ says, "You shall baptize them in the name of the Father, the Son and the Holy Spirit," Mt 28:19. Anyone who is baptized in this name receives outward baptism to show outwardly before everyone that he confesses the triune God whom he takes to be the Creator of heaven and earth, who can and will give him everything he needs and which is good for him, and everything he promised.

But where this righteousness is not in the spirit, there the sign is wrong and disregarded by God. Therefore, old people cannot take comfort in their baptism when they fail to sense the decline of their life. For this reason a spiritual person is not bound to externals. Neither is it essential that inner oneness must be confirmed and attested to by an external sign, nor that the spirit must accomplish its life and work with the aid of corporeal things, Jn 4. It can simply be without comfort and trust in externals.

Now, if you know of some who think that blessedness and true union may be found in external signs, you should attempt to disabuse them of and get them to hate external signs—but easy and with skill, as did Paul with circumcision, Jeremiah with the ark and with God's house, and David and Isaiah with external physical practices.

No one can unite with God through externals [//]

Take another example from ceremonies, such things as physical devotions or spiritual displays. God did not speak of sacrifices on Mount Horeb when he gave the law to his people, Jer 7. God also had his prophets reject sacrifices and external gestures, as may be found in Isa 1 and Ps 50 and in several other places. By this he intended to show and teach that his eternal will cannot be satisfied by external sacrifices and that no creature can unite with God through externals. There is another meaning contained in ceremonies which is that the Jews were to be kept from idolatry and drawn to God through such manifold external exercises and obligations, Lev 17; Isa 19. In like manner Christ draws people away from pride through short prayers. These examples help us understand that God's eternal will is not a temporal will and that the permissive or wrathful will is not always identical with the temporal. For to render sacrifices was, in my estimation, God's temporal and not his wrathful will, unless we wish to deal in subtleties.

The nature of God's eternal will

God's eternal will is not rooted in any external exercise or physical devotion—all that may be false and deceitful. It does not become true in us until God works his eternal will in human works which means that he brings us to will what God wills and to accomplish the divine work.

Further, everything which God demands, commands, and wills externally is temporal and transitory and small, I venture to think. His gracious will can be done without any externals. Nor [G iij] do we gain anything with sentient or external indications. Indeed, we anger God more whenever externals indicate the inward spirit of God which is not present, since externals deceive.

But that which must be is unchangeable, and is to remain eternally, God created inwardly in the emptied soul, for God is spirit. Therefore, creatures must unite with God's uncreate spirit, with and through the spirit. Accordingly, we must all fathom the spirit of the letter if we are to serve God readily. You must search for the spirit of Scripture which is the eternal will of God and then act or refrain from acting in line with what the letter commands or prohibits—not according to the letter, but according to the comprehended or discovered spirit.

The one needful thing

In this way you would confess that one thing is needful which cannot perish and cannot be taken from us: which is to cling to God. This alone is needful and has to be and shall remain so for ever, if the soul is to do well and live eternally in God. Such union with or clinging to God happens when we are obedient to God's voice, as was the case with Moses; or when we love God, as Joshua said—the one not being far removed from the other.

Reason: if you desire to hear God's voice aright, you must, through faith, give leave to everything, bless the temporal,[34] love God, and cling to him alone. You cannot have a "something" except when it is something that is in God. Christ teaches so, saying, "Unless a person renounces everything, he cannot be my disciple," Lk 14:27. If you wish to unite with God and be a disciple of Christ, you must and ought to give up all things for ever. [//] The soul needs this and it must renounce all things. It means that the soul must be rid of all desires. If we cannot shed creaturely desires, we cannot be apprentices of Christ. And if we cannot be apprentices of Christ because we adhere to something that is created, after which we hanker and which clings to us, we cannot be disciples of Christ. And if we are not disciples, we do not hear God's voice, and if we do not hear God's voice, we are disobedient and sin in all we do or refrain from doing when we are not united with God and cling to God alone.

This is what Christ means when he says, "Whoever believes in the Son of God shall not perish, but have eternal life," Jn 3:16. To believe in the Son of God is God's eternal will. It is God's eternal will that we might and ought to attain to eternal life in faith, as Christ says, "This is the will of my Father who sent me that all who see the Son and believe in him are to have eternal life," Jn 6:39. God's eyes look to faith, Jer 5 and God unites our soul to himself through faith, Hos 2. Therefore, where there is no faith, God is not united with us and God remains unknown, for it is impossible for the created soul to be good and right in itself, Hab 2. Spiritual and divine life, righteousness and everything that is pleasing to God are grounded in faith in God. Just as a bride becomes united with the bridegroom when she is prepared to live inseparably by his law and will, so, the soul unites herself with God in whom she is prepared to place absolute trust, love, refuge, and faith. God's will is grounded in that. To be united with Christ, the groom is to walk attentively with God. It is good for us, Mic 6, to show the neighbor what God's will is and what God commanded. This is good (see the same chapter).

By their fruits we know the friends of God [//]

Where there is the true knowledge of God in faith, there the true love and friendship of God are. And where love of God is strong, there too is love of neighbor and orderliness. To the first Christ says, "You are my friends[35] because I made known to you everything I received from my Father," Jn 15:14. To the other, Christ says, "Those who love me keep my commandments, and this is my commandment that you love one another as I loved you," Jn 15:12. Likewise, "as I washed your feet, so you are to wash one another's feet. For the servant is to be like his lord and the student like his master," Jn 13:14.

By the new fruits, we know a new tree; and by the old fruits, we know an old one. A person who is new and is found to be in God's will sprouts with new work. If he was hard before, he becomes soft; if he used to steal, he now works with his hands and earns his bread by his labor. By our fruits we are able to know ourselves and others. Therefore, we must look to what we do. For true knowledge of God and the acceptance of his will break forth and present themselves as the heavenly Father presents himself, Mt 5. This is the one thing that is needed.

The inner being has one thing, but the external has many

The inner being must remain for ever and simply in the singular, eternal will of God and must concern itself with it at all times. The external being, by contrast, hovers in its physical motion—now up, now down, now to this side, then to the other. Now it is embittered, then sweet; now it is joyful, then in sorrow; now at work, then at rest; now in life, [//] then in death; now in heaven, then in hell. And although there are thousands of these happenings, they are drawn into a unity, nonetheless. Whenever we merge and are absorbed in the divine will, hell becomes heaven for us. The eternal will of God, when accepted with one's whole heart, turns hell into heaven and death to life. It brings about that we desire and want to have God's will alone, and that we hold to and respect God's will alone. In the contrary case, all things become to us like nothing: fire, sword, death, and hell become in our eyes like nothing. This is apparent in David's case. When he was driven out he said, "If I have found favor in God's eyes, he will bring me back to the ark and to the tabernacle." And again, when God said, "You displease me," he replied, "Be it unto me as it seems right in his eyes," 2 Sam 15:26. Eli spoke in a similar manner, "God is Lord, let it be what is good in his eyes," 1 Sam 3:18. And Job spoke likewise, "Though he should slay me, yet will I hope in him," Job 13:15. Moses too is caught up in that same will, Num 27. We are like ships, drifting about in the blustering dangers of the sea, being tossed to and fro without perishing, because all the while we are anchored and the anchor is firmly grounded.

So, a person who is without will is not harmed by anything, however evil it may be, as long as we are anchored and the anchor is grounded in God's eternal will. The anchor is to die and to totally abnegate all creatureliness through the faith that is like a mustard seed. The earth or rock on which the anchor is fastened is God's eternal will which brought humankind into being.

Whatever God does not will is sin, whenever we will or do it

It must be said [H] that some sins are beyond our comprehension, so that we do not consider or want to consider them as sin. Yet they are sins, simply because God forbade them and does not tolerate them. Who, for example, would find in his understanding that to desire someone else's goods is sin. I walk through a fruitful field and think, "If only that were my field." Such a thought or desire is sin, although it harms no one, provided the desire is not acted upon. It is a sin, nonetheless, simply because God does not tolerate it and forbids such desire, saying, "Do not covet your neighbor's field," Ex 20:20.

Who would claim such desires to be sin when Paul writes, "I did not know desire and would not have taken it to be sin, had not the law said, 'You shall not covet,' " Rom 7:7. The law makes known the will of God. No one denies that. It reveals sin, as Paul teaches, so that we recognize sin through the law of God. Yet, if we had no law, we would not recognize sin. Thus the law makes known God's will and teaches us when we act contrary to God's will and sin as a result.

We ought to have searched tearfully and asked why God is pleased or displeased by this or that, instead of disputing with God and asking, "Why did you take it to be sin?" We should be satisfied by the fact that God graciously allowed his will to be revealed to us, so that we know that everything that is forbidden by God's word is evil and wrong, even though it appears strange and incomprehensible to our understanding that it should be evil and wrong.

Just as I am not allowed to ask God, "Why did you create me thus and not otherwise?" so I cannot ask God, "Why did you forbid and declare it to be an evil so that Christians are not allowed to make images or to maintain created images in their sanctuaries?" This goes beyond [//] all understanding. It is, nonetheless, evil and wrong in God's sight. God's law teaches that, Deut 4; 7; Ex 20. That idols should blemish churches, places, and roads is beyond all comprehension, as is the fact that an ignorant person who bows before an image should thus damage his Christian marriage and become a spiritual adulterer. This is a sin more grievous than when he commits physical adultery. No worldly wisdom can comprehend that one sins in the realm of faith when one relies on one's armor or sword, or when one depends on great hordes of people; this seems ridiculous to the understanding. Yet all of the above things are evil and wrong because God forbade them and revealed his aversion to them. There are frighteningly many sins indicated by Scripture which no human wisdom reckons to be sin or evil. Yet Scripture condemns all who wittingly or unwittingly do them without repentance. Paul says that all who sin outside the law shall perish outside the law, Rom 2:12. Not having learned and understood the law will not absolve them.

Then again, all who sin within the law will be condemned and judged by the law. Not to know does not help us much. For God did his part and made known to us what pleases and satisfies him, along with everything he hates and flees. It helps even less if we do not want to know and remain like a mule without understanding. Therefore, we should teach God's word to our children from their youth up, so that they come to know what is pleasing to God, what is good and what is evil, and choose the good and flee what is evil.

The wonderful and hidden will of God does what serves to the good of one but provokes the anger of another [H ii]

God's will is obscure and shrouded in such darkness at times that it is hard for us to know what we should do. We are ignorant of why God credits some with a good thing which in others serves to their harm and disfavor. I have observed that God considers a thing as evil in some which is rated a favor in others, such as the enumerating of people. Moses and Aaron enumerated the people of Israel and God was not angered, Num 1. Joshua, too, counted his companions and God was gracious unto him, Josh 8. Saul enumerated his people and God did not show his disfavor, 1 Sam 11. But when David enumerated his people, it was a sin unto death. Scripture states that Satan incited David to enumerate Israel, 1 Chr 21. For that sin God destroyed 120,000 men through the plague. To top it all, David confessed his sin, 2 Sam 24, so that everyone would know that David had sinned in numbering his people. Is not this the wondrous will of God which held against David, what was allowed to pass to the advantage of Moses, Joshua, and Saul.

Antithesis and Response

You might now say that God forbade enumerations after the time of Moses or that enumerating was permitted before David's time, but forbidden in and after his time. But several stories speak against that. For example, Ahab numbered Israel but was not rebuked for it. Ahab who ruled after David, numbered his people [//] without being punished.

What is more, Nehemiah states that God put it in his heart to gather the leaders and the common people to number them, Neh 7:5.[36] This was a long time after David's years and was to have been a work of God. Yet it was Satan who prompted the prophet and David.

Who can fathom this obscure will of God and confirm with an

oath that David's intent was different from Moses', Joshua's, or Saul's before, and after him, Achan and Nehemiah. God never made his will known; he issued neither commandment nor prohibition. Neither was there any sign or vision to indicate that the one did well and the other evil. Joab alone warned David to refrain from his plan and against enumerating the people which was hardly more than one person resisting another person's common undertaking. Therefore, David undertook to number his people and understood in the end only that he had acted foolishly and sinfully, 2 Sam 24. I do not know the reason, especially since David recognized his folly and sin only when God struck his heart, but I fancy and guess that David forgot his great yieldedness and sought instead to gain victory and power with a great horde and with a multitude of people, as is the case now with all commanders and soldiers. They number their people and assess the usefulness of their armor and of everything else. And when they have plenty of people, and a variety of military equipment, and a good advantage, they hope to maintain their advantage. But when they have few people and weak weapons and defenses, they soon give up their manliness. Their heart drops, I don't know where, and they totally forget over their [H iii] fears that they ought to fear God alone, Deut 2; Neh 7; Isa 51; 2 Sam 17. They do not recall that God has a mighty and strong hand and an outstretched arm and that it is all the same to God whether to beat strong men with a few weak people or whether to devastate a weak, small band with much iron and steel; whether to rout an entire army with rustling leaves or whether to scatter it with thunder claps. Therefore they sin in making God too small and weak and in putting greater hope and trust in their own people than in their God. Or else they depend on their armed people and on God, at one and the same time, which is a grave sin. For this reason, all soldiers must fall, just as Peter sank in the lake because he had little faith, Mt 14. Their hope must be solely and totally in God, 2 Chr 14 and 16, Judg 7. I fear that David's trust (which before he placed in God alone) was divided or lessened when he numbered the people. He came under the judgment of God which God proclaimed through Isaiah as follows, "You trust in your chariots being many." Therefore, he sinned in that he probably numbered his people because he lacked trust; the others did not do that.

Had David remained in his former state of trust, as when he approached Goliath and knocked him down, he would undoubtedly have been above this misdeed. I do not know, of course, whether there was something else concealed in his deed. Nor do I wish to be so arrogant and bold as to take the reason I gave as the truth. I have no desire to intervene in God's secret judgment. May God grant me to know his will which he wishes me to [//] know, and to know it through his own light which he gives and takes away, so that I might know and love what is truly good.

On letting go[37]

Earlier I showed in part that life and death depend on God's will. Thus we all live and exist as dear friends in God's sight if we accept God's eternal will with our whole heart. I also touched on the fact that God proclaimed and wrote his eternal will through his voice on Mt. Horeb and that he subsequently granted ears and allowed it to be understood through his prophets, through Christ and the apostles. He has transmitted it to our forebears in visions and through his living voice. God also had his gospel preached to the dead so that he may judge them justly, 1 Pet 4:6. This is also found in the third chapter of the same epistle.[38]

God has widely undertaken to have us know through Holy Scripture what is pleasing in his sight and what displeases him. But there are certain faults and things which are not contained in Holy Scripture. Yet no one is to begin or do anything wantonly. We will have to give account of all our words and deeds and answer to whether or not we sought God's will in these, and sought it gladly.

Therefore, I do not mind seeing many Christian folk following the accounts of the apostles and not letting go or running away from it any more than they have to, but earnestly desiring to know God's will. And in cases where God did not sufficiently inform them, they would cast lots when through Holy Scripture they were not able to grasp and decide, like the apostles who received Matthias by lot in place of Judas Iscariot, Acts 1, although the apostles could have been chosen according to Scripture. Where there are two or three who are otherwise equal, one ought, in my estimation, bring the matter to God, first of all, praying that God might accomplish his will in the matter.

The ancient fathers asked above all else for God's will

I don't care if my guess appears unwarranted to the Sophists, for I could, if I wanted to, give numerous examples of how God's servants began their activities in the greatest fear of God, before, under, and after the law and that they strove diligently to ascertain God's will beforehand.

But for the sake of brevity, I will refrain from such indications.

However, I wish to suggest that Christians should give their minds to the solution which the ancients practiced widely. They would say heartily, "Lo, my God, my Lord, and my Father, I would dearly love to live for you alone and do or refrain from doing your will, not only in the greatest commandment, but also in the very least to hear and to do it. Let me know what you will and what is pleasing to you. This is the path and this the [//] work of my hands; this is the trouble and labor which I am facing and which you know better than I, O God. Reveal your will to me, that I may not act unknowingly in opposition to you. You know what is pleasing to you and what is useful to me. Bring it about that I may live in your will and do according to your eternal and merciful will. Grant that my lot is in keeping with your will."

When this condition (i.e., a person letting go in God's name and with above understanding) is met, and when we come to be in a state of total surrender of self-will, much good is the result. Joshua cast lots before God the Lord, Josh 18, and divided the land by chance or lot. The book of Joshua is full of this. We, too, should cast lots in all unordered things and eagerly learn to know God's will. God willing, I will say more on this another time.

The dangers of human teaching and traditions
Cursed is everything which prevents us from studying God's will and confounded be the one who keeps us from searching out God's will. Moses held two things before the people of God, a blessing and a curse or condemnation. A blessing he granted to all who are prepared to obey and do or leave undone God's word which he commands or prohibits. A curse Moses spoke on the backs, works, and goods of all those people who disobeyed God's word or commandments, [J] Deut 11. Joshua, Isaiah and others did likewise, Josh 18.

Through Isaiah God speaks as follows, "If you will and desire to hear me, you shall eat the goods of the earth." This is to enjoy God's blessing. "But if you do not want and if you cause my anger to be kindled, the sword shall devour you, Isa 1. We must want God's will and work if we are to receive a divine blessing. Therefore, David says, "Many blessings come to the one whose will is in the law of God and who studies God's law day and night," Ps 1:2.

I don't think that Moses orders anything stronger and richer than to keep God's word always before their eyes and in their hearts. Mark this in Deut 6; 11; 17 and 32, and in several other places. Moses asks, pleads, orders, and urges the people of Israel to make known God's word to their children. Why does he do so? Because nothing is more needed and of use to the people of God than to learn and do God's will. And nothing is more dangerous and ruinous than not to know God's will and to neglect what God wants.

If we stand in God's will, we are well placed before God and whatever we do or leave undone will stand, but if we are outside, we are in a bad way. Everything we think, do, or leave undone comes under the curse. It is impossible, of course, for any creature in heaven or on earth to be able to explain God's will or displeasure unless God first makes his will known. It is a thousand times, indeed, countless times, more difficult for us to discover God's will than for me to discover through my own wisdom the thoughts or will of a mighty king (who is a hundred miles away). I cannot through my reason or power probe the will of a person who is close to me. [//] How then am I to take hold of the secret will of a stranger? How much less can I fathom God's will and good pleasure or know what God (who is farther from me than the heavens are from the earth) wills, if I expect to comprehend it through my cleverness. My thoughts are human thoughts. Even if I were an emperor or a clever Mercurius,[39] I could, nonetheless, not carry out the will of another by learning on my own what I should do or what everyone is capable of doing, in order to attain to God's will through their own wisdom, if the powers and thoughts of humankind and God's thoughts are not alike and the former never able to become divine.

God himself says, "My thoughts are not your thoughts, and my ways not your ways. Yes, as far as the heavens are above the earth, so far are my thoughts and ways above your thoughts and ways," says God to humankind, Isa 55:9. For this reason Christ says that all services which happen in response to human laws are futile and for nought. Surely, it is an uncouth and asinine blindness for human beings to have been so arrogant as to make laws by which we are to serve God in a pleasing manner when he is in the heavens above and we are down here. The deceiving popes did just that. They made laws about God and tied us to their dreams rather than leading us by God's word. They pretended that their thoughts were to God's praise and honor. They tried to lead people to God in manifold ways. They painted the dirty sprinkling-brush and refused to understand that the thoughts of popes, bishops, priests, and monks are deceitful and malodorous. [J ii] For God's thoughts are more unlike theirs than are the thoughts of a clodhopper [Misthans] unlike their princely thoughts. Yet they say, How can a peasant or clodhopper guess this or establish a law for us when he has never been inside the courts of a lord?

What would God say to them other than, "Go and offer such things to your prince," Mal 1:8. Although they had no command to do so, they tried to prescribe divine teachings to the people of God (out of their frenzied heads), as they have actually done (this, unfortunately, is fully apparent). And they kept us poor people from studying and ascertaining God's will (which alone makes God known to us through his own mouth, word, or work). They breathed their will and opinion on us instead of teaching us God's will. Or else, as I firmly hold, the devil brought to light his deceitful word through these foolish Roman priests and brainless ninnies and their ornate words and holy pretense. Just as the devil tempted Christ with supportive Scripture, so he made statutes, canons, rules, and forms of Christian discipline and divine living through popes, bishops, and monks, inserting Holy Scripture and using it against us poor little lambs in the same way he was permitted to use Holy Scripture against our Shepherd Christ Jesus. He achieved that we became perverted and sought God's will in human words.

Therefore Christ says, "The people honor God with their lips, but their hearts are far." Are we not far, indeed, when we do the will of human beings, but not God's will? We are worse off than were the Jews who said to Moses, "Go to the Lord and hear [//] what he says and let us know what he wills and we will do it," Deut 5. For a long time we have said, "Go to the pope and the bishops and see what they write and we will do that." Not what pleases God but what they command. Yet we intend to do God's will as the people of God. To this the vexatious devil and his procurers have brought us. We were as if someone had said, "If you wish to do what pleases the king, then go to a crazy fool, ask him, or learn what he desires, and do that." The devil cast his teaching through bishops and monks like a net over the wings of everyone, catching them masterfully and holding us captive, so that we were unable to discern God's will and, as a result, we were consumed by God's wrath. Therefore, all popes, bishops, and monks who prevented our poor elders from discerning the will of God are readily the pope's track-hounds. They are cursed and damned and have altogether died and been buried through the fierce ban of God. For not only are those cursed and damned who disobey God's commandments and teaching, or who do not hear it, but also the helpers and assenters who assist in leaving God's will unstudied and unknown.

Some day I will ascend Mt. Hebal[40] and pronounce several curses over them. God grant that they will some day taste the sword of Isaiah and that they are brought to justice. May God draw the sword from its sheath and rescue us from these knavish deceivers. Amen.

We have nothing to expect of the devil's procurers except for harm and injury to body and soul. They are not content with scraping, scratching, and robbing us by being spiritual princes [J iii] who bring much ill fortune and assist in nothing that is right. In addition, they try to blind us, though we have eyes to see and they tear us firmly away from God's word and drive us to their lord, the devil, whose vicar is the pope.

O God, redeem your imprisoned people, bring down your out-stretched arm and hit them, so that they can no longer diminish your name. Help, O God, it is high time now. Teach us your will and bring about that we may want and are able to do what you will—be it death or life.

AMEN

Printed, Friday after St. Gregory,[41] in the year one thousand five hundred and twenty-three.

9

Regarding the Two Greatest Commandments: The Love of God and of Neighbor, Matthew 22:[36-40]

How it is that the right love of neighbor is not human,
but divine, and flows forth from God's will.

Andreas Bodenstein from Karlstadt

[1524]

Although Carlstadt preached on the subject of divine and human love at Orlamünde in March of 1523, a printed version of the sermon did not appear until 1524, in a Strasbourg printshop. While some of the polemical tracts against Luther as well as against the traditionalists were printed more than once, generally in different cities, this tract had only one printing. Freys/Barge list the only known sixteenth-century edition as number 121.

The tone is eirenic and full of quotes or allusions to biblical texts which stress the interdependence of the love of God and love of neighbor. The tract is one of Carlstadt's most impressive expressions of true spirituality. A feeling of self-worth and general well-being, enhanced by a time of relative calm in Carlstadt's otherwise rather turbulent life during his Orlamünde pastorate, permeates this tract.

Copies are extant in several libraries. Erich Hertzsch, Karlstadts Schriften aus den Jahren 1523-25 Teil 1, (Halle: Max Niemeyer, 1956), contains the only modern copy of the tract. Our translation is based on the text in Hertzsch; the translation has been compared with an unpublished translation by Calvin A. Pater of Toronto. Some of Pater's work has been incorporated with permission. Page numbers in brackets [ ] refer to the Hertzsch edition rather than to a copy of the 1524 publication, located in the Zentralbibliothek Zurich, signature V.160.14.

To the honorable and steadfast Dietrich of Biel, now in the Joachimstal.

The knowledge of the immeasurable love of God which he manifests through the death of his only-begotten Son as through the highest fruit and the lasting peace of Christ be with you. Gracious brother, I am sending you this sermon on the love of God and neighbor that you may read and assess it. I beg of you to let me know any fault you may find with it, for I can readily accept any well-intentioned, godly reproof from you and all other Christians. You will soon receive a booklet from me on idolatrous brotherly love.[1] I am glad to be of service to you.

Dated at Orlamünde, March 1st in the year of the Lord 1524. Andres Carlstadt [50]

On the two greatest commandments: the love of God and of neighbor, Matthew 22:37-40

The gospel of the love of God and neighbor teaches in a nutshell what the first work of God is which a servant of God must receive and possess above all. It informs us how a person might prepare for and become skilled in receiving this first work of a servant of God.

You should know that the greatest and noblest work of God in the created soul is also the first, in that all works and service rendered to God flow from this best and noblest work; they must be governed by and conform to it. This is true because God places the greatest of all works in the ground of the soul where he dwells, teaches, rests, instructs, and governs—united and in spiritual unity. But since reason differs from divine inspiration, our reason considers it strange, yes, foolish, that God should place his best and greatest work first and foremost in the created spirit, and then build other works upon this highest of works. But let reason think it justly foolish so that with regard to the knowledge of God, it too might be deemed a fool, and that the ground of our soul develop an aversion and bitterness toward natural reason and flee it.

One ought to know, however, that God does not instantly set up his greatest work in the soul, fully grown at the moment of seizing and occupying it. God's gift begins with saplings. Similarly, God imprints his loving knowledge upon a new heart in subtle and small ways, as one might imprint the form of a seal upon a piece of hard and unformed wax, making it difficult to distinguish the lines of the form [51] and hard to read the letters. And this young shoot of the greatest work of God is granted in greater measure to some than to others. God distributes his talents and goods as he wills, desiring that everyone be content with what God gave, provided we are not slothful and bury our talent [Mt 25; 18].

The nature of the greatest work

Someone might ask at this point which is the greatest work of God created by God in his spirits? I respond that the love of God without knowledge and understanding is blind and deceitful. Faith or knowledge of God without love is cold and dead. Hence, the greatest work of God must needs be the loving knowledge of God which Scripture often calls love and to which it attributes the work and nature of knowledge.

This work is also called faith to which the quality of love is attributed so many times that one could say, "Faith without love is worthless." Love without faith does not satisfy. Therefore, the right work is a loving faith or faith-ful love. God recognizes and values such, as one recognizes and values a thing which delights and which is dear.

That the above-named work is the best and noblest, may be seen by the fact that eternal life is contained in it, Jn 6 and 17. That it is the first may be concluded from the fact that love does the commandments of God [Jn 3:35]. Anyone who does not believe is damned. Therefore, God's love must be present, or else the commandments will have to remain. Faith and understanding must be present if God is to be pleased by anything a person does [Deut 5; Jn 3].

That Scripture ascribes to love the qualities of faith and attributes to faith the works of love is apparent from the fact that love alone counts for anything before God. It is active through faith [Gal 5:22]. Put differently, only faith which is active in love counts for anything before God. Faith without love is worthless, 1 Cor 13:13. The godless also know God, as Ezekiel and other prophets keep saying; but they have no regard for God and their knowledge is dead for they are lacking in love. [52]

In short, John ascribes to faith or to the knowledge of God and to love of God one work which is to keep the commandments of God. He says that whoever claims to know God but does not keep his commandments is a liar [Jn 3]. But those who keep his commandments truly have the love of God. Note how the apostle John instructs us that faith and the love of God keep the commandments, and he shows that from the fulfilment of the divine commandments we can know faith and love, just as we know a tree by its fruits. Therefore, anyone lies who says, "I know Christ," but does not walk in his commandments. Those also lie who say," I love Christ," but fail to do his commandments. But whoever fulfills God's commandments knows God, just as those who keep his word truly have the love of Christ.

Faith and love are known by one work and one fruit. That's why I said that the Holy Spirit apportions one character and quality to these two virtues and Paul attributes the best to God's love when he says that love is the best or greatest. Faith without love has no regard for what it knows and is a fickle faith which lacks discernment [1 Cor 13]. Therefore I am on solid ground when I say that the best and noblest work created by God in the soul is a faith abounding in love or a love abounding in faith. It is absolutely true that our love of Christ, as does faith, informs us of Christ and makes Christ known to us.

Again, faith is active and merciful, as is love, and through love, as much as through faith, Christ dwells in our hearts. For this reason Christ says, "Whoever does not love me does not keep my word. But one who loves me keeps my word, and my Father shall love him and we shall come to dwell with him" [Jn 14:15f.]. By this Christ clearly teaches us that God comes to dwell within us through love. For this reason Paul desires Christ to dwell in the hearts of the Ephesians through faith, and that they might take root through love [Eph 3:17]. Accordingly, Christ dwells in created spirits through his love as much as he does through faith.

In this way also he teaches self-understanding and implants himself by strongly revealing himself in the hearts of all who love him, as Christ [53] himself says [Jn 14:15], "Whoever loves me will also be loved by my Father, and I shall love him and make myself clearly known in him." This indicates that the love of Christ is the root of faith and that love receives Christ that he might dwell within and that Christ reveals himself to love.

I have said all this lest anyone confuse the terms *love* and *faith* or mistake a blind love or a fragile, loveless faith for the greatest work. You should know that the Holy Spirit intends to include faith when it speaks of love, just as love promised to God embraces faith as well.

Whenever our gospel speaks of love, you must certainly understand [it to mean] a faith-ful love and not separate faith and love in any way or think merely of a denuded love which neither understands nor leads to understanding. What was said above we wish to demonstrate by the gospel for today. That God's faith-ful love is also the first work which God brings about in his created spirits, I will relate briefly on the basis of today's gospel.

All of Moses and all the prophets depend on this work, says Christ; therefore, God's love has to be the first work, for in God's works there is an order that is also found in his commandments.

You may now ask two questions. The first is, "Christ speaks of the greatest commandment and you speak of the greatest work; how do these tally?"

The second question is this, "Christ says that the law and all the prophets derive from two commandments while you say that all commandments derive from one, namely this, 'You ought to love God with all your heart'; how do you explain that?"

My reply to the first: through God's commandments we know God's work in different ways as through an external thing, and we find the same order in the works that we find in the commandments so that the highest and greatest commandment reveals and demands externally the greatest and highest work. Now Christ has said that the highest and greatest commandment is "you shall love God, etc." [54] Hence, love which is rich in faith must also be the noblest work which God has ever made known through his commandments and which he demands of people. Consequently, God's love surpasses all other works—it is nobler, better, and more precious than all other gifts, surpassing and prevailing over them. This is true, for love is purer and more sincere than all of God's works, immersing the lover more deeply and with greater oneness in God than any other of God's works. There is no other work in which the created spirit disregards self more than the work of love. Love is drawn toward and stands in the beloved. A lover does not look to himself as with other gifts and the soul finds less of itself than in other gifts. Further, God's love is more courageous, bold, and penetrating than the other gifts and works of God. Therefore, it is easily the foremost and noblest work of God and would be the best, even if all our explanations should fail us and we would have to rely on Christ's saying alone in which he set it above all other works and valued it more highly than others, saying, "All prophets and the entire law hang on these two commandments, etc." [Mt

22:40]. Indeed, the second commandment and work regarding the love of neighbor depends on the commandment and work of the love of God. Love of neighbor must be abandoned whenever it obstructs God's love or when both cannot happen. It is possible to hate, persecute, or kill the neighbor out of love for God [Lk 14:26].[2] But to hate and persecute God is prohibited for all eternity and there is not a single instance which permits us to hate God. Whoever loves father or mother more than God is not worthy of God [Mt 10:37]. We have been commanded to love God more than anyone else. We might well taunt our parents saying, "Who are you?" But it would be a devilish question, indeed, should one ask God mockingly, "Who are you?" Therefore, love of God is a work on which love of neighbor depends. For this reason Moses says, "You shall honor father and mother, as God commanded you" [Deut 5:16]—with the same will, understanding, and manner which God commanded you.

Love of neighbor (be they angel, human being, or Christ in his humanity), must be governed by love of God and must be in line with it, just as a carpenter [55] must be in line with plumb line and square. It is totally impossible for one who does not love God to love the neighbor in a divine manner, for we must love the neighbor as God demands and because this pleases God—this is impossible without the love of God. For this reason Moses proclaimed the Ten Commandments and then began to explain the first commandment through the love of God, and that God declares "those who love me and keep my commandments" [Deut 5; 6].

With this I have done justice to the second question as well, regarding the law and the prophets which depend on two commandments which is ever so true. For all commandments and prohibitions deal with love of God and neighbor. It is not sufficient not to hate; love is also required. You must love your neighbor and speak well of him, and not harm him or treat the neighbor as if there were no God who seeks (or might seek) those who belong to him. You must love your neighbor, if you wish to fast, pray, sing, and do good works, acceptable in the sight of God.

Without love of neighbor, God abhors you and your alleged good works. Even then you cannot love your neighbor unless of course you love God—who has shown you how to love—with a love abounding in faith.

Paul's assertion that love of neighbor fulfills the whole law [Rom 13:8], only applies when the love of neighbor fulfills all commandments which concern us and the neighbor, in things pertaining to the neighbor. This is exactly what Paul intends to say in his detailed discourse. Hence, love of neighbor must, above all else, give attention to love of God, flow from and be oriented by it.

Christ never calls love of neighbor the supremest or first, but rather secondary and like the first. Now the first must always be ahead of, or else it must be at the same time as, the second. Hence, the second commandment and work of God cannot be unless, of course, the first commandment and work of God exists. Where love of God is lacking, love of neighbor is also lacking. Love of neighbor is like love of God, as Christ says. Thus it must be oriented by and follow the love of God. Accordingly, it is futile [56] for us to speak a great deal of love of neighbor when we ignore the love of God.

Our love for one another is carnal and human, when we muster a godless love, i.e., our love for one another is selfish. We love the neighbor for the sake of profit, assistance, gain, because of a demand or because of self-indulgence, as do the gentiles and those who have forgotten God [Mt 6; Lk 18; Gal 6; 1 Cor 13]. But when love of neighbor is pure and genuine (as Christ shows it here and there in the Gospels as he points to its likeness to divine love), it surely flows from divine love.

The reason for this is that the second comes after the first and is like the first; it is like the first in kind, nature, and form.

Since love of neighbor follows love of God and is like the love of God, it is above nature and has supernatural powers. It has no place, therefore, in the spirit that does not love God. Therefore, John says, "Anyone who loves is born of God" [1 Jn 4:7].

When the apostle says, "How can anyone love God whom he does not see when he does not love his brother whom he sees?" [1 Jn 4:20] he does not contradict this, but strengthens and supports it. For love of God brings out love of neighbor every time it encounters or hears a brother of Christ. Therefore, the same apostle John says, "We have a commandment that whoever loves God must love his brother" [1 Jn 4:21].

The cause and origin of love of neighbor is that God is love. His love is an independent and uncreated loving power which touches the ground of the soul, i.e., the innermost being, and it reveals God and the soul, teaching the created spirit to understand God and itself. This is like the outgoing rays of the sun which reveal themselves to the eye on which they shine, teaching the eye to understand itself and the sun. It is integral to the uncreated nature of divine love that God loves his chosen creatures. God proves this by sending his Son who became incarnate. Therefore, whenever divine love is revealed and poured out into the human heart, it also teaches love of neighbor and makes us love all that God [57] loves, just as faith has regard for everything that is God's, namely, the poor and forsaken people.

It is impossible, therefore, that we love God whom we cannot see when we hate the brother whom we see. That's why the above-named apostle says, "Let us love one another, for love is of God. And anyone who loves, is born of God and understands or knows God" [1 Jn 4:7]. Note and mark well that the one who loves the neighbor knows God—of which he spoke earlier. In other words, God has revealed himself and his love for us. It is essentially impossible for anyone to love God before his divine, independent love has been revealed in the ground of the soul. But when God's love has given understanding to the heart, it must love God and all the sons of God. Therefore, John says, "We know that we love the children of God when we love God" [1 Jn 5:2]. In short, it is not possible for anyone who does not love God to love a brother of Christ and a son of God. And we know whether we love a son of God when we love God. The love of God, which makes itself understood through insight, is a sure and unerring testimony of love of neighbor, just as the spirit of God is a witness and seal of divine gifts. Now if someone were to say, "I love God," who envies a son of God, he would make of God a false witness and a liar.

Therefore it remains true that love of God is the noblest and highest work of God which is revealed through the independent love of God, and love of neighbor must be measured by and adjusted to it. And it cannot possibly be right and good so long as it does not flow from and exist within the love of God.

The love I speak of sometimes is the independent love of God which makes itself known in the heart; sometimes it is the work which this same love (i.e., God himself) leaves in the ground of the soul after it has revealed itself—just as we call the eternal remembrance of a seen light a light. What I say may dispel the darkness of what has been written and indicate which kind of love is meant. I have said enough here about God's love being the foremost and supreme work which God works in his spirits. In what follows you will see what God's love [58] is and in which creature God does his greatest work in the ground of the created spirit.

The nature of God's love

You should note carefully that love of God (speaking in terms of the works that have been yielded) is a strong and intense longing for God, which is not the natural state of the soul, of which the prophet speaks. "Long for God" [Ps 37:34][3] and also, "I am not well without you" [Ps 16:2]. David felt good when he was in God. Without God he was unwell. David found full satisfaction in God and suffered sheer harm without God and he abhorred everything that was not of God. But he loved his neighbor for God's sake, as the history of Saul demonstrates.

How God creates love

God implants his love or this intense desire (for him) in the heart; at first through small sparks. In other words, God allows small sparks of his love to flow into and unfold in the soul. He stands by his work and fans it until it develops into a huge fire and until even the minutest kernel of the mustard seed has grown into a huge tree which supports the birds of heaven and the company of angels.

These little sparks are hearty longings for the highest good, desiring the good purely for its goodness and not its benefits. As soon as the heart begins to long for and desire God, it has received God's work and can be assured that God, who has graciously given it such small sparks which incline the heart toward God and cause it to long for and desire God, will continue to assist it. Just as we can be sure of the spirit of God the moment we realize something to be evil which before we regarded as good and when we loathe which earlier we desired—wrongly.

The spirit of the fear of God lays the foundation in the soul [Isaiah] and renders the heart receptive toward all treasures from God. That same spirit implants in the heart such noble, gentle thoughts and intense desires for God and creates disgust for all that is evil, as is written [Prov 8:13], "The fear of God despises [59] evil, conformity, pride and turns from evil." It inclines towards the good, and desires goodness and righteousness for their own sake.

This spirit is the beginning of the loving wisdom of God and teaches us to understand the independent, radiating power of divine love. And when it has achieved that the created spirit understands God's love, it returns to God's love. In other words, when God's love toward humankind reveals itself in uncreated light, the soul cannot stay away from loving in return, for it must love God in response. Thus we do not love God seriously unless he loves us first [1 Jn 4:19]. This must needs be small at first, for the uncreated light of divine love which is God cannot show itself in the fullest light and greatest clarity to a blind eye. An impure eye cannot see God and a sick eye does not tolerate clear light.

How we must be prepared to receive God's noblest work

Therefore you must know that a person must be prepared and made ready, above all else, to receive the noble work of God. Christ and Moses point to this preparation when they state, "You shall love God with all your heart, with all your soul, and with all your might" [Mt 22:27; Deut 6:5]. How then are heart and soul prepared and what is this preparation called?

I reply: this preparation is called "wholeness" of heart or soul. When soul or heart is made whole, it is prepared for the work. Wholeness is the preparation. Division is the opposite and a hindrance. For if you wish to know why God allows himself to be kept from creating a small spark of his very best work in your soul, I will tell you that it is because your heart or soul is not whole but divided and fragmented. For where there is multiplicity, simplicity has no room, and where that which is manifold dominates, that which is simple, cannot dominate. The soul is unable to serve two masters [Mt 6:24].

There are many creatures; God alone is the One [Gen 2]. Anyone who clings to creaturely things is not capable of and cannot comprehend the great work of God. What binds us to the One and by which the One is united is the love of God. Therefore Moses, wishing to speak of the love of God, said, "Hear, O Israel, your God is One" [Deut 6:4]. [60]

He gives a short preface on God, namely, that God is the single One and then places the commandment regarding love right after that, so that everyone might know that God's love looks to the One.

If we come to hate multiplicity and leave whatever fragments and divides the soul, we become a unified whole, reach our own unified interior and wholeness, and become capable of receiving the noble work of God.

If you cannot understand this, note that the heart must divest itself of all creaturely clothing or images. In other words, the heart must be circumcised if it is to receive divine love. God must remove any blockage and the foreskin of the heart and circumcise the soul until it is just soul.[4] It is then nothing but soul and a total ground which God finds and reveals by turning the sod and casting off all creaturely things.

The soul resembles the things it loves. Those who attach themselves to a harlot to love her, become like a harlot—one flesh and one body [1 Cor 6:6]. For God ordained that we must become like the things we love. Therefore, in God's sight and in truth, all who love contemptible, useless things, blind idols, deaf stones, or anything abominable become contemptible, useless, deaf, blind, and odious [Hos 9:10; Jer 2:8ff.]. Then the soul does not remain soul, but becomes an idol with the idol it loves—a deaf ear and a blind eye, just like the stone or block of wood which it loves and in which it vainly trusts [Deut 7:25ff.; 18; Ps 115:4-8; Wis 15:7-19].[5]

All these things break and destroy the soul, cover up the ground, and harden the heart so solidly that God cannot accomplish his work. Neither does he intend to plant his paternal works in such covered ground until it has been cleared.

Hence, the soul must first be circumcised and swept clean and attain to its clarity and inwardness before it is capable of receiving the noble work. Moses also taught this in clear words when he said [Deut 30:6], "God will circumcise your heart to love him with all your heart." Do you see that God must circumcise your heart? Only then can you receive his lofty work—inasmuch as Moses clearly says, "God will circumcise your heart to love him with all your heart." It must needs follow from this that no one who has not been circumcised is capable of or fit to receive the precious work. That is hard and [61] disturbing for the human spirit is not fully circumcised here [below]. Therefore, it does not become a place for God, ready to accept the small spark of divine love. This is rather disturbing, for it also follows that in this life no one is able to believe, which means that all are damned. How disturbing and bitter.

Disturbing or not, Moses stands firm when he says, [Deut 30:6], "God will circumcise your heart that you may love him with all your heart." And Christ confirmed these words. Hence, God demands at all times and in all of the commandments a whole and circumcised heart, and God regards no work unless it is whole. For this reason Christ says, "No one can serve two masters" [Mt 6:24]. And Moses and Christ [say], "You shall serve God alone," [Mt 6:24; Deut 6:13]. The half-hearted Asa teaches that God accepts no faith and trust from a divided heart [2 Chr 16:1-10].[6] God demands a total turning toward him, total love and whole works, which means wholeheartedness. Nothing ascends to God from a divided heart. The incorrupt truth says so.

[mar: Circumcision]: Spiritual circumcision must come first, before a work of God can take place, to make known that the soul must be one soul, the heart one heart, and the ground must be opened up, and both youth and old age must vanish.

For this reason Jeremiah says, [Jer 4:3f.], "You must break up fallow ground and renew it. Do not sow among thorns." You must clear the obstructions of your hearts before you sow.

Thorns are a creature's innate desires, as Christ teaches, [Mt 13:22], and everything which obstructs God's seed must be plucked up before one sows. In other words, you must yield [*Gelassen*] the obstructions of your soul before you can receive the work of God.

Note how clearly God's spirit teaches that you must first be circumcised and swept clean, before you can receive God's gifts. Laugh or be angry, that's the truth and this has been the reason why I claimed that we cannot fulfill any of God's commandments on earth, not even the least.

You need not despair, however. While it is true that no one enters the kingdom of God unless he believes, loves God, and does his commandments—as Christ says, "With [62] all one's heart," the consoling savior Christ Jesus has, nonetheless, given us a consolation that in this vale of tears we may believe and love God, and do his commandments in the knowledge of his fullness, even though we have not been wholly circumcised and have not reached complete wholeness and nakedness of our heart.

All who like branches have been grafted onto the vine which is Jesus Christ receive from God through this vine divine waters by which they are sprinkled and cleansed and made fit to receive God's love, faith, and work. This is illustrated by the story of the discovered treasure, for which a person will sell all his possessions to acquire the field.

From Christ Jesus living waters flow down into us. They pervade our souls and well up unto eternal life. For the spirit of fear which Christ had in great measure allows his powers to flow through Christ to all the branches which grow on Christ the vine, creating a total aversion to all that is evil, as I mentioned earlier. It tears out all desire and love of our own life, and replaces them by displeasure and boredom with life, our abilities and desires, creating an aversion to all things which prevent heart and soul from receiving the work of God.

When we have taken on the nature of the vine and experience an aversion to and dread of all creaturely desires, we have somewhat opened up and thirst for heavenly waters, just like the arid ground which is split due to drought. When we are thus opened up, we too are prepared, empty, and free to be filled with God, as he himself has promised. He is a helper in need. When we are prepared to receive God's gift of faith, love, and the like, God gives as much as we are able to receive. If our capacity to receive[7] is great, God gives great gifts. For to all who wish to receive, God gives according to their capacity

[Mt 13:44]. If we are in every way prepared to receive God's work, God gives us everything in rich measure. [63]

But if the created spirit is not sufficiently circumcised—as no one ever is—the consolation of Christ is available, nonetheless, that in Christ we may bear fruit as branches on a fruitful vine. Although our work or the fruits never reach maturity before the final circumcision, they are present, in the soul, nonetheless.

But the Father daily thins the branches and cleans them out, that they may bear more abundant and perfect fruit. It is a pleasant consolation, full of joy and delightful words, that God the Father implants his work and his fruits in our soul, even when our souls have not been fully circumcised and still show coarseness and blindness.

Thus God first gives the heart (which has put on Christ and stands in Christ) small treasures, tiny berries, and subtle sparks, such as a strong desire for and love of God. Or else he presents us with deep sighs for God until the heart is more fully swept clean. And when it is well prepared and trimmed and quite new (as an old moss-covered tree becomes new when trimmed down), God then gives it the full love which God has commanded and which he demands.

At the outset, God's noblest work is small and so insignificant that many people possess it unawares. It grows daily and becomes big, understood, filled, and known. But it exists within the six days which are full of labor and create great unrest.

On the seventh day, when the sprinkling has been completed, it stands fully at rest and without labor and in perfection; it now is a love with all one's heart and all one's soul and all one's strength.

Then we lose ourselves in the snow-white cloth which comes from heaven and enfolds us mightily so that we can no longer find ourselves, either in will, desire, or strength, or soul, when surrender of self [*Gelassenheyt*] is complete.

Thus far you have heard that love is the most prominent and first work which precedes all of God's gifts. Moses verifies this when he says [Deut 7; 5:10], "God is true and faithful who keeps his covenant, promise, mercy, [64] and kindness toward those who love him." And Paul says [1 Cor 2:9][8] that the gifts do not perish in the human heart. And no eye can see what God has prepared for those who love him. Both indicate by these words that love of God is the first of God's works.

That God's love also fulfills his commandments has also been said by Moses a thousand times over. Specifically, God through Moses touched upon the small sparks and shoots of divine love (which keeps

God's commandments), when he says, "Who will put into their hearts to fear me and keep my commandments" [Deut 5:29]? [9]

How the heart is to be prepared and fitted to receive God's love is generally least spoken of and explained, and what great effort is required for a person to become skilled in taking unto himself the love of God, which we learn to do and long for by way of the bitter purgatory of an ardent longing for the love of God.

I should now speak of love of neighbor which alone brings forth external works pleasing to God. But [this love] is somewhat extensive and also rather difficult to grasp, for the simple reason that the commandment "Love your neighbor as yourself" has to this day been poorly explained. God our Lord has explained it frequently enough, but the great masters have barely touched on it. I shall make a few tentative beginnings for you; you may then pursue the matter further and test whether you can grasp its secret and concealed meaning in the depth of your hearts.

Love of neighbor requires two things: it must be like love of God and also like love of neighbor. The love of neighbor must be like the love of God, just as the second commandment is like the first. Accordingly, Christ says, "The second commandment which is like the first and close to it is, Love the neighbor, etc." The other likeness requires that love of neighbor is equal to love of ourselves. If we want to love our neighbor aright, we must understand both these comparisons and know to what extent love of neighbor resembles divine love and how it resembles love of self. [65]

Otherwise, love of neighbor cannot be right and good. For all the works of God must flow forth and take place in the manner, with the intention, will, and thought in which God commanded them. Likewise Moses says [Deut 5:29; 6:6; 7:12], "You shall do the commandments of God as he commanded them," when the manner of doing them is sketched by his commandments which is the one reason why God gave us his law. Thus we should observe diligently how God commanded love of neighbor and how it resembles love of God and love of self.

We should also know who is our neighbor, for Christ, our example, did not say in vain, "Love your neighbor" [Mt 19:19]. To the brood of vipers, he says, "You look for a sign, but you will see none other than that of the prophet Jonah" [Mt 12:39]. To the Pharisees and hypocrites, Christ said, "Those who are well do not need a physician" [Lk 5:39]. He also forbade us to throw precious pearls to the swine, [Mt 7:6] and said, "Let go of the blind leaders" [Mt 15:14], and "Beware of the sourdough of the Pharisees" [Mt 16:6]. Paul too forbade us to have fellowship with those who teach and live contrary to God [2 Cor 6:14]. And another apostle says, [2 Jn 10], "Do not invite to your house nor greet those who do not bring the teaching of Christ."

Now if we are not to have a friendly chat with, greet them, or invite to our homes those who do not have Christ's teaching, then we are also not allowed to love such people as our neighbors. Similarly, if I am not to feed or provide with a drink anyone who strives against Christ, that person cannot be my neighbor. And if I am not to throw the little pearl before the swine, it must needs follow that all animals that have a human skin and the form of a human being must not be regarded as my neighbor, but as swine to whom I must not extend the good works [due to a] neighbor. One must therefore carefully consider who the neighbor is whom we are to love as ourselves, so that we do not act contrary to God's love at the very moment when we intensively practice love of neighbor. For we would only create a love of neighbor which is more unlike love of God than a beam is unlike a human being. This is already too much for one sermon. Therefore, I will merely sketch only the first line of comparisons. God willing, we will later dig deeper [66] and look more thoroughly at God's understanding of love of neighbor.

The second commandment is like the first in that love of neighbor must be as upright and serious as love of God. For just as our love of God must be upright and serious, so also our love of neighbor involves an upright and earnest will and desire. And just as love of God implies an uncoerced obedience which is upright and desires nothing but God, so also love of neighbor implies an uncoerced obedience toward God which is pure and must have the upright intent to love and serve and benefit the neighbor for God's sake, without desiring remuneration or reward.

The term *upright* means that we must walk and see straight ahead. The opposite of this is *return*. Christ's example explains this as follows: You see, I should invite the poor to be my guests for the sake of the One who commanded me to do so rather than invite the rich who are able to return the favor [Lk 14:12-14]. If I have the latter kind of love, it is not upright, but it returns to me, finds my soul and seeks what is mine and my pleasure. Were I to love the neighbor in that manner, I would corrupt my soul, for I am not to seek myself in any of the commandments or works of God at the cost of my soul. Yet, that's just what I do when I love the neighbor for the sake of someone other than God. I must seek no reward nor should I allow the neighbor to repay me. My love must be without reward—only then is it upright.

Let me give another example. Should I invite a poor official to my table or render other works of love without receiving food from him in return, I am not justified just because I invited a poor person and my love is not upright if I expect that the poor official may put in a word for me with my lord or that he might reward me for the food in other ways by overlooking something or through certain concessions. All love that hopes for a reward is not upright; rather, it bends back and returns to what is mine. When you love a poor man and show your love toward him through external works as when you feed or clothe him, and if you want to receive praise [67] from people, you have already received your reward and by no means are you without reward. Your will toward your neighbor is not upright. Rather, your will gives attention to your own praise, honor, and glory; thus it returns to you, for when your love is not oriented to God's will and to the neighbor, so that God alone is praised and the neighbor alone helped by you, your intent is not upright, but crooked and bent on profitting and you aim at yourself and what is yours.

It is somewhat like that with straight desire. Where desire is straight, you are unaware of it and do not find yourself in it, but the person whom you love and benefit with a straight desire senses it.

From this you may learn the meaning of serious love or desire. When you have a serious desire, your desire does not titillate you or puff you up, but you experience a great awe of evil and you stay within the limits of God's work and are a simple servant and a tool of the work of love. You have a swift and serious desire simply to fulfill the commandment of the great king.

This seriousness is the fruit of the spirit of the fear of God and grows from hatred of evil and love of the good. When your love of neighbor shows the neighbor that your works are straight and serious, it is like love of God and very close to it, as you may deduce from what was said above.

But you must not ever forget that I said all along that love serves and benefits the neighbor for God's sake, for the love of God must fill the heart and the love of neighbor must spring forth from divine love. This is why we have a divine and not a human commandment to love the neighbor. Therefore I owe obedience to God, not to the neighbor. And when I serve the neighbor, I must heed God's will and render the required obedience to him alone. From this you can understand again how the second commandment is close to and like the first.

Thus you can understand how love of neighbor equals and resembles love of God, for sound reasons found in both the Gospels and Moses. [68]

You will now hear a brief summary of the similarity between our love of neighbor and the love of self. But it seems strange and unpleasant that we should love ourselves, for love of self has been clearly forbidden and uprooted. In its place envy and hatred have been implanted.

It has always been impossible for humankind to understand what contributes to our true nature. We may well choose whatever we consider to be good, but it does not become good or useful simply because we consider and value it to be good. Take for an example a person with a fever who chooses wine as if it were good for him. But as soon as he satisfies his desire and realizes that the wine was harmful to him, he must revise his opinion and his choice and admit that the wine is not good for him. Now, as it is with the wine, so it is with other created things which a person chooses as if they were to serve him unto a good life and nature. But experience proves to us that we do not know what is good for us, and that we especially fail to understand what benefits us for eternity.

Since we cannot see what is eternally good for us, we are unable to love ourselves any more than we are able to love others for their benefit. Hence, we are unable really to love either ourselves or the neighbor in a way that benefits truly and eternally, rather than in a way that seems good now, but which is harmful and evil later.

Nonetheless, God has given us one commandment of the love of neighbor and of self and enticed us to love the neighbor as ourselves. And God would be fully in his right to damn us if we were to neglect that commandment.

But his mercy is immeasurable and cannot leave off doing good. Therefore God made known his commandments that we might learn what is always and eternally to our benefit and that our well-being may spring forth as we observe God's commandments. For this reason Moses says often, "Keep all of God's words which I command you and do them so that you and your children may eternally benefit and that you may do what is right and pleasing to God" [Deut 10:12-13; 11:1-2; 12:1]. We must at once learn from God how he has proclaimed [69] through his commandment what contributes to our well-being and what is truly good for us. Thus we learn to know how to select and judge by them and how we all can love ourselves rightly and for a lasting benefit. By the same token we must also produce love of neighbor.

Hence, I must not begrudge my neighbor any gifts which God gave me, so that he may enter with me into a divine community, and receive an eternal good. And I ought to wish that he may walk in all of God's commandments and be strong, wise, and holy in God.

To this end I must spare no labor or expense. Rather, I must stretch out my hand and provide food, drink, and clothing, instruct and do everything that I would wish to happen to me, so that I may come into the right grace.

That's how passages of Scripture which deal with avoidance of people, who are not to be greeted and with whom we are not to eat, agree with the texts that urge us to approach neighbors who are not close to us, that in God they may be our siblings and children of God, redeemed by the precious blood of Christ, to seek their benefit, help them, and be at their disposal.

For someone who does not confess Christ, but wishes to hear of him, is close to me, even when he does not have the title, name, and baptism of Christians.

This too is a love of the creatures, when we follow God our Father and do good to people—be they good or evil—since he lets his sun shine on them all without distinction.

And this is a work of love of the neighbor, to do good to one's enemies and pray for one's persecutors, as Christ and Stephen did.

But one must not be blind and foolish in these matters. We should not eat with those who are against Christ nor associate with those who turn us away from God, lest they become our downfall [2 Jn 10; Deut 13]. You ought to know, too, that Christ refused to pray for those who were of the world.

Love without salt is foolish and dumb and belongs underfoot. Note from this that brotherly love is a carnal and devilish love when it displaces the love of God.

You now understand how a person may love himself for his own benefit and then love his neighbor as himself, [70] and that the saying which bids us love the neighbor as ourselves makes us equal.

For now this is all that needs to be said, in brief, on the two commandments of the love of God and the neighbor. God willing, you shall hear more and I shall say more, to God's glory, at a more appropriate time. Amen.

Preached at Orlamünde in the year 1523.

Printed at Strasbourg in the 1524th year. [71]

10

Whether We Should Go Slowly and Avoid Offending the Weak in Matters Pertaining to God's Will

Andreas Carlstadt

1524

After Carlstadt's expulsion from Electoral Saxony, a period of severe turmoil ensued. On a challenge from Martin Luther, his erstwhile colleague at the University of Wittenberg, Carlstadt wrote feverishly on several issues regarding which they had developed different positions. Notable were their differences on the right understanding of the Lord's Supper—a debate reflected in several of Carlstadt's tracts. Another issue was the extent and speed with which reforms were to be undertaken. Luther's was a "go slow" policy on account of "weak consciences." Carlstadt countered by charging Luther and his camp with a new popish attitude.

The tone was initially still rather moderate, but would become more shrill especially after Luther's polemical tract "Against the Heavenly Prophets." "Whether we should go slowly" [Gemach] was published in Basel with no known reprints having been made. A copy of the tract is found in Zentralbibliothek, Zurich under signatures number V.160.15 and Ms S 12.

The Zurich copy has several glosses which have not been incorpo-
rated in this translation. Scripture passages appearing as marginalia,
however, have been inserted into the text in brackets [ ]. References
added by the translator will appear in footnotes. The only modern re-
print of this tract to date was published by E. Hertzsch, Karlstadt I. We
used this publication for our translation. Freys/Barge list the Basel pub-
lication of 1524 as number 138.

To my especially beloved brother in Christ, Bartel Bach,[1] city
clerk in Joachimstal, Andreas Carlstadt wishes God's grace through
Christ our Lord.

Dear brother,

In response to my intimation that several changes have taken
place here, you write that you wish to go slowly in your place. By this
you give me to understand privately that, in order to avoid offending
the weak, one ought not move ahead quickly or suddenly, but slowly.
This is nothing other than what the entire world is now doing, shouting, "Weak, weak, sick, sick; not so fast, easy does it, easy does it." I
cannot reproach you. In this case you speak with the great majority—
"easy does it, the sick"—although you do so more politely and more
reservedly. However, I must say to you that neither in this case nor in
other matters which pertain to God should you look to the way the
great mass speaks or judges. Rather, you should only look to God's
word, for it is more than apparent that the chief scribes and the entire
population erred in the past and were capable of error. This is why
God stipulated what the princes and all of them together or a council
had to sacrifice due to their ignorance and error [Lev 4:13f., 20f.].
God has clearly shown by this that everyone—even the learned
princes—are capable of stumbling and error. Therefore, God said in
general, and also in particular, that [74] everyone must pursue righteousness for himself [Ex 23:2], and that no one ought to follow the
example of others in deviating from what is right. God calls it harlotry
and whorishness to have eyes which look to other than his guideline
which is the word of God. God forbade us to follow our own thoughts
[Lk 15:1f.]. All our good intention is altogether undone when we
speak or do as other people speak and do, or as we ourselves think fit
[Isa 2:5; Mt 16:13ff.; Deut 12:1ff.]. The wisdom of the wise must cease
to exist if divine [wisdom] is to reign. Not only your own wisdom, dear
brother, must come to nought and become as folly, but also the wisdom of all other human beings. In this way you will not allow either
learned or ignorant people to influence you and you will, without any

agent, come upon the pure truth which sets you free and which in all eternity will not allow you to fall. Note here that you have become your own liability which you must avoid; in the same way, all learned people are to become to you an unreliable prop, to be avoided. Pure truth alone is to be your foundation and rock; when you have it, you will remain unconcerned and unchanging even though all scholars should change and the apostles break away—if that were possible. This is in line with what Paul says [Gal 1:8], "If I or an angel should teach otherwise, let him be banned." Anyone who thoroughly understands and comprehends the truth remains in that truth even if Paul should preach against it. Therefore, let everyone who must withstand the winds and the waves of the water be intent on experiencing the true foundations of God. This is the reason why God, through Moses, ordered all Jews to have pinions, tassels, and small yellow cords [Num 15:37] hanging from their garments by which they would constantly be reminded to think on God's commandments as often as they were aware of such tassels which they had to look at daily.[2] From this it follows that we are bound to Scripture so that no one can be guided by the whims of his heart [Num 15:37ff.]. Those who look to things other than the word of God are engaged in harlotry [Jer 23:16ff.]. However small and insignificant such looking about and desiring may appear to the flesh or to reason, it is nonetheless genuine harlotry and spiritual adultery, inasmuch as God, the husband of the created spirit, ends up being despised, or ignored and forgotten as soon as the soul looks to things other than his word in divine matters. If it [75] is true that no one can serve two masters and that a servant of two masters will leave the one by as much as he clings to the other, then spiritual adultery is an even greater devilish vice. And all human beings succumb to this vice when they value the word of the princes among scholars or of a great mass of people such as a council more than they do the word of God. The same is true of those who look to something other than God's true sayings.

Therefore, dear brother, you are obligated no less than the least to look promptly, directly, earnestly, and diligently to God's judgments which in themselves are just and true; you are not to look to the strong or to the weak. The great multitude may err, and they can cause one to err. The anointed, too, set limits on their anointing, for it is applied externally, and they too are prone to error which displeases God. Since it is true that you have experienced divine righteousness and truth, you must give direct attention to what God says. All those wise in Scripture must be as nothing to you, and you must not wait for one another or until the other follows your lead.

In whatever one does, one must also not look to others

As I have just now shown through scriptural proofs, no one should look to another or wait for others to follow one's lead in knowledge of the truth [Jn 5:39ff]. This applies to one's deeds. We are to keep all of God's commandments to the best of our ability and are not to wait until the unwise or the weak act on them. For God continuously bids all of us to teach his covenant and do accordingly [Deut 4:2 & 5:1]. For it is written thus, "Teach them and keep them; and act in keeping with them." The doing of what God asks of us is commanded of us all, even if the entire world were to hold back and be unwilling to follow.

I ask you whether a son should refuse to honor his parents until all the weak agree, understand, and show a willingness to honor their parents? You would have to reply, Indeed, those with understanding must not rob their parents of the honor due to them while waiting until all immature persons are ready and willing to follow suit with understanding. I ask whether a person should not stop [76] coveting other people's goods until the others are ready to follow suit. Is one allowed to steal until all who are thieves cease stealing? And so I ask, repeatedly, regarding all the commandments, whether it is fitting to wait until others are informed and are willing to follow suit before doing what God wills. And what I asked regarding the commandments which deal with love of neighbor, I also ask regarding the works and deeds which concern God's honor without any mediation. And I ask whether I ought to leave the idols standing which God commands me to remove until all the weak follow suit by removing idols. Likewise, whether I ought to slander God until all others stop slandering. If you should say yes, the enemies of Christ could say with equal right that murderers can murder, thieves steal, and adulterers commit adultery and knaves commit all sorts of vices until all knaves have become righteous,[3] for the same reasoning and foundation goes for all the commandments. That knaves might sin, I do not wish to assert, especially since I know that they also sin who backslide or break God's commandments [Lev 5:17] because of ignorance. They will have to suffer punishment because of it. How much more, then, will those who associate with adulterers, thieves, murderers, and blasphemers [Ps 50:18] be punished. The Lord says [Lk 12:47] that the servant who knows the will of his master and acts in opposition to it shall receive a beating. God shall punish the one who sins out of ignorance. How much harder and more seriously [will the one be hit] who sins against his commandments to please a knave. Paul says, "Have nothing in common with idolaters, adulterers, and the like."[4] Yet, you tell me that you think one should go easy and depart gradually from evil. I also know that St. Peter will turn the key—which he is supposed to have to open heaven—very slowly; that he will twist and turn it in the lock and will open to them just as slowly as they are approaching.

What shall I say? Are we to learn God's commandments slowly? Are we to wait for the big throng? Should one look to the other person and wait for one who wants to be first? Just think how the great princes would like it if people attended to the tenth, to taxes and compulsory service, as slowly as they attend to God's service! They would throw the disobedient ones [77] into towers and place them in stocks and would chain them until their subjects became obedient. By their ragings they pronounce upon themselves the judgment which God would pronounce and which they show toward others on account of their disobedience. For which master can tolerate his employees standing still with none wanting to be the first or willing to start something he has ordered to be done?

God shall punish all who stayed away when he gave them orders, even though they might have had valid excuses and rallied the very best reason of brotherly love. While there should always be a great and special love between marriage partners, Christ says, nonetheless, that the one who excuses himself on account of his wife, etc., is unworthy to come to the meal. Everyone who understands what is right ought to do what is right, without hesitation and without looking back.

To say that one should make concessions to brotherly love means nothing, because it is not clear whether their sort of brotherly love is an unchristian cover-up, readily as evil and harmful as any of the little inventions of the pope. I shall leave that matter undecided for the moment and say that Christ has cancelled and nullified all brotherly love if it stands over against his commandments or turns one even slightly away from God. For love fulfills God's commandments, and it is impossible for a person to love Christ and to act against his commandments or not to do what Christ commands. This flows from the following saying, "If you love me, then keep my commandments" [Jn 14:21ff.], and from "he who is not for me is against me" [Mt 12:30]. "Anyone who does not hate father and mother, wife and children cannot be my disciple, etc."[5] Thus it is written that it is impossible for a person to love Christ and not to live by his commandments, or to stand still and look to another, waiting to see whether the other would do, or not do, what pleases God. Accordingly, they will not be able to tie a blindfold or curtain in front of my eyes to stop me from doing something that God wants, or to do something God forbids, even if they should preach and write for a thousand years about offenses and brotherly love.

The truth says [Lk 9:62], "Whoever puts a hand to the plow and looks back is not fit for the kingdom of God." Christ said this to the one who, when called into discipleship, answered as follows, "Lord, I want to follow you, but permit me to bless my people or bid them farewell." Now, if the one [78] is not fit for the kingdom of God who looks back to persons whom he might readily have bid farewell at another time, how fit will those be who administer God's commandments and hold them back because of those who are not prepared to start [Lk 17:32]? Lot's wife looked back and was turned into a pillar of salt [Gen 19:26]. What might become of those who look back to their slothful and lazy brothers who at the moment remain indolently blind and lazy?

When Christ said to Peter [Jn 21:19-22], "Follow me" and Peter asked, "And what about this one?" Christ answered, "If I want him to remain until I return, what is that to you?" Understand here that God permits some to be lazy or unwilling to learn and do what is right. But did he not call you sufficiently? Do you want to enquire what the others are doing or when they will come? No. It says, "Follow!" Do not stand still and do not wonder whether the others follow or not.

What did Peter care about the fraternal love of those Christians who were aggrieved when he baptized the Gentile Cornelius [Acts 9-11]? He did what he understood to be God's will and asked no one about it. And when his brothers talked to him about what he had done, he gave the answer which God wanted. Nonetheless, there were things in Peter's doings worthy of rejection or reprimand, because Christ said, "Do not walk in the ways of the Gentiles."[6] Because of this, Peter might well have considered his offense; but Peter had no regard for the offense. What are we to do in matters which God does not command or prohibit in unmistakeable words? Are we to avoid offense? Now someone might say that Peter is not a pattern for us, but Christ is; therefore, give me an example from Christ [Jn 4:9]. I can say to that: Christ spoke with a Samaritan woman and yet the Jews were not in the habit of speaking with Samaritans, so his disciples were astonished by it. But Christ paid no attention to their being offended and he freely did what his Father wanted him to do. I shall demonstrate this further with examples such as those regarding the Sabbath, the temple, sacrifices, fasting, prayer, and the like.

They involve Paul so strongly in the matter of offending and in the things by which they want to force one to the conclusion that in matters which pertain to God one ought to go slowly. They shout all day long, "The weak, the weak, etc." But I know how to hush them, and I can say without hesitation that Paul [79] did not go easy in matters that were more important than ours here have ever been; and he had no concern for the few who took offense or for those who were sick, ignorant, and weak [Acts 21:20]. We read that many thousand Jews at Jerusalem became believers and were aggrieved by the fact that Paul taught and preached departure from Moses, namely, that children were not to be circumcised and that one was not to walk according to tradition, etc.[7] In this you see that Paul ignored the offense which so many thousand Jews had taken, and he freely preached without regard for the weak. You may want to respond, "I think preaching and doing are two different things." To that I say that preaching is a work like any other and does not happen for nothing. Furthermore, Paul actively prevented circumcision from happening; so how can we say that we want to be Pauline when we do not actively undertake anything that might go against fraternal love? What Paul does later by which he silences some of the clamor against him does not compel me to state that Paul therefore did not physically stop circumcision. His epistle to the Galatians is too revealing to be concealed by anyone. And from that epistle one can see that Paul did not have any concern for the weak. Rather, in sharp words he pulled them away from Moses when he said, "You foolish people, are you having yourselves circumcised?"[8]

Here then you have clear grounds that we were not obliged, either in word or deed, to hold back in doing God's commandments until our neighbors and those gluttons at Wittenberg are prepared to follow suit.

Every congregation, be it small or large, must see for itself and do what is right and good without waiting for anyone

God issued a general law by which the entire believing community, every congregation and each person, is to be guided and directed. That same law, which God also calls a covenant, is spoken or read to the entire people. Not that the whole multitude or community is a dead body as that which these blind lawyers invented for the body of the community, when they say that this body cannot hear, nor see, nor do anything. Rather, it has [80] ears to hear, eyes to see, and bodily parts ready for righteous living, to do everything that is pleasing to God [Deut 29:3]. For this reason God complains about the slothful ones and threatens to punish those neglectful ones who do have ears, yet do not hear; eyes, yet do not see; and bodily parts which do not function. Accordingly, it is quite true that Moses called the entire multitude of Jews together to recount God's commandments for all of the Jewish multitude [Deut 4, throughout; 5:1; 6:1-9; 8:1; 11:1, 8:18ff.]. And he always says that they are to do what he teaches them; that they are to be satisfied with his teaching and his works and are not to add anything to the teaching or take anything away from it [Deut 13:1]. In like manner they are not to think of doing any other work in the service of God except that which he taught them to do [Lev 16:2ff., 29-34]. Moses bound his people so firmly to God's teaching, customs, rights, and to the works of the law that they were not allowed either to teach or to do other than what they had heard. And because of this bond and other reasons as well, Moses called the law a covenant.[9]

That God's covenant included all separate communities and in addition every household; and that, in addition, no community or house was to hold back until other places became wise and active has been stated so often in Deuteronomy alone that I consider it unnecessary to present any proof. How often is it written, "Keep the rights and customs of God within your gates" [Deut 17:8-13 and 26:16-19], "You are to choose and place judges who are to punish the transgressors of the covenant."[10] Did God speak the following words to the multitude or assembly alone [Deut 5:29], "The Lord your God commands you to do according to all these statutes, customs and ordinances, with all your heart and with all your soul, as you explained it to your master? Who can say that God's commandments are to be kept in certain places only or that we break God's laws in other places?
[mar: The covenant of his Ten Commandments]

If you insist on saying that God ordered the Jews to erect stones in certain places [Deut 4:2; 6:5-8], I, too, will say that God ordered and commanded that we are to write his covenant, not only in certain places, but also onto the posts of our houses as a memorial and onto the gates, so that it might be held up before the eyes of all the servants and of the entire congregation [Deut 26:16; 27:1-3; 28:1, 14], that they might be reminded to guard God's commandments and, not only certain ones, but [81] all commandments. This applies, not only to the Jews, who heard Moses at that time, but to their descendents as well—for Moses says, "Your children and children's children" [Deut 6:7]. And not just one day, but all the days of your life, Moses says. Each community is to have its Levite who proclaims the covenant of peace and truth. Every housefather is to teach his children God's word, recalling and narrating it. From this it follows that every community and household must take care that it understands God's commandments and acts accordingly. And God wants so much that we not wait until others follow suit and become righteous that he commanded that the godless be punished as one punishes other vices, Deut 13:1-19 and 17:1-7. In addition, entire cities which catered to idolatry or refused to walk in the right path were to be destroyed and devastated.

I am very much surprised by our rulers and those learned in Scripture who punish carnal adultery but leave spiritual adultery unpunished. Spiritual adultery they intend to conquer with their breath and wind, but they fend off carnal adultery with swords, iron, fire, and wheels. Is not this a rather miserable endeavor for Christians? Is it not a devilish affair that they consider the dishonoring of persons greater, and apply severer penalties to it than to the dishonoring of God? Moses commands that idolatrous or spiritual adulterers are to be put to death just like carnal adulterers [Deut 13 and 17]. If they would only look to their Paul properly, they would surely find that Paul punishes those who are enslaved to idols no less severely than those who are enslaved to whores.[11] Yet it has to be right because they want it that way, and they defend their honor and their beautiful image of themselves.

The deed must always and immediately follow understanding

Our gracious God brought forth several created works thereby showing his paternal love [Deut 4:2ff.], among these the divine wisdom and understanding which God gave to our forebears through wondrous visions and stories and through his most precious word. Therefore, all people should readily say that it is indeed an excellent nation which has such great knowledge and such just [82] customs and laws. God gave us his covenant so that we should, in everything we undertake, work, live, and direct ourselves with wisdom and understanding. For God desires in all things to have knowledgeable servants who know what they are doing and what they leave undone; why they do it and to whose honor. And we ought to understand in sweet and bitter ways, in an active or passive manner, what and why God sends what he does. As Moses says [Deut 29:8], "Keep then the words of this covenant and do accordingly, that you may be wise in all you do." And Paul [Eph 5:15], "See to it that you walk with foresight, not as those who are unwise, but as those who are wise. And do not become foolish, but understand what the will of the Lord is." For this reason God complains through Isaiah that they do not look on his works [Isa 5:1-7]. And for this reason Christ often reprimanded his apostles for not understanding his works and his teaching. The same understanding and wisdom should be maintained, not only when you do something, but also when you suffer something, so that you know what you suffer, why, to whose honor, and for whose benefit. For this is the nature of suffering, as Isaiah says [Isa 28:19], "Affliction or being driven about lead to understanding." And Moses says [Lev 26:40], "God tests you so that you may be ashamed on account of your sins." And Paul says [Rom 5:3-5], "Suffering produces patience and patience brings knowledge, or experience"; for experience is a form of knowledge and the perfect work about which James writes [James 1:4f.], "Without knowledge none of God's works is perfected." Without knowledge we are like a mule[12] or a horse in whom there is no understanding. Accordingly, God's word has been revealed to us by sheer grace and in order that we might become wise, knowledgeable, and discerning—mark this well, through yieldedness [Gelassenheit]. It is a great thing, and highly to be valued, that God's secret has been made known to us. The wise of this world consider it a great privilege to become the adviser of an earthly prince, and everyone looks to the one who is loved by such a prince, etc. How much more highly is the one to be held, and how greatly such a one ought to esteem it, when God has made his secrets known to him? Especially since he has divine and superhuman wisdom. This is one of the reasons why God has revealed and made known his secrets to us [Deut 4:11ff.]. [83]

The other is to give us an everlasting and unshakeable recollection of all his words and stories so that at no time throughout our lives any should be forgotten, and that we may fear God and cling to him always. Recollection ought to be heady, busy, and strong, never standing still, but ready to break out with passion and be active. It is a widely known saying, "Cursed is the one who does the work of the Lord indifferently or who works deceitfully" [Jer 48:10]. Although this is said in relation to God's revenge, "Cursed be the one who spares his sword by not shedding blood," it applies to other works as well. For if it is true that God desires swift punishment, although he is merciful in forgiveness, how much more are we cursed and an abomination in God's sight, if we are tardy in coming forth with works which are to be to the betterment of our neighbor. God wants to see a free and cheerful giver who gives swiftly and willingly. A ready and willing heart which is inclined to deeds pleases God greatly [2 Cor 9:7]. All this flows from a continual and intense recalling of God's words. A person who is clearly mindful of divine teaching must not stagnate, nor be idle or slothful, since God's words bind him and drive him to action. Should he hold back in a case where he can and should do something, this is a sure sign that he is forgetful or that he does not have the kind of total heartfelt recall which he ought to have [Deut 29:28].

Here one may say, You seem always to link a servant of God to action, etc. [Deut 4:2 and 11:1], which undoubtedly is grounded in what is written, "You should at all times, and throughout your life, act and work according to divine law" [Tob 4:20]. "You ought to speak well of God at all times" [Ps 34:2]. I shall speak well of God always. One who is a friend loves his friend at all times [Prov 17:17], i.e., a friend acts out his love at all times as Christ teaches [Jn 13:35], "By this they shall know that you are my disciples, when you love one another." Over against this I also see it written [Eccl 9],[13] Everything has its season. In other words, nothing can go on forever; for a while it happens; then it stands still. So also God has set up certain commandments to be kept for a time, but not all our life or every day, as the Hebrew text and you, would have it. Among these are the Sabbath on the seventh day, the seventh week, the seventh year, the fiftieth year—all of which are based on the number seven [Gen 20:9; Deut 16:1ff.] [84] the paschal feast for a certain time of the year; the festival of booths for a certain time, and the like [Lev 25:1-23]. These had to happen for a specific time, but they were not to last forever.

My answer: Even if such figurative speech unites us according to the letter, as it united the Jews in times past, God's word, nonetheless, stands, which says [Deut 11:1], "You shall keep the commandments of God daily." The phrase "daily" means that everyone is to keep God's commandments at the time, and in the place and situation for which God had commanded them. There is a time for being alert and active. And there is a time for sleeping. If there are poor people, we must help; and if there are no poor persons, the hand is at rest.[14] In any case, we must act or work daily in line with the commandments of God, celebrate every seventh day, etc. We must at all times come to the aid of the poor, destitute, imprisoned, naked, etc., and should we have any such debtors, we must forgive the money debts of those who are without any possessions. If we have none, then God's commandment does not bind us; just as the poor, unlike the rich, were not committed to make costly sacrifices. So it states that you must do God's commandments daily, and show your love of God and neighbor continually.

So it is with the removal of God-blaspheming and Christ-blaspheming images or masses in places where we are in control. If we find idols among those who confess God, we are to take them away and deal with them, as God commanded.[15] This is to be done daily throughout our lives. Yes, if we find them in our community, then each congregation in its own city is obligated to keep them away from its own [Deut 14; 15].[16] It is always right and must firmly stand that we are to act daily in keeping with God's commandments. This is right and good when properly understood.

Figurative commandments catch and entangle the weak only, and it is on account of the weak that figurative commandments were kept and are still being kept, as Paul says, "All things are fitting, but not all things build up" [1 Cor 11].[17] By the same token, even if you have right knowledge or understanding, not everyone does [1 Cor 8:2]. Nor do you as yet know as you ought to. Since the understanding of many Jews was limited and their blindness great, they were not free and were held captive. They were obligated to keep God's figurative commandments, even though God's intent was different from what his words sounded like and thus the weak failed to observe the eternal will of [85] God. As a consequence, they had to observe the Sabbath and other celebrations and carnal righteousness such as water baths, etc.—in keeping with God's words and his hidden will—until they were capable of knowing God's true righteousness and his just truth more fully. One who broke and transgressed such figurative law of God had to have good explanations, as Christ did and as David did when he did not make an external sacrifice, Ps 39 [40:7-9]. This does not belong here, but I mention it so that we might know how God's commandments are to be kept daily. "Figurative" means at an appropriate and opportune time, but we must keep God's commandments properly every day as the case may demand. There are several commandments which call for a time, a place, or a situation. These have to be kept daily, i.e., in keeping with the situation and no one must look back to another who was amiss and deserved punishment. Several commandments—such as the following—do not relate to occasion, time, or place. These we must pursue forever and at no time depart from them or act contrary to them: "You shall not make, have, or suffer images; you shall not steal, or murder, or commit adultery, or bear false witness, or covet the property of others and so on."[18] Such commandments bind us always and to the very end. Whoever for a time, in any given place, acts contrary to one of these is a transgressor, a disobedient, unjust despiser of God. Nor should we look around at the multitude or at a council, for we know the commandments which we must not transgress. Hence, we must not ever make an image of any kind, nor must we tolerate those that have been made in the parts where we are in control, whether they signify, God, Christ, or one of the saints. Neither must we blaspheme God or do anything which God's covenant prohibits (which Moses explains and whose explanation the prophets further expound). Unless, of course, we have received a sure and nondeceptive command from God to act contrary to a commandment such as the one which Moses received from God to make images of birds above the throne of grace and of twelve oxen who were to hold the sea and to erect a serpent in the wilderness. If we do not have such a commandment from God, we know that we sin and that we disobey the voice of God who commanded that we are to make no image nor [86] suffer those that have been made in all those parts in which alleged believers rule. Similarly, no one ought to steal, murder, commit adultery, or desire the goods of others. If we act contrary to one of these, we are disobedient, unrighteous, and we sin. We will not be able to excuse ourselves by [pointing] to any number of those who are weak or sick. But if we should be bid by God to steal, rob, murder, commit adultery, or covet the goods of others, and if we are sure of the divine intent, we ought to steal as the children of Israel did when they stole from and murdered the Egyptians [Ex 12:35f.; Acts 7:24], and as Moses murdered the kings of Seir and Heshbon, etc. [Deut 2:26-36]. But without God's command, we must do all that God has put in the Ten Commandments [Deut 29:6f.]. We must give attention to nothing other than God's commandments and to ourselves so that we do, and refrain from doing, in order always to please God.

God always speaks within the limits of the Hebrew tongue. But there are a few who add, contrary to God's commandments, the phrase "not daily." We ought, so they say, to tarry on account of the weak and not to go on with anything. But what is this other than to say that we ought to allow a council to predetermine what we are to do and in which manner we are to serve God? We are constantly hearing that, on account of the weak, we should not fulfill God's commandments immediately, but rather wait until they have become wise and strong. This would have substance were Paul's teaching interpreted correctly. But it is strange that they want to move the weak along by delaying and setting aside the clear commandments of God. In fact, they set them further back with their horns and debtors, as Ezekiel prophesied regarding the moon.[19] They have no foundation for this in any teaching. Paul whom they so clumsily and illogically set up as an example in support of being lenient toward the weak is against them with all his might. What shall I say? I say this: their babble "not so fast, not so fast; soon, soon; lenient, lenient; the weak, the weak, the sick, the sick" is a glaring addendum to the word of God against which we are not to set anything [Deut 4:2]. Furthermore, the excuse, "I restrain myself, I am lenient, and I tarry until the weak catch up" is an impairment of divine works and stands against the statement, "You shall not add or subtract anything from it," as it is against the saying, "You shall do all that God has commanded you, and you are to do so always" [Deut 11:1]. [87]

Giving offense and love of neighbor are devilish coverups of wickedness

It is wrong to use the giving of offense and brotherly love as excuses for maintaining idols, and allowing the mass and other blasphemies to blossom and flourish under the pretext of not wanting to offend or of showing brotherly love. How this is, and what meaning it has, I shall write about in a booklet *Concerning Offence*.[20] For now, let it suffice to say that images are given or set up to ensnare people and to cause them to fall and be destroyed, as God said through Moses and the prophets. Moreover, idols are more perditious in Christendom than are carnal houses of pleasure, and they lead more quickly to spiritual adultery than any whore or knave. Therefore, those who bid us keep idols (which lay persons call saints) in God's houses, atop mountains, in valleys, and at crossroads under the pretext of fraternal love until the weak become strong do not exemplify genuine brotherly love. They preach fraternal harm and not fraternal service or love. Such excuses are nothing other than a roguish cover and a hidden snare which, if God speaks the truth and Paul says what is right, serve the poor soul unto its destruction, for in the matter of offending, he teaches the very opposite.[21]

We ought to take such harmful things away from the weak, and tear them out of their hands with no regard to whether they might cry, shout, or flee because of it. For the time will come when those who now curse and swear will thank us. For the one who breaks the will of a fool by force shows him the right and best brotherly love. Let me point you to a parable on the matter. Isaiah says of the fools who maintain idols that they do not understand their folly and that they do not know that they maintain a dangerous thing.[22] I wanted to say this first. Now I ask you, when I see a small infant holding a sharp, pointed knife in its hands, one which it would love to keep, do I show brotherly love toward the child when I yield to its will and leave the harmful knife, so that it might hurt and kill itself, or rather when I break its will and take away the knife? You will have to say, when you take away from the child [88] what could harm it, you do a fatherly or brotherly Christian deed. Christ has delineated true Christian and brotherly love when he said [Mt 18:8], "If your hand offends you, cut it off and cast it away from you." Christ said this in order to show what true brotherly love is. And Paul agrees with Christ when speaking of offenses. It is true then that I am under obligation and that it is everyone's duty—as long as God and the neighbor are dear to us—to take away from the foolish their dangerous and offensive things with no regard to whether they are angry, and whether they weep, or curse. How much they speak of brotherly love and that out of brotherly love we ought to leave idols and other offenses alone and untouched until the weak have caught up! What they call brotherly love is in fact brotherly harm and offense. Their love is the kind of love which senseless mothers show who let their children have their own will, thus leading them to the gallows. Christ never said anything about us being soft on offenses when we wish to do away with them and cast them from us. He says, Cut away, chop off, throw from you, so that they no longer offend you. Moses also says [Deut 13:9f and 33:9], "Let not your eye protect him and have no pity on him or hide him." Rather, you are to kill him; your hand is to be the first that is laid on him [Mic 7:17]. Moses says this with regard to people who cause offense. How much more should such saying lead to the removal of offenses which have neither flesh nor spirit, blood or breath, and for whose reform no one can hope, but through whom ignorant souls are brought to a fall. Moses would clamor loudly in this case, "Do not protect them, kill them and let your hand be the first."[23]

Anyone who wants to add anything to these words by saying that we ought to go easy and not act in haste and that we ought to be lenient toward the weak and not go against them suddenly nullifies the words of Christ and Moses and adds his own against God, thus making of them a false Christ and a false prophet. Christ says, "If your eye offends you," i.e., when you perceive that your eye offends you, "tear it out and cast it from you."[24] When does he say, "Go slowly, don't be too hasty, or go easy on the weak"? What great and harmful blindness! If the world only knew what harm comes to simple [89] spirits because of idols and other offenses, it would bite off its own hand before tolerating such deceit. And is not this a roguish cover-up when one preaches and promises hellish brotherly harm under pretext of brotherly love? O devourer of the world. Christ says that it would be better for you to cut off, tear out and cast from you, than to be cast into the fire of hell along with those offensive things [Mt 18:8]. I wrote against that miserable and pitiable billy goat Emser at great length and breadth of the damage that comes from preserving those devilish saints which our neighbors call saints and which we call idols.[25] Because of the new papists, however, it was suppressed.[26] But all who now read and understand the Bible know well how they treated me with force and in opposition to God.

The devil invented this roguish cover-up, just as he also invented the claim that images are the books of the laity.[27] Thus the devil robbed the honor of God's word and handed it to these dreadful, abominable, and idolatrous creatures. Thus he likened the word of God to idolatrous mud puddles which God hates and which he wants us to avoid and flee. It goes beyond saying that idols insult God and that the weak are corrupted [Ex 23:24; Deut 29:15ff]. Let any patron of idols step forward and tell me that the slaves of idols have a root which contains gall and vermouth. If they knew that, they would spit at themselves (I say this as an aside). Shame on you, despoilers of Scripture and catchers of souls. If there were as little danger and damage caused by idols as you claim, God would not have forbidden them so frequently through Moses and the prophets. Neither would he have warned them, "You will destroy yourselves if you make images or some form or likeness of me, etc.," [Deut 4:15ff.]. God calls it our destruction, and "papistical sophistry." But they call it an expression of brotherly love, in opposition to God. There you can see how they understand Paul when he says that the weak, i.e., those who are unwise, will perish from the food of idols.

Nothing can be proved from God ordering the Jews not to eliminate their enemies, the gentiles, hastily or quickly [1 Cor 8:11], but gradually and at leisure, or in good time, and that, as a consequence, Christians, too, ought to act gradually and slowly when removing offenses.

I should probably have retained a good arrow [90] for a stubborn and wanton enemy and I fear that I might not meet any scholar or that I will not fight cleanly with God's word or sword when I enjoy making fun of my enemies. It does not take much to handle the pure word of God dishonestly. I should, therefore, like to get ahead at this point to indicate to the enemies of divine righteousness what they could say if they would only open their eyes. And yet, I will remove their foundation at once by asking them, Do the servants of idols and the protectors of images not have good reason to keep their idols from the fire for a time when they cannot protect them forever? God says [Ex 23:29f], "For a year I will not cast them out, lest the land become desolate and wild beasts multiply against you. Gradually and in time, unhurried and slowly, I will cast them out before you until you increase and possess the land." God said this of the gentiles whose land the Jews were to occupy, saying, "I will not cast them out for a year. Gradually and slowly will I drive them out." This fits and rhymes well, as a start and for an example, with the removal of images. For if the Jews were to destroy gradually and in time, their enemies who could do them great harm, how much more[28] gradually should they remove the idols which cannot harm them at all. And that it is fitting to go easy and not destroy the idols for a year, is given by the text which reads as follows, "You shall not join with them and make no covenant with their idols. Do not allow them to remain in your land so that they cannot cause you to sin against me," says God.[29] If you serve their idols, it will be your downfall. Decide now whether we, too, should proceed slowly in removing idols. We are not to enter into a covenant with false gods, just as we are not to mingle with gentiles. Neither are we to allow idols to remain in our land; yes, in time and gradually on account of the weak, we are to cast idols and gentiles out. We must not be rash, therefore, or rage, or be hasty. Is not this a good, sound and strong foundation? Who can topple this wall of steel? [91]

Answer

O pitiable blindness! You mend your coat with strange patches. You cannot get out of your bind with tricks. We are prepared to meet you on behalf of the truth, even though you may have good reasons to practice your trade a bit longer and to cover your face with greater glory. The passage of Scripture you cited sounds as if the staff of the abbot at Begaw[30] had recited them—he can color his reasons that way.

Let us take a look then at what sense your text makes: it is true, first of all—as these patrons of idols say—that God had no intention of casting out the Gentiles for a whole year and that God forbade the Jews to act quickly, in haste and suddenly. But for you to say that because of this we should also go slowly and leisurely in removal of idols is your own invention. I do not mean you, dear brother, but the patrons of idols. But when you speak on behalf of the weak, you bring your wisdom and your additions, and not God's. I ask you, where is it written that the Jews are to drive away their enemies slowly because of the weak? God had his reasons. And if God is wise and faithful enough then his reasons are upright and sufficient as well. But God never said that we ought to go gradually and easy because of the weak. On account of the weak, God might have destroyed all the Gentiles at once. God forbade the Jews to befriend and to associate with Gentiles, so that the Jews might not fall away from him and that the Gentiles might not be for them a pitfall and ensnarement [Deut 7:2ff.]. God gave a reason and we ought to stand by that more firmly than by a wall and not nullify by human additions the reason God gave [Josh 23:11ff.]. God says, "Therefore, you must not kill them hastily and all of a sudden, so that the land not be laid waste and the wild beasts not multiply against you" [Ex 23:29]. Here you have the reason which is divine, upright, and sufficient. Moses narrates it also in another context and without any addendum [Deut 7]. I do not see anything at all which is different from that. "God would uproot these people, one by one, so that the beasts, etc." Yet, the patrons of idols are able to say that the enemies have hands, too, with which they can strike and hit and they cause great offense, as Moses and Joshua say. [92] It is apparent that Gentiles can cause offense through false teaching which idols cannot do, etc.

I reply: in order that the people of Israel might practice on Gentiles and become wiser, God allowed the Gentiles all the more readily to remain, so that the Israelites might learn to fight against their enemies [Jdt 3; Josh 1, 2, 3] and to understand through external warfare how the spirit can overcome and subdue the flesh and how it must fend off the beasts of the field and overcome falsehood with the truth and with wholesome teachings. If idols could defend themselves, they would not be as dangerous and not as much of an ensnaring yarn for a fall, as they are. Furthermore, it is wanton for a human being to give reasons for divine statutes when there is no divine foundation for them. It is sufficient simply to say, God wills it. There the crafter of idols may see that he put the headgear where his feet are and that he looked at Scripture through a gauntlet. That he bases his argument on parables I could have overlooked, provided he does not violate Scripture or harm the simple. But since his speech strives openly against God's righteous words and entices the ignorant man to his fall and ruination, I am not willing to do so. I must state that it is against God.

When he states that the Jews must not leave the idols of Gentiles in their land, he speaks correctly. But when he adds his own bit by saying that the Jews had to go easy and not be hasty; that they had to cast out idols gradually and in time, he makes his own addition. God says that they were not to leave the idols in their land as they were to leave the Gentiles, probably because they could not kill any worm or beast and were only prepared for sin and corruption. Therefore, whenever they were able to do so and were in control, the Jews were to destroy the idols of the Gentiles and not allow them to remain.

So God commanded the Jews two kinds of expulsion: one was the expulsion of their enemies; the other, the removal of the gods and idols or images of the Gentiles. The first was to happen at leisure; the other, immediately and suddenly [Ex 23]. The text says, "Do not allow the idols to remain in your land," i.e., you must not move gradually and slowly, as with the Gentiles, but quickly. That this is the correct and true meaning [93] and understanding is indicated by the context of Scripture. Earlier we read, "You shall not do their work, but you shall utterly break them. And their titles and the things they established you shall utterly overthrow." God does not say that they are to break idols gradually, as they were to do in destroying their enemies, immediately. Although God, in speaking of human beings and of the idols of the Gentiles, says that they are not to destroy enemy folk in one year or quickly, it follows, on the other hand, that they were to remove idols as quickly as they were able to. I prefer to prove this with Scripture rather than with human statutes. Hence, I point the reader to the seventh chapter of Deuteronomy where Moses repeats and renews above-mentioned text as follows [Deut 7:22], "You cannot and should not devour them all together or in haste, so that, etc." This sentence is complete and whole and has its ending. In that we are of one mind.

This is followed by a special clause which points to the removal of an offense; it reads as follows: "The graven images of their gods you shall burn with fire, etc." [mar: the end of Deut 7:25f.]. Nothing is said of going easy, as was said above. Rather, it is to be at once. You are to destroy them. This is clearer still, earlier in the seventh chapter [mar: Deut 7, at the beginning]: "You shall tear down their altars, and break in pieces their pillars and cut down their bushy trees[31] and burn their gods." When? At the same time they were destroying the Gentiles gradually. Why? So that they would not learn to serve other gods [mar: Ibid, Ex 23] or cause the idols to sin against me, says God. It would serve unto their damnation should they leave idols standing. Do you see now why one has to act quickly in suppressing offenses and why Jeremiah says [Jer 4:14], "Israel, if you remove these offenses from you, you will not fall?"

Gentiles cannot offend when they do that by which they cause their own destruction, which is to hold something in their right hand without acknowledging that they hold folly in their right hand [Isa

44:20]. It all depends on the offense.[32]

Therefore one ought to remove quickly anything that has been erected to offend and corrupt the neighbor; one must not go slowly. For this reason God sent an angel to the Jews to let them know this interpretation: I brought you out of Egypt into this land which I had promised to your fathers so that you might strongly adhere to my covenant and not nullify it. And I imposed on you [94] not to enter into a covenant with the Gentiles. Rather, you were to overthrow all their altars. But you did not heed my voice, etc. These stories show clearly that the Jews were neither to enter into covenants with the Gentiles nor to go slowly in overthrowing altars and that God persecuted them and harmed them because they were negligent. God is wise enough and will add to what he said, when and where one is to go slowly, and not quickly or suddenly. It is therefore a great and anti-Christian sacrilege to fault God's wisdom and to add something to his words, especially when the addition is contrary to God's will and serves to harm the neighbor's soul, and where they say, "There and here one ought to wait and go easy because of the weak," although God never said that we are to go slowly and gradually. This is especially so when, because of our slowness, the weak are led further from the truth and into grave error. It is written [Deut 27:18], "Cursed be the one who confounds a blind person on the way." How much more cursed is the one who confuses the blind soul with regard to God's way and word. And this is done by everyone who leaves standing an offense for his brother, be it a mousetrap or the devil's lures. Blessed, on the other hand, the one who removes what might destroy his brother, even against his will, thus saddening the one for whom he is doing a good deed, so that he might benefit him—just as a father will anger the child whom he loves when he removes a sharp knife from his hand.

With regard to offenses in the faith, the one who has a strong spirit which is able to endure a great deal would wish to tear out, throw down and break before he preaches like Gideon, although he was timid and broke the altar of Baal during the night [Judg 6]. Nonetheless, I say that it is unnecessary to attack public offenses through preaching before the deed is done. This is indicated by Gideon's action, or by Asa who sweeps out abominable idols and dethrones his mother; by Jehoshaphat, Jehu, Hezekiah, Zedekiah [2 Chr 12; 2 Kings 15], or by promises, as was the case with Shadrach, Meshach, and Abednego [Dan 3] and by many others. For though Paul and Barnabas had short sermons, they were nonetheless not bound by their example even though they might have preached many a long sermon.

The example of Christ is as strong as theirs. He drove the buyers out of the temple immediately, saying at the same moment, "Why do you turn my Father's house [95] into a den of thieves or a market place?" Look to God's commandments and teaching and you will find this. Destroy all places at which the Gentiles (whom you shall conquer) served their idols—be it on hills or mountains or under green trees—break up and devastate, do away with, etc. God never commanded the Jews to first preach to the Gentiles ere they removed their idols. And what more than double Gentiles are our idolatrous Christians? It is unnecessary to teach them first before removing from them what might destroy them. Even though they may be angry now, they will rejoice later. God did not order the Jews to do it in the entire world, but only in the places which they were to conquer and in which they were to rule. Accordingly, the conclusion is that where Christians rule, they are not to look to any magistrate, but are to strike out freely and of their own and throw down whatever is against God even without preaching. Such offenses are numerous such as the mass, images, meat offered to idols which the priests now devour, and the like. But in a case in which a matter is based on the figurative sayings by God, one ought to preach first to indicate the hidden and steadfast will of God before one acts contrary to some Scripture or at least at the same time or shortly after, if there are likely any people who might be offended by the example that goes against Scripture and who might report reasons for the new example. This is as Christ did when his disciples broke the Sabbath according to the external letter and appearance and as Stephen did when he spoke against the temple, or Peter when he baptized Cornelius, or like Paul when speaking and acting against circumcision, and so on. All of them expounded the law of God as the prophets had done.

It is for this reason that Paul wants to be considerate of the weak i.e., of those who lack understanding. But at this point I want to ask why Paul did not allow the Galatians to be circumcised until they and others were strong or wise enough? Human tradition may well be broken when it is not rooted in divine truth, although we must not suppress it in any other way than by the word of Christ. Every single plant which my father did not plant shall be torn up. Human statutes are the dung which the Jews had to carry outside their dwellings to bury them there. Whatever God has prohibited, which causes us to sin against him and corrupts the neighbor, must be removed—the sooner, the better. [96] Thus we serve God and benefit the neighbor, even if he should complain and object because of it. It results in our seeking his best; God help us to that. Amen.

Of the many other offenses I shall prepare a small special booklet, since I can see a need for it.[33] There I will show clearly that the very persons who clamor daily to go easy on the weak so as not to cause offense, are the worst offenders and aggravate the sick most of all. [97]

FINIS

Three Peasants in Conversation, engraving by Albrecht Dürer.

11

Dialogue or Discussion Booklet on the Infamous and Idolatrous Abuse of the Most Blessed Sacrament of Jesus Christ

Andreas Carlstadt [Carolstat]

1524

Carlstadt's polemical writings focus on the alleged abuses that had turned the simple "meal of remembrance" instituted by Jesus into an "idolatrous mass." Such strong attacks against traditionalists and reformers alike were not to go unchallenged. The published debates were caustic enough to elicit reactions from several individuals.

The Strasbourg preacher Wolfgang Capito published a tract toward the end of October 1524 in which he wondered, "What we are to make of the split between Martin Luther and Andreas Carlstadt." [Was man halten und antworten soll . . .].

Valentin Ickelsamer, a friend of both Carlstadt and Schwenckfeld, on the other hand, published "A Complaint About the Injustice Perpetrated on Carlstadt by Luther." The tract repeats succinctly some of the complaints Carlstadt himself had voiced earlier against unfair treat-

ment by the authorities which he believed Luther to have instigated.

*However, Luther's rather virulent "Against the Heavenly Prophets" was still to come, but the battle lines were drawn and the gloves were off. The tract was printed three times in Basel, Bamberg, and Strasbourg. It is one of Carlstadt's most extensive tracts from this period. Freys/Barge list two editions of this tract. Cf. number 126 and 127. But see A. Zorzin, **Karlstadt als Flugschriftenautor**, p. 105. Erich Hertzsch reprinted the tract in his edition of Carlstadt publications from the years 1523-25. An English translation by Carter Lindberg was published in MQR 53 (1979). Our translation is based on the Hertzsch text.*

I wish for all true believers in Christ the grace and knowledge of God.

No one, my dear brothers, must think that I write from impertinence and insolence about the anti-Christian use of the most Blessed Sacrament in an unheard-of manner, though I am fully aware that the majority will think that I sought nothing but innovation and strangeness—all the more since this my work stands over against so many thousand scribes; especially since the princes of these highly learned and Scripture-wise people adhere to the old papistical abuse. Common people run after them and dance up and down according to their tune, considering everything they hear from these Scripture-wise people to be a firm foundation of righteousness. They think that they always do the right thing when they sing the tune of those highly learned precentors or dance according to their tune and babble what they do, saying "yes and amen" to each bit of their advice. Now if these bound consciences were to free themselves of some of their bonds, allowing these personages who are esteemed by the world to pass by and if instead they were to cling to the unsullied truth and would recall that it is unseemly and wanton to direct the truth according to human bogeys or to judge Scripture by what people think, they would never again trust in the arm of a person but rely on the unerring foundation of truth. They would thus attain eternal peace and drink from the water which Christ gives and which fully satisfies them and springs forth unto eternal life. I desire that the truth be seriously considered, and I have no doubt at all that many would then think the better of it and receive said sacrament more worthily than it has been received up to now.

And if you, brothers, could take to heart how divine love, along with faith, hope, and trust in [7] God, is cut off, disappears, and comes to nought because of the abuse of all external well-intentioned signs, everyone would say that it was neither impertinence nor innovation nor self-glory nor anything else that called and brought me to this labor. Rather, it was simply the fact that through the false use of the sacrament, God's love has been extinguished, faith obstructed, and the consciences imprisoned because of this awful error, who sought by long-cherished practices to confirm themselves in God's love and faith and rid themselves of all anxieties.

God understands all things better than we, no matter how clever we are or may become. For this reason he has often suspended the use of external things or fully prohibited it, though he himself instituted these things, for he could see how the simple were offended by them because of their ignorance. Thus God rejected sacrifice, fire, smoke, temples, the serpent, and the ark, [2 Kings 18:4] saying, "What do I care for your sacrifice and your incense?" [Isa 1:11]. What does it mean when you say, 'The temple of God, the temple of God, the temple of God'? You shall not name the ark again [Jer 3:16]. Hezekiah removed and smashed the uplifted serpent because of the abuse, quite apart from the fact that God himself had erected it and that it had been a peculiar sign of the body of Christ who was to be given into the hands of evildoers and nailed to the cross. What, my brothers, do you think that we should do, we who see so many abominable abuses of the most Blessed Sacrament; we who understand how miserable and blind Christians treat and handle the sacrament so that they fall into the error of treating the host as if Christ had suffered in it for our sin? Or as if Christ washes and forgives our sin in the host? Or as if Christ remains eternally with us in the sacrament? We can see that some celebrate the sacrament more than they do the death which Jesus Christ endured. My material may appear new to you. But I intend to present the truth to you as I would present it before the eyes of God and before his severe judgment seat. I therefore admonish you by the obligation of your oaths not to look either to me or to anyone else except only to the foundation of my booklet, and to judge the truth in itself earnestly and wisely. [8]

You must not think that I berate you or seek a diversion in creating a dialogue booklet. I am greatly concerned with your salvation and take the matter most seriously. I therefore invented persons who for the sake of brevity dialogue with each other about the sacrament. In such a conversation the arguments can be kept shorter than in a single straightforward speech. You ought to know then that I sought brevity, your benefit, and, above all else, the glory and honor of God and not derision or diversion. It is up to you to apply great diligence to each of the points and to ask God to keep and protect us, through the discernment of his truth, from all forms of dishonoring him which are most prominently contrary to God in a perverse mind and will.

(Dialogue partners: Gemser [Gem], Victus [Vic], and Peter [Pet], a lay person)[1]

Gem: Dear brother Vic, why are you so downcast?

Vic: What is the use of complaining to you? You cannot help me in any case.

Gem: Do you not know that it is written, "When in anxiety, call on a saint"? When in need, you ought to call on a saint.[2]

Vic: Someone who was a companion just like you must have said that, wishing to turn disconsolate Job away from God and cause him to flee to creatures. And methinks that you are more devious than he was, for your advice suggests that I should flee to you as if you were a saint.

Gem: What harm in that?

Vic: A great deal. For you are immersed in sacramental teachings and you take that to be a sign of health which to me is a sickness and an abominable ulcer.

Gem: I sense that you have doubts regarding the sacraments.

Vic: You have found me out.

Gem: We have seven sacraments. Which of them gives you trouble?

Vic: I know neither of one nor of seven sacraments.

Gem: Well, well.

Vic: I do not know what sort of word "sacrament" is, much less what it means. It is possible therefore that I might err or stumble, as Aristotle says, *Ignorantes virtutes herbarum defacile*—those who are ignorant of the virtues of herbs, easily....[3]

Gem: *Sacramentum* is a Latin and not a Greek word, although the Jews claim that it is a Hebrew word which in German means a false, fabricated image. *Seker* [9] in their language means false, fabricated and useless. *Ment* allegedly means image.

Vic: I thought you were an advocate of the sacraments and you turn out to be a scoffer.

Gem: I informed you of what the Jews say about the word sacrament and wanted you to know what it means in Latin, but you interrupt me like a peasant and try to put me to shame.

Vic: Your speech and your facial expressions appear as if your mind was in tune with that of the Jews.

Gem: God help and protect me!

Vic: What then does the word "sacrament" mean?

Gem: *Sacramentum* is a Latin word which in plain German means a sign of a holy thing, as the master of the lofty mind teaches, saying *sacramentum est sacre rei signum*—sacrament is the sign of a holy thing. The Latins say *hoc est sacramentum militare, hoc castrense, nihil ad propositum*—this is the oath of a soldier; it pertains to a camp and has nothing to do with the subject.

Vic: You are master of lofty thoughts—one of those who do not think highly of God's word and to whom God does not reveal too many things. In fact, God hates them and corrupts their minds and wisdom. I prefer to have a good, clear biblical word.

Gem: *Hoc sacramentum magnum est* [This sacrament is important].

Vic: Rhyme *Eisenhut* and foot. You know full well that our old translations have many invented words which are inappropriate to the Greek and Hebrew and that the sentences of our Latin Bible at times are not in agreement with the original tongue. You cannot therefore dismiss me with poor words; introduce me to these languages as Jerome teaches.

Gem: The Christian church uses that particular word.

Vic: That's why I want to know how the term "sacrament" is rooted in the word by which the church lives, and for that reason I want a divine and true foundation.

Gem: We have seven sacraments. Among these one is the greatest and most unsurpassed, namely the sacrament of the body and blood of Christ.

Vic: God delights in his words, as the prophet Nehemiah says. Tell me therefore, whether God, a prophet, or an apostle uses the term sacrament pertaining to the things you call sacraments. God always gives his creatures their own proper name.

Gem: God led all animals to Adam and had them named by Adam.

Vic: Is this why you intend to give to the church the power to name stories and works as Adam named the animals?

Gem: Right and proper.

Vic: Improper and wrong; it is much too slow. [10]

Gem: How too slow?

Vic: Christ and the apostles named baptism and Lord's Supper long before the high-minded church came to be in existence. You tarried and were born too late.[4]

Gem: We have the same powers Adam had.

Vic: I conclude then that you have the power to call white "black" and evil "good," thus to correct Christ and his apostles, as you have done for several hundred years now, though Adam never had such power, or ever used it.

Gem: *Propter bonum sensum* [On account of good sense].

Vic: Thus the apostles and Christ must have had a poor mind and understanding; nor could the apostles and Christ have been clever enough to name correctly those things which you call sacraments.

Gem: I gather you are vexed by the names.

Vic: Not for myself, but because of the sick and weak who are led onto thin ice with such words and are prevented from advancing and coming to God. One or the other has to be the case: either Christ was not clever enough or else not graciously sufficient enough when he instituted the Lord's Supper and omitted to leave behind the information that his bread and chalice were to be called a sacrament or a sign of holy things—though when understood aright one might allow that baptism, bread and wine be called signs of the things they represented at the time of the apostles, Rom 6; 1 Cor 10. If you papists would leave such interpretation alone, there would be no danger.

Gem: You discovered your sickness, Victus.

Vic: Let me hear it.

Gem: You are downcast on account of the most Blessed Sacrament.

Vic: If you hit home, I'll shout.

Gem: You are worried whether Christ in his humanity is in the sacrament.

Vic: You guessed it. For to ask whether Christ according to his divinity is here or there is to ask whether Christ is in every creature according to his divinity. That is nonsense, for God is in hell as well as in heaven and fills all of creation.

Gem: The priests declare the bread to be nothing. They retain only the form of the bread and put the body of Christ into it in place of the bread.

Vic: I perceive that it is not *sacramentum*, but *fermentum* of the Pharisees. For the shape of the bread always remains small or big or thick—in every way as before [11] the priests breathed or blew on it, chattering like geese. I ask then whether the body, arms, chest, thighs, and legs, along with the crown of thorns, the nails, and the spear are in the piece of bread which is smaller than the size of Christ's baby finger?

Gem: Yes.

Vic: Does he have to make himself small and distort himself, then, when the priests blast forth these words?

Gem: What kind of pontificating is this! [*was pfaffestu*]? [5]

Vic: I doubt, therefore I ask.

Gem: You should not scold.

Vic: I do not know what other words to use.

Gem. We must not probe.

Vic: That's what you priests say when you are not sure of your case. But I think that if what you are saying is true, we ought to search the Scriptures and find those which testify of Christ, for Scripture praises the Thessalonians because they searched. For if the Scriptures report on other matters pertaining to Christ and teach us how Christ was miraculously conceived by the Holy Spirit in his mother's womb and how he lived and spoke, suffered and died, was raised and ascended to heaven, Scripture should also tell us how Christ is in the sacrament, which is as miraculous as any one of the things of which it speaks.

Gem: Where I shall go to, you do not know, says Christ.

Vic: Duck, you are about to hit your head.

Gem: Is it not fitting?

Vic: Just as fitting as the saying that one ought to preach long enough for the carved, molten, or painted idols to run out of church; but one must not lay hands on them before that.

Gem: In such things one should not investigate.

Vic: Why then does the truth bid us to search the Scriptures and in another place say, My lambs hear my voice, but the voice of a stranger they do not hear? And again, You are not to hear the words of false prophets, but the word of God we are to study day and night. You never said to a single stone or piece of wood that Christ is in the host when he was on the cross.

Gem: The body of Christ is as fully in the host as he was hanging on the cross.

Vic: Your tune is like that of a raven. Yet I am unable to believe it. I would be more prepared to believe that the body of Christ is as small in the host as it was when he was conceived or born. But I believe neither unless, of course, you can present me with the word of faith. For if I were to trust your wind, my case would be worse than that of a reed. [12]

Gem: How so?

Vic: A reed only has twelve or thirteen winds that blow at it. I, however, would have to endure as many winds as there are heads were I to hear and believe every priest.

Gem: Anyone who does not believe is condemned.

Vic: Shout yourself hoarse. I believe in Christ, his suffering, and in all his words. Anyone who does not believe in Christ is condemned. Show me Christ's word or a letter of faith in the Bible which says that the body of Christ is in a small host and see whether I will not believe.

Gem: You are tied to the Bible.

Vic: I seek God in the Bible and not Scripture in writings.

Gem: What good then is Scripture to you?

Vic: As a testimony of the truth.

Gem: Let us talk Greek, Hebrew, and Latin.

Vic: Do you know these tongues?

Gem: If need be.

Vic: What need is there?

Gem: Don't you see the peasant behind us? He eagerly laps up every word and speech we make and weighs each one.

Vic: Is that so bad?

Gem: It is quite bad. All the lay people first come into their Christian freedom and then do not give a farthing any more for a priest with regard to a sacrament.

Vic: I gather that you have something in your quiver which you could and should empty out.

Gem: I do not complain, for you can see that God now makes several revelations to the simple which he hides from the wise.

Vic: Are you interfering with God's power?

Gem: In no way! But I should like to save my honor and my uppermost position.

Vic: Instruct me. I shall be as silent as a watermill.

Gem: The text *Hoc est corpus meum* ["this is my body"] was understood for a long time to mean "this bread is my body" as if it were *Hoc panis est corpus meum*; but the Latin does not sustain that.

Vic: Is that not the text with which the priests—the old and new papists alike—patch and mend, and behind which they cover and hide, trying to preserve that Christ's body is in the bread and his blood is in the chalice?

Gem: You hit on it.

Vic: Have you perchance covered yourself with the cloak of a fool?

Gem: Don't scold me and I will tell you an amazing thing.

Vic: You are a learned scribe.

Gem: I am kidding.

Vic: You can't back out.

Gem: Why not?

Vic: The verse "This is my body which is given for you" is a perfect saying which Christ placed in the Gospels alone, though in different words. [13] But there he did not speak of the sacrament; see Mt 16, Jn 3 and 6.

Gem: Prove that.

Vic: Easily. The pronoun *hoc* is capitalized. And a capital letter means the beginning of a new sentence and verse. Thus this verse has been inserted in our Lord's speech about bread, as one happens to insert something which enhances a speech or sermon, though it is complete in itself.

Gem: What then is the purpose of this verse?

Vic: So that the disciples might learn what the remembrance is based on, in which the Lord ordered his bread to be eaten.

Gem: But where did Christ speak about his body to be given for us which now has been given?

Vic: In all the prophets and gospels which speak of his suffering.

Gem: This does not ring true.

Vic: The old violins and the pope's laws and practices and your honor have filled your ears with creaturely thundering, that's why you cannot hear anything. Why don't you clean out your ears and instead offer cleaned and free ears to God's speaking and then see whether what I have just told you does not ring true for you.

Gem: It is hard to abandon old habits and one's honor.

Vic: That's why the way to the kingdom of heaven is narrow and bitter.

Gem: Since you have started this, keep going.

Vic: I should learn from you.

Gem: Go on from here.

Vic: Greek serves this separation well, as it does the verse in its entirety. It shows it to be a special verse by dividing, *hoc est corpus meum*, etc., through punctuation and letters, much better than the Latin.

Gem: *Vide quomodo omnia rusticus ille perpendit*—See how the peasant carefully ponders on everything.

Vic: Why don't you search and read and I'll listen.

Gem: *Touto estin to soma mou*—this is my body.

[Vic]: Translate these words.

Gem: *Istud est hoc corpus meum, quod pro vobis, etc.*[6]—This is my body, broken for you.

Vic: Give it to me in German.

Gem: Don't you see how this peasant stands open-mouthed, as if he is about to swallow every word we are saying?

Vic: That's why you must talk German.

Gem: It is no good when we make all these things known to lay persons. Before too long, peasants will be as important as priests.

Vic: That does not harm me or you. I bet you that a God-fearing person would love you on account of the truth. But even without that you should testify to God's righteousness to your own hurt, yes, even by your death.

Gem: In [14] hopes of that I say that I would translate it into German as follows, *Tuto* [*sic!*] is "my body which, etc." It would have been helpful had one left the Greek pronoun *tuto* and mingled it with the Latin.

Vic: Why?

Gem: So that one might have read it as follows: *Tuto est hoc corpus meum*—this is my body.

Vic: I am asking why?

Gem: People would then have wondered what the word *tuto* is.

Vic: This would not have been inopportune for the priests.

Gem: All the better.

Vic: You always want to trod the path of the priests.

Gem: Are you making fun?

Vic: I have reasons. For it would have been questionable or a delusion had there perchance been a thing called *tuto* which very same thing would have had to be the body of Christ.

Gem: Would it have mattered?

Vic: Quite a bit. You priests would have tried to convince us laypersons that Christ had I-don't-know-what at that Supper which he then transformed into his body and to which we would then have attached silver and gold.

Gem: You must not believe that.

Vic: Not believe? I see clearly what you have made of the cup and how you insist that you must have gold and silver vessels, thus drawing silver and gold out of our pockets.

Gem: As far as I am concerned, I should like to inform you and let you know that *tuto* is a Greek pronoun.

Vic: Who knows what you might have done had the old women brought their nickels and dimes.

Gem: I am much too righteous for that.

Vic: But greedy people and fools would actually have turned the small word *tuto* into a box of silver or gold.

Gem: It would still have been a fine speech. *Tuto* is my body, as all the evangelists have it.

Vic: But what do you make of the Greek reading and what does it mean in German?

Gem: *Tuto estin to soma mu,* etc—This is my body, etc.

Vic: Speak German.

Gem: Hush, be quiet, say nothing. The peasant might take note, *quia verba sunt apertissime contra nos sacerdotes*—for these words are most clearly against us priests.

The layman Peter: Dear gentlemen; I take leave to speak. Do not take it amiss when I ask, but I gather that you are discussing the body and blood of the Lord and the bread and cup.

Gem: *Prius, O Victe, dixi de rustico quod audiret et ruminaret verba nostra*—I said before, O Victus, that the peasant would hear and chew over our words.

Vic: What harm is there?

Pet: Dear gentlemen, I note that you are quarreling about a small word with which I am not that familiar.

Vic: That's why you should speak German, Gemser, and tell us what *touto estin to soma mou, to uper umon didomenon*—this is my body which has been given for you—means in German.

Pet: I too desire this [15] greatly.

Gem: *Tuto* means "my body which is given for you."

Pet: That's a rather strange saying.

Vic: Truly a rather mixed saying.

Pet: I will ask and hear whether or not you are able to enlighten me.

Gem: If it appears like this and when "*tuto* is my body, etc.," is translated thus, it is all right.

Vic: What if some had come and said that *tuto* means "golden bread," just as you have turned "chalice" into "golden drinking vessel"?

Pet: Dear gentlemen, speak more intelligibly and in good German, for though I understand you up to a point, I do not understand you fully.

Gem: In plain German the Greek statement means the following:

This is my body which was given for you, etc. But it seems that it is better to leave the pronoun *tuto* as is and as I said.

Pet: But it would sound funny.

Gem: Each language or tongue has its own peculiarities which one cannot translate in another language. When we want to stress the peculiarity of a foreign language, we must use the terms of that language; that's why we have so many Latin terms in the language of chancery. So now too we took recourse to the Latin and Greek tongue, but will have to speak to you of the hidden content and meaning of both. Yet we are forced to speak to you by means of Latin and Greek terms.

Pet: Go on. Who knows whether I will be able to note anything. I am defeated by Greek, Hebrew, and Latin tables, and I seem to learn less than I forget.

Gem: Did you understand what we said? You are probably peeved and annoyed with us.

Pet: Speak for yourself.

Gem: Greek has articles and pronouns which show the nominative; they inform us so that we can clearly see which word belongs to the article or pronoun and which does not.

Pet: This looks like quite something. Go on.

Gem: *Touto* is a Greek pronoun which indicates the neuter of a name. Now the term *artos, panis* in Latin, "bread" in German, is masculine. Thus the pronoun *otutr* [*sic*!] cannot be applied to it; nor will it sustain the opinion of some who say that bread is the body, etc. For Greek does not allow for it any more than it is proper to say in Latin, "*istud panis est hoc corpus meum*" or in German, "*Der brot* is my body."[7]

Pet: That's good.

Gem: [16] Do you like it?

Pet: Yes, indeed. For I could not find out for the longest time how it might be that *das brot* could have become *der leib* of Christ. I always figured that Christ pointed to his body when he said, This is my body which is given for you. For Christ did not point to the bread, nor did he say "the bread is my body, given for you." But those who say that the bread is the body speak on their own and they lie or else they are mischievous, to say the least. Give heed. Jesus took bread and gave thanks to God and broke it and gave it to his disciples, saying that they are to eat it in remembrance of him, establishing in the midst of his saying the reason for and manner of this remembrance, namely, for the reason and in the manner that his disciples were to recall that he had given his body for them. Paul holds this position strongly and anyone who teaches differently perverts God's word and is a perverse person.

Gem: Who taught you this?

Pet: The one whose voice I hear yet whom I do not see and of whom I do not know how he came to me and how he left me.

Gem: Who is this?

Pet: Our Father in heaven.

Gem: If only I too had learned this from him.

Pet: Was it not you who promised his spirit? Aren't you the poor person who gives the living voice of God a creaturely form?

Gem: At one time, but not now.

Pet: If you really have a sincere delight in righteousness as righteousness and a passionate heart to boot, then the Greek Scriptures, which you have just read, is a welcome gift to you.

Gem: What assurance did you recall that you relied so heavily on your delusion and remained in it until now?

Pet: I suffer no delusion, but I have truth and certainty and I can assure you that the text is true.

Gem: That's why I am asking about assurances.

Pet: If Christ is to have redeemed us through his body when he was one with the bread, as you say, Christ would have suffered in the host or in the bread or with the bread. Without bread he would never have been on the cross, nor could he have suffered other than in the bread which is all openly wrong.

Gem: Who ever said so?

Pet: All those say so (though in ignorance) who say that the body of Christ was united with the bread or in the bread or under the form of bread.

Gem: How does it follow?

Pet: They speak as follows, Christ [17] said, "The bread is the body which was given for you." Is not this saying as much as the bread is given for you and shall suffer, or my body under the bread, or my body which is the bread is given for you? And does not this sound like my body shall not be given for you unless it has become bread or when it has come in the form of bread? From this follows that Christ suffered secretly and in hiding just as he is secretly and hidden in the sacrament, which is contrary to God's truth and all the prophets. It follows further that Christ did not give his body for us on the cross, for you priests are unable to produce a person who at the same time would have brought the body of Christ into the bread. If you intend to show Christ, tell me how he took bread when his hands were nailed to the cross? If you intend to single out an apostle, then prove this and show that the apostles consecrated the sacrament at that time as you say when they were all scattered and had fled their Shepherd and when they were offended at Christ? Thirdly, it would have to follow that a loaf of bread baked by a baker would have had to be the body of which Scripture writes so often that it was to have been given for us. This, however, would be in stark contradiction of all Scripture.

Gem: If you were so sure of your case, how is it then that you were so happy when I told you what the Greek meant?

Pet: Because I received an external testimony through which I may now lift up and edify the fallen, and silence and overcome those who resist. As for myself I did not need the external testimony. I should like to have my testimony which Christ promised through the spirit in my innermost self.

Gem: Where?

Pet: Do you still not know that Christ speaks as follows, "The Spirit, the Comforter, shall testify for you and you too shall testify of me."[8] This is what happened to the apostles who were assured inwardly through the testimony of the Spirit and who then preached Christ externally, confirming through the Scriptures that Christ had to suffer for us and that the same Christ Jesus of Nazareth was the crucified.[9]

Gem: This was spoken by the apostles?

Pet: If we were not to be like the apostles, why then does Peter say of [18] Cornelius that he had received the Spirit as they had?[10] Why does Paul say that we ought to be his followers? And did not Christ promise his Spirit to us as he did to the apostles? The Spirit alone leads us to an understanding of what God says. It follows therefore that all those cannot understand what God says who do not hear God's Spirit speak. Nor are they Christians, as Christ says. All those are Christ's who have the Spirit of Christ. Therefore God's Spirit alone testifies and assures, Rom 8:16. This is the reason why God's Spirit is called a pledge, *arra* and *arrabo*.

Gem: Note, when the Spirit testifies, you too are to testify. Why then did you not bring your understanding to the light of day before this?

Pet: The Spirit does not drive me fast enough. Had he driven and convicted me more forcefully I should have kept back or hidden much less than if I had a devouring fire in my bones. At times the Spirit has to be kept hidden on account of his honor and at times one has to struggle with externally accepted testimonies. I know right well that you and all the world, especially those "Scripture-wise" types, laughed at me saying that I was an enthusiast when I would have preferred to break away. But now that the tongues have become more cunning and vulgar, I should give those skilled talkers their own medicine.

Gem: Because you speak so earnestly and sincerely on behalf of divine truth, I, in turn, will let you know that the proclamation "This is my body which is given for you" is contained within periods; it has periods at the beginning and the end.

Pet: Does this suit what I said?

Gem: It is extremely good.

Pet: Why then did you not tell me earlier?

Gem: I was afraid of the rage of certain princes who claim to be well versed in Scripture though they read little or nothing of it.

Pet: You are to give joyful testimony of what God says.

Gem: I lacked the fortitude of spirit. Furthermore, I paid little heed earlier to what I now treat with great respect.

Pet: We are to be watchful and do nothing in haste and look carefully at full stops and other things with leisure and diligence.

Gem: Nor must I hide from you the fact that the saying "This is my body, etc." begins with a capital letter in Luke. By this is indicated that the line "This is my body which is given for you" is not connected to the preceding words, but is a self-contained speech.

Pet: The kind that God might often have spoken to himself?

Gem: Yes, yes; this is why [19] I almost have to agree with you and confess that Christ simply said, "This is my body," pointing to his own body and not to a loaf of bread.

Pet: If you can suggest anything to the contrary and overcome or undermine the reasons I have advanced, do so.

Gem: Though I cannot say anything against them, I will not be silent, either.

Pet: Let us continue and further discuss the matter of how one eats Christ's bread worthily and how his body is given.

Gem: Tell me what it means to say my body is given for you? When, how, why is it given? Is this a unique way of speaking and not at all united with or tied to the bread as you and Victus said and as I have to confess.

Pet: Are you to have partaken of the Lord's bread and cup as dogs eat grass?

Gem: My dear, don't make fun of me.

Pet: Anyone who does not eat the Lord's bread worthily spews out the body of Christ and is guilty of the Lord's body.

Gem: I am a priest who prepared and offered it in the sacrament.

Pet: Aha. Four boots in a dung heap. Shame on you, you forgotten priest.

Gem: Are you slapping my wrist?

Pet: Of course and gladly.

Gem: Why?

Pet: Because you are so stark blind and because you do not know that the priests have murdered Christ.

Gem: We are talking about receiving the sacrament worthily.

Pet: I thought we were to talk of the handing over of the body of Christ.

Gem: Not long before this you said that these two articles should be handled together.

Pet: I concede that point.

Gem: Why do you accuse me as if until now I had eaten the sacrament unworthily?

Pet: You claim to be thoroughly Pauline and do not know that?

Gem: I often eat mustard so that my eyes start running and the sweat pours forth, but I hang tough, nonetheless.

Pet: You are a courtier and you are able to ignore and keep silent when you are ridiculed.

Gem: Come on, tell me why you said that I ate the Lord's bread unworthily?

Pet: O you Paulinist! Yet, you do not know what all of Christendom harps on, which is that everyone is to eat the bread of the Lord in the light and discernment of the body of the Lord? And if anyone eats without the knowledge of the body of Christ, he is guilty of the body of Christ.[11]

Gem: Clever!

Pet: How so?

Gem: I was going to use the words of Paul regarding the eating of the Lord's bread without discernment against you, to trip you up and to get the better of you, [20] so that you would have to confess that the body of Christ is under the sacrament and that we must bow down before the sacrament and bring it divine honor and that we are obligated to do everything which Christians now do. But you are crafty and escape from the battlefield, undertaking to beat me with my own defenses.

Pet: I beg to differ on the term "crafty." For I fight you in truth and not with cunning. But in a thorough housecleaning it should soon become clear whether these words of Paul belong to and serve you or me.

Gem: Don't make fun of me for I have letters from Wittenberg.

Pet: Nonetheless it is ridiculous and disgraceful that you should boast with Paul as if he were exclusively yours alone. You bank firmly on this and boast of him daily without knowing what you are dealing with. Were I to keep silent, the dead Quintus Mutius[12] might rise and say, It is unbecoming such a brave man who seeks to be true to the gospel not to see and understand Paul correctly when he speaks and writes of him daily.

Gem: Do you think that I do not understand Paul?

Pet: The constellation suggests ignorance and blindness.

Gem: Allow me to bring Paul against you.

Pet: On with it!

Gem: Everyone is to eat the bread of the Lord worthily. Whoever eats it unworthily is guilty of the body of Christ; and whoever drinks the cup of the Lord unworthily drinks judgment [upon himself], 1 Cor 11:29.

Pet: What's so new in that? Solomon said that better when he stated, Whoever eats the king's bread is to eat it in great fear and reverence so that he does not arouse the king's anger. If I were eating with a prince, though I were to eat my own bread or such bread as I have, I would have to sit with greater respect and eat more politely and with greater caution and modesty than if I were in my own house. How much more then should I eat with due respect the bread of the most supreme king, my Lord Jesus Christ, who allowed himself to be killed for my sake though he was innocent?

Gem: To eat the bread of the Lord worthily means that I ought to know what kind of bread it is and how it is the bread of the Lord and how the Lord is in and under the bread. I ought to beat my breast, honor him, fall on my knees and anticipate and receive with certainty forgiveness of sins through the sacrament, as I receive the sacrament. I must let go of all my doubt [21], depend on and be comforted by this.

Pet: You took hold of the sword by its edge, and you show me its sheath. The faster you fight with it, the deeper you wound yourself.

Gem: How come?

Pet: Anyone who abuses God's word uses it to his own detriment.

Gem: But I use it properly.

Pet: According to a priestly and popish rule.

Gem: Isn't that good?

Pet: It is evil and devilish.

Gem: Why?

Pet: Because such person robs God of his honor and glory like a thief. He opposes the truth, ravaging Paul's teaching and causing people to be irrational.

Gem: You are an enthusiast.

Pet: I'd rather be an enthusiast in your eyes but true and wise before God.

Gem: You have made quite a few points. Tell me then why the pope's teaching makes people irrational in this case?

Pet: When wise persons eat the bread of great lords at the table of great lords they never fear the bread. Nor do they bow to the food, but they bow to the lord; they are respectful of and behave fittingly toward the lord. They do not look what kind of bread it is but wonder why and how they come to eat with the king. Now the pope expects this of those who eat with him. But when he speaks of the bread of Christ, he talks of how we are to know, honor, and respectfully eat the bread, though we should never think of Christ. Now this has to be a stupid way and that's why [we say] that the pope creates silly people. He teaches how they are to clean their teeth and rinse their mouth; but this antichrist does not teach how they are to look to and honor the body of the Lord.

Gem: How does he rob God of his honor?

Pet: Like a thief.

Gem: Why?

Pet: Because he says that we are to say to the form of bread, My God, be merciful toward me.

Gem: Do you have anything else to say?

Pet: The pope nullifies and turns to naught the suffering of Christ.

Gem: In which way?

Pet: If Christ has forgiven our sin and redeemed us in the form of the bread, then his death on the cross was for nothing.

Gem: How does the pope contradict the truth?

Pet: He says that we ought to be mindful of the bread which Christ never bid us do. And he causes us to forget the body of our Lord which we are to remember whenever we eat the bread of the Lord. Therefore no one but the papal lot has ever eaten the bread of the Lord more unworthily.

Gem: Did you not eat the bread of the Lord according to the pope's institution of it?

Pet: Not in twenty years.

Gem: How did you come by [22] such great fortune?

Pet: I was under the papal ban to my own salvation and learned what is written, I will speak well of their ban and condemnation.

Gem: How does the pope destroy the teaching of Paul?

Pet: Paul applied greatest diligence that he might clarify and hold before us the death of the Lord. This the pope tears down, presenting us with his form of the bread instead. He elevates it so high that we forget the body and death of the Lord for all the fear and concern and knowledge of its form. We come to regard as nothing all that the Lord suffered on the cross, though we ought to esteem it most highly. Paul, on the other hand, keeps us sane as he instructs us that we are to enjoy the Lord whom we do not see and the bread and wine which we neither see nor feel, in the fear of the Lord as the food of the most supreme Lord.

Gem: Now I know that remembering makes one worthy.

Pet: You have to add something else.

Gem: I have a wonderful memory in view of the fact that I think the form of the bread to be the body of Christ.

Pet: Did Christ command you such a remembrance? Does he say, Do this in memory of me or does he say, Do this in remembrance of the sacrament? Or, in remembrance of the form of bread under which my body is? Did you not say yourself that the pronoun *hoc* does not refer to the word *panis*? Does not Christ intend to say that we are to remember his body which was given for us? Is this form of bread that you talk about given for us also? Has it been crucified and did it die? If we lay persons should confess to that, we would be as bad as the worst priests. You are a priest, and you must sense what will be your portion.

Gem: Go easy on me.

Pet: Go easy yourself. We are not fighting over money, but for the truth.

Gem: All my life I heard again and again how we are to get ready and prepare that we might receive the sacrament and the body of Christ. Thus I took one for the other as did those from whom I heard it all.

Pet: We do not speak either of your preachers or of your hearing. We are simply discussing whether you heard correctly or not. If you insist that you speak correctly you would have to show through divine righteousness and truth that it is right. Without that I shan't believe you.

Gem: My, how often have I heard "prepare yourselves worthily to [23] receive the body of Christ worthily."

Pet: I readily believe that. But give me just one word of Christ or one of the apostles who speaks in that way. I know that Christ did not give his body anywhere to receive it, as our subsequent discussion shall show. Christ further says that his flesh is of no avail to us. But he also says, It is good for you that I leave you, for if I do not go the Comforter will not come. If all this is true, then it is equally true that we do not receive the body of Christ either naturally or sacramentally.

Gem: Make that clearer.

Pet: Did Christ say anywhere, Receive my body, as he did say, Take bread and eat, etc.? Therefore your dried-up preachers[13] would have preached more fittingly had they said, "See to it that you receive and eat the bread of the Lord worthily," as Paul preaches.

Gem: Is it not written that unless you eat the flesh of the Son of man and drink his blood, no life is in you?

Pet: Did Christ say that when he said, Take the bread and eat, etc.?

Gem: No. But it is written elsewhere.

Pet: Yes, in the place where Christ says that the flesh is of no avail.

Gem: Yes.

Pet: Thus receiving of the flesh of Christ is of no avail either. Further, I wonder whether Christ does not mean by above words that we shall feel no life within us unless we eat his flesh and drink his blood.

Gem: Correct.

Pet: If you concede that point, you will also have to concede that eating the flesh of Christ is an internal tasting of the suffering of Christ. And that its meaning is that the Son of man is lifted up so that everyone who sees him, i.e., believes, might not perish, but have eternal life.

Gem: I rebuke you unfairly.

Pet: To receive Christ thus is to accept Christ which means to know Christ with heart and soul.

Gem: That fits the sacrament.

Pet: Even if we were never to receive the sacrament in all eternity, we would be saved, nonetheless, if we are otherwise justified. But to gain salvation without tasting Christ is impossible. No one can be justified without the work of Christ, Isa 53:3f. The sacrament is not necessary, but the knowledge of Christ is. You also know that long before the institution of the sacrament, Christ said, "Unless you eat the flesh of the Son, etc." Thus, you did not correctly use the words of Christ. [24]

Gem: There is this term *sacramentaliter* which answers many a question.

Pet: For simpletons. Among those with understanding it cuts no ice, for those who know God better speak with Christ, and they will say *spiritualiter*, i.e., that we must eat the flesh of the Lord spiritually. *Sacramentaliter* it has no more use than the natural, external flesh of Christ.

Gem: You pour out everything that's in your innards.

Pet: It gets better still. For those who want to eat Christ in the sacrament are worse than those who left Christ or those who wanted to devour Christ physically such as unicorns and lions whom Christ would have carefully avoided according to what is written, "Deliver me from the horn of the unicorn and save my soul from the mouth of the lion."[14]

Gem: Keep talking.

Pet: The body of Christ is useless in a sacramental manner, for one cannot find in it either the death or the resurrection of Christ. Therefore, understood in this sacramental manner it has no use either carnally or spiritually, and it is nothing.

Gem: You really boxed the pope's ear with this so that his entire face has turned black and blue.

Pet: And all papists to boot.

Gem: And the new papists as well. But what do we have to do to receive or accept the body of Christ spiritually?

Pet: We must *verlassen*[15]—let go, and not do anything.

Gem: This is too deep for me.[16] Tell me simply how we are to receive the bread of the Lord worthily as you call it?

Pet: Whoever has a sincere remembrance of the body of Christ which has been given and desires to show this externally in the congregation in that he is ready to eat the bread of the Lord is worthy to receive the bread of the Lord as Christ says, "Do this in remembrance of me." Whoever does not have the right remembrance is not fit in the manner in which Christ desires to have him fit.

Gem: Be good enough and patient to carry on.

Pet: Look, do you want to repeat the same speech?

Gem: Yes, it won't hurt, for this matter is strange. In which of the articles is the remembrance clearly stated?

Pet: You are a master; you ought to answer me. Instead, you are asking.

Gem: Don't worry about anything—neither my dignity nor my loud clamor; just answer my question.

Pet: Remembrance has many parts in Christ, but one article is above all others; we will have to understand that and be mindful of it every time we desire to eat the bread of the Lord worthily. [25]

Gem: Name it.

Pet: The body of Christ given is that which everyone who seeks to eat the bread of the Lord without judgment will have to remember. In good time and at the right place we shall speak of that.

Gem: What does Paul call this article and the knowledge of it?

Pet: Paul calls it the death of the Lord, and the remembrance he calls proclamation. But you should understand that by what else I am going to say.

Gem: Speak and I shall hear.

Pet: You do this from humility.

Gem: From necessity.

Pet: Paul's words are as follows, Take eat, this is my body which was broken for you; do this in remembrance of me. This [cup][17] is the New Testament in my blood. This do, as often as you drink, in remembrance of me. Paul says clearly that we ought to do everything in remembrance of Christ such as eating the bread of the Lord and drinking of his cup. By this Paul indicates that the remembrance of Christ is to kindle and urge us to take the bread and the cup of Christ.

Gem: You skip over this as a frightened hare skips over a bush.

Pet: What is that?

Gem: You are afraid of the term "broken."

Pet: Why?

Gem: Paul has strengthened what we priests think, for he says this is my body which was broken for you. Now this has no point if you do not allow that the body of Christ comes in the form of bread, for the bread is broken, whereas the body of Christ in itself cannot be broken, though in the form of bread Christ's body is broken by inference.

Pet: You poor benighted man. Do you think that Christ's body has to be broken as bread is broken? Don't you know that it is written, You shall not break a single little bone of his? Don't you know the manner of speaking as when one says that you have a broken heart or a crushed spirit? If you insist that Christ was broken in the form of bread, you cannot win. Tell me who broke him. If you were to say that Christ himself broke the bread, I should answer that Christ was not in the bread when he broke it. Therefore, nothing in his body was broken when he broke the bread for his disciples.

Gem: The nature of Christ in the sacrament is different from the nature outside the sacrament.

Pet: That's why you priests have another Christ in the sacrament than the one we laypeople have on the cross. Anyone who has broken bones broke them where [26] he is. Now I ask further did Christ break himself without someone else's hands?

Gem: No.

Pet: Then you are not able to point to an apostle who broke the body of Christ in the bread, although you can point to their having eaten the bread. Moreover, it is false that Christ's body was broken in the bread, and it is a lie to say that Christ's body was broken on the cross in the form of the bread; go then and hide, you Sophist.

Gem: Let us stay with the matter we have begun and look further at the words which Paul spoke of the remembrance and of that which we are to remember.

Pet: Paul calls the broken body and the shed blood the death of the Lord; this we are to remember. But the remembrance he calls proclamation, as I said.

Gem: Say some more and lay the words of Paul before me.

Pet: As often as you eat of this bread (Paul says) and drink from this cup, you are to proclaim the death of the Lord until he comes.

Gem: Explain that.

Pet: It is as clear to me as a bright light.

Gem: I clearly note what we require in order to worthily receive the Lord's bread and cup, namely, the remembrance and proclaiming of the death of Christ. And yet, I do not understand this very proclamation.

Pet: Learn to understand it. We believe in the heart unto our righteousness and with the lips unto our salvation.

Gem: Relate this verse to remembrance and proclamation.

Pet: The remembrance of Christ cannot be without faith and knowledge of Christ, just as it would be impossible to recall my father if I had not known him. Therefore, remembrance comes after knowledge or faith, both in nature and kind. If the knowledge is lively and pure, the remembrance is fervent and pure. If it is based on hearsay, the remembering is likewise derived.

Gem: Can the remembrance also justify?

Pet: Why not?

Gem: Demonstrate that.

Pet: Isaiah depicts the Messiah who is derided and killed in all gruesome bitterness. Then he goes on to say that this Messiah makes righteous many of his servants by his grace.

Gem: Is the text, "By his knowledge he made many righteous," Isa 53:11?

Pet: You said it.

Gem: Do you still insist that remembering Christ as he was derided, laughed at, nailed, and killed makes as righteous as does his grace?

Pet: Yes, I do, for it is [27] written, "It will be said that they have done this in remembrance of me."

Gem: What then do you make of the statement, "With one's mouth one believes unto one's salvation"?[18]

Pet: The proclamation of the death of Christ. For proclamation is a statement of faith which goes forth from the heart through the mouth. Therefore, the external confession or preaching of the death of Christ is a sign or the fruit of the inner righteousness so that everyone who hears such external proclamation will have to say, "God is in the person who preaches" or "God speaks through him."

Gem: I understand then that the remembrance of Christ has to be so rich, so overflowing and so powerful in the one who wants to eat the bread of the Lord that a person is driven to preach publicly before the congregation, or to proclaim the death of Christ in some other way and then only eat the bread of the Lord (from great love and remembrance).

Pet: You guessed it. Don't you know how Paul preached Christ at Troas and how the people were then compelled to eat the bread of the Lord?

Gem: Yes, as told in Acts 20:7.

Pet: Do you also know how the disciples remained steadfastly in the teaching and in the breaking of bread?

Gem: Well.

Pet: But do you know that there always ought to be first the proclamation of the death of Christ before one should begin to break and receive the bread of the Lord?

Gem: From whom and wherefrom?

Pet: Preaching the death of Christ is essential, as Paul says, "You are to proclaim the death of the Lord, as often as you take it."[19] Acts also indicates this.[20] Sermons on the resurrection and birth of Christ are not at all fitting for receiving the bread of the Lord, however well one might mix in the articles of the birth and ascension of Christ.

Gem: Who should preach?

Pet: One who intends to break bread or another one.

Gem: But I consider it superfluous that all who receive ought to be examined, since Christ gave his bread to Judas who betrayed him.

Pet: You have now heard enough of me. And I consider it good enough if one understands how the words of Christ and Paul agree and what a person needs in order to take and eat the bread of the Lord worthily.

Gem: Dear brother, in things one has not experienced, it is not too much when a matter is brought out twice.

Pet: What do you mean?

Gem: Let us talk once more of the worthy [28] receiving and taking of the bread of the Lord, for I notice that you have something else up your sleeve.

Pet: What?

Gem: The term *diiudicare*, which Paul used, in translation means "to judge correctly, to esteem highly, to judge severely." The Greek term *diakrinon* also means "to discern well" and "to judge." Anyone who seeks to discern a matter well has to look at it from within and without and must wholly determine that which he wishes to distinguish.

Pet: What do you refer to?

Gem: I refer to what Paul said which is as follows, "Whoever eats and drinks unworthily eats and drinks unto his own judgment, for he does not discern the body of Christ."

Pet: We have dealt with that term in a timely fashion.

Gem: Please oblige and let us deal with it once more.

Pet: I want to hear how you heard me.

Gem: You say that anyone who desires to receive the sacrament without harm must hold Christ in remembrance and must discern the body of Christ with great diligence. He must proclaim the death of Christ externally—all of which we priests have usurped, as you say, by applying it to the sacrament.

Pet: What are you sacramenting? Where in Scripture did you learn the term?

Gem: Bear with me for not being able to express myself and do as if you hear "bread" whenever I say "sacrament."

Pet: Continue.

Gem: We spiritual priests and monks say that the sacrament forgives sins and we preach as follows: O sinner, whenever your conscience frightens or presses in upon you on account of sin, and whenever you cannot get rid of your anxiety and burden, go and take the sacrament for your sin and be at peace.

Pet: You false prophets. You promise people the kingdom of God for a piece of bread. What would you promise for silver and gold, if you had no shame at all? You promise peace of mind to the simple-minded through things that are smaller than the conscience and which cannot give or create peace.

Gem: Go easy.

Pet: It is true. I know that even with your secretive breathing and hissing you cannot change the bread for the better or into something else. Why do you say that it forgives sin after you have breathed over it? Would it not be as easy for you to say, People, if your sins press in upon you and you desire to have peace, then take a handful of rye and eat it in God's name [29] and you shall be free and rid of your sin and at peace in your conscience?

This is how the pope granted letters of indulgence and how some false prophets at one time took wheat and rye, and our priestlings took offering money for sins. Human consciences were at peace in themselves and in people's eyes. But what

was it in the sight of God? Did they not have a false peace and
security which gave neither peace nor security? You must not
be surprised therefore that these foolish people believe and
are pacified by lies, for they allow every wind which blows at
them to lift them, whirl them about and set them down. But in
the end they shall come to nought when they see how they
have been deceived.

Gem: But Martin Luther himself gave this advice.

Pet: It is most harmful when simple people who have regard for
certain persons sell themselves short, for they do not cling to
the unalloyed truth, but to a person. Therefore they cannot
hear or see the unalloyed truth, for they have such a thick
foreskin over their ears and their eyes.

Gem: The bread contains the body of Christ.

Pet: Although I am prepared to concede that the body of Christ is
united with the bread, I would speak deceitfully and wrongly,
however, if I were to attach to wafer-thin bread so much power and strength as to be able to forgive our sins and bring us
peace. What I grant to the bread, I take away from the suffering of Christ. Further, Christ's body or death would be of no
avail, if Christ had not been God, sealed by God the Father
when he was human (which he still is) and if Christ had not
fully known his suffering and death. Now think, dear Sophist,
and note how Paul directs us to know the remembrance of the
bitter death of Christ which we recall whenever we think
back some fifteen hundred years, even though our knowledge
and memory extend beyond time and place. No one should be
bound to these anyhow, for they contribute nothing toward
the forgiveness of sins.

Gem: I fear you are right and that we play an apish game every time
we adore the sacrament and hold it in a silver or gold mon-
strance, carrying it about in our cities and villages that it might
protect us and whatever belongs to us and drive out the
devil.[21] For whatever we attribute to the external bread, we
take away from the death of Christ. [30]

Pet: Well, what do you now think of all this?

Gem: I think it a lousy trifle and an artful deception to have talked
thus of the sacrament for so long. For the sacrament is an external thing which cannot save us, nor make us holy, or good,
or better, or more just, or free, though we look on it a thousand
times. I fear that the prophet Haggai [2:12] prophesied of us

when he says, They attach a piece of holy meat to the hemline of their clothes and say that what they then touch is holy.

Pet: You are less steady and you vacillate more than a feather in the wind. Now you are wholly on my side, then you are with the priests; for a while you talk like a papist, then again you speak truthfully with regard to the sacrament. At times you come over to me; then again you step away from me. What a Proteus you are![22]

Gem: Great subtlety has made me as quick as that. It comes in handy, for thus I am able to flee the cross and I am enjoying a wonderful time amidst the great.

Pet: I believe you.

Gem: If I did not have this skill, I would long have been despised.

Pet: But it is not very civil nor very Christian. It would be more becoming an easy-going liar than you.

Gem: I still say that Haggai prophesied concerning us.

Pet: How so?

Gem: We say that once the bread is blessed, it is capable of forgiving sins and sanctifies everything that merely clings to it. Thus we give the sacrament the same honor, praise, love, and fear that we give the body of Christ.

Pet: You have no basis for that in Scripture.

Gem: Not a single letter. Christ said, Anyone who loves father and mother more than, or as much as, me is not worthy of me. What would he say to us for equally honoring, fearing, and loving a lesser creature which has neither soul nor body, namely a piece of bread?

Pet: Anyone who regards the bread of the Lord as much, or fears, honors, and loves it as much as the bitter death of the Lord is not worthy of the death of Christ and does not comprehend it. He also takes and eats the bread of the Lord unworthily unto his judgment, harm, and fall.

Gem: If it were right to adore or fear the bread of the Lord and honor it so greatly, the prophets too would have prophesied of the holiness and righteousness of the bread, and they would have foretold us that the bread can bear our sins and pain and that it should be visited whenever our [31] sins frighten or distress us.

Pet: You speak well and correctly. John the Baptist, too, would not have pointed merely to Christ if Christ, cloaked in the host, was to forgive our sins. And Christ himself would have been good enough toward us to have shown us how we ought to eat his bread in order to be sure of the forgiveness of our sins.

Gem: How is it with Paul?

 Pet: He directs us to the recalling of the death of Christ when our sins weigh us down. That's why he says, Many have been made righteous by the obedience of one person.

Gem: Continue.

 Pet: Anyone who wants to be sure of forgiveness of sin and to eat the bread of the Lord worthily and without harm—what you call "receiving"—must be sure in the knowledge of the death of Christ. This means to understand and accept the death of Christ in the measure by which God our Father has promised it, and they must affirm with their heart that God is in truth. Anyone who is thus skilled is well skilled, but anyone who lacks one of these is unfit and unworthy. It were better for such a one to eat ordinary bread than to eat the bread of the Lord.

Gem: Why?

 Pet: Because of his pretense and unworthiness.

Gem: Continue.

 Pet: As often as you eat of this bread and drink from this cup, you are to proclaim the death of the Lord; it is the Lord's death Paul speaks of and not the Lord's bread when he impresses upon us memorial and proclamation, until he comes. With this Paul casts to the ground in one heap all monks and priests who celebrate mass. For Paul says that when the Lord shall come, the Lord's bread will no longer be eaten nor will there be preaching before the reception. With this he proves that the Lord does not come in the bread or sacrament; and should he come, the sacrament would then disappear. Therefore Christ cannot appear in the sacrament. He remains in heaven above and occupies the same until the time of refreshment has come. And anyone who eats this bread and drinks the cup of the Lord unworthily is guilty of the body and blood of the Lord.

Gem: This is frightening.

 Pet: A person must examine himself and only then eat of the bread and drink from the cup of the Lord.

Gem: Do I hear then that I must be sure of the matter?

 Pet: Anyone who [32] is to examine or test himself must know and not conjecture. Whoever eats and drinks unworthily eats and drinks unto his own judgment for not discerning the body of Christ.

Gem: It is better then to abstain than to take.

Pet: You said it.

Gem: We have gone rather far afield and note that the sun is about to set. Let us turn back therefore and put aside the matter of the handing over to a more convenient time. Then I will be happy to hear and learn how Christ is handed on, to whom he has given himself, for what reason and for whom or to whose benefit he has given himself, what we must understand and know in all of this, and how our spirit must be assured by God's spirit.

Pet: What then shall we discuss now?

Gem: The matter which we have now touched upon when you said that Christ does not come in the sacrament which would be too close for every priest and monk.

Pet: Are you the great giants and children of Anakim who can pull God down from heaven?

Gem: We are able to and do it by another's power.

Pet: Who gave you this strange power?

Gem: Christ when he said, do this in remembrance of me.

Pet: Did Christ also bid you to put his body into a piece of bread?

Gem: Yes.

Pet: I thought so, and I know it for a fact that you priests lie, for Christ never bid you to force his body to enter your host.

Gem: What then?

Pet: Christ says that you are to take and eat his bread, and he adds that as often as you take and eat it, you are to take and eat it in memory of him. You are to do as Paul says; and this all Christians can do—the unsmirched ones better than those besmirched bald heads [*blettinger*].²³ They are truly the lusty giants who with such words stole by force their alleged and falsely praised power by which they pretend to be able to put Christ's body into a small piece of bread.

Gem: Methinks Paul confirmed our power well when he said, I received from the Lord what I have given you. For the Lord Jesus in the night in which he was betrayed, took bread, gave thanks, broke it and said, Take, eat this is my body which is broken for you. Do this in remembrance of me. There, there see, Peter, how Paul celebrates mass and repeats the words of the Lord, [33] bringing his body into the bread and giving us power too to fetch and bring the body of Christ into the sacrament.

Pet: My, my, how ridiculous your prattle seems to me.

Gem: Why?

Pet: Did Paul give you the power with these word, "Do this, etc.," to conjure the body of the Lord into the bread, and to celebrate mass? A blind person can grasp this in utter darkness that Paul does nothing other than to recall the words of the Lord and the occasion when Christ instituted his Supper and that he wants to teach us not to eat the bread of the Lord like other bread, but in remembrance of him. If from such recalled words you want to take power unto yourselves to drive the body of Christ into small pieces of bread, as Christ was to have done according to you, I would say that Moses has given us power to create heaven and earth and that Moses created all creatures when he began to describe the creation of heaven and earth. If you undertake to assume the one, you will also have to accept the other. If you can now prove the creation of a new world through a deed, I too will believe that you or some other bald head is able to order or bring the body of the Lord into the sacrament.

Gem: And what did Paul achieve with the word of the Lord?

Pet: Much good. For he reminds us of the time of the suffering of Christ and the appropriateness and manner in which we are to eat the bread of the Lord.

Gem: Make yourself clear.

Pet: On account of the time we are not to eat the Lord's bread like pigs. For when he handed us the bread in remembrance of him, it was the night in which he was betrayed innocently for our sake. It is right therefore that we stand in the bitterness of life when we eat his bread. Because of his suffering it is apparent that we should think on the greatness and severity of our sins and on Christ's boundless obedience and intense love. The manner is found in the remembrance and proclamation of the death of Christ, as has often been said. This is the reason why Christ points to his body, saying, The body which has been given for you. Before that none was given; therefore there was none that might have been given. Nor will there be anyone after me, for I am [the body] and my body is like and truly the body which will be given for you. Now the one who, having considered everything, takes and eats the bread of the

Lord [34] surely has enough reason to eat the bread of the Lord more solemnly, though it is neither holier nor better than any other bread.

Gem: And yet Christ blessed the bread.

Pet: It is written that he thanked—mark this—God his Father. For this reason there are some who call the sacrament a eucharist as if the sacrament alone were a "giving of thanks"—these people follow their thoughts more than God's word.

Gem: This thanksgiving has ever been the real power by which Christ brought his body into the sacrament.

Pet: Prove that. You have abandoned your former defense and have found another protection for yourself. Had your first foundation been sound when you made yourself heard with the words, do this in remembrance of me, etc., you would have taken the battleground. But because your foundation left you and brought you to fall, you look for this, Christ gave thanks. It will sustain you like the previous one.

Gem: I have three foundations or swords. If one of the foundations gives way, I resort to another. Is it not wonderful that when I break one sword, I grab another to protect myself?

Pet: Proof positive that the vanished foundation and the broken sword were not firm and strong. But the one who fights with truth on his side has the firmest foundation and the strongest sword, for truth is the strongest of all.

Gem: I don't care that much about it as long as I protect myself and resist you.

Pet: You are a born Sophist then. A deceiver. A spoilsport. Yet, according to your reputation, you should be able to accomplish your task, compel your enemies, press and frighten them, and catch them by force. You are to gag them with truths so that they cannot contradict you.

Gem: My foundations are mere show.[24]

Pet: You ought not have appearance alone, but truth to back it. Put forth your appearance and let us see how light and bright its sheen is.

Gem: One is as follows "Jesus took bread and blessed it." The other is "This is my body which is given for you." The third, "Do this in remembrance of me."

Pet: It barely shines and is so dim that I cannot see how one of these foundations could serve the priests.

Gem: Your eyes are weak.

Pet: If yours are keen, then lead me to your alleged shine. I reckon, however, that your [35] eyes are so keen that in their keenness they see what isn't there.

Gem: Jesus took bread and blessed it or thanked God.

Pet: Are you taking "blessing" and "thanksgiving" to be the same?

Gem: Yes. One of the gospel writers has "to bless" at the very end where the other has "to give thanks."

Pet: But show me your appearance that Christ turned himself into the sacrament by his blessing and that you priests through Christ's blessing are able to bring his body and blood into the sacrament.

Gem: This is so clear as to be beyond proof.

Pet: But to me it is so obscure that I am unable to believe anything the priests say.

Gem: Show me the obscurity.

Pet: You boasted of the light but could not point to it. I am not obliged therefore to point to the darkness. Anyone who boasts of light or appearance must support his case through Scripture or witnesses.

Gem: Christ gave thanks and by those very words of thanksgiving, he transported himself into the sacrament.

Pet: Since you talk so much of thanksgiving, I ask you what Christ said when he gave thanks? When Christ raised Lazarus, he also thanked God and the form in which he gave thanks is contained in the very same story.[25] But of this thanksgiving I cannot give the manner or the form; if you know the form, tell me.

Gem: All my life I did not hear of it, nor did I pay attention to it or ask for it.

Pet: You boast then of not understanding. But it is essential that you know the words of thanksgiving which Christ used if you claim that through the thanksgiving of Christ you are able to bring the body and blood of Christ into your sacrament.

Gem: Do you find many more faults with me?

Pet: Many.

Gem: Out with them.

Pet: If Christ brought himself into the bread or the cup through the blessing which you use, it would follow that Christ was in your sacrament before he could have spoken the words, "This is my body, etc." Hence, the words "This is my body" cannot serve you in bringing Christ into the sacrament.

Gem: More of the same!

Pet: Had Christ entered the sacrament he would have had to leave the place where he sat. Christ always left the previous place when he came or went to a new city or place, as the Scriptures verify, Jn 6. For instance, [36] when Christ went to the mountain, he left the valley and when Christ ascended to heaven, he left this world, physically speaking. Is it not written, I shall leave you and return to you?

Gem: All that is true *naturaliter—naturally speaking*. But the truth is *sacramentaliter*—sacramentally-speaking, and *supernaturaliter—supernaturally*, according to which Christ is in many places at the same time.

Pet: Do you have a foundation for this in Scripture?

Gem: No.

Pet: Then you are a liar.

Gem: Then all of them are lying.

Pet: That's possible and human, Lev 4, Ex 19.

Gem: Have you poured out all of your opinion?

Pet: No. I have kept some back and on hold. But one thing I will not keep from you, namely, that it is rather sandy ground on which the priests stand when they claim that the words of blessing or thanksgiving which they don't even know are so strong as to be able to drive Christ into their sacrament. For if that would hold, it would also have to hold that the priests of the old law would have brought their bodies into food and drink, as well. Yes, into the people, when they blessed them. In sum, it would have to follow that you priests and monks would bring your bodies into your food and drink when you bless your food and drink or when you read the *Benedicite* and that you and your guests devour your bodies and your own flesh and blood. You would have to bring yourselves sacramentally into the food and drink which you have blessed or which you receive with thanksgiving. For Paul uses the same word "eucharist," 1 Tim 4:4, when he speaks of the common use of all sorts of foods. You can see from this that your first light and foundation is a dark lantern and a sandy trap to you, for you misappropriate clear Scripture.

Gem: Well then, the other foundation, "This is my body, etc.," will have to serve me.

Pet: Little. In fact, in no way.

Gem: How come?

Pet: You priests say that Christ is in the bread or under the bread or in the form of bread; therefore above words cannot serve you any longer.[26]

Gem: But it is written, "This is my body, etc."

Pet: That's why it is against you. For since it is written "This is my body" the words are different from "under or in the bread is my body." Had Christ said under the bread or in the bread is my body, you would have a light.

Gem: Is it a sin to add "in"?

Pet: A grave sin, to be sure! God says that we ought not add anything. Yes, [37] it is a falsification. The supreme priest burns persons who falsify his bulls with one such little word, bringing another meaning to it from the one Christ had intended in his saying. If you priests want to defend your sacrament with such coinage, you would have had a better foundation in the words for the cup, since the words for the cup are as follows: The cup, the New Testament in my blood, etc." These words would have given you a somewhat brighter appearance to say that the cup is in the blood and that it must be in the blood by virtue of the words of Christ which you read and say, "The cup, the New Testament in my blood." For you to say that the body of Christ is in the bread or in the form of the bread is not right; for there is no "in" in the saying about the cup.

Gem: Yes, my dear, we hit it right on.

Pet: It's not "hit"? You would have thoroughly veiled everything with scriptural sounds had you said straightaway that the cup is in the blood which the text states and which, furthermore, is a new covenant.

Gem: Yes, well covered up. What would the peasants have said? Not perhaps that "I see no blood in which the cup is? The cup I see, but blood I do not see." They might even have stoned us.

Pet: Goodness, no.

Gem: Goodness, yes.

Pet: I don't believe it.

Gem: I know it for a fact, for they would not have seen any blood in which the cup would have been.

Pet: Could you not have talked them into it by saying, Control your reason and subdue your senses and pretend that you do not see, taste or understand?

Gem: You ridicule.

Pet: You have convinced lay people that they taste bread and wine, yet are not allowed to say that they taste bread and wine when they receive your sacrament. In like fashion you could have achieved to make them believe that your cup is in the blood which nonetheless they cannot see. You say, don't you, that faith comprehends all things, understands all things, and can do everything. Therefore faith is also able to see blood which cannot be seen by the eyes of angels or human beings.

Gem: I don't know whether you ridicule us or not.

Pet: How dare I?

Gem: What about when he says right out, "The bread is my body," as Christ did?

Pet: Christ never said that the bread is his body. The Greek does not tolerate that we relate these words to the bread, as was pointed out above. [38] Moreover, it is ridiculous to say the bread is my body, etc. For it sounds in this way as if the body of the Lord which was to suffer and be given for us is bread and not a natural human body. It is not the body that was born from Mary the mother, but bread made by a baker. And moreover, it is against the stream of all of the prophets who wrote about the handing over of the body of Christ and against all the gospels and apostolic books. For it is ever true that one who is not with Scripture scatters and is against Scripture.

Gem: Let me present the third foundation then.

Pet: The one, "This do in remembrance of me"?

Gem: Yes.

Pet: I recently heard some great clods [*hanffbutzen*] who used these words, "Do this in remembrance of me" in a way by which they hoped to support the priests's loading the body and blood of Christ onto the papistic sacrament and confining it there.

Gem: Who are these clods?

Pet: They are called "doctors" and wear beautiful round and pointed hats, walk about in long gowns and stand about like strawy and wooden hemp clods which are covered in beggars' rags.

Gem: Go easy.

Pet: How can I go easy on them as long as they claim that bishops consecrate priests with these words, "Do this in remembrance of me." Yet another claims that the priests conjure Christ into the sacrament. A third does it in yet another way.

Gem: I think that Christ has given us power by these words, "Do this, etc.," to order his flesh and blood into the sacrament whenever we read these words.

Pet: O pitiful blindness. Is it one and the same to you whether it is to read or to do? Did Christ speak of reading or doing? Or did Christ say what his disciples were to do before he said, "Do this"?

Gem: What are we to do?

Pet: You are to take the bread and eat and you are to do that in remembrance of the Lord, as Paul says: "You are to proclaim the death of the Lord as often as you eat the bread of the Lord and drink from his cup."

Gem: Let us speak some more of several of the foundations.

Pet: Which ones?

Gem: Of thanksgiving.

Pet: Do you think that Christ by his thanksgiving has changed his body into bread?

Gem: Yes.

Pet: Then you will also have to confess that Christ changed his body into the five loaves of rye bread since Christ [39] gave thanks there, too, or blessed, as you say. For in that very context, you find the word, "He spoke well."

Gem: Stay on track.

Pet: Was the blessing or benediction of Christ the power by which Christ brought his body into the bread and is this the power Christ was to have given to the priests? Then Christ instituted his sacrament long before the night in which he was betrayed which is contrary to all those learned in Scripture and Paul. It would follow, moreover, that Christ fed several thousand with his body and that he gave it to the others before he gave it to the apostles. You would then have to admit that Christ pushed his body into the body of Lazarus when he awakened him from the dead.

Gem: You bring me close to doubting.

Pet: Now assume that Christ brought his body into the bread, as you say, on Thursday. Do therefore the priests have the same power as Christ?

Gem: *Maiora his facietes*—the same and greater.

Pet: Now I hear that mangy priests are able to bring the body of Christ into their alleged form of the bread which Christ was unable to do.

Gem: No. Christ too changed himself into bread, but with clear voice. The priests however bring Christ into the bread through soft blowing.

Pet: That's good. Hold on; let me clear my throat and spit before I kill myself laughing.

Gem: Christ said, "This is my body."

Pet: Christ stood in their presence when he said, This is my body, etc. Therefore, when a priest says, "This is my body, take and eat the bread" and when we then eat, we devour a miserable priest. But when priests speak of the body of Christ and recall how Christ stood and said of his body that his body was the body that had been promised to be given for us, they speak correctly. But he is not stuck in the bread as they claim.

Gem: That's why I spoke of the humanity of Christ.

Vic: I really doubt whether the body of Christ is in the bread and his blood in the cup.

Gem: Why?

Vic: Because they claim that his natural body, conceived in his mother's womb and later nailed to the cross, is in the sacrament as large, broad, thick and long as it was on the cross.

Gem: *Oportet credere*—one must have faith.

Vic: *Maledictus qui credit verbis mendacii*—cursed is the one [40] who believes in lies.

Gem: It is the truth that Christ is as large in the sacrament as he was hanging on the cross.

Vic: I know nothing of that truth and cannot believe it unless you can show me God's own true sayings which indicate this freely and clearly.

Gem: You have not been a priest, for priests have certain words (they call them *verba consecrationis*—words of consecration) which are so powerful that they could bring the body and blood of Christ down to earth into a small host from the high heavens. If you could understand such speech, you would talk a bit more intelligently.

Vic: You have given me a lot about which I must ask you. One of these is when you say that priests or monks could bring the body and blood of Christ down from heaven. This is contrary to what you said earlier when you said that Christ is as large in the sacrament as when he hung on the cross. Therefore you would have had to bring Christ from the cross into the sacrament when he died and shed his blood. In heaven Christ has no shape nor is he spread out as he was on the cross. One has to be wrong. Secondly, you speak of certain small words which you call *verba consecrationis*; I have never read of these; I suspect that the priests invented them. Thirdly, you speak of a host. Explain these articles to me.

Gem: The host is bread which the priests bless to bring Christ into it.

Vic: I still don't understand.

Gem: Do the priests have no commandment to bring Christ's body into the bread?

Pet: We read of many commandments and several articles by which God has granted his apostles much authority. But among all these we do not find one which says that Christ has given power to priests to fit his body into bread and his blood into a cup.

Gem: Is that it?

Pet: I would say yes, for Christ gave his disciples power to preach, baptize, drive out devils, heal the sick, shake the dust off their feet, and raise the dead. But among all these commandments put together, there is not one which goes as follows: "You ought to or shall bring my body into small pieces of bread." I would love to see a single letter which you ink guzzlers could boast of or base yourselves on and which says that Christ commanded you to bring his body into the bread or the form of bread. Therefore, [41] I say that you have appropriated this power by stealth and deceitfully, like thieves.

Gem: Must Christ then remain up there forever?

Pet: It has ever been concluded by Paul, as noted above, and by us that we shall not need the sacrament or bread of the Lord longer than until the coming of the Lord. When Christ returns from heaven, the sacrament and all external things shall pass away.

Gem: Christ comes into the sacrament secretly. But Paul speaks about the clear and apparent coming.

Pet: If Christ comes into the sacrament secretly, he would have to be ashamed of his future or be afraid of you.

Gem: It is to us priests that Christ comes secretly.

Pet: Indeed, he comes so secretly that you yourselves don't know whether he comes into the sacrament or not. For there is not a single priest who can maintain with an oath that by his binding Christ has come into the sacrament as large as he was hanging on the cross.

Gem: I have celebrated many a mass and frequently, but I never felt that he had come.

Pet: I know that.

Gem: Would Christ not come down from heaven secretly?

Pet: No.

Gem: Cite Scripture.

Pet: Two men said to the apostles, "Christ shall come again as you have seen him ascend. Christ ascended to heaven visibly, thus he must also return visibly." I shall not allow myself to be convinced by any more than that the apostles neither hoped for nor desired the secret coming into their bread.

Gem: I don't know who the two men were. Therefore, I should prefer to hear Scripture.

Pet: Take Christ's word who spoke as follows, When they say Christ is here, Christ is there (as you priests did and spoke for a long time, Christ is in this host and in that host and in every corner), do not go out, nor believe it, for Christ's coming shall not be secret, but it will be as apparent and visible as lightning which shines from end to end.

Gem: Christ says that of the second coming.

Pet: There are no more than two comings: one in the form of the cross and suffering here on earth, the other in glorified form. A third I must not invent, and I could not add either of the two to the host. Christ shall possess heaven until the day on [42] which all things shall be finished as Peter says in Acts and as we stated above.

Gem: I gather that you find it hard to believe that Christ might be in several places at once.

Pet: No. I believe just as readily that you can bring and place him in several places at one time as I believe that St. Anne had five heads and an innocent little child a beard twelve yards long [*elle*].

Gem: Don't you believe that Christ can be present in ten thousand places at the same instant?

Pet: Essentially I don't. But I do believe that you would dearly love to bring him down from heaven if he were so forgetful as to come down.

Gem: Do you not believe either that Christ stands at the same time in many *ciboria*? [27]

Pet: In your jails?

Gem: What are you jailing?

Pet: You are accustomed to lock in your God with several external doors; and you affix many iron locks and bolts to them so he won't escape. By this you inflict great ridicule, mockery, and affrontery on Christ our Savior.

Gem: Ridiculous.

Pet: You invented a God for yourselves who is no God at all.

Gem: It is Christ.

Pet: Christ is in heaven, bodily. If you can cite Scripture to show that he is in your bread, I will change my tune.

Gem: We bring him down.

Pet: O you powerless priests, do you really ascribe such great power to yourselves? It takes greater power than that to bring Christ from heaven into the sacrament, to drive out the devil and then cast huge rocks into the sea—none of which you are capable of. I know that. Should you try to drive out devils, you would quickly suffer the fate of the seven sons of the Jew Sceva, Acts 19:13ff.

Gem: Whatever we do, we do with good intent and to the honor of God.

Pet: You honor Christ as a cat honors the mouse it has caught.

Gem: Of course not.

Pet: Now even though you may be well-intentioned, humanly speaking, you should leave behind your good intentions if you are not sure that God the Lord is pleased by your good intentions. Remember Peter who was wonderfully well-intentioned, humanly speaking, for he was appaled by the fact that Jesus was to be handed over and tortured. Nonetheless, he had to hear, "Get away from me, Satan."

Gem: We thought it would honor God and benefit us to bring Christ into the bread and to hold him within it as in a wonder- [43] ful temple.

Pet: Where do you find a basis for this undertaking?

Gem: In Scripture.

Pet: Produce those Scriptures.

Gem: What shall I produce? Don't you know that Moses erected a tabernacle for God and that Solomon later built God a house?

Pet: Where do you find the basis for building Christ a house of bread?

Gem: It is an argument from similitude.

Pet: With such a bun [*Semmel*][28] you might ravage Scripture and devalue the precious suffering of Christ.

Gem: Is it contrary to Christ and Scripture?

Pet: There are too many things contrary to Scripture for which you will find no basis therein. But it is against Christ when you priests want to build him a temple which has been wrought by human hands. Christ is the supreme priest who through one sacrifice and one death entered the eternal tabernacle which was formed by God's hands alone without the aid of any creature. Out of that temple and tabernacle you bold characters dare order Christ into a thing that at times is devoured by worms, at times by fire, at times by mice and sows and fatted pigs such as you priests are.

Gem: Is that wrong?

Pet: What kind of house are you planning to build me? Am I to rest in your bread? Christ says. Did you not devise and think up all this? Did you not choose these ways and abominations yourselves? Away, away you butchers of dogs.

Gem: The cup which we bless is the communion of the blood of Christ. Note and absorb that we bless the cup and that this cup is the communion of the blood of Christ.

Pet: The blessing is in the remembrance and proclamation of the death of Christ, as Paul expounds in the following chapter and as we noted above; other than that I do not know what form the blessing took, but I would like to know.

Gem: Answer my claim that the cup is a communion.

Pet: In this the communion is found that no one ought to drink from the cup except one who understands why Christ shed his blood. He is to drink from the Lord's cup with great love and gratitude and in sincere remembrance, for without the communion of the Lord it cannot be drunk unto salvation.

Gem: The words of consecration do it.

Pet: Who invented them?

Gem: *Fingere licet.*[29]

Pet: *Lapidare ius est.*[30] How many such strong words are there?

Gem: Five, just as there are five [44] wounds. Anyone who leaves out even one cannot consecrate.

Pet: How many of these do you have in Greek?

Gem: Four.

Pet: The apostles did not consecrate then.

Gem: Are you surprised by that? Are we not to increase daily in the knowledge of Christ?

Pet: It is said that Christ spoke a mixture of Jewish and Syriac. If this is so, you may have trouble retaining two words.

Gem: Our power has been expanded and strengthened.

Pet: I like to see that.

Gem: What are you thinking about! Are you going to choose other words?

Pet: I am quite certain and know it to be the truth, that the body of Christ without suffering would have been of no use to us, as Christ says, The Son of man must be lifted up so that everyone who sees him thus hanged should not perish. It is for this that the clause "given for you" is so firmly tied and equal in power to the clause "this is my body." I will demonstrate this with the remembrance, though I do not hold or believe that these words are words of consecration.

Gem: You are stubborn.

Pet: With regard to lies yes, but I am soft on the truth.

Gem: Is Christ not likely to come into our sacrament then when a priest reads words like these?

[31]**Gem:** Should Christ get onto the back of every priest then because of his foul breath?

Gem: Why not?

Pet: Is not the greater number of priests a pharisaic generation and a brood of vipers whom Christ does not intend to come close to and with whom he wants to have little to do!

Gem: As far as the words are concerned, Christ has to come.

Pet: Even if the Pharisees had God's word and were good enough for Christ to say, "You ought to hear them," he would still not go near them.

Gem: He was afraid of them.

Pet: Christ should be more afraid now, for now the priests tear Christ apart with their teeth and kill him for three pennies. God says to such sinners, Why do you take my word into your mouth? Therefore it avails you not, etc.

Gem: I have always thought that Christ should enter into the sacrament.

Pet: Christ would surely have restless days and would be tossed to and fro by the priests in a more derisive way than a conjurer's wand.

Gem: Are you comparing Christ to a conjurer's wand?

Pet: No. I am merely saying that drifters handle their wand more skillfully than priests handle their Christ. My reason is that these drifters abstain, and remain more sober and enunciate their ditties clearly. But the priests smell early of wine and beer [45], like vinegar bottles and some of them are still so full in the morning that they cannot hold up their heads or control their tongues to speak properly; they babble but do not read. Some of them sleep during silent mass like one who has fallen asleep and talks in his dream saying, Methinks I am dreaming of being in a wine cellar. Yet another finds himself standing during silent mass in his dream, saying, Deal the cards. See for yourself now whether the conjurer's wand is not handled better by drifters than the words of Christ are by these priests. And who can believe that such a wino is able to bring Christ into the sacrament? And if Christ is indeed in their power, his cause would be worse off than the conjurer's wand.

Gem: I myself do not believe that Christ would have communion with such priests.

Pet: Why then do you bid us poor peasants fall down and beat our breasts when you drunkards lift up the bread of your idol?

Gem: Make yourself clear.

Pet: You priests imprinted a disgraceful image of Christ onto your bread with a waffle iron. This stains every conscience. Yet God considers all images an abomination, hates and flees them. It is for this reason also that I do not believe that you are able to transform Christ into your sacrament. For he has always done his Father's will here; that Christ now should be opposed to that same will I do not believe. Your bread is the bread of idols —an abominable and rejected bread.

Gem: Go easy.

Pet: The image also brings about that simple people think that Christ was changed into an image and that the feet of the image are the feet of Christ and that it is the head of Christ where the head of the image is found. Some even think that the priests empty Christ's stomach when they turn the image upside down, and so on.

Gem: We know that images are nothing.

Pet: And we know that they are less than dirt and a rope to bring someone to a fall.

Gem: How then would it be if we used bread that is not the bread of idols?

Pet: Into that you could not manage to lure and change Christ. To make it short, I ask you whether you are able to bring the mortal body of Christ or the glorified and immortal one into the sacrament?[32]

Gem: Your question is a snare thrown out to catch and entrap me.

Pet: But you owe me an answer.

Gem: Christ is in the sacrament in his glorified and immortal body.

Pet: Why?

Gem: Christ died once and shall [46] never again die, as Paul teaches in Romans and in the Acts of the Apostles.

Pet: You are a strong Paulinian.

Gem: I am that.

Pet: But you know little of his teaching.

Gem: More than the whole world.

Pet: You are so learned, yet you do not know that Paul says, "The Lord took bread, etc.," and said, "This is my body given for you." It was the mortal, not the immortal body, which was handed over into the hands of Jews and heathen alike to be killed.

Gem: Yes, that is true of when Christ changed himself into the sacrament.

Pet: It is true in the morning when you are sober, but in the afternoon when you are full it is a dream.

Gem: Why do you ridicule?

Pet: Are you able to bring another body of Christ into the sacrament than the one Christ himself was to have brought into it?

Gem: No, but in another form and shape.

Pet: In which one?

Gem: Christ brought himself into the bread in the form of poverty and in the shape of a servant. But I and my ilk bring Christ into the sacrament in his glorified state.

Pet: Where do you find support for this?

Gem: Support or no support, it is so nonetheless that anyone who does not receive my words cannot be saved.

Pet: No. With such tune you could never entice me into your net. Let the devil accept your words in every detail.

Gem: How else are we to defend the words of consecration?

Pet: I rather suspect that you are unable to bring it off.

Gem: How so?

Pet: If your words of consecration are true, they mean the following: "This is my body, given for you" is the one done in and given to death at the hands of evildoers, but they cannot serve you in your delusion.

Gem: That's why we have only five words which we call words of consecration.

Pet: Count them.

Gem: *Hoc est enim corpus meum* [for this is my body].

Pet: But you have left out the attached words "given for you."

Gem: Naturally, we insist on that.

Pet: As butter does in the sun, or thieves do on the gallows.

Gem: Not as bad.

Pet: A thousand times worse.

Gem: Why?

Pet: Because you interpret Christ's word differently than he does.

Gem: Prove that.

Pet: Easily. Christ says that it is the body in the shape or form which is capable of suffering and willing to do so. But you pervert that and say that it is the body which cannot suffer.

Gem: What causes you to be so vehemently against me?

Pet: The truth and righteousness of God.

Gem: If I could hear it from you.

Pet: Christ had intended to redeem us and lead us out of the kingdom and [47] power of the devil as out of Egypt into the kingdom and power of God. But Christ could not accomplish that except through his death as God had ordained it. He had to take on the form of the Paschal Lamb and stretch out his hand to the wood.

Gem: Say more.

Pet: In this way Christ had to concern himself with us and by his righteousness justify us from our sins; and this had to be achieved through death.

Gem: What is this righteousness?

Pet: Obedience unto death.

Gem: Would you have Scripture?

Pet: By the obedience of one person many have been made righteous. And this obedience Christ demonstrated through his ignominious death when he was obedient unto death, the death on the cross.

Gem: Do we not have this righteousness through the resurrection?

Pet: No. We have the righteousness of our dying through the death of Christ and not through the resurrection.

Gem: It is written that Christ was raised for the sake of our justification.

Pet: That is the righteousness of the resurrection of the spirit which here has its beginning only and will break forth after an accomplished death. The righteousness of dying comes first; the other follows.

Gem: You have almost got me onto your track.

Pet: If Christ's glorified and immortal body was in the sacrament and got there by virtue of his words, we do not have the first righteousness. And one who does not have the first does not have the other either and then it is also false to say that his body was given for us. And if Christ's mortal body was in the sacrament, you cannot bring his body into the sacrament by virtue of the spoken words of Christ in any other shape and form than the one by which he brought himself in. You must say therefore that Christ's mortal body is in your sacrament and that Christ dies daily whenever you sacrifice. And that is totally against God's truth.

Gem: I soon saw these snares and realized that you would catch me out before I could answer. If I say that Christ's mortal body is in the sacrament, you close the noose and catch me out demanding, "Is Christ still mortal then?" And if I say that Christ's immortal body is in the sacrament, it would follow that we have no words of consecration and that the ground on which we built our case crumbles.

Pet: Confess the truth and [48] say that Christ's body is not in the bread and his blood not in the cup. Yet we ought to eat the bread of the Lord in the remembrance or knowledge of his body which he surrendered for us into the hands of the unrighteous, and drink of the cup in the knowledge of the blood which Christ shed for us. To sum up, we are to eat and drink in the knowledge of the death of Christ.

Gem: If I could escape the snare held out to me?

Pet: All right with me.

Gem: But how?

Pet: Christ never spoke of the resurrection when he gave the bread and the cup. It is not necessary for the receivers to concern themselves with the resurrection. Christ shall drink a new and different cup and give it to us when he shall bring his resurrection to its full fruition within us. Then the bread and wine of dying shall cease. Therefore Paul said, You shall proclaim the death of the Lord until he comes, as if to say that when he comes your dying with Christ shall come to an end. But now before we have sufficiently died to our own strength, whenever we eat the bread of the Lord and drink his cup, we must confess the death of the Lord with heart and mind, i.e., we must sense the death of Christ within us and experience the righteousness of Christ and not ours.

Gem: God be praised.

Pet: God help us to a vital knowledge of the death of Christ.

Gem: Amen.

Whoever is able to guide us better, do so and soon, for God's sake, for we are softened and willing and desirous to accept and honor the truth of God to whom be all honor forever.

Whoever desires to read this matter in a continuous dialogue and without opprobrium may read the booklet on *Whether It Is Possible to Prove Through Holy Scripture that Christ is in the Sacrament with Body and Blood.*[33] See also, *An Exposition of the Eleventh Chapter of 1 Corinthians.*[34] Further, *An Explanation of the Words of Christ, "This Is My Body, Given for You."* [35] And, *That the Sacrament Is Not a Sign by Which People Can Strengthen and Confirm Their Consciences.*[36] Further, *Against the Old and Popish Mass.*[37] *Finally, faith in the promise and the sacrament which the new papists claim is a false faith; it breeds sin and does not forgive sins. You will find more and other arguments in these booklets.* [49]

FINIS

12
Regarding the Sabbath and Statutory Holy Days

Andreas Carlstadt

1524

JENA

"*Von dem Sabbat und gebotten feyertagen,*" *published early in 1524, must have been popular. It was printed at Jena, by Carlstadt's printer Buchfürer, formerly of Erfurt. Other editions originated in Augsburg., Strasbourg., and Constance. Three reprints are also known. Amidst the proliferation of humanly instituted festival days which encouraged undue feasting and the cessation of all work, Carlstadt sought to strike a biblically sound balance which would encourage people to find physical and spiritual renewal without, however, becoming enslaved to excessive and unwarranted practices.*

The tract is not strongly polemical but reflects the kind of pastoral concerns which undoubtedly occupied Carlstadt in his Orlamünde parish, where he sought to encourage a style of Christian living that would manifest the simplicity of the gospel while not acting too aggressively against established religious practices.

Freys/Barge list four editions of this tract, all from the year 1524. See numbers 115-118. Erich Hertzsch reprinted the tract in Karlstadts Schriften, vol. 1. Our translation is based on that text and has been compared with an unpublished translation by Calvin A. Pater who has given his kind permission to have his translation used in this way.

Table of Contents

1. The Meaning of the Term Sabbath

Sabbath is a Hebrew or Jewish word which means the cessation of labor, or to rest and be idle. Therefore, the Sabbath or holy day derives its name and comes from rest and idleness and simply means a day of rest during which all creatures are to rest. Note that God created and worked for six days, but rested on the seventh. In like manner, we are to work for six days and rest and be idle on the seventh [Gen 1—2:2]. It follows from this that we are not to celebrate created spirits such as angels and saints. For the feast day is a day of rest of God our glory. The Lord alone, and no angel or saint, is our Lord and God.

2. Why God Commanded the Sabbath

God laid out before us all commandments and prohibitions to make us aware of our inner image and likeness, and to understand how God created us in his image to become as God is, i.e., holy, tranquil, good, just, wise, strong, truthful, kind, merciful, etc. All commandments of God demand of us to be godlike; in fact, they have been given us so that we might be conformed to God. As it is written, "You are to become and be holy, for I, your God and Lord, am holy," says God, "keep my commandments and do them," [Lev 20:26]. From this we are to learn that God has given us his commandments and counsels that we might become holy and conformed to God, which is to be like God and as he is. Thus the Sabbath has been instituted by God that we might desire to become holy as God is holy and rest like him, letting go of our works as [23] he did and yet perform God's work in a passive manner for eternity, so that God may do our work [*wircklichkeyt*] without ceasing.

This is a spiritual reason for the Sabbath which was commanded to honor God and to benefit us. For God is honored when his children become like him who is our Father. We should regard this foundation alone and not our own benefit. Just as God is concerned about our benefit and holiness, so we, too, are to be concerned about and seek God's glory, honor, and the benefit of the neighbor, not of ourselves.

When we have eyes only for our benefit, we defile ourselves and make ourselves unholy, neglecting the reason for the Sabbath. Isaiah understood and declared all this when he said [Isa 1:13f.], "I cannot suffer or tolerate your Sabbaths and holy days. Your deeds are impure and wicked. Remove from before your eyes your evil thoughts and cease to do evil." According to this, the finding of our soul must cease and our eyes must directly behold and focus on God and not on what is ours.

When the soul does not become aware of its clarity and inwardness and does not surrender darkness, impurity, wickedness, and unholiness, it is far from and alienated from the reason for the instituted Sabbath. God then hates its Sabbaths and rejects its holy days [Amos 6:4f.]. For in all commandments, the reason and spirit must be sought and nothing else; that means God alone, who commands and whose will is to be sought and known in the commandment, is to be taken seriously. Whoever loves something else fails the commandment and deceives the self.

Above-mentioned reason is eternal and unchanging. No person must change it, and no creature can alter the honor of God and slander God without harm. This reason is spiritual, invisible, and eternal. Thus understood, no person is lord of the Sabbath, but a servant of God or a servant of this Sabbath. Therefore, we may not, without notable diminishment, stray even by a hair's breadth from the reason for the Sabbath.

Faith and the love of God focus on this reason. And just as little as we are able to shorten faith or ignore God's love without bringing about our perdition, so little can we ignore God's Sabbath without condemnation. [24]

A Second Reason for the Institution of the Sabbath

There is yet another reason why God has commanded the Sabbath, namely, love of the neighbor which the masters of the house are to have for their servants and laborers. It flows from the love of God which is to be understood as follows: God loves his people and is gracious and benevolent toward them. He knows full well what benefits and helps his own and serves to strengthen them and make them whole. He also knows what robs their strength and weakens them and that no work can last very long and endure without rest. Therefore, God ordered the seventh day to be celebrated for the well-being of humankind. Employers of laborers and owners of beasts of burden are to leave the seventh day free for their rest and leisure, that they may renew their strength and be refreshed.

This is a physical reason for the Sabbath over which human beings are masters, as much as in them lies, as I shall note subsequently. And this reason must conform to the spirit, i.e., it is to be turned into spiritual rest and must be subject to and serve the first reason. [mar: Note this, for I know it to be true] We must also remember that too much work, done too fast, tires the mind and causes it to be slow and slothful and rather reluctant to stretch and to desire the work of God, so as to suffer and taste it while at rest. I know, of course, that rest and leisure are just as useless as having to put up with unrest and work, when we fail to comprehend what purpose putting up with unrest and work may have.

In this reason for the Sabbath, changes occur in that a person may effect some change in line with God's counsel, as we shall show. But that which external things signify must remain unchanged. External forms are merely signs between God and humankind. They indicate that God alone, not our works, sanctifies humankind. And whatever is thus indicated through externals is true for angels and human beings alike.

3. For Whom the Sabbath Has Been Commanded

The Sabbath has been imposed upon the whole people of God, which means all the citizens of the divine city, both human and angelic [25] spirits alike. Since it is true, as Paul says, that we are able to judge the angels through divine words, proclaimed through Moses, the prophets, Christ, and the apostles, therefore the angels must bend their knees before God's word and confess that they, like we, are subject to the divine word. They have to concede further that it has been said to them no less than to us human beings, "You shall celebrate Sabbath, you shall not commit adultery. You shall not desire another's goods. You shall not kill"[1]—all of which the fall of Satan points to. I stress therefore that the intended meaning and spirit of the Sabbath must be observed by angels and human beings alike, as I shall show, despite the fact that angels are above the law and the commandments.

Therefore, the commandment "You shall celebrate Sabbath" applies to angels and human beings. You may see this from the fact that angels are freer from external work and unrest than we are and that God sanctifies and blesses the Sabbath when he ceases his work of the first Creation. In short, just as God will judge all creatures through one word and one law, so all commandments of the short law[2] apply to all members of the people of God. All who desire to be saved have been given and commanded the Sabbath. To them the word of Paul also applies, when he says [Gal 2:16f.], "You are no longer under the law, but under grace," for the law soon turns into an external testimony and does not remain a commandment.

4. How the Sabbath Is to Be Celebrated

What we must do or leave undone on the Sabbath and how we must act toward God and our brothers can be said firmly, for Scripture is clear. But it is more difficult to experience and test than it is to understand, because it exceeds any natural powers. In our relationship with God we must have rest and peace and pray and wait for all holiness from God. That the Sabbath is a day of rest is given by his word and voice, as was stated above. Moses likewise calls it "a Sabbath of rest to the Lord" [Ex 35:2; Deut 5:12; 16:8; 23]. This rest consists of knowing that one cannot attain to any holiness save through Christ and that one ought to be holy as God is holy—[26] which we are incapable of. Therefore, we are without peace, restless and full of labor and toil and cannot have peace, rest, or leisure until we yield to God irrevocably. When we know truly that God sanctifies through Christ alone, without any work or merit, and when we know and understand that God sanctifies without cost, we are at peace with God and enter into the rest of God.

Accordingly, the form of the Sabbath and everything about how we ought to "sabbatize" God and be at leisure is contained in the reason for the Sabbath. It indicates that creaturely spirits rest in God aright and laudably when they understand and know, through a highly valued, intense, and strong grace and knowledge, that God sanctified them through Christ. Those who know this with a creative wisdom know the manner, customs, and traditions of the Sabbath which has been commanded. They do what ought to be done, are still, and wait for how and when God deigns to sanctify them in conformity to himself, for all that is external is merely a figure and sign of the internal holiness, as Ezekiel prophesies [Ezek 20].

It should also be noted that the Sabbath prepares us for the first commandment as spiritual circumcision prepares us for all works.

Leisure has or is rest and removes the rough skin and the blockage from the heart when we understand that. Hence, leisure is the knife of circumcision.

The most direct way of celebrating the Sabbath is to understand in a loving manner the abundant glory of Christ, the firstborn of all creatures, [Col 1:15]. Anyone who enters through another door, or even more directly, in observing the Sabbath, is a thief and murderer. Christ is the perfection of the Sabbath. Angels and souls must learn from him how to celebrate and they must sabbatize through and after him.

[mar: Gelassenheyt] To celebrate the Sabbath of God blamelessly we must not have our own will, but must let go of our will, and accept and do God's will. That's the right and proper way to celebrate and to sabbatize, as has often been stated. If we desire to celebrate a delightful and God-pleasing Sabbath day [27], we must abandon our delight, will, desires, ways, and our own soul and mind and everything that delights us. Instead, we must take on the delight, will, desire, ways, and thoughts of God. Only then do we celebrate well. In other words, we must unite ourselves with Christ who is the perfection of the Sabbath, as God says through Isaiah [Isa 58:13], "If you turn your foot from the Sabbath on which you pursue your own desires or will on the holy day, and if you call or accept a happy Sabbath on which to praise a gracious God by not doing your will or desire and by not finding your way or speaking your word, you will then delight in God and be carried or led through to every height on earth."

Similarly, if you keep my Sabbaths and choose what I will, you celebrate aright; as if God were to say that if you choose what pleases me and not you, you keep my Sabbaths. Thus, the Sabbath must break self-will.

The holy day means an illumined and bright spirit which is enlightened by the light that illumines all people [Jn 1:9; Isa 58:8]. Such a spirit is lifted above all the highest hills of the earth and does not delight in created things. Its delight is solely in God and goes where the reflection of the lofty sun leads it, for conversion enters in God through light, as Christ says, "Where I am, there my disciple is also" [Jn 12:45ff.]. The delight and light are not at all absorbed by what delights the self. Rather, it is a firm and earnest desire in God who abhors anything that is not God or that leads away from God.

This is what had to be said about how and why the Sabbath day was commanded, and of the appropriate and most diverse [*uberbuntigen*] meaning of the Sabbath which celebrates God.

But do not wonder when I call the holy day an illumined spirit who by God's grace has become a light and a day, since such a spirit is also called a temple of God [1 Cor 3:16]. For the diverse figures of Moses commonly point to one thing. Now, it is undeniable that a believing person is called a priest, a sacrifice, and a temple, why not also a holy day? For it is [28] written, "This is the day which the Lord has made, let us rejoice in it" [Ps 118:24]. God must always be praised in spirit only [Jn 3:6].

I must now consider briefly how the Sabbath is to be celebrated in relation to the neighbor and our brothers, whom we must grant their leisure. Hence, on every Sabbath day we must allow our menservants and maidservants, horses, oxen, donkeys, and all other beasts of labor who worked through the week to be idle and to celebrate.

This is the other reason for the Sabbath, namely, for your laborers and beasts of labor to refresh themselves and to cool the heat of their labor and to refresh their bones and restore their strength. This has been clearly stated by Moses. Six days you shall work and on the seventh day you shall cease to work, so that your ox and donkey might rest and the son of your maidservant and the foreigner might relax [Ex 23:12].

What God says for the benefit of oxen and donkeys, Moses applies to all other animals who help us complete our work, be they buffaloes, elephants, etc. Moses says that God demanded that all working animals are not to work on the Sabbath. Why? The reason is that they might rest. When Moses speaks of the son of a maidservant, he means all workers. Your children, too, should be idle and refrain from all work on the Sabbath, says God. Why? To be refreshed and to relax by resting [Deut 5:12].

Male and female cooks must have this freedom, too. On the seventh day, they are not obligated to kindle your fire. The same is true for stokers and others. For God says, "You shall not kindle a fire on the Sabbath," which has been said for the benefit of laborers [Ex 35:3].

In short, God bound all householders to let their workers go idle and free on the Sabbath. Even more are poor people to be freed from all bonded labor. And their masters must not prod them to do anything or serve on the Sabbath day, be it with horse and buggy, on foot, or whatever. To force their subjects to work or serve is to act against the will of God and to violate and tyrannize their neighbor, thus giving sufficient cause to their subjects to oppose their authority. [29]

5. The Desecration of the Sabbath

This leads us to note the desecration of the Sabbath which is rather common among today's Christians, seeing that they carry out on the feast day all the things they would avoid at other times. Neither cattle nor manservants nor maids are safe from them—in that I am as guilty as they.

On feast days they use their horses which all week long pulled plows or vehicles. Then on the seventh day, the Sabbath, they ride cross-country to visit their friends, seek out merry company, or they collect their debts and do things which are openly against God who gave us work horses to let them work for six days for our food. On the seventh day, however, we must let them rest because the One who gave them to us, granted them leisure, that they might regain their strength and be able to do the work that is to come. Disregard of this leads to contempt, not only for the will of God who desires that we give the working animals a chance to celebrate, but also for the gift of God, which we ought to accept and use with thanksgiving.

Yet, we are neglectful and stubborn to do what God demands. From this comes the horrible vice of disrespect for God when people neither seek nor respect God. God often punishes this vice on the cattle through whom we sin, when our animals are stricken and allowed to die or perish. Yet, we refuse to acknowledge responsibility or sin and we blame warlocks and witches instead. But our resentment toward God we do not take to heart, deeming our inattention a small sin. Therefore, God, too, considers us as nothing, which is why things happen, as we can see.

Similarly, it is an abuse when we force our servants or children to work on a feast day by tearing them away from their rest. I speak here of the rest of God and not of play, drinking, high living, and swearing. Those who rest in this manner celebrate with backgammon, dice, cards, chessboards, drinking bouts, high living, and bad company; they work against God and [30] the neighbor. Such rabble should be prevented from having their devilish rest, and be enticed or forced to do something better. It is better for them to till the field than to throw dice, curse, blaspheme, get drunk, fornicate, gossip, ridicule, fight, steal, and murder. Such devilish feast days I do not commend—they provide no rest. This is readily apparent in drunken servants who cannot lift head or limb the day after, because of the heavy work they did on the feast day, tapping beer kegs or in wine cellars.

But when servants or maids wish to relax or refresh their weary limbs or rest in God, the head of the house owes it to God to let them rest. How Christians observe this, however, I need not tell you. It is obvious that the masters of the house, because of their gluttony, force their male and female cooks to greater work and less rest on a feast day than on a work day.

And they aggravate their children and servants ten times more than on work days, forgetting their obligation to God which they accepted in their baptism. They contravene God's commandment and voice and show themselves at odds with their faith, for the leisure which a householder must grant his employees on the Sabbath is a work of faith for all who understand God's mercy and hold vividly in mind what goodness God has shown. We should ever be mindful of God's gracious deeds and that God has freed our forebears from the laborious and unbearable service which oppressed them in Egypt and led them to rest and leisure [Ex 13:6]. Therefore, we in turn should respond with works of mercy and willingly allow our employees to rest and be idle on the seventh day. For this reason God says, "You shall not work on the seventh day, etc., so that your servants and laborers might rest" [Ex 20:10f.]. You must recall how you served in Egypt and how God brought you out of the furnace of servitude and that therefore God commanded you to keep the Sabbath [Deut 5:12-15].

[mar: What faith can do] Faith is a strong wisdom which truly tastes God's goodness and knows how God has liberated from servitude in Egypt; it empties itself toward the neighbor [31] who serves us, and makes us want to afford him rest and freedom also, because we know that this pleases God.

Therefore, those who force their servants and employees to work on the Sabbath are not believers at all. For this reason the spirit of God says, "I desire mercy and not sacrifice" [Hos 6:6]. Speaking of external works and practices, it is better for you to allow your employees to rest than for you alone to refrain firmly from works of necessity. This must be stressed and means that you must be merciful just as God was merciful toward you. Therefore, it is against God, their own faith and Christian obligation, and a terrible abuse, indeed, when the masters of the household coerce their servants.

It is especially abusive and contrary to the nature of the Sabbath when debtors are made to pay their debts on feast days. [mar: Note this, you rich usurers] For a debtor becomes even more agitated (when he is reprimanded on the Sabbath because of his debt and is unable to repay) than if he is warned on a weekday when he works.

Those who would gladly pay up but cannot, are most aware of how this saddens and wearies them. How can I rest in God when I cause my brother unrest and upset him with my restless work? If we would rest in God we must forgive our debtors, not only their transgressions, but also their monetary debts, which they are unable to repay, as the gospel story indicates which tells of the servant who oppressed a fellow servant because of a debt [Mt 18:24-34]. The reason is that we must be of one mind with God who wants us to forgive. Thus we should wish to be sanctified by God on the Sabbath also and to forgive sins, just as we want our sin to be forgiven by God and to be sanctified [Mt 5:20]. That is what we call keeping the Sabbath holy externally, when we are united with God inwardly and desire to receive forgiveness of sin and holiness from God. It is an unchristian vice and shame, therefore, when Christians and usurious priests reprimand their debtors from the pulpit on the Sabbath and then harass them and so rob others of their rest. Divine Scripture amply supports and demands that such dealings be avoided and stopped on the Sabbath from the very start, else they do not keep the Sabbath holy, but defile it [Deut 5; Lev 65; Isa 58; Mt 5]. [32]

It is a terrible abuse among Christians to demand repayment of monetary debts on the Sabbath [Isa 1:13; 56:2], but it is just as offensive to hold hearings on legal matters which involve penalties or payments. The exception might be hearings that lead to peace or avert unrest and involve no greed. For the commandment of brotherly love and unity is greater and higher than the external Sabbath. Therefore, we need not heed the Sabbath when peace can be achieved and nothing but peace is sought.

To sum up, I would like to see ungracious householders and raging or unbelieving Christians to be persuaded as they are told, "Look, you want to rob me of my rest and harass me today on the Sabbath. But for God's sake I am not obligated to serve you today." In a similar way a debtor might speak out against the lender, "Look today I should rest in God, but you are out to torment me, contrary to the rest and freedom granted by God. Therefore, I refuse to answer you today."

But servants should not turn this freedom into carnal disobedience, as they are wont to do. When it is said, "You are free on the seventh day and not obligated to work," they forget that they ought to work six days. They then seek to have a good Monday as well and in addition work unfaithfully on the other days, too, while still wanting to enjoy the freedom of the Sabbath. This is just as much against God as when they are forced by their masters to work on the seventh day.

For six days servants are to work faithfully—not for the sake of appearance, but wholeheartedly [Col 3:22]. None of the six days is free or given to leisure. Lazy servants should accept this as much as that on the seventh day the servant must rest or be idle. Both householders and servants must heed God's commandments and honor them to the best of their ability. Then everything will be well and no one will harm the other. [33]

6. Whether We Have the Right to Break Sabbath Observance

The external Sabbath has been instituted for the benefit of those who work, that they might renew or restore their strength and that people and livestock—and not only they but the housefather—might be refreshed, as we said earlier. However, God does not care much for external behavior and customs, but merely that no one disadvantage or harm another. Therefore, the external celebration has not been commanded so rashly and seriously that work which might benefit another could not be done on the Sabbath, or that we should suffer loss or disaster rather than do an external work and so forfeit celebration. For God does not look to external things and sacrifices, but to the internal ones. When these are upright, what follows externally is right, too, and everything a person does or leaves undone is right as well. Similarly, God prefers a broken heart—where that is found it matters little whether we fast or eat, drink or suffer thirst, sacrifice or not, celebrate or work, as long as we do not come to God while we are empty within [Ps 51:17]. Although we might come empty-handed externally, it does not endanger us before God.

Thus, I may kindle a fire, cook, and eat in God's name, as long as I am in God's rest uprightly. For God has no need of my external leisure which does not add to, or take anything away from God. But my internal leisure God can praise or scold, despise or magnify. He can consider me merciful or cruel and call me truthful or deceitful. Therefore, God gives attention to the inner rest and leisure—if that is honest, we can stand before God even though externally there may be no celebration. Thus Christ defended his disciples for gathering and eating grain on the Sabbath [Mt 12:3ff.] when the Pharisees complained about it.

7. The Son of Man Is Lord of the Sabbath

In response to this Christ said, "The Son of man is lord of the Sabbath and the Sabbath has been commanded on account of people," [Mt 12:8] i.e., we have the freedom to [34] work on the Sabbath as often as our need or welfare calls for it. This the disciples did when on the Sabbath they plucked and ate the grain because they were hungry. All external practices have been instituted for the benefit of people, and a believer is lord and has power to take or leave them, as his need dictates and his spirit comprehends.

Moses and Christ concur. Moses says, "You shall not do any external works so that your servants and maid servants, your children and you might rest and restore your strength." And Christ says, "The Sabbath was instituted for humankind" [Deut 14; Ex 20; Mt 12].

For your need or benefit, you may work on the Sabbath and do a good deed for yourself as much as you might do one for someone else —kindle a fire, cook, eat, drink. But see to it that you do not forget God in all of that. Know that God loves mercy more than a burnt offering [Hos 6:6]. Celebrate and enjoy your leisure, but in such a way that you do not neglect a better or greater thing.

If hunger prevents you from experiencing God's grace, then

pluck ears of corn on the Sabbath and eat them in God's name [Lk 6:1-5]. The Sabbath has been instituted for your benefit and betterment. You are lord of the Sabbath, and the Sabbath exists for you and not you for the Sabbath [Mk 2:23-28]. Hence, you may give herbs to another and prepare them for medicine on the Sabbath, and you must help the neighbor and show mercy, which is more and better than to sabbatize and celebrate externally. In this way servants should help meet the immediate need of their master and prevent future damage by foregoing their freedom and ignoring the Sabbath. One owes it to another out of Christian brotherly love to help up livestock that has fallen down [Ex 23:5].

When I said that one may do on the Sabbath on account of need what apart from need ought not to be done—in other words, that in an emergency we may ignore and break the Sabbath—I did not endorse the breaking of the Sabbath with works of mercy and brotherly love which I call works of necessity. For I spoke of breaking the Sabbath in the sense which Christ used against the Pharisees who [35] thought it unseemly and detrimental to the Sabbath to have a sick person made well on the Sabbath. Christ countered them, saying, "Look, if it is not fitting for me to do good, why then do your priests kill the sacrificial [animals] on the Sabbath and break the Sabbath with their killing and butchering?" Likewise I respond to those who think that a person might defile Sunday through a work of brotherly love: It is right to break the Sabbath to help another person in his need, even though such works of mercy might break the Sabbath. However, it is impossible for a work of love to break the Sabbath, for God has put an order in his commandments. Some command great and highly valued things; some command lesser things. Those that command works of love, faith, mercy, and the like enjoin the very best and highest works. Those that speak of sacrifices and Sabbaths and similar ceremonies, enjoin what is of lesser value.

God never commanded us to keep all the commandments at once—speaking of the letter of the law, but that we are to do the best works first and foremost. Among the best is the commandment and work of love and mercy toward the neighbor which God prefers to the Sabbath, sacrifices, fasting, singing, baptizing, and the like. If we observe the latter works but neglect to show love and mercy, we anger God who would say, "It never was my will or order that you keep the lesser commandments while omitting the major commandments, or that you sacrifice other than with a good will and intention." God wants us to keep the highest commandments and works, above all.

Now, if we have done the greater, but have not done the lesser, God is not angered therefore, if we had no time for them. Therefore, the lesser are not commanded for times when the greater would have to be left undone. Stubborn servants should know, therefore, that they do not break the Sabbath when they help their masters on feast days if they observe that their landlord's goods would spoil if they were not tended in time or were not saved and secured through [36] work.

God subordinated the Sabbath to brotherly support. Employees along with other people are obligated at all times to prevent harm to their neighbor, on a feast day as much as on a working day. They are to spare no effort or diligence. How much more then are they obligated before God to do the very best for their masters whose bread they eat and whose wages they earn? They do not break the Sabbath of God when they work in such situations, for the external Sabbath is disregarded whenever you must come to your neighbor's aid—the external Sabbath is then no longer a Sabbath. So, servants and maids may not appeal to the Sabbath when their masters are in need or suffer harm, for they are obliged by God to work on the Sabbath. Should a servant see that it is going to be wet or that a devastating thunderstorm is coming and that his master's hay or grain would get wet or spoil in the field unless it is gathered in on the Sabbath, the servant ought to harness the horses and help with the loading and diligently bring in the crop. He cannot use the Sabbath to cover and excuse himself.

God speaks as follows [Deut 22],[3] "When you see your brother's donkey or ox falling on the road, do not ignore this, but assist in helping it up. You must help up your neighbor's cattle when they fall and you are present, be it Sunday or Monday." You must not leave without having helped, for God spoke without specifying a day. And when you see that one of your neighbor's donkeys or animals has fallen, you must not go away and leave it there, but you must help it up. Had God intended to exclude the Sabbath, he would have named certain days and he would have said that you are to help them up every day except on the Sabbath. But God did not exclude the Sabbath. Rather, he made a general commandment to prevent harm to your neighbor. Thus we know that servants must not allow their landlord's hay to spoil because of the Sabbath, for the donkey and other animals would perish without hay, and human beings—who are more important than animals—would die without grain; and God's commandment would be for nought.

You masters of the house owe more to your servants, and you menservants and maidservants owe more service [1 Pet 2:13-18; Eph

5:21] to the masters of the house [37] than to anyone else. Therefore, you must protect their cattle and goods ahead of anything else.

Hence, female cooks cannot excuse themselves and say to their masters, "It is Sunday today. I am not obligated to work," if fire and food are a necessity. Therefore, maids and stable-hands, and all servants are obligated to God to take care of their master's cattle on a Sunday and not allow them to perish. Assume now that a landlord hates his servant and vice versa, the servant or maid is nevertheless obligated before God to help up the master's cattle. Even if someone with whom you have made no agreement to work hates you, you are obligated nonetheless to help up the donkey or cattle of the one who hates—Sunday or work day—when you see that the cattle might be harmed. Since everyone should prevent harm to his enemy, even at the expense of the Sabbath and since servants are more obligated to their masters than to anyone else, slothful servants and maids cannot excuse themselves by appealing to the freedom of the Sabbath and so neglect their master's beasts, as some do who spend an entire Sunday with the tavern keeper or at a dance, leaving their master's cattle hungry and thirsty. For they are obligated—Sunday or work day—to look after their master's cattle and goods to prevent damage—each according to his contract [bestellung]. The negligent will have to do penance before God.

I had to make this known to the dishonest servants and maids lest this booklet cause them to yield to the freedom of the flesh or to be ensnared by the devil by being disobedient and by breaking off their covenanted duties. For the master has the power to force his servants to work on the Sabbath (if necessity demands).

It is obvious from this that a person can break the external Sabbath whenever need demands, and that we ought to break it, as we heard. Especially since it is important that the great matters of the law be done before all others and the lesser ones afterwards, and since God demands mercy more than sacrifice [Hos 6:6; Mic 6:8]. Since God demands one kind of activity and work more than another and since we are to relax the least and do the greatest when we cannot do both at the same time, we ought to break the Sabbath [38] and put it off to help our neighbor and be merciful without fearing any person's criticism in the matter or heeding anyone, as Paul says [Col 2:6-16]. We ought to help ourselves as well, rather than celebrate, as long as we understand that external leisure prevents God's grace from reaching us and that the spirit of God—who leads people in all things to God—directs and leads everything, although this may appear foolish to carnal people who lack the Spirit.

8. One Sabbath Is Another's Slave or Servant

Truth says that the Sabbath is the rest of the Lord. It follows from this that one Sabbath has been instituted on account of another and that human beings are both slave and lord of the Sabbath [Gen 1]. If a person is to rest in God and is to ask of and expect holiness from God, then the Son of Man is a servant of the Sabbath, just as he is a servant of God. And just as God is lord of humankind and not we lords over God, so the Sabbath is lord over humankind and not vice versa. These words refer to the inner and spiritual Sabbath which is celebrated to the honor, glory, and praise of God.

As the soul is greater and better than the body, so God is immeasurably greater than the soul. Similarly, God's honor and glory are greater than the soul and the Sabbath greater than the created spirits. As the one who sanctifies is greater than the one who is being blessed, so also is the sanctified Sabbath greater than the sanctified soul. Therefore, the Sabbath is lord over us and we are servants of the Sabbath—this is true only of the Sabbath which includes God, i.e., which contains the spirit of rest.

The external Sabbath, however, on which human beings rest from their work and refrain from physical labor, has according to God been commanded because of humankind. Hence, the external Sabbath is lower than the inner and serves the inner when needed. It is merely a sign of inner leisure and is there because of humankind. We stand between both Sabbaths under the spiritual [39] and invisible and above the physical and perceptible—servant of the higher and lord of the lower.

The external Sabbath (which the Pharisees imposed on Christ and his disciples), exists on account of humankind and the spiritual Sabbath. Thus one Sabbath is higher than and lord of the other, while the other is a servant. Just as the inner being is master of the external, and the spirit [master] over the flesh, so also the soul or spirit is above all lower creatures. The external human being is perishable, relates to perishable things only, and will pass away with them [1 Cor 3]. But the inner person can deal with and handle eternal things, and is above all things temporal and perishable. Further, it is not always good for [the inner being] to be bound to time and place, wherefore, God set him above all external Sabbaths.

9. What We Must Do on the Sabbath or Holy Day

Someone might now ask what a person is to do on the Sabbath to pass the long time or [overcome] boredom. Answer: We ought to be idle, do nothing, and endure the long time. The Sabbath has been instituted for the spirit to reach a point of boredom and learn something during the idle time.

For idleness and getting bored is a spiritual circumcision and preparation to receive God's work, since boredom and ennui drive out human desires.

It would be good if on a Sabbath we were to put our head in our hands, bow down, and acknowledge our misfortune and weakness with great sorrow; thus we should rush more quickly to the One (who alone cleanses and sanctifies).

God forbade human beings to work on the Sabbath [Ex 20:10]. And everything we, our children, and our cattle might do, God has canceled; everything is to be at rest on the day on which we pray God for holiness. This undoubtedly indicates that we must remain surrendered [*in der Gelassenheyt bleyben*] and that we must add nothing of our own to God's works, [40] lest we defile God's work through our own works. God's prohibition moreover indicates that our works impede God's work. Therefore, God demands that we cast off all our works whenever we desire his work; the visible ennui serves that purpose, as is said, "You shall chastise yourselves, keep yourselves down, and humble yourselves on the Sabbath day, if you desire to be cleansed and sanctified by God or to receive the gifts of God" [Lev 16:30f.]. The burdens that are in our house we must bear [Jer 17:21ff.], but other burdens we must not pick up or load upon ourselves. As Christ says, "Take up your cross and follow me" [Mt 10:39].

On the Sabbath you are to do nothing but suffer and when your ability to suffer [*leydlichkeyt*] has been reached, God's spirit will fill you with his work. You might say now that everyone who does God's will does some work. I answer that all work issues from God, but it is found in us only in a passive manner, i.e., we receive God's work, but if we are active, we are not at rest [Jn 6].

To speak generally, all evil works are prohibited, for anyone who does an evil deed defiles the Sabbath of God and does not celebrate.

10. Which Day of the Week Must Be Celebrated

If servants have worked for six days, they are to have the seventh day off. God says without distinction, "Remember to celebrate the seventh day." He does not say that we must keep Sunday or Saturday as the seventh day. It is no secret that human beings instituted Sunday. As for Saturday, the matter is still being debated. But this is clear that you must celebrate on the seventh day and allow your servants to celebrate whenever they have worked for six days. Now if every householder were to appoint a special seventh day for each of the servants, there would be disorder in his household, especially if he has many servants. And if every household in a given city were to have its own Sabbath, the city order would be disrupted and as a result preaching would also end up in disorder. [41]

Now, if it is not to the detriment of the word of God or to preaching, or if there should be daily reading or preaching of the word of God, each householder would be entitled to select a seventh day that suits him and his household best and is of greatest advantage to his work. For a householder does always have greater power in his own household to order the worship of God than any pope or bishop—yes, even the entire community [Num 30].[4] And if a householder is scrupulous about the time and allows his servants freedom from beginning to end to hear God's word, he should be able to select and set the seventh day as he pleases. This must be done so as to avoid the risk of cheating his servants and forcing them to work for more than six days; this applies to the external Sabbath. But when the external cover is removed and we look at the spiritual Sabbath, then every day is a Sabbath and one Sabbath flows from the other. For the more we exercise in spiritual celebrations, the more Sabbaths follow and flow from one another [Isa 56]. Because we need God's blessings every day and hour, we must therefore keep all days holy and be without work on every working day and experience tranquillity [Gelassenheyt] and ennui, as noted above.

11. On the Diversity of the Sabbath

The Sabbath means nothing other than a time of rest, and the Sabbath of God is to rest in God. Although in our mortal body we do not rest in God with all our strength—nor are we able to—yet we ought to rest in God with all our heart and might. Then perfection is bound to follow on imperfection and the whole to come after the parts and that which impedes the whole will perish. The soul will be emptied and the vine, provided it has been well tended, will bring forth a perfect work. The spirit of fear will be replaced by the spirit of rest [Jn 15]. The small and low spirit will become so big as to be able to enter the kingdom of God in order to experience a perfect Sabbath [Heb 8:11; 9:11-14] with all the angels. Everything we do on the tabernacle of God, we must gauge and do by the highest [42] model and example. Therefore, there must be a variety of Sabbaths, as God's mouth indicates when he calls the Sabbath under heaven a day of reconciliation and purification, tribulation and discipline [Lev 16; 23]. The spirit of fear works all this and this is signified by the external appearance of the Sabbath. Our Sabbath contains fear and work. Since we must be careful and guard against clinging to or becoming attached to anything which may hinder our readiness for salvation, but instead flee all that could work against holiness—but fleeing evil involves its own work—therefore, we must know fear and bitter resignation [Gelassenheyt] of all that clings to us temporally. We then do not mistake creatures for God, by seeking comfort, joy, help, or counsel in creatures and so rob God of his honor [Jn 12]. In this, surely, we toil and labor for as long as we are in the night, and we catch the light only with great effort and travail and follow it so as not to err in darkness.

Now this temporal work must pass away, and anguish and fear must cease; resignation [Gelassenheyt] must enter our unresigned state and we must become unconcerned about anything that might prevent us from receiving sanctification from God. Future rest, therefore, will be a bright and meaningful day of rest without work—like light without darkness. For the higher Sabbath has its roots in the period of greatest rejoicing when there will be total love, complete rest, and nothing but inexpressible, heavenly, eternal joy and freedom. Then we shall forever recall all the pain and evil we suffered (in this life), namely, all that prevented us from experiencing God's grace; and we will be assured, henceforth, that during the highest Sabbath no obstacle shall hinder or bother us. We know this through the spirit which fills us with peace; for the spirit of fear which taxed and stretched the created spirit to the limit has been brought to an end [Isa 11].

Here we experience the first interval and beginning of the Sabbath and we are servants. There we experience—everyone according to his measure—a wholly joyous perfection of the Sabbath [Ex 35]. [43]

Not in vain does God say that the seventh day is the Sabbath of Sabbaths, according to the tenor of the Hebrew language. If ever there should be a Sabbath of Sabbaths, it is one which is higher, more noble, purer, holier, and better than all other Sabbaths. By it we are cleansed and sanctified so that we can no longer approve of and persist in what is unholy, for we have been placed beyond occasional temptations. For that reason I suppose that God used two different words when he commanded the Sabbath [Deut 5]. For he says, "You shall keep the Sabbath," or "preserve" and "take heed to keep it." This is indicated by the word *schama* which includes notions of worry, anxiety, and labor. This indicates that our Sabbath here is kept and celebrated with labor and anxiety.

[mar: Labor and anxiety on the Sabbath] The other word is "Remember and be mindful of the Sabbath to keep it." In Hebrew this is *zachar*, which does not imply pain and labor to the same degree as the previous word. It is merely the remembrance of former troubles, but not that which can actually happen. At that point we experience eternal rest, and we labor no longer as we did earlier. We merely recall our labors and the struggle between spirit and flesh and all carnal experiences [Jer 23]. We have entered God's high Sabbath and enjoy the inheritance of Jacob which is secure. In our Sabbath [here below] this was merely promised and indicated from a distance. [Above]the small spark of the Sabbath has become a major fire. There is then only one bright shining day and an eternal Sabbath. May God help us to attain it. Amen.

12. On Designated Feast Days for Saints and Angels

[mar: The pope is the devil's first begotten son] The reasons and names for the Sabbath which I narrated above make it more than obvious how the devil or the son of the devil invented feast days, contrary to the honor, will, and commandments of God, and how they thoroughly deceived us to establish sabbaths for saints and angels. Sabbaths are to serve to the honor and praise of God alone and the external Sabbath is a simple figure to indicate that God sanctifies and that by celebrating the feast day aright, we shall [44] be sanctified by God. Now a figure that points to holiness when the will to become holy is not found there must be a lie and deception. Just as the sign pointing to wine being sold is a lie and deception when the inn keeper has no wine or cannot serve any, so also the Sabbath is false, deceptive, and a lie whenever it is celebrated or attributed to one who cannot sanctify us, which happens every time we celebrate the saints.

On judgment day the saints will sit on the twelve chairs of judgment and render the verdict of unbelief and condemnation against those who help create celebrations for the saints. They will rightly charge them for having slandered their God when they courted him with their customs and solemn observances which they themselves fled and detested.

Sabbaths for saintly creatures are true signs that those who celebrate a saintly person or angel reject Christ. By the solemn deed they indicate that they intend to attain to holiness through someone other than Christ which is nothing but a rejection of Christ. Likewise those reject and scorn Christ who dare say that righteousness comes from the law [Gal 2:16f.]. Then it would follow that Christ had died in vain, which is totally opposed to God. Those who celebrate saints interfere in God's creation and pervert the works of creation, since no saint is capable of creating a single hour. Those who attribute a single day to a creature rob the Lord of his created work and place it with one who did not and could not create it. This then is a sin against God's power and works directly against God's omnipotence.

I shall not even mention the damage suffered by householders who, because of priestly abuses [*pfeffische tyranney*] are robbed of their authority and of the services which their servants are obligated to render their masters for six days. These duties and obligations are broken by the feast days of the priests who give masterful reasons in place of obedience for such diverse vices as slander, drunkenness, swearing, theft, murder, and every sort of evil, all of which could be detailed in many more words. [45]

13. How the Commandment of the Sabbath Leads to the Recognition of God's Mercy, Drawing and Bringing Us to Christ

We ought to note especially that God has shown us great mercy in relieving us from the serious and strict command to work daily. For God ordered Adam and through him all of mankind to earn their livelihood and the bread they eat from the earth, as punishment and atonement for disobedience [Gen 3:14-19]. This commandment also means that we must earn our daily bread by daily work and that we must not eat our bread on any given day unless on that day we obtained it through new work. For it is said there, "In the sweat of your brow you shall eat your bread."

Now if we are to eat our bread in the sweat of our brow, we have to work every day and make up for Adam's desire by our disinclination and labor which would be rather too hard and unbearable. For not only is Adam's disobedience atoned by us, but the constant labor also means that in the long run we must die, for Scripture says that unbearable work ages us and leads to our death. It would not be unreasonable for God to do away with us and kill us through work. God is fully in the right to strangle us with work and reduce us to ashes. But God our Lord has shown paternal love and unmerited mercy toward us. He does not remain angry forever nor does he want to exterminate us. Therefore, God issued the commandment of the Sabbath by which we are to work for six days only. The seventh day he set aside for a Sabbath and a day of leisure for our benefit, so that we might revive and strengthen ourselves and restore our exhausted strength [Deut 26:11]. For this we cannot sufficiently thank the merciful God. Blessed are they who experience the spirit of mercy and rejoice in God's praise, name, and glory.

Again we must consider diligently that leisure brings forth boredom and was commanded that we experience tedium and ennui when we rest in God and experience leisure like God. Through leisure, among other things, God commanded those who are tougher and stronger and well able to work (and who greatly delight [46] in their work), to break their delight and fall into listlessness and dread of life and on a feast day think on how evil, fragile, foolish, weak, loveless, and without faith in God they are; how they pursue greed and are full of anxiety and do not seek God's honor uprightly nor take God's commandments to heart or do them when they work. Such reflection of their evil will is caused by idle ennui or boring idleness.

Therefore, we must observe the Sabbath diligently and learn how ennui or listlessness is useful and why God urges us to be idle. But we must be careful not to turn leisure into pleasure for the simple reason that it is better to enter a house of mourning than to enter a house of pleasure [Sir 7:2], for God has imposed idleness on us to make the Sabbath also a day of renunciation, sadness, and tribulation.

Never forget that the Sabbath includes forgiveness of sins, for we cannot be sanctified and enter into God's forgiveness before we obtain forgiveness of sins. And this must happen through the six spirits of God, after which we enter the seventh, which I will speak of in another booklet.[5]

May God enlighten all pastors of his poor little sheep and with them lead all of us graciously to a true knowledge of his divine holiness, which we so greatly need, and may he enlighten us eternally. Amen. 1524

13
Several Main Points of Christian Teaching Regarding Which Dr. Luther Brings Andreas Carlstadt Under Suspicion Through False Accusation and Slander
1525

After his expulsion from Electoral Saxony, Carlstadt traveled to several places in hopes of finding a more permanent settlement. He lived in Rothenburg ob der Tauber, Strasbourg, Zurich, and Heidelberg. During December 1524, Carlstadt received the first major attack on his position from Luther.[1] It was followed in January 1525 by a second part.[2] Carlstadt responded to these tracts with three tracts, one of which was the document, "Anzeyg etlicher Hauptartikel," published by an Augsburg printing house.

As with other tracts from this period, interest in Carlstadt's appeal was limited—he managed only one edition. In fifteen sections the au-

thor sets out to defuse the charge against him of having taught errors, and he attempts to give a reasonable account of main articles of faith which would show to his Christian brothers and sisters that his position is in line with the pure teaching of the crucified Christ whom God chose for the redemption of humankind.

He further alleges that he was driven out of Saxony without having been able to defend himself. Since the best defense is a good attack, he, in turn, charges that Luther's teaching is erroneous when measured by the yardstick of "inner" and "outward" law—a distinction which would in no way endear him with Luther and his camp. The topics he focuses on are faith in Christ, the necessary mortification of the flesh, love of God and of neighbor, true Christian freedom, and truth. More than elsewhere in his tracts, Carlstadt unabashedly names Luther as his antagonist and holds him in large measure responsible for the misfortune that has befallen him. The widening gulf between the two men is clearly apparent.

Freys/Barge list this 1525 publication under number 145. A copy of the booklet in the Zentralbibliothek Zurich, signature V 16024, was compared with the text in Erich Hertzsch, *Karlstadts Schriften aus den Jahren 1523-25, Teil II*, pp 61ff. We used Hertzsch to prepare this translation.

Page references in brackets [ ] are to the Hertzsch edition. Scripture references in the margins have been incorporated in the text in brackets [ ]; those supplied by the translator appear in endnotes. R. Sider included translated excerpts from this tract in his monograph on Carlstadt. Our translation was made independent of his.

Contents of This Booklet

Andreas Carlstadt, exiled on account of the truth without a hearing, yet called and chosen by God the Father to the true proclamation of the cross of Christ.

To his brothers on the River Saale and to all who seek, or would like to seek God, the true way.

Love, grace, wisdom, understanding, strength, and consolation from God our Father who knows us and from Jesus Christ our Lord be with you. Amen.

My dear brothers, although Dr. Luther knew and praised me before our falling out as one who knew something of the articles of Christian teaching, the poor man now allows his anger to get the better of him. He defames me as one who knows nothing of these articles of which even children talk now.[3] He does not care much that it ill suits him to convict his own mouth of lying and to negate that which my many booklets and disputations at Wittenberg publicly attest to and which he himself acknowledged. All this might be forgiven and understandable. But he defames me against his conscience and acts as if God were blind and unable to see into our hearts, and so unjust as not to punish Dr. Luther's malice, or so weak as not to be able to avenge me, or so unmerciful as to want [61] to forsake the afflicted and not save those who depend exclusively on divine help. In short, D. L.[4] acts as if he knew nothing of the fact that all those who overcome and devour Israel sin and hit the very apple of the eye of God when they hit the least of God's servants [Jer 2; 30:16; Zech 7:12; 12]. Dr. Luther brazenly accuses me against his own better judgment of not knowing or caring about the main articles of Christian teaching, treating me unjustly before his own conscience (for that I call on God as my witness). He hits me more severely with this than if he had hit me with swords or guns to finish me off.

I must charge this against him before God and ask God to be our sole judge. He knows what is in our respective hearts and will not allow an evil to go unavenged. Far be it from me, however, to defame anyone, as Dr. Luther has defamed me. For I esteem divine wisdom, justice, power, and mercy more highly than, without cause and against my own conscience, to tell lies about and defame the least of all who live, as Dr. Luther has lied and defamed me. I am quite sure that he neither fears God nor esteems the God whom he confesses, for I can and must judge him by such fruits, since I know that true faith in God does not tolerate such devilish lies.

I can accept it when Luther calls me unlearned. For I know that he himself is unable to pass the great sea which we all have to cross, to gain health and understanding [Ezek 47:1-14]. But I cannot judge in his favor when Dr. Luther challenges me on articles of faith. Just as little as I consider it acceptable when he says Carlstadt is a blasphemer. I will prove through my books and oral testimony (should I be called on to be examined), that Dr. Luther has done me gross and insufferable violence. I dare him to appear together with me before a Christian congregation and to allow that the assertion of my innocence be heard.

Should I not know that the law of God is spiritual, just, holy, and good, and that it makes the inner being spiritual, just, holy, and good—when God writes and imprints his law upon the heart [Rom 7:6; Ps 19:7-10]—when God's spirit leads into [62] truth and speaks into the heart what the external voice shouts into the ears, so that sin is then rightly known and fled as an evil [Jn 16; Jer 31; Rom 7; 8]?

The true exposure of sin comes through the spirit who gave that which is external, and not through the external letter. A right understanding of evil or sin abhors sin. It springs forth and flows from the acknowledged grace of Christ. Thereafter the acknowledged grace of Christ (shown on the cross) liberates from the external law and breaks its sting and power [Rom 6; 1 Cor 15]. For anyone who understands the law of the letter without the revelation through the spirit does not hate evil and has not become its enemy. Rather, through the law a person increases in that which is evil. Thus it is the grace of God through Christ by which we know sin as it is. This grace alone leads a person away from sin and from the power and might of the letter and the law which really kills. For God's law, known through one's understanding, exposes sin in such a way that one who comes to know it becomes worse than he was before. He really comes to delight in sin and develops animosity toward the righteousness of God, thus achieving that sin becomes a thousand times more prominent. Therefore, there is a marked difference between the exposure of evil through the spirit of Christ and the exposure of sin which the flesh points up of its own strength. The external exposure of sin through the law enflames the sinner with lust and animosity, and strengthens sin. The internal exposure through the grace of Christ breaks lust, cools animosity, and destroys sin. If I cannot distinguish what one is able to achieve who is under the law and what one can do who has been freed from the law by the grace of Christ, I should be a poor Christian, indeed. Yes, I would be a senseless fool who does not understand his own resources, paper and ink. In short, I have known it longer than Dr. Luther (I think) that the law is spiritual in that it reveals the righteousness of

God and the unrighteousness of creatures. And I know nothing better than to be more sure of my case than Dr. Luther even. I also understand Paul more thoroughly than Dr. Luther. I should have thought that Dr. Luther knew that I wrote a booklet at Wittenberg entitled *De spiritu et litera*[5] in which I proved that Dr. Luther wronged me gravely when he accused me of not knowing what the [63] law is capable of. I have written other books on the subject of which I must now boast because of the great plight I am in. Though they are not as fine and ornate as Dr. Luther's books, they are nonetheless truthful and godly, just like the books of the prophets and apostles.

Although I wrote on all main articles [of faith] and although my books convict Dr. Luther of untrue slander, I nonetheless wanted to write a special booklet (for you, brothers) on the main articles of faith, so that all those may learn of my faith who do not know me as well as you, my brothers. I sense that there are several unchristian souls who do not as yet know Dr. Luther as I do. They refuse to believe that Dr. Luther has lashed out with such malice and untruth. They blame me before having examined me—quite contrary to the teaching of Christ not to judge [1 Jn 4:1; Mt 7:1].

Then there are several others who are so blinded and in error that they can read my booklets without seeing that all my arguments against the sacrament flow from my faith in Christ. They fail to note that the true and pure faith in Christ is so upright and pure that it cannot bear the tainted popish sacrament as it has been used till now, but knocks it down instead. But just because I attack and deal with the sacrament, those who are envious of me should not ever be led to accuse me of unbelief or charge me with having forgotten the faith. For there are not a few examples in Scripture in which a few articles are specifically dealt with, such as the article on the law which is dealt with in Romans and Galatians where it becomes clear that faith is put ahead of the law.

Note how Paul drives the Jews away from the law through the grace of God. Similarly, I drive the papists from their sacrament through faith (in the grace of Christ). I find it strange therefore to hear of certain people who otherwise want to be informed and who notice for what reasons I turn the sacrament into a pure supper of the Lord (i.e., I do not attach it to the grace of Christ). Nonetheless, they judge me on the basis of Dr. Luther's untruthful writing who considers me an enemy. Not that I care much about their false judgment. I must put up with their blindness. There are not many of them whom I thus single out; and even if there were many, I know full well that the

[64] smallest portion will be saved. Can they not clearly see from my booklet (written against the sacrament), that knowledge [*Erkenntnis*], as Isaiah has it, or faith in Christ the crucified, as Paul says, is so rich and perfect that we need not seek forgiveness of our sin or salvation anywhere else but with Christ who died on the cross. Is this not a true confession of my faith? Is my faith not Christian? Let them show me theirs. If their faith is different from mine, I will demonstrate that it is dreamed up and unchristian. Did I not produce a rich fruit of my faith in writing when I wrote this? True faith in Christ is a loving knowledge of Christ the crucified, the mighty and rich Son of God. Would I have hidden my faith?

Yes, some malicious voices will say, where in all of this is love, where the mortification of the flesh? My reply: If I always have to speak explicitly of the love of God and neighbor, lest I destroy love, Dr. Luther has a better claim than I, for he does not do so, yet gets away scot-free. But you will discover on the day of judgment that I have always written of the love of God and neighbor in all my books when I taught the right faith in Christ. For to believe in Christ and not to love God and Christ means not to love the neighbor either. This is less likely than to find a cold fire. Nor would I give a farthing for the kind of faith that does not dearly love God, Christ, and one's brother for whom Christ died.

Now if I wrote of faith in the above-named booklet, why then do they accuse me as if I wanted to destroy or dampen through silence the love of neighbor? No righteous person can truthfully ascribe this to me. I wrote in a booklet on the sacrament called "Of Three Kinds of Food," [6] that everyone who is not well-practiced in fraternal love, should abstain from the Lord's Supper. I also published a separate booklet in which I wrote on the love of God and neighbor.[7] What then do you false Christians have against me? Are you free to lie? Is your faith so precious as to permit you to hurl untruths at a poor brother? Keep your faith then, for I would much prefer [65] your animosity than to have to associate with such loose faith which judges before it has any understanding and accuses without knowing what for.

On the mortification of the flesh and the old Adam I produced several special booklets.[8] I am trying to have them published, and I have scattered a few bits and pieces here and there in other books of mine on similar matters. What can I do when those who falsely blame and slander me do not read them? For I know well that they will take a yardstick by which to measure me and that St. Paul considered it a small matter when the Corinthians judged him; the Lord is my judge.

For the sake of the poor Christians, I must boast and confess that I have written on the mortification of the flesh in a nuanced way so as to harm no one, and I have unveiled the very core of the gospel, of the books of the apostles, of Moses and the prophets. I often accuse Christendom for not having many preachers who proclaim sufficiently the mortification of life. I also point out that some mortification comes before faith, but that some—and this the best—comes with faith, while some follows in its wake. I have written many such books.[9] Hence I know that you, my brothers, have heard some of my speeches and read some of my writings, though I am not a book dealer so as to take my books to everyone.

But even if I had never written a booklet, should I therefore be called an unbeliever, one who suppresses love and who does not know anything of the right articles of our faith?

What have those written who pass judgment on the basis of Luther's lies that Carlstadt is incapable of writing or speaking of faith?

I now turn to you, dear brothers, since you heard me, and I beg of you to be my witnesses before God, the supreme and severe judge, against Dr. Luther and his good-for-nothing Christians. Vindicate me as one who is God-fearing, and testify how I instructed you—orally, as the text warranted—in the faith, and in love, on how to recognize sin, on the lawful revelation of the righteousness of God and on human righteousness, on the mortification of human nature and the right use of the sword. [66]

I would be happy to have your testimony, for you saw and heard me and sought my advice. Those others, however, who never heard me and have never heard me talk about above-named articles, yet judge and punish me, nonetheless, ought to know that I despise their judgment and their justice as being of the devil and the flesh, but not of God. I know well that they are the prickly burrs of my adversary to whom they cling.

I intend, nonetheless, to write on the main articles of Christian teaching as soon as I can settle down to that, so that you might have a reminder of the things of which I spoke to you and which you learned, and that my wicked judges will have to eat humble pie for having given me such an evil, devilish name, which is that I do not know the very God who is my only Lord and on whose account I suffer want, though I live contentedly under his shelter and protection. This time though and in this booklet you shall be made aware of Dr. Luther's arrogance and weakness who has dared present his articles to the world with such [self-]satisfaction as to assume that Christians will not have to—indeed, ought not—look for any other. For I will write Dr. Luther that he did not set up sufficient main articles and that no Christian could be nurtured by them as they now are. And whether these gathered articles are grounded in the truth, I will show as briefly as possible and [also] that Dr. Luther offends and defames me with a great deal of venom. May the almighty, eternal God preserve you well according to his will. Amen. Regards to your wives and sisters in Christ.

What knavery Dr. Luther uses in his booklet *Against the Heavenly Prophets* I will briefly note.[10] He leans on the backs of critters or washers, and uses clever tricks which prove me right in calling him a subtle Sophist. The trick of the critter he uses as follows: Attorneys whom the peasants call "critters" have the habit of washerwomen—fast tongues and sharp words. And when such "critters" bring evil and unjust matters to court and fear that their antagonist will support his good cause with firm [67] arguments, they reach down into their bag of defamations which is chock-full of curses, lies, slanderous words, and defamations. These taunts and lies they throw about as a hedgehog throws about his bristles. They do not do this in the hope of saving their cause, for they themselves know that it is a lost cause, but rather to force their adversary to direct much energy and work to their defamations so that his cause is left undefended. Or ele, he is so moved by anger that he no longer knows where he stands.

This is what Dr. Luther does. Wise parties, however, shake off such words of abuse and do not justify themselves. They keep silent unless their cause or plight demands a response. This is what I do. So much on the weapon of the critter which Dr. Luther employs.

The Sophists work in a similar fashion. When they cannot bring enough material against a case or when they are too weak and unlearned, they turn to another subject which they know better. Then they apply great skill to get their opponent onto this case. Dr. Luther seeks to do this, too. He actually accuses me of suppressing the main articles of Christian teaching. For what reason he accuses me thus, I cannot quite figure out, other than that he might wish to trip me up. He therefore brings forth a few reasons which he mixes into his writings. The first of these is that the main points must remain untouched and be forgotten while we write of idols, the mass, baptism, the sacrament, and similar articles. The second is that Carlstadt turns God's order upside down, for he puts the last first, the hindmost up front, and the lowest at the top. The third is that Carlstadt is incapable of writing or speaking on the chief articles.

I can see the reasons in Luther's defamatory booklet (called

Against the Heavenly Prophets). Not one letter of honest argument to support what Dr. Luther writes can I find in this slanderous booklet. But Dr. Luther always assumes that I am sufficiently convinced as soon as he writes something. In this he is way off the mark, for he heaps such untrue words and so many unproved items upon my back that I cannot believe Dr. Luther [68] even if he were to praise me and be my friend. But now that he is my enemy who is not ashamed of any disgrace or untruth, what am I to do? Who can trust his empty words?

That Dr. Luther should consider such reasons significant enough to accuse me of having allowed the main articles to be forgotten while doing what I reported earlier, I cannot believe.

But I do believe that Dr. Luther crawls into his old sophistical hole to use a sophistical gag by which he might lure or drive me away from the articles (on account of which he picked a fight with me and entered the arena) after the fashion and craft of sophists, that I might begin to quarrel with him about articles which are in line with truth. And that on account of enmity I might depart from the truth (which he upholds in his malice) as I distanced myself long ago from his wicked life and tricks, even though he still extolled and praised me. It pleased him, of course, when I began denying the laws of God, as he had already denied the laws of Moses. Furthermore, he departed from the holy gospel that he might have cause, afterward, to revile me with the truth just as he reviles me with lies now. But the devil shall accomplish nothing.

To sum up, there are three reasons, I reckon, for which Dr. Luther draws me to these main articles. The one is to produce many and large books with which to acquire new fame among fools or to sustain the old. The second is to cause me to let go of the article on the sacrament about which I am quarreling with him, so that he might have his peace. The third is that I should begin to criticize that which he has in common with the truth and that I should congratulate him with all my heart for having it and being like me.

That Dr. Luther pretends that the main articles should be ignored and forgotten while we quarrel over above-named articles does not matter. For there will still be preachers and writers (there are some now who preach and write in the time we spend debating the other articles), even if Dr. Luther and I were asleep. Dr. Luther need not worry. The world does not depend on us. Dr. Luther ought to know this, one way or another. [69] For we cannot deal with these matters properly, unless we also deal with several of the articles which he calls main articles. How can I prove that the sacrament or the fictitious faith in the sacrament and in the sacramental word does not forgive minor sins or strengthen consciences, if I cannot prove it through right faith in Christ, the crucified, and through God's word? How can I destroy faith by indicating, praising, and setting up true faith? When I call for removal of that which deadens faith, do I then destroy or obscure true faith (if I, a poor earthen vessel, could do it otherwise)? The same is true with regard to baptism. Anyone who refuses baptism, and refuses it to those who do not believe until the time when they have become believers, enhances rather than deadens the main article of faith.

How else am I to destroy idols or write that they are to be destroyed, except through the love of God and of neighbor, and especially because of fraternal love. Dr. Luther must have read all this in my books. Yet he slinks about like a cancer or a spider around poison and behaves as if he could not see anything that might maintain my Christian honor.

The mass is glaringly against faith in Christ in name and deed. Therefore, anyone who eliminates the term *mass* and all mass-like activities enhances faith. One who removes the smoke or tarnish from the silver does not ever blacken the silver.

In the third place, Luther thinks he could strike me with the reproach that by engaging in external matters I cause the main things to be forgotten. Yet he does not know that he detracts from the apostles, prophets, and Christ, and hits them by hitting me. For it is known that apostles, prophets, and Christ discussed and talked about external things among themselves and with others. Accordingly, the main articles would have lain dormant during that time. This is contrary to the prophet who says, "You ought to remember the Lord and not be silent. You are not to be silent in his presence" [Isa 62].[11] [70]

That the apostles discussed external matters and for a time debated the above four articles among themselves, and sent some with letters to Antioch in order to disclose their thinking to them, we are taught in the Acts [Acts 13; 15]. But what do these apostles have to hear from Luther? Indeed, the very thing I hear; during that very time they kept silent on the main articles.

Paul used not a little time and writing when he spoke of the meat offered to idols and when he taught the ignorant how they were to deal with such meat [1 Cor 8:1ff.; 10:7f.; Rom 14:3ff.]. But in addition, Paul talked a great deal about baptism [Acts 19:4ff.]. To wit, he had a special sermon on the Lord's Supper [1 Cor 11]. To wit, [one against] circumcision, new moons, the Sabbath, to the Galatians and

Colossians. Did Paul do something wrong? Dr. Luther passed this sentence, saying that Paul did wrong. For St. Paul ought to have preached on the Lutheran main articles. Or else what is right with Paul must be wrong with Carlstadt. Thus Paul is not left alone by Luther. Or else I must suffer for Paul's associates, and that which serves to Paul's honor is my disgrace. That which enhances St. Paul's books is not becoming my books at all. But it is not enough that Paul and the apostles must hide in the presence of Dr. Luther; the prophets are taken to task as well.

Beware, all of you together, for we all know without being informed of your prophecies that you have written or prophesied a great deal about circumcision, altars, and sacrifices and also against sacrifices, the Sabbath, the ark of the covenant, temple, priests, and rulers. Take special care, Moses, for Luther rightly says that you have always said a great deal of nothing regarding the gospel[12] when you wrote of external things. You cast a great deal of haze upon Scripture when you taught how court cases are to be handled and how the neighbor is to be served. How will all of you servants of God stand before the severe judge Dr. Luther when he teaches—inspired by God—what words we are to use in despising, destroying, and ridiculing idols? For you have caused the main articles of Luther to be forgotten. If you were still alive, your heads would have to roll over the cold blades into the young grass. But you would not be martyrs now but transgressors, for Dr. Luther has discovered the right to [71] kill the innocent lawfully. Thank God that Dr. Luther was not appointed a judge over you.

It does not stop with you and me, though. Christ himself has to appear before Dr. Luther's judgment seat and receive his sentence. Christ has befogged the gospel because he spoke about and spent some time with the Jews on such external matters as handwashing, the Sabbath, the temple, and other things.

Wait all of you together, you servants of God. Run, run, and flee Dr. Luther's judgment, for if he catches you, you will all become his target without mercy. Once Dr. Luther has sounded the trumpet of his judgment, you will no longer be able to escape him. He is master of all laws; before him divine and human laws dwindle to nothing. He has new bulls from Wittenberg and Rome and power to rebuke and condemn you as he pleases, as those who have obstructed the gospel. Haste, flee; he thunders already from afar, growls, hails, and throws about thunder bolts as one who intends to judge you and your lost generation.

As for me, I would rather stand on your side and suffer Dr. Luther's thunderbolts and die with you than rejoice and be glad with Dr. Luther. If it is obstructing the gospel when one proclaims the grace of Christ purely, I will gladly suffer all the shouting. And if writing against abuse and false trust in creatures means to create vapor and smoke, I will gladly blow up some steam and throw about soot and smoke thus to deaden the devilish trust in creatures, so that God's honor be known.

Dr. Luther can see now whom he besmirches and who will complain about his bad judgment.

Therefore, it is either Dr. Luther who falls short of the truth, or else Moses, the prophets, the apostles, and Christ know nothing of the main articles of Christian teaching. We know well, of course, that all these persons, foremost among them Christ, did sufficiently know these main articles—especially when they directed erring people to the right understanding of God and creation and when they led them in the right use of external things through their diligent and proper instruction.

I am sure therefore that Dr. Luther shoots winged words from the barrel [72] of his frivolity and that it is not necessary for me to appeal from his worthless judgment.

The other matter on which Dr. Luther accuses me is worthless, too. He says that I pervert God's order by placing the bottommost at the top, and by taking the lowliest for the best, the last as the first, for I have not as yet debated with him the order of his main articles. Had I been asked, I would have given such an answer as Dr. Luther attributes to me, so that Dr. Luther would have had to excuse himself. Now, however, he stands as one who has burdened me with an attribution he himself thought up. And if he had wanted to know, he could have refreshed his memory from my booklets to see that I never subscribed to such errors since I left the papacy. I have since written booklets in which every sincere reader may see that Dr. Luther tries through untruths to make me appear abominable in the eyes of Christians. He will not succeed, for I have been blessed before him and all his devils and I know that whatever case he will mount against me, God will tear down and bring to nought—that the godless are against me, I leave to God, of course.

But if he always wants to hear things a second time, let him know that I consider faith and love of God as the foremost and greatest articles—as I have written a long time ago.[13]

Thirdly, Dr. Luther interprets my writing against sacramental grace, the abuse of baptism, idols, and the mass as if Carlstadt is not able to write anything else: "If he knew as much about the main articles of faith as I, Dr. Luther, do, he would hold back." O Luther, how totally you have forgotten your own fame when you yourself boast that you achieved more, etc., with your writings against idols, mass, etc. Did you not ever think then that you might write later that anyone who writes against idols and the mass does not understand the main articles? How terribly a blind swordsman can hit himself. He aims for me, but hits and wounds himself. So be it. We will see in time how learned Dr. Luther really is in the main articles, for I have always known them better than he thinks. This time I would only like to know how he is going to sustain his argument that one who writes against idols, usury, the mass, and the like therefore knows [73] nothing of the other main articles. Should it stand, the Holy Spirit will have a hard time, for through his prophets he has preached many whole speeches against abundance and abuse of externals. And how is Dr. Luther himself going to stand, who also wrote against the mass, etc.? If the Holy Spirit and Dr. Luther in his former writings will stand, I, too, shall remain and Dr. Luther and his untruthful big mouth, which he now has opened against God and me, shall be put to shame.

Now Regarding the Main Articles

Dr. Luther says further: I will briefly relate here the main articles of Christian teaching which everyone ought to note and in which we are to remain, above all else.

Carlstadt: And I shall surely listen with diligence and zeal to what the great mountain Israel is about to bring forth. My only fear is that he conceived an elephant and will give birth to a mouse.

Dr. Luther: The first is the law of God which must be preached in such a way as to reveal sin and make it known, Rom 3 and 7.

Carlstadt: I had hoped that Dr. Luther would remove the true kernel of the law from its shell and present the perfect spiritual content of the law—what it is capable of and how far its power reaches and spreads. I waited eagerly for Dr. Luther's product. But I note that he merely tore one line out of the context of St. Paul's teaching without providing the full content of Paul to which we ought to have looked and on which we ought to stand. How much less does he get to the heart and core of the whole law which Moses, the prophets, and the apostles show here and there. My hope has been dashed. For when I am to learn from the law, above all else, that sin can be revealed, yet remain in it without ever looking back, I will soon fall from one error into another and into the many contradictions of the law, which not only the law, but Paul as well, rebukes. [74]

The law always maintains that sin cannot be understood through the law. For there is Moses who in this case is no evangelist and says, "I have not given them an understanding heart, nor ears that hear, nor eyes that see" [Deut 29:4]. Therefore, the law cannot sufficiently reveal sin, for anyone who acknowledges sin or that which is evil is disgusted by sin and leaves it or turns away from it [Isa 6; Mt 13].

This, however, is God's [doing] and not of the writings of the law, as God says, "Who shall put fear in their hearts that they might fear me and keep what I command" [Deut 5; Isa 36; 43; Jer 32; Ps 51; Ezek 36]. The law indicates this as follows, "I am your God," which is explained through the prophets.

Neither preaching nor the proclamation of the law, nor beatings, nor anything else is of any avail when God does not send his spirit into the heart of the godless to expose the offensiveness of his wickedness and to cause him to begin disliking sin. Preach what you will, it is impossible for the law to unveil the meaning of a single sin, which is what the revelation of evil is to be, namely, to hate and dread what is evil [Rom 6; 7; 8]. This is the prerogative of the spirit of God. Indeed, if the law were capable of imprinting upon or pouring into the heart an understanding of sin (which is what is meant by "reveal" in Christ's way of speaking), the law would be God, as indicated above, "I, I," says God, "eradicate and forgive sin."

I conclude all this from the following writings: Preach to the people and harden them, and they will not understand in their hearts that they are to turn to me, so that I might heal them [Isa 6:9]. Likewise, I know them to be a stiffnecked people [Mt 13:13; Deut 10; 31]. God says, I know of your disobedience and of your very stiff neck. Likewise, they turned their backs on me and plugged their ears so as not to hear. They have made their hearts adamant so as not to hear the law and the words which the Lord in his spirit sent through his servants [Zech 7:12]. Likewise, to whom shall I speak and whom shall I support, that I might be heard [Jer 6:10]? Their ears are uncircumcised; that is why they are unable to hear. These words are also words of the law and of those who preach the law.

That sticks and beatings are also lost on them in bringing about [75] true repentance or abhorrence, and dislike of one's own sin (when the Spirit of God does not reveal) is shown by the fact that God indicates how he has to beat his people seven times, ere they repent and begin to show shame [Lev 26:14ff.]. Does not Isaiah say [Isa 1:5;

9:21], "Why should I continue to beat them?" The hand of God is stretched out; is there no one who will turn to the one who is beating? Likewise, "I have beaten them in vain, for they have not learned discipline through it" [Jer 2:30] Likewise, " I burned coals, bellows, and lead [Jer 6:27ff.], yet their wickedness has not been removed or repentance made for it."[14]

That it befits the spirit of God to reveal sin as sin so that sin might be known, hated, and fled (is to be noted in above-named chapters in Deut 5; 29; 30), and as follows from the prophets. I will note the clearest only. "I will remove from you the heart of stone and give you one of flesh and pour my spirit into you, etc." [Ezek 36:26f.]. "You shall come to despise your depravity and wickedness. They shall be an abomination to you." One might wish to add to this what Ezekiel writes in chapters 18 and 20. Likewise, "I shall put my fear[15] into their inmost [being] and they shall not depart from me, i.e., they shall leave everything which separates or distances them from me, such as the doing of sin [Jer 32:37-40], and they will be guided by me." Here you note that it is characteristic of the fear of God to unveil and make sin known. This fear does not come from the law, but is the righteousness from God, the ark of all of God's gifts which brings about abhorrence of and flight from all that is evil and guards against falling. It is characteristic of the knowledge of sin, and adheres and is integral to the revelation of sin, to drive away from and wash off sin. Just so, it is integral to the revelation of the Son of God that we cling to him and that the heart is transformed in Christ, as it is characteristic of fire to warm. To this article belongs what Paul writes at length regarding the freedom of the law through the grace of Christ, in Romans 6, 7, and 8.

Through the law one might readily learn that sin is evil, just as a thief might recognize the wickedness of his thievery. But what sort of knowledge is this? Nature knows only itself and the damage that results; but it does not know and fear God who has prohibited sin. [76]

Now when Dr. Luther writes, we must preach so that sin might be revealed and made known through the law, he writes a rather imperfect thing. One is not to build upon it before the right and appropriate understanding is added which is missing from Dr. Luther's main articles. For when Dr. Luther says that the law reveals sin, I could at the same time say in so many words and truthfully, that the law is not capable of revealing sin. Paul intends and teaches the same thing, yet is diametrically opposed to Dr. Luther's main articles. Likewise, the law does not reveal sin any more than Scripture reveals Christ—merely as a testimony. Hence, if I move from the law to the spirit of God and do not look to the law, above all else, as Dr. Luther's devilish teaching advocates, and if I do not remain under the law, but turn to the one whom the law points to, as Paul says, then the law is an instructor leading to Christ [Jn 5; Gal 3].

By this you might note, dear brothers, that Dr. Luther has set a false foundation for his first main article when he continues to write as follows, "Everyone is to note and remain in my articles, above all else." Yet, anyone who remains in his main article without further looking about makes an idol of the law and moves far away from the grace of Christ, yes, from the law itself, and denies Paul who writes contrary to such Lutheran bits of law. One can derive from this that Dr. Luther himself does not know how to speak of the main articles properly and that he is not able to present them in writing so that one might bank on them freely and without fear. Now in case Dr. Luther wishes to say that he did not fully explain what he intended to say (which he must, or else accept the charge that he is a deceiver), I answer by asking why then does he insist that one should and ought to remain with his articles? Is he the bright star which illumines all things? How dark then is he in those main articles from which other articles are to be derived, when otherwise he can scold and ridicule in clear and firm words? Why does he present us with dark, lean, and hungry judgments? It were better if he did not write at all than to write deceptively and erroneously. Should Dr. Luther say that Paul wrote such things word for word, I must reply, "But not with this particular meaning." Dr. Luther should have made a wholesome brew[16] from Paul's teaching and [77] should have put this together with a whole sentence from the law and then submitted it as his main article.

Even if Paul had taught such words regarding the revelation of sin, with no other meaning than the one advanced by Dr. Luther, Dr. Luther ought to have held these words up to and compared them with other writings before drawing a main article from them, so as not to endanger and harm the faith.

It is apparent that Paul uses statements such as "Through the law we know sin," or "The law reveals sin" against the Jews who boasted excessively of the law and who claimed that they could be justified through the law, i.e., that they were able rightly to know and abhor sin. Paul set himself against these, saying that the law cannot create enmity toward or hatred of sin. It makes sin known, but cannot protect from sin. Because of this Paul concludes that the manifestation of sin through the law is not suited to or sufficient for justification. This is the proper understanding of the law inasmuch as it reveals sins. I sent this out into the world in writing some years ago in my little book *De spiritu et litera*,[17] though this insolent mouth still likes to create envy and hatred of me among people. Nonetheless, I do not pretend to have hereby given the whole content of the law so as to forestall further enquiries about the nature of the law. But as soon as I have some breathing space and leisure, I will get to Dr. Luther's main articles and give an honest account of myself, demonstrating that Dr. Luther violates the text.

How the Law Reveals Sin

St. Paul's view regarding the manifestation or knowledge of sin is as follows: through the law sin is known; it is lustful,[18] powerful, and frequent. The one who has thus come to know sin through the law outside the grace of God develops anger and disaffection toward the law [Rom 3; 4; 5; 6; 7 and 8]. He then commits two sins in place of only one. [78] This is Paul's true view. I gathered this from the many places of Paul's teaching in which St. Paul writes about the revelation or knowledge of sin through the law, without the revelation of the Holy Spirit [1 Cor 15; Gal 5].

Now place this view over against Dr. Luther's main articles and you will note that Dr. Luther has not even moved an inch toward this article, even though this article is drawn from St. Paul's teaching and indicates the view and intent of St. Paul regarding the law, inasmuch as Paul introduces from Moses the power of the law against the Jews who wanted to be justified through the law. Paul, however, concludes masterfully that laws awaken the unrighteousness of the flesh, making it lustful and alive, giving power and strength to sin and [causing] the unrighteous person to sin exceedingly much through the law, in fact, sinning beyond measure [Rom 3; 4; 5; 6; 7, and 8; 1 Cor 15]. For by the law come enmity, resentment, and disgust. Thus the sinner walks not only in the lusts and desires which the law prohibits, as he did before, but actually runs in them and does them with greater intensity than before. And on top of this, he wants the law—not just anything—removed, trampled, and burned. Indeed, reason, in addition, reproves the righteousness of the law and through the law follows the true God who created the law and gave it in his exceeding grace. This is what God said through Moses [Deut 9; 10]: I know well your stiffened neck, your obstinacy, and that you go your own way and murmur [behind my back]. All this is written exceedingly well in Moses.[19]

That this is the true kernel and Paul's basis and view, I will indicate through the following words of his. They are: "The law creates anger toward the righteousness of God which the law indicates in writing" [Rom 4:15]. This is a more heinous sin than carnal sins, desires, or lusts—however intense these might be—for they are done without retribution contrary to the law, for if rebellion against the righteousness of God is not blasphemy of God, it comes certainly close.

The law had to be set aside so that transgressing it might increase until the seed would come, etc. [Gal 3]. How the transgression of the law [79] is increased by the law is partly dealt with and amply indicated in other places of St. Paul's teaching, as follows.

The law has come in, so that sin might be victorious or increase [Rom 5:20]. In other words, that sin might rule within you and that you become slaves of sin and thus obedient to it unto death [Rom 6:23] and give over your members and your body to sin, to serve unrighteousness which is prohibited by the law. Anyone, then, who understands sin through reason alone, with the aid of the law only, without knowledge and illumination of the Holy Spirit, understands sin and what is evil in such a way as to have more delight in sin than ever before. Sin which before had lain dormant rouses itself within a person through the law, for the evil desires of the flesh are quickened first of all by such revelation through the law, stirring, binding, and leading the members of the body by force and through their fruits driving them unto death.

For when we were outside the grace of God, says Paul, in the mere powers of the flesh, the sinful desires (which were stimulated through the law) were stirring mightily in our members [Gal 6], driving the members to yield fruit unto death, doing works worthy of death which lead unto death and hell. Regarding them it is written that anyone doing those things shall not enter the kingdom of heaven.

By this I have amply shown that the law—which is evil—is incapable of revealing the nature of sin. Anyone who recognizes evil as it is abhors and flees it.

Of such knowledge of sin through the law (which loves sin and goes after it), Paul concludes as follows: "I did not know sin apart from the law, for I would have known nothing of its desire and lust had not the law said, Thou shalt not covet, etc." [Rom 7:7f.]. This is a reasonable knowledge of sin through the law (of which Jews, Pelagians, and non-Christians boast). But that such a revelation is very harmful and increases unrighteousness, Paul teaches as follows, "When I heard that desire and lust were sin, then only my desire increased on account of the prohibition by the law. It now took occasion to do evil and aroused a host of lusts within me. For before I heard the law, sin lay dormant within me as if it were dead. However, as soon as the law [80] came and prohibited sin, sin was quickened, just as suffocating vapor [*Schwad*] [20]—which normally lies dormant—rises to our death when inhaled. Similarly, the law which was to be unto life served unto my death."

Hence, the law is a power or force of sin (not of its own account), for the law is ever holy, right, and good [Rom 7:12; 1 Cor 15; Gal 3]. But those who are under the law are sheer reason and flesh outside the grace of God. They are kept under the law as under an enemy who prohibits and threatens and drives the hungry dog to rage. They do not enter the holiness of the law until they are sanctified by the one who gave the law.

The flesh (such as carnal wisdom and will), cannot attain to, reach, or desire the holiness of the law. Yet it can strengthen its wickedness with that which is good, just as a spider increases its poison from a flower.

This is the meaning of the law, as far as St. Paul explains it against those who suspect the spirit. And if one reads his books aright, this conclusion would appear more convincing than Luther's main article. Through the law sin can obviously not be understood. Rather, the spirit of God must reveal sin if one is to understand sin as sin and know evil, as was said above. It is written therefore, "When you showed me my transgressions, I was ashamed and beat my thighs," [Jer 31:19]. This is as much as to say that neither law nor reason will help me to be ashamed. But when God himself reveals my sin, then shame, regret, sorrow, penance, and improvement and everything that goes with understanding evil come my way.

And when shame, horror, envy, hatred, and the fleeing of evil do not follow in wake of acknowledged sin, God is displeased, regardless of whether a person is in the law of God or under rebuke from God. The law, however, is not capable of this. On this account Paul says that the law elicits anger—anger in the flesh and against God [Rom 4]. For the law causes reason to complain and fume against the righteousness of God, which, as we said earlier, is a great and formidable sin, Num 14 and makes God out to be a liar, 1 Jn 5. And when God afflicts the sinner with plagues and great suffering without the person changing for the better as a result of persecution, the punishment is wasted. In other words, if the [81] persecuted is not prepared to feel ashamed on account of his sins, God bemoans this, as is written, "Wherewith shall I beat them? For none of them is ashamed" [Isa 1]. They are unable to be ashamed and even if they are put to shame, they do not feel any shame [Gal 3] and many say, "Say, what have I done?" Therefore I will, says God, be opposed to them, persecute, and afflict them until they are ashamed of their sins, etc. [Jer 8]. Everyone can gather from this that the revealing of sins is lost if a sinner does not show shame for his sins [Lev 25; 26]. That is to say that the consequence of the revealing ought to be the removal of sin. What good is knowledge of poisons when you eat poison because you are blind? What good is it for you to know your sin when you neither hate it nor are ashamed of it?

Now it is in the power of persecution to reveal sin, though persecution is ever more likely than the law to create dissatisfaction with the old life. It is therefore much more difficult for the law (and the law itself teaches this) to reveal this, for God alone can rightly manifest sin and elicit resentment, abhorrence, dislike, hatred of and flight from sin through knowledge of sin. These things are essential to know. But since Dr. Luther has kept silence on such essential things, I dare say that his main articles are neither Pauline nor legal and that through the law he has written against the law. It would have been better had he abstained from writing because he is so blind. This demonstrates further that Dr. Luther's order[21] regarding the mortification of the flesh is also wrong.

In all this, you honorable bastards[22] who preach the law wrongly should understand Dr. Luther well, for you preach it according to lines taken out of context and not in line with its true content. You undertake to preach the law, frighten consciences, cast them down and destroy them, yet you do not even know the right way to it. Yes, when you think that the consciences have been frightened, you have instead merely comforted, warned, and strengthened them in their wickedness. You preach that the law manifests sin and thus you intend to bring consciences to an abhorrence and dismay of sins. Yet Paul writes that sin together with the flesh is strengthened through the law, yes, that the flesh becomes angry with the law and shows greater delight in sinning than before.

I dare stake my life on whether you are capable of finding the really frightening parts of the law, let alone that you are able [82] to preach them. For I fancy that you do not know how to find them. Yet, however unskilled and foolish you are, you still demand the appropriate interest and tenth. You gather in rents and moneys and thus put the poor under great pressure whom you cannot teach but whom you know how to cheat. This is said to you, you usurping wolf at Orlamünde and you devouring murderer of souls at Kahla, Hellingen,

Uhlstädt, and Dienstädt,[23] and in other places. The devil led you close to pious Christians, to the detriment of the salvation of poor peoples' souls, to whom the essence of law and gospel had been preached earlier and whom I will now have to warn against you. What should you preach if you can do no better than to limp behind your master of all error, having no concern about what you are still doing wrong. And you preachers in your gilded shirts, look out for me. As soon as I find some leisure, you shall have no peace and you shall have trouble with me until your preaching is more firmly grounded and you have ceased or changed your carnal living.

For it is necessary (as your master of blindness ought to write), that in all your preaching you must preach the law which in its right understanding I consider to be essential. I know then that you short-change your preaching when you preach the law contrary to the law and intention of the Holy Spirit. I would like to tell you something here which might benefit the small flock of God. But I know full well that you have so much to do with your large incomes, rents, and registers, that it would be more beneficial for me to write to pigs and dogs than to you. However, I shall pray to God that he send into his harvest apostolic workers, for you are wolflike preachers.

Whom will you frighten off sin when you wallow and delight in your sins and preach delight in sin?

If you preachers would properly carry to market the pieces pertaining to the law (of which Moses writes exceedingly well and which Christ also had in his preaching), the small people of God might be led to the right pasture; but you give them chaff and sugar-coated poison to eat.

Dr. Luther: But these prophets do not have the right understanding of it.

Carlstadt: Dr. Luther is one of the false prophets who frightened and scared us for a whole year with the coming of the last judgment. [83] But now we see that he proclaimed lies and the visions of his own heart.

But these prophets know well that Luther is so blind that he cannot even understand his own writing, for he uses the following Scripture passage, "Repentance in the name of Jesus ought to be preached." But he relates this saying to the revealing of sin which happens through the law. By this he proves that he knows nothing about how the law makes sin known or that he does not know what it is to call for the preaching of repentance in the name of Jesus. My sinners at Orlamünde know much better how to speak of this. They know that it is one thing to learn how to recognize sins through the law, and another to do so in the name of Jesus and that these are two different parts, like those which St. Paul juxtaposes in his letters to the Romans and Galatians. O blindness, O shame! If the teachers are in error what will their students do? God, help us and grant grace. I will subsequently explain what it means to preach repentance in the name of Jesus.

Dr. Luther: For this means to preach the law in a truly spiritual manner.

Carlstadt: Spiritual? Does this mean that human tradition in revealing what is evil is equal to the law, as when one prohibits vices?

What sort of spirituality is there in such revelation if the desire for sin grows or increases through it? Or does spiritual preaching consist in this that the internal being develops delight in the law and comes to be of one mind with the law, devoutly saying, "The law of God is holy, spiritual, good, and just." I cannot see this happening without the intervention of the Holy Spirit. I have to be saved through Jesus our Lord. Jesus the Christ of God removes the burden and power of the law from me. Is this what is meant by preaching the law spiritually or is it simply to preach the revealing of sin? Is it not impossible for reason to carry out the task of the law without God's grace?

I would dearly like to see the preachers come down from the broad realm and lofty heights of the law into the valley, which is to speak of sin in small portions and then not only of grave sins which the world also considers to be sin. Rather, they must present those things which the wisdom of the world considers to be good and not [84] sinful at all—sins in which the Pharisees remained and which they defended as right. Of such sins there are so many that I do not know one single prophet, evangelist, or apostle who spoke of each particular sin. It is true, nonetheless, that we can speak of unrelated sins on the basis of those that I mentioned above. I see well, of course, how the prophets worked in proclaiming sins and what effort and work they had with the supreme princes, kings, and priests of the Jews in making them recognize their sins, and how they failed in this. It would be good if simple Christians could understand such secret and treacherous sins, for there are several who have such good appearance in the eyes of the world that Dr. Luther himself refuses to acknowledge them as sinful and wicked, though God is truthful and Luther a liar.

For it is ever true that the revelation of the law, as the law itself states, is lofty, good, spiritual, and just, whereas we are low, untimely, carnal, and unjust. As a result, we are less likely to attain to the spirit of the law than we are to reach heaven. Not in vain is it written, "My people who call you blessed deceive you" [Isa 3:12]. Woe to those who call evil good and who pervert the word of the living God [Isa 5:20]. I know a saying in Moses (which I contemplated for a long time), and everyone I asked knew the saying before me, yet does not understand it any the better. I know well, therefore, that it is called spiritual preaching of the law when sin is made known. Indeed, if the preachers were to preach God's people into grace by way of the law, they would be truly spiritual and lawful preachers. I have the feeling, though, that they do not understand me. As human beings, however, they must, nonetheless, reveal invisible and insidious sins, diligently calling on God to teach the heart to know sin.

On the Other Main Article

Dr. Luther: When sin is known and the law is thus preached, faith follows. [85]

   Carlstadt: On this article I have also written so much in my recent booklet,[24] that everyone can readily understand Luther's mind and how right and true he is when he writes that these two items are not and cannot be found in these prophets. But is not this article contained in the saying "Christ shed his blood unto the forgiveness of our sin" [or] "Christ has redeemed us," which means that he obtained forgiveness of sin? But this quarrelsome spirit cannot write four lines without lies. At times I have to lash out with unreasonable words, for Dr. Luther writes so much through scolding words about my not confessing Christ. Therefore, I must say that whenever Dr. Luther writes or says this, he lies like that son of the devil Belial who is not worthy of honor, and who does not love the honor and praise of God and cannot bear to have the suffering of Christ known or exalted.

   It is true that sin must be quickly discredited and set over against the wrath of God and that the grace of the cross must be preached so that the abject sinner may esteem the grace of Christ the more highly and hurry and run after it the more.

   But the entire gospel of Christ does not consist in the proclamation of the grace of Christ alone which has been proffered for the forgiveness of sin; it is much richer. For there are immeasurable goods and treasures in Christ which Christ has obtained for us and desires to communicate to us if we believe in him [Eph 3; Titus 2]. What does Dr. Luther think is written in Hebrews regarding the New Testament? Does not Paul write of treasures other than forgiveness of sin? Is this no gospel which says that we are all together to receive of the fullness of Christ [Jn 1:16]? Where is the gospel of the spirit of Christ? Where are the rich gifts of the Messiah of which Isaiah writes? Is not this a special piece of the gospel which says Christ has given power to all those to be sons of God who receive him and that Christ is the end and perfecting of the law?

Now, if it is something to have become sons of God which we now are, what we are to become is more still—this, too, Christ obtained for us. What Dr. Luther writes is well-written, but it is wrong to limit it to one piece with which we are to remain without looking beyond. Paul [86] did not only write that we are liberated from the law and power of sin by the sacrifice and death of Christ's body or that the spirit quickens us in Christ and sets us free from the law of sin and death and that he worked this and accomplished what the law was incapable of doing. He also wrote that Christ saved us from the entire law and that he brought about the end and perfection of the law. A Christian person must look to such statements, too. It is not enough simply to know how Christ saved us through the forgiveness of sin. We should also know that we must draw the entire wealth of all treasures from God through Christ. Dr. Luther does not indicate this. But he coins one phrase as if the entire gospel of Christ rested on that phrase and as if no one should desire to be further taught by God about grace, truth, wisdom, strength, goodness, and suchlike treasures, which have been placed in Christ so that they might flow into us through Christ. Of such treasures of Christ, one should write, so that we might believe and be saved.

Dr. Luther: These two items Christ himself teaches in this very order in the last chapter of Luke. Repentance and forgiveness of sin in his name must be preached.

Carlstadt: The text just now presented does not suggest that the law must be preached or that sin is revealed through the law. Rather, the opposite is suggested, namely, that which is above the law and which the law is incapable of. What is that, Dr. Luther? Is it not the one thing Paul often teaches in Romans, which is that by the grace or the body of Christ we are set free from the law? Is it not that through the spirit we are made alive in Christ and set free from such things as law, death, and hell? Is not all said when we affirm, the spirit of Christ or grace leads us to the right; and true knowledge of the law of sin, death, and hell and sets us free? Does not the internal being (through the spirit of Christ) delight and take pleasure in the spiritual, good, and just law while at the same time showing abhorrence and dislike of sin and its fruits? Does not the heart spit out its dirt when by God's grace it understands that that is dirt, which before this knowledge it considered to be delicious food and consumed as such? What tears the heart away [87] from itself and its sin? The law? No. The knowledge of Christ? Yes, truly yes. And is not this knowledge, faith in Christ the Savior who gave himself for us? If it is fitting for the grace of Christ to proffer repentance in the name of Christ, how can the law do so fittingly when it is incapable of doing so, as Paul teaches in Romans 8 and 7 and frequently elsewhere?

You can see and touch Luther's blindness—he is a blind leader. He hears the ringing, but not the combined sound; and he does not know how lute and harp are to be attuned to each other. I have thought for some time now that Dr. Luther and those burrs that cling to him will treat the grace of the name of Christ so badly as to say, "To repent in the name of Christ means to learn through the law what sin is." You poor knaves. Don't you grasp who repents in the name of Christ and that through Christ's suffering one perceives the extent and severity of one's sin better and more thoroughly than if one had read, heard, or wallowed through the law for a thousand years? I ask you, brothers, whether it is ever possible truly to understand sin as sin and as something evil, without comprehending the suffering of Christ and without the favor which comprehends the excellent grace of God and of Christ crucified? Pitiable Christendom which has to make do with such poor, blind teachers who know not how to write well and how to differentiate between the law and the grace of Christ. How little these teachers understand the fifty-third chapter of Isaiah, Moses, the prophets, and apostles.

Who can believe that some sin or other kindles the wrath of God when he does not comprehend the reason for Christ's death?

Thank God that I was able to reveal and make useful the name of Christ to those at Orlamünde, more fully and better than for them to compare knowledge of sin through the grace of Christ to the law, or to run from grace to the law when they wish to repent. And I know that the peasants at Heilingen, Dienstädt, Freienorla, Zeutsch, Uhlstädt, etc.[25] could speak of repentance in the name of Christ in a more Christian and skilled manner than Dr. Luther, unless, of course, he has secretly torn them away from the grace of Christ through his delegated honorable [88] bastard.[26] I should deeply regret that.

Anyone who repents of his sins through the law repents so little that he actually sins more grievously by totally disregarding God and his divine righteousness. When he passes by, he leaps over it. It can therefore not be called repentance in the name of Jesus when one recognizes sin through mere laws; it is rather to disregard the name and grace of Christ.

But anyone who repents in the name of Jesus recognizes his sins at the same time and improves his ways. The sin which he once loved he now hates. He flees his desires which before he sought out, so that it is quite a different thing to hear confession in or through the name of Christ than through the law, as Paul expounds in clear and rather extensive words.

Luther must not know this one thing, therefore, that repentance through the law does not justify and that it does not yield fruit unto life. Or else, he does not know that repentance in the name of Jesus is a fruitful and divine repentance. Luther puts the two statements together: repentance through the law alone and repentance in the name of Jesus. Thus, this know-it-all gives more to the law, indeed, the very thing which Moses, David, other prophets, Christ, and the apostles took away from it. Or else, he takes from repentance in the name of Christ that which the apostles and disciples grant to it in the Acts.

You ought to know that the name of Jesus is a name of salvation. To repent in the name of Jesus means not simply to call on the name of Jesus in the manner in which those call on him of whom it is said that not everyone who says, Lord, Lord, etc. Rather, this is what calling on or repenting in the name of Jesus means, namely, to know the Lord Jesus, as Paul says, "No one can say Jesus is Lord or the Messiah, except in the Holy Spirit."[27] In other words, those who then repent in the known name of Jesus, that is those who know Jesus the Savior have a blessed repentance and a godly turning away from evil. And as soon as they repent, they attain to the forgiveness of their sins. Therefore, repentance in the name of Jesus is quite a different and a much higher recognition of sin than what a creature is able to achieve through the law. [89]

The highly learned Dr. Luther should have learned this from Paul's teaching. St. Paul teaches quite well and amply what baptism in the name of Jesus is [Rom 6]. He says that whoever is baptized in the name of Jesus has died to sin and has been buried in his death. To wit, our old nature is crucified with Christ. Here Dr. Luther will have to see, firstly, what it is to be baptized in Jesus and then that it is one and the same thing to be baptized in the name of or in Jesus and that "in the name of Jesus, etc." means as much as to be baptized in the knowledge of, or in the faith in, Christ [Acts 2; 10; 11]. From this then follows the death to the old life and to sin.[28] In other words, one leaves the old life and all its desires, lusts, and works and comes to stand in a new life, which, of course, means to repent. In this new life, sin and the old life are not simply abhorred and hated, but a person actually crucifies his life through the known crucified Christ [Eph 4; Col 3; Gal 6]. Thus we do not simply live in the world as those who are dead or who have died. Rather, we choke lusts and desires through affliction and persecution which befall us and by living daily according to the will of God. All who have the spirit of Christ do this. For they have crucified the flesh and their desires [2 Pet 1]. Faith which recognizes Christ does all this, as Paul clearly indicates, Gal 2. Their life is the life of Christ. Now all those who are thus baptized in the name of Christ also have repentance in the name of Jesus. But such repentance is above the law and accountable to the spirit of God only.

For to be freed from the clutches of the lusts of the flesh or to die does not belong to nature or to the law, but to the spirit of God alone, Gal 5.

No one properly mortifies lusts except through Christ, Gal 2; Rom 6. Moreover, any mortification of the flesh is useless. But all who are driven by the spirit of God and walk about are not subject to the law, Gal 5. Rather, they are free from the law, Rom 5; 6; 7; 8.

Repentance is indicated and demonstrated by this that right repentance does not come through the revelation of the law, but through the name of Jesus and the spirit of God. This foundation is amply contained in the prophets, the gospels, and the books of the apostles. [90] I am greatly surprised by how Dr. Luther can grope in the dark when he is the one who thinks that he stands most uprightly. I don't even think he knows what it means to be baptized in the name of Jesus. This perhaps is the reason why he takes the baptism of Christ so lightly as to baptize children who do not understand their desires, let alone the death of their desires through Christ.[29]

Dr. Luther: And the spirit shall punish the world on account of sin, etc.

Carlstadt: The application of these words of Christ to Dr. Luther's use is not confirmed as yet. If it would not take so much of my time, Dr. Luther would have to see that such Scripture does not serve him as well as he fancies.

Dr. Luther: The third is the judgment which will mortify the work of the old nature.

Carlstadt: Here Dr. Luther introduces an example from Christ who drove the devil out of the world through his suffering [Jn 12]. Nonetheless, he accuses me disdainfully that I make the example of Christ a main article. Thus the reed is bent this way and that by its own dreams. When properly understood I willingly grant that Christ judged the devil through his suffering and cast him out. In Jn 12:31 the Lord says, "The judgment of the world is now and the prince of this world will be cast out, etc." We, too, must overcome the devil through suffering and through the truth which we have come to know. Through such suffering we must subdue, break, and subordinate to the spirit our untamed flesh in order to assist hope, strengthen faith, and firm up the word. For tribulation brings about patience and patience leads to a certain knowledge and experience. Experience leads to hope and hope does not disappoint.[30]

Now I know well that we cannot achieve anything without the love of God and without truth, however much we may suffer and through suffering engage in warfare. For Christ overcame the devil, not so much through suffering and death as by professing the truth and love of God [Isa 58; Rom 12; 1 Cor 13]. Indeed, had not his suffering glorified the name of the Father, the devil would not have been cast out.

Therefore, one must be well-versed in suffering and know and understand the truth and love of God. For this reason St. Paul teaches us that we must be equipped with the truth [91] in order to overcome the devil [2 Cor 10; Eph 6]. The weapons of our knighthood with which to destroy the fortification are not carnal, but mighty before God. Through them we overcome all attacks and all obstacles which rise up against the knowledge of God. We hold captive all reason in the obedience of Christ; and we must overcome devil, reason, and flesh through the truth which we know, and we must suffer tribulation in love and understanding, otherwise suffering is of no use to righteousness, Isa 9; [1 Cor 13; 15]. Where this skill does not exist there flesh and devil are victorious, Isa 5; 11 and 27. I wrote a lot about this in a sermon which I preached at Orlamünde and arranged to have printed.[31]

But when Luther equates the works of suffering with those of love, I want him to explain that. As for myself, I would not be as bold as to set myself up as the advisor of the Holy Spirit and to impose on him an order without clear testimony of Scripture. The fact that mortification must follow is not a rule, for the cross often comes before the law, as was said earlier.

The internal mortification of the flesh is much quicker and more unbearable than the external—by as much more as internal righteousness surpasses the external.

I also know fully well that we must undergo external castigations with a great deal of caution, and I also know that Dr. Luther proffers some shaky arguments concerning the internal cross and invisible mortification and that there is no one who can properly understand what the yielding of one's soul[32]—which Christ teaches—is unless he has himself endured it.

The outward[33] cross such as fasting and castigation one must begin when moved by the spirit. Blessed is the person who follows the spirit. Woe to the person who disregards such movement. Anyone who desires to benefit from such control of the flesh must subdue himself as the spirit of God leads him, whether this results in rejoicing or sadness, whether it is withheld or poured out. For shame and pride creep in before one becomes aware of them.

If Dr. Luther is of a good spirit, let him write me how he felt in his heart when he suffered the loss and destruction of his great wisdom of which Mt 15 and Isa 29 write. I will then further deal [92] with this article. However, I would, God willing, write something for Christians from my own experience.

I do not believe that God leaves a person untested in accepting inner mortification. However, few there are who understand this and fewer still who accept it. But it is true that anyone who has a right and true faith must be able to tell something of the dying of worldly wisdom or else he must hear me say, "You do not believe correctly, for the gospel of Christ does not miss the mark."

Dr. Luther: These prophets do not accept what God sends their way, but what they themselves choose.

Carlstadt: I have always written that we must accept persecution when God sends it to us. Dr. Luther has been informed through a copy of a letter I wrote to the people of Orlamünde and which was sent to him. Still, Dr. Luther writes [concerning me] that he does not state it anywhere; in other words, he writes what he pleases. Though it cannot possibly be as he writes, he is not greatly concerned. As long as he causes me, poor Christian brother, anxiety, envy, hatred, and disgrace, he is delighted.

I know fully well that we must not desire any change in the cross that befalls us. If I look for a change or an end to the divine rod, I have my conscience and God as judge over me. I have to account for this, not Dr. Luther.

But who is not aware of the fact that God the Lord has fully forbidden and taken from us this self-appointed and chosen mortification and service? Does not Scripture clearly state that we ought not do what we consider or look upon as good? Deut 12; Num 15; Mt 15 and Isa 29.

Likewise, you ought not serve me as masters, Deut 18, nor choose that which I did not command you or which I do not will, Isa 58; 65 & 66.

Likewise, you ought not mark or tear your skin, Deut 14; Lev 19; Jer 16 and 47. I teach, preach, and write this. If I were not also to act accordingly, Dr. Luther might reprove me, though he likes his own work to be uncorrected when his teaching is right. I hope, however, that by God's grace both [93] my teaching and my work are evident enough so that I can speak without boasting.

I also specifically pointed out to my brothers in Orlamünde the hidden danger of a self-appointed cross and, by contrast, the precious benefits that come from acceptance of the tribulation that may befall one, and I directed them to exercise themselves in this. I can prove and verify this. Dr. Luther, however, despite his sincerity and following, cannot verify anything he accuses me of (in mockery of God, whose I am) pertaining to this article and many others. But revenge is and remains God's.

Dr. Luther: They wear gray coats.

Carlstadt: What harm is there in wearing common dress, since a gray coat does not indicate potential holiness, as Dr. Luther in his sanctimonious cowl suggests.[34]

Dr. Luther: They impose this, carry on, and lie.

Carlstadt: I think that Luther is not well when he has to speak the truth. Tell me, Luther, where I have insisted on anything? Who has ever bought me a gray coat to please? Had I ever attributed salvation to a gray coat, I could hardly have ridiculed a monk's cowl or cast off the cloak. But I know too well that simple folk are often deceived by dainty clothing and that many a fool judges a person, his skill, and holiness by his clothes. One who wears modest clothes is the world's fool and ape, however skilled he might be. And when a fool wears velvet clothing, he is considered clever and upright. But when I am able to endure the world's despising, what concern of Dr. Luther is it? It is nevertheless not altogether unbefitting the example of Christ and the apostles to wear a peasant's gray coat, rather than the scarlet, satin, brocade, Angora cloth, velvet, and gold tassels. And those who preach in plain clothes do not create an offense or obstacle for the word, and entice no one to come to the word through costly pomp—to its dishonor—lest it is said, "You seek the word not because it is true, but so that you may wear gold-embroidered shirts."

Now Dr. Luther must further know that I now have a gray coat (thank God) in place of the finery which at one time greatly delighted

[94] me and caused me to sin. I am grateful to God for this though, of course, no piece of clothing either condemns or sanctifies me.

How does Dr. Luther think he can condemn the desire for superfluous clothing when I write thus? To wit, that we ought not have more than one piece of clothing and food? Anything above that is excessive and not any less a sin than excess in food. A handsome cloak encourages the proud flesh. How well I know that! To strut about in costly clothing is suspect—it shows up poorly the inner frame of mind.

Dr. Luther: They want to be like peasants and such like foolishness.

Carlstadt: Here Dr. Luther berates me for something which Scripture attests to for many people with great respect. Let it be so. For Dr. Luther must berate everything I do, so that his word might come true that nothing in Carlstadt is good.

But I thank God that Dr. Luther cannot condemn me. The judgment he renders over me will harm him, not me. Nor must he think that I shall surrender the least bit of what I consider to be true in God's sight on account of his slander. Would to God that I were a real peasant, field laborer, or craftsman, that I might eat my bread in obedience to God, i.e., in the sweat of my brow. Instead, I have eaten from the poor peoples' labors whom I have given nothing in return. I had no right to this nor could I protect them in any way. Nonetheless, I took their labors into my house. If I could, I should like to return to them everything I took.

God commanded Adam to work and the commandment related to work in the field. All of us are equally responsible to obtain our food from it in anguish—no one is exempted, however highly placed he is or may be, unless God chose him for another office or has prevented [such labor] by divine law.

And such work is the genuine mortification of the flesh, commanded by God. Blessed is the one who accepts and carries it out, for God's sake. That Dr. Luther forgets himself and does his own thing once more, when he claims that I chose such mortification of the flesh myself, I have to tolerate even if he should project an even greater falsehood onto me. [95]

But I am grateful to God that his divine grace has given me the mind, through grace, so that now I work gladly, without fear of what the world might say. What do you think, Luther, would blisters on our hands not be more becoming than gold rings?

When some people leave work in order to preach and go idly as a result, I am surprised that they do not read that Christ was a carpenter who did carpentry work [Mk 6] and that many prophets were simple peasant folk and that it was prophesied, " I am a tiller of the soil." Who was the greatest among the prophets? Was it the one who preached most? Is it not the one, rather, who said, "We did not eat our bread for nothing"? What will our pastors say to this? Will they not say, "See, we work? That's why we take money for it." I then ask whether Paul acted in this way. Had he done so, why then does he say, "I never ate any bread for nothing, but I worked for it, laboring day and night in order not to burden anyone"? How do you like that, Luther, when you dare write, as I reported, that a preacher may demand and take two hundred guilders a year?

Where is your written counsel? There? Is it that the prophets teach for money? Is your counsel better than the counsel and teaching of St. Paul? Are you perchance God's new counselor? Christ permits evangelists and apostles to take food, but you go beyond Christ in granting to some a lordly and abundant table and two hundred guilders in addition. Paul says that we ought to stay clear of such inordinate bellies, but Luther encourages such inordinate beer bellies. Paul says that one ought to imitate him by preaching and working, and he leads preachers to look to the poverty of Christ. But Dr. Luther says that it is a fool's lot to labor, and he leads the tightfisted bellies away from Christ by means of a money chest in which their God lies hidden whom they seek to please or serve through their preaching by keeping silent or by preaching according to what greed demands.

Paul says to the elders of Ephesus, "I did not desire any of your silver, gold, or clothing, for you know yourselves that my hands served in providing my necessities." But Dr. Luther not only lines his own bastard nest with silver and gold, etc., but desires the poor man's sweat and [96] blood and extracts it by force. I will write about this some other time.

Dr. Luther: Fourthly, works of love toward the neighbor must begin.

Carlstadt: This is a new order when one separates works of love from the mortification of the flesh, especially when putting them in a different place and category. For it is fully apparent that works of love toward the neighbor tame the flesh better than many of Luther's tribulations. Further, it is also apparent that one ought to suffer because of love toward one's neighbor. These steps could then be confused and become an obstacle. I say therefore that works of love toward the neighbor strongly break and mortify the desires of the flesh and are extremely useful in the knowledge of God. I am surprised therefore when Dr. Luther places the mortification of the flesh on the third, and works toward the neighbor on the fourth level; especially when he destroys St. Paul's teaching like a spider web by saying (though privately), that love is not the greatest. I will abruptly break off here, for I am waiting for the widely known Dr. Luther as David waits for Goliath. God willing, I should like to write down for you brothers a genuine major work and present it to you in a sequence which has an obvious foundation in Scripture. And I will serve you as if the scoffing Goliath no longer taunts me.

Dr. Luther writes at the outset of his articles that he intends to relate the main points of Christian teaching succinctly which everyone ought to remember and keep above all else.

Carlstadt: What ignorance and damage would result were we to remain with above-named three articles without searching Scripture further and more thoroughly and reflecting upon it, I have indicated in part. Again, on the fourth main article enough will be indicated so that Christians will become aware that they cannot rest on Dr. Luther's main articles without fear and harm. Rather, they must seek another, more perfect main judgment in Scripture.

I say then that Dr. Luther's piece leaves much to be desired and that it is a blind, foolish article—a line taken out of context as a child in grade one might take it out of context, without the sense, sap, [97] and power of what the spirit of God intends. For who can say that he understands the difference between divine and carnal love? Is not carnal love prohibited and divine love commanded, as is written [Rom 8] to be healthy in the flesh is death and enmity toward God? Then again, the commandment closest to "you shall love God with all your heart" and one that is equal to the greatest of commandments is "you shall love your neighbor as yourself." Here Dr. Luther is to have written when and how we are to love ourselves, for we must also hate ourselves. Which love toward neighbor is carnal and prohibited and which is spiritual and commanded we all must know if we are to remain firmly grounded upon the article regarding love of neighbor, especially if we desire to be well taught in the doctrine of the love of neighbor. It would have been better and more Christian had Dr. Luther left his articles alone, instead of not making them clear enough and driving us to his main articles as if they rendered the right understanding. This mistake is so grievous as to render Dr. Luther's main article unworthy even of a fragmented, broken article.

But what Dr. Luther attaches to the end when he says, "As Christ has done for us" is not sufficiently justified and upheld in his main articles. For you know that Dr. Luther does not esteem the example of Christ more highly than that of any other saint, and even if he were to esteem the example of Christ as highly as I do, it does not help Dr. Luther at all.

It is not good enough to serve for nothing and do good unto the neighbor as Christ did and Dr. Luther says. One must also do good from the understanding or wisdom of God which Christ had and from such truth as Christ. We must, above all else, be like Christ in our inner being and have the likeness of Christ. These are higher and more essential articles than to love the neighbor for nothing in word and deed. This stock-blind Dr. Luther simply does not know that the example and wisdom of Christ went before us, commanding us to walk in such wisdom. I know that Dr. Luther does not understand how Moses wrote of Christ in this case and what God [98] demands of his people above all else; that is why he pulls his load as a blind old horse pulls his cart.

The people of God must be a reasonable, wise, clever, and understanding people [Deut 4; 5; 6; 29; 30; Eph 4]. And Moses wrote this in a way that a certain one will come who will fulfill the law in all aspects and who would be our example. We must, of course, look to this inwardly. There we must learn how the example or work of Christ flowed forth or was set up out of the wisdom of God, truth, love, and suchlike virtues.

Without such understanding all love is blind and mad, and all works of love toward the neighbor are neither divine nor Christian. God therefore commanded that we must season with salt all our works toward the neighbor or others [Lev 2; Heb 13].

On such justification of his love I have spoken a bit, especially to you, brothers, at Orlamünde and Kahla. You know well how much honesty attaches to Luther who can blacken for me the great honor of God and who would like to get me to the point at which I could no longer boast in my God. But it does not depend on this. His lies do not stick and will accomplish nothing.

Dr. Luther: The fifth and last concerns the law and the doing of its works. It is not for Christians, but for the uncouth and unbelievers.

Carlstadt: I think it demonstrates that Luther does not practice this article. Indeed, he esteems the law of Moses as he does the *Sachsenspiegel*[35] and he sets human laws above the laws and judgments of God. Further, I fear that he will disavow the laws of Moses as he already has disavowed the covenant of Moses. And I know this for a fact that he cannot stop with this main article, nor ought he to. I am certain also that he cannot see as far as this article reaches. That Dr. Luther sets up peace as the reason for external piety or punishment and that he writes in a gloss on Romans that temporal authority is set up for the sake of temporal peace, etc., shows what an ignoramus he is. He does not know what causes laws and legal rights. He has invented a dream in his own brain, and though peace might have been indicated in his prized books as a [99] cause, Dr. Luther would have to look around a bit more for what are the fruits of love of God and neighbor and define them more carefully.

Dr. Luther: One must watch in all this how to preserve Christian liberty.

Carlstadt: Here Luther uses caution in the hope of blowing me over. Little does he know that my understanding of Christian freedom is as true, sound, and certain as Dr. Luther's ever was. To become involved in a quarrel with this troublemaker I not only place Christian freedom in the knowledge of Christ, but in the divine understanding of every truth of God. Paul and Christ teach thus. Nonetheless, the greatest freedom and true salvation is in the knowledge of the truth which is the Son of God.

Since freedom comes without works, it is soon abused or betrayed (that it is not freedom) when its works do not follow [1 Jn 3 and 4]. Therefore Christ says, "Either be a good tree whose fruits are good or an evil tree whose fruits are bad" [Mt 7:17]. It is impossible for anyone to have the true freedom of truth and then produce a work which is full of lies, evil and against the nature of the known truth. Nor can freedom last very long without its own works.

The fruits of true freedom are in keeping with the nature of each judgment or truth. It is the property of all fruit to bear witness to the inner nature of the tree. Yet it is not the testimony that makes for a good tree, just as little as apples and leaves make a good apple tree.

Anyone who knows Christ has been set free by the knowledge of Christ. He walks in good works, but does not become a Christian through these works, just as no one ever became a Christian through humble service, good deeds, help, charity, etc. By the same token, lack of such works proves that a person is still held captive in his heart by the things [100] that perish and by the devil, and it shows that he has not yet become free in the truth.

The truths that are known set the heart free from error and from the prison of the devil and of creatures [1 Jn 3]—not further though than truth is able to reach and take hold of a person. Therefore, the heart remains bound by other things. This happened to St. Peter who was called blessed and a devil at one and the same time [Mt 16]. It happened to Joseph and others of whom Acts writes that they understood truth in part and were free. In other matters, though, they were not familiar with the truth and captives to error.

The Jews did not understand the correctness [*gerechtigkeit*] of figurative speech. For this reason they were captives. But God sent them prophets who unveiled the hidden meaning of the law, so that they might have true freedom which is grounded in the knowledge of the inner core of Scripture. Those then who accepted the truth were set free and praised, while the others remained captive.

Let me take the Sabbath for an example. Those who truly understood the Sabbath were the lords of the Sabbath and had genuine freedom—not that they were allowed to do or disregard all works or the will of God (which was to be fulfilled on the Sabbath). Rather, they did not have to bear the burdens of the Sabbath, yet did what the will of God was. These were free from the law to interpret the law, as Paul says on occasion, "Use the law spiritually, as those who are spiritual." In other words, they sanctified the Sabbath, as I have written regarding it.[36]

There are other judgments of God, though, which must be clearly understood according to the text. These, too, set free when they are recognized. They have their good works, too. One of these judgments pertains to authorities, what an authority is, and how it lives and functions. For the judges who know God's order in which they have been placed become free and righteous judges by knowing the truth through an understanding of their office, just as the bishops do by understanding theirs. But both must result in good works—not, of course, that they become judges and bishops because of their works. For the right understanding [101] brings forth good works; but good works do not bring forth the right understanding.

These works now (as the fruits of a good tree), manifest the understanding or tree and glorify God. And the rest of us judge by the works so that we can say, "This one is a righteous prince or judge, for he has no regard for persons, accepts no gifts, does not plug his ears. He hears the lament of orphans and the destitute and helps everyone to his right."

But when we do not sense such fruit in our rulers or see the very opposite, such as when a ruler accepts gifts, and favors one person ahead of another, barks at the poor, scares them and such like, we know him to be a false judge, captive to the devil, and of a perverse nature.

No one will ever hear me giving someone a [bad] conscience through some work or other, for I base righteousness and freedom on hearing and accepting—as Christ and Moses both teach. But I judge on the basis of works. And should I judge someone unjustly, it is because of my lack of understanding and not because of the works; for there truth stands. You shall know them by their fruits. Had I known the fruits aright, not an iota would be missing from my trial or judgment.

Indeed, what is greater still, one can examine oneself and find out from the fruits how it is with one's righteousness, and how the righteousness of the heart is to bring forth works or fruit. It is certainly true that regarding works Scripture does not teach that we are to serve ourselves through them, but others. Nor that we become righteous through them, but merely that we bear external testimony to the power of our righteousness and how it is to show itself when it is true. For a free person does not only stand before God and his conscience, but on earth before the congregation of God.

Those who insist on works do not do so—provided they are believers—that freedom might be born through works or that the conscience might be saved through works. They do it, rather, that freedom might serve unto the glory of God and that the neighbor be kindled to glorify and praise God. On this there is a bag full of writings. [102]

It follows from above-mentioned articles that some cling to the word of God, yet lack the truth. Therefore they remain captive to error. Others again see word and content, break through shadow and mist, and hit the bright sun. These are strong and free, clever and understanding. They do not give anything for that which is not, while those others lay store by something which is not at all.

There are two types of people: the clever and strong and the ignorant and weak. But no one is his own person alone. Everyone is for others also. The strong should bring the weak to himself through sound teaching and so lift him out of error. The weak, on the other hand, is not to quarrel and judge. The clever who is the greater, ought to humble himself, testify to his freedom by standing by the truth and whatever he is capable of, he should not use to bring another to the fall [Rom 14; 1 Cor 8; 11].

The ignorant should not be caused to fall or sin. Dr. Luther, however, is so free and righteous that he is no longer in need of looking out for the weak which may be seen from his articles.

Dr. Luther: One must not harp on the consciences of Christians.

Carlstadt: I take consciences to the point [of saying] that no one who satisfies the desires of his flesh shall inherit the kingdom of God. I intend in my preaching to expose evil works as evil and so to set consciences free, for Christ creates consciences. Women are not denied to a man, but to desire a woman other than in the manner in which God ordered, is prohibited. It is true also that God did not prohibit wood and stone. But to make idols of them and to do so in order to bring the ignorant to a fall is not only against Moses but also against Paul.

Dr. Luther compares idols to clothes and food, places and persons. I would much prefer to hear some scriptural proof for his comparison or else I will see to it that if he cites Scripture he receives an appropriate answer in due course and with greater justification.

Dr. Luther: What you write is not true, for you state that idols are the same as clothes.

Now, my brothers, you have heard that God punishes our enemies with those same plagues which they afflicted upon you and me [103] and that even Dr. Luther's ranting and raving is a horrible punishment from God. For surely when it comes to the place when a person undertakes to defend his cause through unlawful activity, lies, deception, raging, and blaspheming, it is an unmistakable sign that such a person stands outside the grace of God, even though blind reason does not heed or understand this. Look, if an honorable man were to allow himself to be carried away during a table talk so as to express only half the words of blasphemy and false opinions against his opponent which Dr. Luther hurled against me by the loadful, would one not say, "What fool is this fellow?" How soon will he end up being seated on a donkey? Is this an intelligent chap? Where did he leave his senses? I think that Dr. Luther prophesied when he wishfully said, "If the donkey only had horns." Carlstadt is not to be driven away except he be asked.

But he attacks with the sheer force which in Scripture is indicated by horns, and like an ignorant, senseless man which is indicated by the donkey.[37]

We may recognize God's anger when we see the poor, horned donkey and ask God to permit him to come to his senses again, should Dr. Luther desire it, and that God might protect all God-fearing people from such grave punishment. Amen. [104]

14

Apology by Dr. Andreas Carlstadt Regarding the False Charge of Insurrection Which Has Unjustly Been Made Against Him

With a PREFACE by Dr. Martin Luther
Wittenberg, 1525

Luther's preface to Carlstadt's Apology, *one of the last of his tracts to appear in print during his years in Germany, is an indication that approval had been granted for a public clarification of Carlstadt's stance. The document, published in 1525, attempts to differentiate between the sound teaching which Carlstadt advanced on the foundation of his interpretation of Scripture and the "unchristian attitude" Müntzer had come to adopt in the course of 1524. He also clearly distances himself from violent peasant groups with whom he was commonly associated.*

Significantly, Carlstadt says little about his own beliefs or practices, undoubtedly to avoid further theological quarrels. The short tract seems to have found few takers. In light of the defeat of the Franconian peasant uprisings, Carlstadt is almost forced to make his relationship to them clear. Hence the opening greeting "to all dear Christians." He is anxious to distance himself from their destructive activities. To prove his good intentions to the authorities in Saxony, he slips in "Dear gentlemen and friends," obviously aimed at the "princes, citizens, and peasants" he names in his concluding remarks.

*The pamphlet was first printed at Wittenberg around July 1525, when Carlstadt was back in Saxony. A second edition was printed later that year at Augsburg. Freys/Barge describe the tract in numbers 146 and 147. Erich Hertzsch reprinted the tract in volume two of Karlstadts Schriften. See also A. Zorzin, **Karlstadt als Flugschriftenautor**, p. 104. This translation is based on the Hertzsch edition. For Luther's preface, see WA 18,431 ff. For a translation of the preface, see appendix A below.*

To all dear Christians grace and peace from God the Father and from our Lord Jesus Christ.

Dear gentlemen[1] and friends:

From common talk and from some writings, it has come to my attention that I am accused of the uprisng in Allstedt and of several others, as if I had been the leader and captain of the rebellious peasants. This has been to the detriment of my teaching, my service, and the name of Christ.

Therefore, my conscience prods and drives me to bring my innocence to the light of day, so that I might once more gain a better reputation by means of this truthful intimation, and that the name of Christ be no longer reviled on my account. Everyone who loves honesty, innocence, and righteousness, or who fears God's vengeance will no longer, by word or deed, accuse me falsely of any uprising.

That I have become implicated by such rumor may be attributed in the first place to the fact that I housed people with the best of intentions, in order to discover what was going on. I did not know, of course, that they might be party to causing an uprising, though they were suspected of being seditious.

Further, I fear that the honorable, respectable, and most learned Dr. M. Luther bears not a little responsibility for this. He proclaims openly to the world that I am a sectarian and troublemaker[2] and calls me Müntzer's associate. All this with such strong words and well-formed speech that the simple are firmly convinced that I am guilty of

Müntzer's uprising.[3] This has led to neighbors shouting across the street to each other that I am a troublemaker. [109]

Thirdly, the great danger and unbearable persecution, because of which I often stayed in hiding and was not seen by anyone, drove me all the deeper into the bog of this dreadful reputation. Since I was nowhere to be seen, many people believed that I was in the very place in which these unchristian babblers had put me with their lies.

Although I know that this is high-handedly and unjustly being imposed on me, I ask God, nonetheless, that he might forgive them. But may God, to whom all vengeance belongs, punish all who persist in their fury.

Regarding Müntzer's unchristian attitude, I can write with a good conscience before God that I find Müntzer's undertaking, so far as I understand it, as offensive and regrettable as anyone who now lives—whoever he may be. Those who can still be reached who saw the color of my face and who heard how quickly I spoke against and complained about Müntzer's writing are my witnesses. How I cursed Müntzer's folly and made known what disaster would come of it and what harm to many innocent people and death to some, and that the gospel would suffer irreparable damage, etc.! All this—I bemoan it before God—has come true and everything happened exactly as I had prophesied. And what I also feared has befallen me: though I am innocent, I am under suspicion and I am being accused of and have to suffer for Müntzer's uprising—something which I never liked all my life and did not want to be part of. But I must leave all this to God who, because of my sins perhaps, washed me so thoroughly in the bath of tribulation that I nearly lost my life over it.

That I tried to desist and stop Müntzer's uprising the people of Orlamünde can vouchsafe. When he turned to the congregation of Orlamünde to ask for their aid and support, they, in turn, sent him a reply which was Christian and above reproach.[4] With divine sayings drawn from Scripture, they earnestly warned Müntzer and strongly sought to prevent him from fighting with swords of iron instead of the word of God. I added approximately one or two lines to said letter, helping to cool and extinguish Müntzer's fire, in the same vein as the people of Orlamünde.

One can see effortlessly in that very letter whether Müntzer's impudent demand[5] pleased or troubled me. The reply can be obtained easily, for the letter of the people of Orlamünde was published in Wittenberg a year ago and is not unknown in the German nation. Therefore, everything contained in it is undeniable. On the basis of that very reply, all reasonable and honorable lovers of both justice and innocence ought to be able to judge me readily and decide whether to excuse or to accuse me.

It is also true, of course, that in addition to the letter which Müntzer sent to above-named congregation, he wrote me, too, attributing the same or even greater folly to me. But as soon as I read Müntzer's letter, my blood curdled in reading it, and I got so frightened that I impulsively and out of sheer fear tore said letter to shreds from top to bottom. Afterwards I reflected that I should at least have shown the letter to someone, so that someone else might have known what folly Müntzer dared attribute to me and how lightheaded and unwise he thinks me to be when he assumes that I would assist him in such foolhardiness.

Consequently, I soon got onto my little horse, rushed toward Hellingen to Master Boniface[6] to complain about Müntzer's letter—its unchristian impudence, evil suspicion, ruination of my name, and slander of my life. All of this Müntzer allegedly presumed of me. Thereupon we pieced together the letter on a table and after we read Müntzer's letter, Boniface became as aroused and angry with Müntzer as I had been. I then told him that Müntzer had written to the congregation as well. I quickly returnèd to Orlamünde where I met several people whom I advised to equip themselves with sharp replies to answer this fool harshly; this happened as I said earlier.

Personally I wrote a reply to Müntzer in Latin. I wish everyone to know what I wrote and to have my letter in hand so that my innocence or guilt might be determined from [111] it and I hope that a copy of that reply will be in Orlamünde.

In short, I know that I am innocent of and uninvolved in Müntzer's uprising, and I rely on above-mentioned letters which the congregation of Orlamünde and I sent Müntzer in reply. I appeal to the people of Orlamünde and to all who knew what I did at that point and earlier.

But anyone who can and wants to say something different should know that I do not seek to avoid the law. I am prepared to appear with him before a court of justice, as long as I am granted safe-conduct and the assurance that I will suffer only what is appropriate. But should my accuser not be able to substantiate his charge adequately, he ought to suffer what I would have had to suffer had he sustained his charge in line with the orderly course of the law.

I dislike writing this self-defense after Müntzer's death; I would rather praise Müntzer in excess than scold him a little with the truth.

But necessity forces me to write the truth, and I do not doubt that Müntzer—were he still alive—would have to excuse me, and I have no doubt that he exonerated me if he was properly interrogated.

Concerning the other peasants in the Rothenburg yeomanry and in Franconia, I request to be fully exonerated and I intend to describe my lodging arrangements and other conduct in a way that puts me above suspicion by any reasonable person. At this point, though, I will give a brief intelligence only, so that it might become clear what favors I enjoyed with the new squires, the peasants, and that I never was their captain nor would ever have been considered good enough, had I desired it.

I was in hiding at Rothenburg until the peasants had encamped in the fields. I can prove this. How then could I possibly have instigated them? How can it be that I was their leader and captain from the outset? I don't believe that a single peasant even knew me, and I doubt that there were three burghers who knew me. What association then could I have had with the peasants? And I would have remained in hiding for an even longer time, if a good friend, one of the City Council, had not led me out. [112]

If someone wishes to lie or say that I encouraged the peasants through letters, let him present those letters that it may be determined whether they are mine. What more do you expect of me in this matter? Is there another way of proving something that does not exist?[7] Does the fact that I was not seen by anyone allow them to suspect me? If such suspicion is warranted and if such tittle-tattle is valid, then neither princes nor lords are free of the suspicion of uprisings, since they, too, were not in everyone's field of vision.[8]

I hope that no one will suspect me any longer of having begun an uprising. But anyone who still suspects me and wishes to protect his honor must know that he owes it to God and the world to substantiate his suspicion. Such testimony won't be forthcoming, even if he were dressed in velvet.

Now, as to how I pleased these peasants and villagers after I came out of hiding and whether I was considered worthy in their eyes to be tolerated by them as advisor or captain will be shown by the following account which, for the sake of brevity, I will narrate in part only.

I once walked from Tawbarzal[9] toward Rothenburg and approached an inn in which a number of battle-ready peasants with guns and firebrands had gathered. One of them called out, "Carlstadt, Carlstadt." I walked on as if I had heard nothing, for I was afraid. One of them, gun in hand, then pursued me and brought me to his companions. When I reached them, one of them asked, "Are you a brother; then read the messenger's letters. If you are not a brother, we will have you give account of yourself." The peasant said this with such vehemence, defiance, and haughtiness that I was glad to be able to read. When my companion and I had read the unsealed letters and the headings of the sealed ones, the peasants allowed us to go on. But on the very same day the same peasants (I believe) spread a rumor in the town that Carlstadt opens letters and exculpates the messengers. This was the reward those desperate knaves gave me, although none of them coerced me or bid me open any of the sealed letters. Had my way companion not exonerated me before the comission or council, these peasants could have brought me anguish and grief. Well, does this story and that very group of peasants not [113] demonstrate what the peasants thought of me and how they loved me? They would much rather have used me as a bullet in their guns than to have made me a captain of their band and used me in that way.

At Rothenburg one of the peasants wanted very much to knife me; another would have liked to run me down. God, however, graciously protected me.

Between Würzburg and Karlstadt near Tungersheim, several peasants with their guns and other weapons were gathered against Carlstadt, intent on taking from me and my wife whatever was left to us. As I understood, several of them had just separated from their band. They were heard to say that they had been informed by their band that a certain fellow by the name of Carlstadt and his wife were coming along whom they intended to relieve of what he had brought along, etc. Had I not had a letter of safe-conduct from Würzburg through the intervention of my dear patron which I gave these peasants to read, they would have robbed me, probably imprisoned me, and done to my wife and child whatever they wanted.

From this it is once again truly apparent how well I fared with the peasants. I was among the peasants as a hare among ferocious dogs. Let anyone deduce what he likes, I know for a fact that the peasants would have choked me to death on several occasions had not God protected me.

Many times I would have liked to get out of the area of the peasants. For this reason I would have liked to move away from my mother in Franconia. But whenever I tried to go to Saxony, I had to turn back.

At Stetten, half a mile from Karlstadt, a peasant called me a mail carrier. He knew me well and said that Luther and I were indebted to them. I took leave of him and other peasants on good terms. Soon after, not far from Tungen, I walked along the path ahead of my wife when she was accosted as follows: Where do you come from? Do you carry goods belonging to a priest? My wife replied: This is not a priest's belonging. I and my husband acquired it in the sweat of our brows. The other peasant then said, Take it quickly; it is the goods of a priest. My wife: Will I now be robbed in my gracious lord's own territory when I have come all this way without being robbed? [114] What a pity. I shall lay charges with my gracious duke against this bastard. Retorted another peasant: God's suffering on you for that. Do you still want princes and lords? We are intent on driving all princes and lords out of the land. Do you still bank on princes and lords? My wife: How was I to know that we are no longer to have princes and lords? I will gladly desist and give princes and lords no further thought. Thereupon one of them, You had better do so if you want justice in the land. And another, Off with you; God's suffering be upon you.

Are not these excellent signs which prove how the peasants would have liked me as their captain? These signs happened to me in a part in which I am known and from where they go to market in Karlstadt. If those who know me did this to me (and it is true), it is certain that the great mob, without knowledge of my message, would not have accepted me. Any decent chap can gather then that it is not likely for me to have been the instigator or captain of the peasants.

I was not very long at my mother's when someone accosted me in the market square, and after a sermon of mine, a brother-in-law advised me to get myself to a village. What shall I say? When I wanted to go to Frankfurt and when I waited for my wife at Framersbach, several robbers from among the peasants gathered—they knew me well and were known at Karlstadt as well. They conspired and decided on the eve of Trinity Sunday that they would tie me to a tree in the Spessart or kill me. Afterwards they would take everything my wife and I still possessed. But God made their counsel known to me and led me by another way.

It is unbelievable how strangely I fared with the peasants. But I do not want to say any more about common peasants. I consider this sufficient to prove my innocence, provided an understanding and upright person happens upon these examples or stories. The peasants never chose people unknown to them and never undertook anything without the testimony of those they knew. Who then is so bold as to stand up in court and dare say that the peasants chose or engaged Carlstadt to be their captain? Where was Carlstadt chosen? What is the name of the witnesses? Who saw it? Speaking of conjecture, [115] it is a fairly sound conjecture that known [peasants][10] would have liked to rob and then kill Carlstadt. Little do I care if you do not believe any of this. If I could afford it, I would prove all this amply and sufficiently, though it is not my responsibility to do so. Somebody else would leave it unproved, although he ought to testify.

I often preached at Rothenburg on the article concerning the sacrament. Let anyone impudent enough say like an honest person that I preached a single line, one word, or one syllable to incite uprisings. And let him prove this through witnesses who are beyond reproach and who heard me, lest he be shown to have a deceitful tongue. Nor did I ever sit on a commission or on the council.

That I lodged with peasants and ate and drank with them and at times helped them extol injustice or castigated sin too often and too severely, I cannot do anything about. I had to eat and drink, and I was not prepared to endanger the life of my wife and child. I would have been a fool had I stood up to the peasants; they would have cut me into pieces for a single word.

I moved to my mother's from Rothenburg because I could no longer remain in Rothenburg on account of the danger I faced there. Whereto and to whom would I move more logically than to my natural mother? That I was in Würzburg is explained by the fact that I needed a letter of safe-conduct which stood me in good stead, too.

That's all regarding the peasants and me. Now with regard to their leaders. The peasants sent some of their leaders to Rothenburg. Among them was one who boasted at table to have stirred up the entire Main valley. He accomplished so much that a petition was presented to the honorable City Council in the name of the entire community of Rothenburg in which the expulsion of Carlstadt was requested. I only know that said leader was an instigator and troublemaker and that the gate keepers caught me at the gates because of this supplication of the previous day, ready perhaps to put me to death. Said captain [116] enjoyed a great deal of respect, and had I been among the peasants when I was caught, he would undoubtedly have succeeded in driving me out with guns and spears, so that I would be cold and stiff by now. I well recall also how another captain or advisor of the peasants at Schweinfurt honored me on their country day; but I shall forgive him.

I wonder though what I did to the peasants and their leaders, so that I rarely had a day when I was not beset by anguish and fear or at least had to endure ridicule. I cannot think of a reason for this, except, of course, that it may be the letter which I wrote to the band in which I reminded them all of the mercy they were to show and warned them to beware of the wrath of God. I pointed to the stories of Assur, Nebuchadnezzar, and Moab—some twenty—with the brief comment that the Lord God raised such people in order to punish his people, but that God destroyed all such people, if only for the reason that they had killed too many, etc., in other and shorter words, of course. I honestly wrote such a sweet letter that I fear I might have lost favor with the other side. But I undertook to write it for the benefit of both peasants and lords. One of the advisors of the peasants whom I know well suppressed this letter, telling his militant band that Carlstadt is not a good peasant. This same advisor blackballed me and all my supporters, whenever he found one, calling them Carlstadt's knaves. This may be the reason why the peasants and their leaders persecute me, but I do not know for sure. But this I know well that both the peasants and the lords had a poor image of me. The spiritual lords chased me as if I were game, and the peasants imprisoned me and would have devoured me, had not God protected me. And yet there was not a single one who dared to guide me. That is how both bishops and peasants regard the precious parable of Christ which they ought to heed and for the sake of an erring sheep leave ninety-nine sheep in the wilderness.[11]

I hope that princes[12] and lords will take this defense seriously and clear me of any suspicion. Should it be too short, I request a trial by law, that I might submit a complete [117] list of where I took shelter during my travels and give account of what I am able to recall. I hope, however, that this report and voluntary account will help and protect me.

Should it not help, however, I rejoice in my innocence and boast of it, for I know that my God will also hold court when princely lords, citizens, and peasants alike will have to answer to me. They will then receive what they deserve for what they have done to me. I do not say this because I am without sin, for I sin before God even when I do good. Little wonder then that I sinned when I was among the peasants and surrounded by dangers. But this sin does not come before the courts of the world, but under the forgiveness of God. May he be merciful to all of us. Amen.

Dated, St. John the Baptist Day,[13] 1525.

Andreas Carlstadt

15

On the Incarnation of Christ. A Sermon Preached by Dr. Andreas Bodenstein from Karlstadt, Archdeacon at Zurich, on the Occasion of His Farewell, in the Year of the Lord, 1534

John 1:14, "The word became flesh."

The following farewell sermon, preached sometime in 1534, has been virtually disregarded by scholars. Calvin A. Pater rediscovered it in Konrad Füssli's **Sammelband zur schweizerischen Kirchenge-schichte des 16.-18. Jahrhunderts.** *Noting its significance for an understanding of Carlstadt's extensive biblical knowledge and for his solid trinitarian thinking, published it with an Introduction in* **Zwingliana** *XIV/1 (1974), pp. 1-16.*

In addition to reflecting an orthodox Christology, the sermon also shows that Carlstadt cannot be identified with the spiritualist tendencies of contemporaries like Hans Denck or Caspar von Schwenckfeld.

As Pater rightly notes, the fact that most citations are accurate would allow for the conjecture that the manuscript was probably a copy of Carlstadt's sermon notes. The sermon was preached at Zurich prior to Carlstadt's departure for Basel where he had accepted a teaching post.

The manuscript was overlooked by Freys/Barge. Our translation is based on the text edited by Pater. Page references to the text in Zwingliana and biblical citations are noted in brackets [ ].

A sermon recently preached at Zurich by Dr. Andreas Bodenstein Carolstadius, archdeacon, in the year of the Lord 1534.

John 1:14 The word became flesh.

John speaks here of two natures in Christ, namely, the word and the flesh, and of the word becoming flesh. Therein is our salvation. Therefore, we must look at this properly and consider it well: for anyone who does not understand this will hope in vain for eternal life. Those who do not have this understanding of the two natures in Christ are children of death and the wrath of God is upon them [Jn 3:36]. On the other hand, all who understand why the word, i.e., the eternal Son of God, became flesh, i.e., a human being, are children of God.

Holy Scripture often speaks of Christ and of these two natures in Christ, but often focuses on only one of the two natures, either the humanity or the divinity.[1] We must carefully note this, learn it through faith, and hold it as our greatest treasure.

"The word became flesh." The word is the eternal son of God, as John himself testifies, "which dwelt in us, and whose glory we saw as of the only begotten son of the Father, full of grace and truth" [Jn 1:14]. The word that we speak comes from the heart; it is in and with us. Through it we indicate our will. So also, to speak by means of comparison, the Son of God goes forth from the heart of the Father, is in and with God, and indicates the will of God. This, too, John indicates in this chapter, "as the only-begotten Son of the Father, who is in the bosom or heart of the Father who revealed his will to us" [Jn 1:18]. This word was from all eternity before the creation of the world. And if it was from the beginning, it is eternal. "And this word was with God," namely, a person in the Godhead. The meaning of this, that God became a human being, and also the power of this word [9] John himself narrates, "By this word all things have been created" [Jn 1:1-3]. In other words, through the Son of God all things were created: angels, principalities, etc., as St. Paul indicates [Col 1:16]. Further, "God the Father set his Son to be an heir of all things, who is the image and splendor of his glory and nature" [Heb 1:2-3]. For whatever is in the Father appears in the Son. As the Lord Christ himself says, "I and the Father are one" [Jn 10:30]. One cannot compare the Son of God by means of any natural thing to God the Father; rather, he is God himself. Whatever is in God the Father is in God the Son also. For he is the splendor of the eternal God. As the splendor comes with and from the sun and points to the sun, so God the Son relates to God the Father and the power of God is known through Christ.

He is the one in whom the Godhead dwells bodily and essentially [Col 2:9], as St. Paul says of Christ. He did not consider it robbery to be equal to God, but lowered himself [Phil 2:6-7]. If we say Christ is equal to God, we speak correctly, for he is in truth of one nature with God the Father and the Holy Spirit. Thus Isaiah the prophet says of him, the Messiah is and shall be a strong God [Isa 9:6].

All those who handle the mass, disparage and belittle this power of Christ—for they still do not know the power and strength of the Son of God, though they boast that they alone know him. They behave like the Jews who said they knew him, and that they knew well where he came from and who he was and who his father and mother were [Mt 13:35-56; Mk 6:3]. Yet they did not know him at all, as Christ rebukes them, nullifying their claim when he said, "Yes, you know me and whence I come" [Jn 7:28; 8:19], namely, you know me only as a pure human being. But my Godhead, strength, and power you do not know, nor whence I came, for I did not come on my own account. Yet, the one who sent me is true, whom you do not know. But I know him [Jn 7:28-29].

Therefore, let no one boast of his faith or that he knows Christ if he does not have the meaning of Scripture of which one may learn properly and understand the divinity in Christ who indicates Christ the true knower of God, yes, who is Christ in all eternity who became flesh, i.e., a true human being. He says, "The word became flesh" and not "he became a human being" so that he might [10] properly indicate the foolishness and weakness in human beings which Christ took upon himself so that he might suffer, die, feel, and do satisfaction for us. As St. Paul says, "Christ has redeemed us through the body of his flesh" [Col 1:21-22]. He says "body and flesh" to show his true humanity and that Christ took the foolishness and weakness of our flesh upon himself that he might suffer and die for us, etc. [Rom 8:3]. For through him all the patterns of the Old Testament had to be fulfilled and be brought to light. These we ought to learn well from Scripture and then believe them absolutely firmly and henceforth live unto the one who died for us which is Christ [2 Cor 5:15-16; Gal 2:20]. Yes, believe how Christ died and was raised that we, too, may henceforth die to sin and become wholly new persons and henceforth know Christ in the new life, as St. Paul teaches, "Once we knew Christ according to the flesh, for anyone who is in Christ is a new creation" [2 Cor 5:16-17]. For Christ rose to a new life, has taken on an immortal, glorified body, and hence does not live in weakness any longer, but in the glory of God. Henceforth, he cannot suffer or die any more, as he did once when he was born into the world to save, since the one who saves us must be God. Eve also knew this when she said, "I conceived the man of God" [Gen 4:1], meaning the seed which God had promised her[2] and who was to crush the serpent's head [Gen 3:15]. Though she was wrong about the person, she was not wrong in her faith. For the seed, who was Christ, came only later, as Paul expounds it for the Galatians [Gal 4:4].

This Christ took on a mortal body which was like our body in every way, with weaknesses[3] and afflictions, except for sin [Heb 4:14-15]. Though he appeared and was seen in the form of a sinful body [Rom 8:3], no sin or deceit was found in him in any way [Isa 53:9; 1 Pet 2:22; 1 Jn 3:5]. For Christ knew of no sin. But for the sake of our sins, he died [2 Cor 5:21]. The Son of God, though he was in the form of God, accepted, nonetheless, the form of a servant [Phil 2:6-7] who was under everyone's feet and suffered a great deal of derision and shame for our sake. [11]

We must learn well, therefore, that Christ is true God and human being, for the reason that if Christ had not been true God he could not have saved the world.[4] Further, Paul testifies that he is true God [Rom 9:5]. For surely God was in Christ, etc. [2 Cor 5:19]. Similarly, in Christ the full Godhead is and dwells essentially [Col 2:9]. Otherwise he could not have reconciled the world to God his heavenly Father.

Therefore, all those err grievously who seek to be reconciled through their works—with them Christ counts for nothing. Rather, they set themselves above Christ. For the one who paid for our sins and made peace with God has to be true God and human being. Therefore, we are not to look to any creaturely work or merit, but alone and solely to Christ Jesus our Lord, the eternal word of God incarnate—the one who took our impotence upon himself. The Godhead is the head in Christ. Anyone who does not believe the Godhead in Christ and does not understand his flesh and blood is a child of God's wrath and an unbeliever. God grant all of us the right understanding, etc.

For your sake I referred to both natures of Christ and stated that we must be diligent to learn and understand these. To wit, the reason why Christ had to be God is that his work and deed should stand and last forever so that he might touch and placate our consciences. Therefore, he had to be the supreme and eternal priest whose sacrifice is good to eternity.

And he had to be a human being, so that he might initiate this salvation and be able to suffer and die. If he had brought a body from heaven, he could not have redeemed us. And he had to suffer and die so that all who believe in him should not perish [Jn 3:16], but, etc. Anyone who intends to speak of Christ aright must really know what the suffering of Christ brought and achieved. Christ had to take on impotent flesh, so that he could die to fulfill the righteousness of the law and to nullify all our disobedience,[5] [Rom 8:3].

The righteousness of the law demanded all this, as St. Paul points out to the Romans, for it was impossible for the law, i.e., it could not achieve that we be sanctified. God then sent his Son, in the form of sinful flesh that he might destroy sin in the flesh, i.e., the sin of the entire [world][6] with his flesh, and that he might give it as an offering for sin, redeem sin, and all flesh, as St. John also says, "Behold the lamb of God which takes away the sin of the [12] world" [Jn 1:29]. He made satisfaction for the sin of the world. Those who believe in him shall be sanctified and in his death have assurance of eternal life. Through his suffering and death, he took away sin.

The holy prophet Isaiah explained this well [Isa 53]. God thus ordained that Christ should take upon himself our sin and experience our suffering. For God laid upon him our sin and guilt, i.e., he became an offering for our sins; therefore, he had to take upon himself the impotence of our flesh so that the righteousness of God and the law be fulfilled, which is all of the righteousness that is in the law. And whatever God demands of us is carried out, completed, and accomplished through the sacrifice which Christ made on the cross through this impotent flesh.

Therein lies the righteousness of the law that it directs and teaches us what God has placed before us, i.e., how we are to live and follow his will. For righteousness is grounded in the law, i.e., in the eternal will of God. It is the eternal wisdom to which Scripture points. Thereafter Scripture shows you what God demands of you and which on our own we are not capable of doing. This is what Christ accomplished by his terrible death.

Now those who have knowledge of this very work of redemption,

God credits as if they had obeyed and fulfilled the law. For faith shall lead and form according to the spirit of Christ and in full surrender [Gelassenheit] to God all who believe in Christ and daily honor his name and are eager to obey his will. The one portion of the law which God demands of us is "you must be holy, for I am holy" [Lev 19:12]. Such holiness is far from us. Of ourselves we are not able to attain to such holiness, though we may have the will to serve God and walk according to his will and exercise in it. Nonetheless, there are daily imperfections, tribulations, weaknesses,[7] and flaws.

This holiness Christ obtained for all who believe in him and in his bitter suffering by which he presents God to us pure, without spot and wrinkle, as if we had no weakness; as St. Paul says of the bride of Christ which has no spots or wrinkles [Eph 5:25-27]. Not that we could become or be that of ourselves, but rather, that God takes us to be holy and righteous for the sake of his Son who earned this holiness for us. All who know and understand the work of redemption which Christ has achieved in impotent flesh, God considers to be blameless. For they shall order all things to God's honor. [13]

In like manner we also speak with regard to good works for which we have been created in Christ Jesus [Eph 2:10]. Therefore, the world errs with its good works through which it intends to be holy in the sight of God, turning things upside down. For all who want to do good works must first have life within them. That life is Christ who quickens us. Therefore, one must have the knowledge of Christ. And then all who put on Christ shall walk in good works [Rom 13:14; Gal 3:27, etc.], for he cleansed them in their consciences from all dead works [Heb 9:14].

Christ offered himself blamelessly to God through the eternal spirit in order to cleanse our consciences from all dead works. For where death is, there is no life; where there is a dead tree, there will not be any fruit. So also is it impossible for any good to come from us [Ps 14:2-3] unless death is taken away through Christ and we be made alive and believing through his spirit. Then only can we serve God and everything we do will be pleasing. For the work which Christ accomplished on the cross is eternal; indeed, it has an eternal power, for he is the supreme priest forever [Heb 7:17; Ps 110:4]. Whatever has been sprinkled with his blood shall live; indeed, it shall rise in a sanctified life. Therefore, those hearts which have been touched by the finger of God are a people of the new testament, for by the faith of their hearts,[8] they have the right understanding of the work of salvation which was only possible through Christ on the cross.

To wit, on account of the disobedient will, it was necessary that the eternal word take on human impotence to remove our disobedience by which we perished. But by the obedience of Christ we were brought back to life, and he thus reconciled us anew to God his heavenly Father.

To wit, on account of the food, he took on flesh and blood, that Christ might become our food, dwelling place, and the true living bread: Whoever comes to me shall never hunger [Jn 6:35]. For this reason St. Paul calls him our Paschal Lamb [1 Cor 5:7], not that we have to eat him bodily, but rather that we know him through faith. The Paschal Lamb of which Paul writes has become bread, a fire of the inexpressible love which was shown on the cross. He was prepared to die in his physical body so that we might know the food in our hearts. [14]

To wit, for the sake of redemption—that we might be guiltless in the sight of God, the heavenly Father, that he may remove our sin, satisfy the law, and make peace between God and us and become our comfort—he had to shed his blood on the cross and die the most despicable death. All this was possible because of the impotence of the flesh. Therefore, he took upon himself a true and impotent body.

Now, anyone who desires a quiet, peaceful heart must understand and know this and keep it in his heart with a true faith, seeking forgiveness with God and no one else besides.

From all this, dear friends, you may perceive the great error which those commit who say that sin is forgiven by the sacrifice of the mass in which they offer up Christ for the sin of both the dead and the living. For if they sacrifice Christ, he would have to die first; but then the sacrifice and death which happened once on the cross would be in vain [Heb 10:12]. And that is blasphemy.

Those who with their masses want to do satisfaction for sin or who eat physically do not believe that everything which Scripture says of Christ Jesus our sole and eternal Savior [Heb 9:12] is true: that he redeemed us, died on the cross once, and found our eternal salvation. They are blaphemers who deny the truth. For Christ himself said that he had to die and be lifted up, so that all who believe in him should not perish, but have eternal life [Jn 3:14ff.] and that repentance and forgiveness be preached in his name [Lk 24:47]. But these say that Christ did not have to die for sin, for we are able to remove sin through eating and celebrating mass. This is utter blasphemy and their sacrifices are deceptions and lies. For Christ is the truth [Jn 14:6] who cannot lie. Because of sin Christ had to give his body on the cross. This is the work of redemption: anyone who teaches you differently misleads you and is a false and deceiving prophet, etc. For Christ offered himself and shed his blood that he might thus cleanse us. Therefore, Paul says, "Through Christ we have redemption through his blood, namely the forgiveness of sins according to the riches of his grace" [Eph 1:7]. Hence, their sacrifices are deceptions and lies.

Moses and all the prophets declare this: "Christ is the eternal word and wisdom of the Father" [Col 2:3; Heb 1:3]. Similarly, the voice of the Father calls from heaven, "This is my beloved Son with whom I am pleased" [Mt 3:17]; similarly, the four evangelists, here and there; similarly, the apostles in their epistles. A sinful person would have to contradict all of these—which is the ultimate blasphemy. [15]

Therefore, hear and believe God's word more than human words. If you lack wisdom and understanding, ask God faithfully for them that he might increase your faith in every way and form your life in keeping with his will. Persevere to the end and you shall be saved [Mt 10:22]. You need not fear death or purgatory, etc.

[Postscript]

I trust thus to have given you, by way of a farewell, the teaching of God's word, as best I could. Almighty God grant you eternal health and all that will benefit you in body and soul. Dear folks, I commend to your prayers your honorable council and your pastors. Amen.

Appendix A

Martin Luther's Preface (1525) to Carlstadt's *Apology*

(translated from WA XVIII, pp. 436-438)

Whether Carlstadt had returned to Saxony toward the end of June 1525, after nearly two years of exile, (as Barge contended[1]) or whether he merely was given temporary residence, it is a curious fact that Luther wrote an introduction to "Entschuldigung des falschen Namens des Aufruhrs"—our Apology. Not only had Luther responded affirmatively to Carlstadt's request, made early in June 1525, but he actually provided lodgings for Carlstadt and his wife on their arrival in Wittenberg—albeit without making the fact known.

Luther's preface is not, of course, an unqualified endorsement of Carlstadt. It is premised on the assumption that the latter's regret is sincere. Luther does not condone violence or uprisings on the part of the peasants—with whom Luther and others associated Carlstadt—and he objects strongly to the handling of the peasant uprisings by princes and prelates. At the same time, he clearly distances himself from Carlstadt's theology, while extending him the opportunity of apologizing, so that "God not be tempted and tested any further."

To all dear Christians who receive this writing, grace and peace
From God our father
and from the Lord Jesus Christ.

Dr. Andreas Carlstadt transmitted a booklet to me in which he defends himself against the serious and grave rumor that he is guilty of uprisings or that he has been a leader and instigator of the uprisings. He earnestly pleaded with me to permit the publication of this booklet so that he might clear his name and not be condemned so lamentably without a hearing and totally unmerited, and having to live in constant uncertainty regarding himself and his possessions, especially since it is now being said that many poor people are dealt with too hastily. From sheer anger, blameworthy and innocent people alike are being executed without a proper interrogation and without matters having been resolved. I gather that fainthearted tyrants who earlier feared a rustling leaf have now become so bold as to satisfy their wantonness. In his own good time, God will cast them to the ground.

In matters of doctrine, Doctor Carlstadt is my greatest antagonist and we have clashed so fiercely in these matters that all hope for reconciliation or for further dealings has been dashed. Nonetheless, since he placed so great a trust in me in this his trial and tribulation—more even than in his friends who directed him to me—I will allow him, as far as I am able, to find this trust in me satisfied, and oblige him in the matter. All the more so since Jesus Christ teaches us to act thus and by his own example directs us to do good unto our enemies and to love them. We must follow him if we desire to be Christians and if we want to participate with him in his kingdom. Nor would I know how to maintain a good conscience with God, should I discover that he has to endure harm to body and possessions without guilt and if I could have helped to prevent this but did not. This would be regarded in God's sight as if I had done the evil myself, since Paul teaches Rom 12:20, "If your enemy is hungry, feed him; if he is thirsty, give him to drink, etc."

I oblige him all the more readily in the hope that God may grant grace that this good beginning is followed by better things still and that Carlstadt may in the end come to know himself and depart from his error regarding the sacrament and return to the full truth, along with many others. Christ says that a day has twelve hours. We must not lose hope for any person while he is alive, however badly he may have fallen. And we know how wonderful God is in his works—for which we cannot set a time or [436] limit, apply a measure or establish a goal, or give them color or shape. I do want to make crystal clear, however, and state that I do not endorse, nor in any way subscribe to, Carlstadt's opinion and teaching, especially with regard to the sacrament. Rather, I have written against him before and stand by that now. And I would most earnestly plead with everyone to guard against [his teaching], notwithstanding the fact that many others write on these matters in a similar manner. They do so without foundation and with deliberate cunning, so that I have no other thanks to offer except to say that they confirm me all the more strongly in my own understanding.

But should someone be full of suspicion and wish to find fault with me for believing Dr. Carlstadt too readily, suspecting him of not being serious but to have other things up his sleeve, I reply, "It is neither mine nor anyone else's to judge a person's heart." St. Paul states in 1 Cor 13:5, 7, "Love is not jealous" and again, "love believes all things." Even though love is often deceived because of such trust—as the saying has it, "Trust rides off with the horse"[2]—it does not let go. Let me say what I think: as long as Dr. Carlstadt is prepared to stand trial[3] and to suffer what he ought to if he is found and convicted of being rebellious, I must believe his booklet and confession, even though I tended to think earlier that he was a rebellious spirit—as did several others who were with him—before I heard his solemn affirmation. At this point I must leave room for his own offer and not prevent, but rather promote, a hearing.

If I were to speak the truth and look at this matter in the light, I must say that this misery and rebellion cannot be blamed on the peasants alone. Raving princes and foolish bishops must take some of the blame.[4] For when common people[5] had good preachers and gladly heard the pure gospel through which they were learning faith and obedience, our squires would not tolerate them. They expelled righteous preachers without cause and placed uncouth donkey heads over the people who knew nothing and frivolously incited the people against themselves. God then allowed rebellious preachers to rise up among the people. These started the misery by which dissatisfaction has taken hold of common people. There will naturally be no end to this until the tyrants too end up in the dirt. For there can be no permanence when a people does not love its master, but merely fears him. The saying becomes true which states, "The one whom many fear must fear a lot."[6] He can never be sure or happy among those who are not fond of or love him. [437]

Yet our squires and false gods are not to hear or accept any of this. Rather, they continue to blame the gospel for that which they are responsible for and are guided by the fool's jingle which states, "I pay no heed to anything until someone comes along who sets another jingle over against it." I seriously intend neither prince nor bishop to remain under the dome of heaven. Therefore, let go whatever goes. They will soon find what they have long been looking for. It is now on the way. May God grant their timely conversion. Amen.

So I plead with both lords and every man to let Dr. Carlstadt have his say, since he is so anxious to clear himself of the charge of insurrection, in order that God be no longer and more seriously tested, and that the displeasure and anger of the populace[7] toward the authorities not increase and gain the appearance of right. It is never good to bring the common prayer[8] and clamor upon one's own head, especially since the One cannot lie who promised that he would hear the cry of the oppressed and not tolerate oppression, and that he has power enough to avenge and punish it. God grant us his grace. Amen.

Notes

Abbreviations

1. Most biblical references in Carlstadt's tracts appear in abbreviated form. In order to retain the flavor of the originals, the practice has been retained throughout this volume. The abbreviations used conform to those of the NRSV.

Editor's Preface

1. The tracts in question are: *Reason for Carlstadt's Silence, The Two Greatest Commandments*, and *Regarding the Sabbath*.

Introduction

1. The correct spelling of Carlstadt's name has never been fully established. While some reference works list him by the original family name as Bodenstein, most German, and some English, works refer to him as Karlstadt. We have chosen Carlstadt, his own adopted spelling in a variety of adaptations, whenever we refer to his person, but spell Karlstadt when we mean the town of his birth. When citing articles or monographs we have, of course, retained the spelling chosen by their respective authors.

2. Erich Hertzsch, *Karlstadt und seine Bedeutung für das Luthertum. Gotha, 1932,* bemoaned the lack of sense and clarity regarding Carlstadt's life and thought. Nonetheless, Hertzsch considered certain tracts by Carlstadt significant enough to publish them in 1956-57 in a two-volume edition as Karlstadt's Schriften aus den Jahren 1523-1525. Halle: Max Niemeyer.

3. Bubenheimer, Sider, and Zorzin provide detailed bibliographical references to the relevant literature.

4. See Ulrich Bubenheimer, *Consonantia Theologiae et Iurisprudentiae. Andreas Bodenstein von Karlstadt als Theologe und Jurist zwischen Scholastik und Reformation.* Tübingen 1977.

5. Calvin A. Pater, *Karlstadt as the Father of the Baptist Movement. The Emergence of Lay Protestantism.* Toronto 1984.

6. Ronald J. Sider, *Andreas Bodenstein von Karlstadt. The Development of His Thought 1517-1525.* Leiden 1974.

7. Alejandro Zorzin, *Karlstadt als Flugschriftenautor.* Göttingen: Vandenhoeck & Ruprecht, 1990.

8. Between eighty-five to eighty-seven known publications appeared in at least

156 editions, published mostly in the sixteenth century. The majority of these had been composed in German, Carlstadt's preferred language of communication. See Freys/Barge and A. Zorzin. The latter lists eighty-six publications, but has overlooked the Farewell Sermon preached by Carlstadt in 1534. However, he does give a detailed breakdown of Carlstadt's Latin and German publications and shows peaks and low periods in his publishing activities.

9. One of the most important of these is Carter Lindberg's translation of "Carlstadt's Dialogue on the Lord's Supper" of 1524, in *Mennonite Quarterly Review* 53 (1979), pp. 35-87.

10. An analysis of his use of the Scriptures and an examination of the version of the Bible which he used would be most desirable.

11. See A. Zorzin, op. cit. Teil II, pp. 85ff.

12. As a corrective to F. Kriechbaum's *Grundzüge der Theologie Karlstadts* of 1967 which is inadequate because the author sought to fit him into theological norms which were Luther's rather than Carlstadt's, one would have to do a thorough new analysis of Carlstadt's theological stance.

13. Clear signs of a theological change are apparent in the 1521 publication of *De legis litera sive carne et spiritu*. Carlstadt suggests that, in addition to a literal understanding of Scripture, there must be the deeper understanding which comes through the inspiration of the Holy Spirit.

Chapter 1

1. We have retained the term *Gelassenheit* in the title, but will use a number of synonyms such as yieldedness, abandonment, detachment, and surrender, to express the many nuances Carlstadt seems to have had in mind when he used the term and its derivatives.

2. Carlstadt quotes the Vulgate; we have simply corrected his citations to correspond to modern English Bibles; hence, Ps 11 in the Vulgate is Ps 12 in a modern Bible.

3. "Tribulation is foremost." This statement is not from the quoted Psalm.

4. Throughout the document, which has numerous marginal notations, we will incorporate these in the text in [. . .]. When we identify biblical references not given by Carlstadt, but alluded to, cited, or paraphrased, we shall give the textual reference in a footnote. Citations which he gave in the body of the text will appear there, with the verses added where this seemed appropriate.

5. In this section Carlstadt paraphrases Scripture, often beyond recognition. The dominant note is psalm-like and some of the quotations are blended from a number of possible texts. For this quote see Ps 126; Ps 22:26.

6. Ps 15:15

7. Ps 21:13 [Ps 22:12] in the Vulgate speaks of *Thauri pingues*.

8. Many of Carlstadt's tracts are poorly paginated. While, in general, every second page has a letter or Roman numeral, there is no consistent pattern. Hence, we provide his pagination in [. . .], but indicate the end of page in the original text thus: [//] when there is no page number.

9. Carlstadt refers to Pope Leo X, one of the Medici of Florence, as the Florentine lion. While Leo supported the arts and promoted the Renaissance, he did not seem to have had too great an appreciation of the theological distinctions that went into the making of the Reformation. Nonetheless, his political gamesmanship seems to have advanced the cause of reform.

10. James 1:18.

11. Frequently throughout Ps 119, *vivifica me* occurs in conjunction with specific affirmations; so verse 159, "Preserve my life according to thy steadfast love, etc."

12. Ps 22 once again.

13. Ps 22.

14. These words are not found in Matthew, but in Luke 23:46.

15. Carlstadt cites from the Vulgate, Ps 118:42, *et respondebo exprobanti mihi sermonem, etc."*

16. *Spottvögel* is the original German term, here translated as "mockers."

17. *Pax multa diligentibus legem.*

18. According to the MSS of his acts, Symphorianus suffered martyrdom by beheading about 180 C.E. for refusing to worship Cybele. His mother encouraged him to remain steadfast. His feast day is August 22. See Smith & Wace, *Dictionary of Christian Biography.*

19. The correct form would be *Scomma in pagan.* It is an invective against the pope.

20. Carlstadt does not seem to have a particular situation in mind, but simply uses this illustration by way of contrast, but he probably meant John I of Saxony, 1468-1532, who shared responsibilities with Frederick the Wise, 1463-1525, and was Elector of Saxony after Frederick's death. He was succeeded by John Frederick, born 1503.

21. Carlstadt does not follow the Vulgate verbatim. His interpretation, as a result, is not in line with the usual interpretations of the text.

22. An allusion to the words of Christ in Gethsemane, Mt 26:39.

23. Ibid.

24. Carlstadt uses *werden*—become, the plural of "to be," a rather uncolloquial form in translation.

25. John Hus, a Czech nationalist and Reformer of his church in the fifteenth century, was burned at the stake during the Council of Constance in 1415. His name was held in high esteem by 16th-century reformers and also among the Radicals.

26. Mt 10:34.

27. Mt 10:37.

28. Jn 15:13.

29. A line of text seems to be missing here. The author does not mention the specific trials he had in mind.

30. Mark 11:24 reads in the Vulgate *orantes petitis credite quia accipietis*—whatever you ask in prayer, believe that you receive it.

31. The text has *neyden* instead of *meyden.*

32. 1 Tim 1:15 or Mt 9:13 and parallel passages in Mark and Luke.

33. John 1:29.

34. Probably Isaiah 43:25.

Chapter 2

1. Albrecht Dürer the younger, May 1471-April 1528 of Nuremberg was renowned for his graphics, paintings, and drawings. His numerous altar pieces and his exquisite woodcuts established Dürer as one of the great artists of the new era. He also contributed significantly to art theory which he pursued throughout his life.

2. Actually Heb 11 almost in its entirety.

3. This is a key text for Luther's understanding of the centrality of preaching; it was important for a majority of the Reformers.

4. Since Carlstadt often cited from memory and worked under pressure, his translations do not always correspond to the text in modern English versions of the Bible. In each case we transmit the rendition he gave, but note significant variants from the NRSV.

5. Probably Mk 11:24.

6. The play on the words *beten—anbeten* [pray to—worship] is not possible in English.

7. George [Jörg] Reich was addressed by Carlstadt as "a supporter and especially dear brother." The booklet *Von beyden gestalten der heiligen Messe* was published in several editions in 1522. See Freys/Barge, numbers 71-74. Different editions show variations in spelling.

8. Carlstadt here follows the account in Mt 26:26.

9. In the Roman Catholic liturgical practice the *Engelmesse* also known as *Engelamt* [*missa de angelis*], is a high mass in honor of the angels. The liturgy may be celebrated as a votive office in honor of the blessed virgin during the season of Advent.

The name is also used for the midnight mass on Christmas Eve, and may be celebrated at the funeral of children.

10. The words here ascribed to John's Gospel are actually found in Mt 20:28.

11. The RSV reads, "She had done a beautiful thing."

12. Mary and Miriam are interchangeable.

13. Carlstadt paraphrases 1 Cor 11:18ff. using the term *secten* for the RSV terms "divisions" and "factions."

14. 1 Cor 11:29.

15. Literally, "bite its own fingers."

16. *Von beiden gestaldten der heylige Messze* was first published in Wittenberg, late in 1521 and appeared in three further printings in 1522. The book was dedicated to Jörg Reich of Leipzig. See Freys/Barge, numbers 71-74. Extant editions are found in several European libraries.

17. Jn 20:28.

18. Mt 8:8.

19. Lk 19:6.

20. Carlstadt here retains the notion of the real presence, but does not wish to promote the medieval teaching of transubstantiation.

21. Carlstadt attacks the medieval sacramental teaching as the result of erroneous thinking by "the papists," i.e., everyone who adheres to the notion of transubstantiation. In his later writings on the Lord's Supper, he will distinguish between the old and the new papists, meaning by the latter term the followers of Luther's interpretation rather than that of writers like the Dutch cleric Cornelis Hoen, the Swiss Huldrych Zwingli, or his own.

22. "In *Christo hafften.*"

23. The number 14 was inadvertently omitted from the text.

24. Carlstadt means Jesus.

25. This appears to be a slightly altered reference to Mt 13:16-17.

26. Carlstadt collapses Gen 9, the account of the rainbow, and Gen 15, the story of Abraham's cattle.

27. This narrative is found in Judg 6.

28. The NRSV does not bring out the note of vexation and astonishment in 1 Pet 2 which Carlstadt may have found in Luther's September Bible or in other texts at his disposal.

29. The NRSV translates this passage as follows: "that he himself is righteous and that he justifies the one who has faith in Jesus."

30. Mt 28:20.

31. 1 Cor 10:17.

32. Carlstadt's uses *brot* and *leyb* interchangeably, as both terms are often used in German for bread, analogous to the English "loaf of bread."

33. The Piccards originated in northern France in the early fifteenth century. They rejected ecclesiastical structures and frowned on the veneration of saints and sacraments. They were ostracized and sought shelter among the Hussites in Bohemia. Hence, in common parlance Bohemians were generally labeled Piccards in the 16th century. Jean Calvin as well as B. Hubmaier referred to the Hussites by this name.

34. In a rather complex sentence, Carlstadt uses the term *unversuocht*. Although it literally means "untested," the context suggests unperturbed, i.e., without interference, control, or the allure of ecclesiastical carrots.

35. *Beutelfeger*—literally one who cleans out a purse. An English equivalent may be "purse snatcher."

36. In German usage "evangelical" generally means "Protestant."

37. *Hostien*—the wafers used in the mass.

Chapter 3

1. The kastner was a manager of grains and often receiver of revenues and administrator of the same.

2. Kitzingen is a district town not far from Carlstadt's birthplace in Lower Franconia.

3. John Pfeffer, Gutman's son, appears to have been well known to Carlstadt.

4. Carlstadt paraphrases 1 Jn 4:1 "test the spirits to see whether they are of God; for many false prophets have gone out into the world" in a plea to lay persons not to rely on the words of others in matters of the spirit, but to become discerning Christians.

5. This may be an allusion to Ps 145:10, "All thy saints shall bless thee."

6. The marginal note reads Ps 06—an obvious inversion of numbers for 60 in the Vulgate.

7. As so often in Carlstadt's biblical citations, the text he uses is a paraphrase rather than an accurate rendition of the text he has in mind.

8. Carlstadt prefers to read "saints" for *sanctorum*. The RSV reads "holy ones."

9. Carlstadt's rendition of Jer 7:18 differs slightly from the Vulgate and from the English translation in the NRSV.

10. Carlstadt quotes from Esther's Prayer; cf. The New Revised Standard Version, The Apocrypha, Addition C.

11. The so-called Shema which is spoken by every devout Jew to this day and must be recited at the moment of death.

12. The term *erdichteten glauben* was also used by Thomas Müntzer.

13. The NRSV reads, "Unless the Lord guards the city, the guard keeps watch in vain."

14. Carlstadt mistakenly cited the last chapter of Deuteronomy for a statement attributed to Moses regarding the tribe of Levi, recorded in Deut 33.

15. Do not share a meal with the worshiper of idols—misprints in the Latin text have been quietly corrected. "*Cum simulacrorum cultore ne quidem cibum capiatis.*"

16. Carlstadt uses the term *vicarien*, meaning assistants, messengers or, as we have translated here, representatives. I have avoided the English "vicar" since it has a technical meaning which Carlstadt did not intend.

17. Carlstadt's reading of Num 30:1 differs in several instances from the NRSV rendition.

18. Carlstadt paraphrases the text for which he provides a marginal notation.

19. The specific instruction is in Lev 27:1ff.

20. One silver shekel was equivalent to four Roman denarii. Its approximate modern value is $ .64.

21. The suggestion of restricting church buildings, one to a community, is rather revolutionary for the 1520s.

22. The author is here guided by church rules pertaining to vows. According to the *Corpus Juris Canonici* (CIC) (Rome:1918), 1307:1 and 3, vows are deliberate promises which can be made by persons after their eighteenth year, provided they have a sufficient use of reason. Several types of vows are recognized. See also *CIC* 1309.

23. Originating in the Lowlands, beghins were communities of young women and/or widows who lived in cloister-like institutions. Those who affiliated with an established religious order were tolerated by the Roman Church, but others were suspected of heresy and suppressed since the Council of Vienne, 1311.

24. Widows in Bible times were protected by legislation and granted privileges such as gleaning in fields and orchards. In early post-biblical Christian communities, they were frequently organized into ordered groups who ministered primarily to women.

25. It is difficult to establish what he intended; he probably means the censure of one who exercises dominative power over the maker of a vow to invalidate a vow. See CIC c 1321.1.

26. Carlstadt may be thinking of the Cluniac Reforms in the eleventh and twelfth centuries, out of which came the Investiture Controversy and some major reforms to which Pope Gregory VII (1073-1085) contributed significantly.

27. Carlstadt paraphrases rather accurately the law concerning vows found in Lev 27.

28. Whether Carlstadt equates "sickness" with "sin" is hard to determine from the context. He sounds almost sarcastic, not to say derisive.

29. This freely rendered passage of Lev 5 is taken from verses 4-7.

30. It is not clear which Augustine text Carlstadt had in mind.

31. Carlstadt's text has *Propter fornicationem unusquisque ducat suam.* The Vulgate reads, *Propter fornicationem autem unusquisque suam uxorem habeat.* We have simply corrected Carlstadt's text.

32. Carlstadt's more circumscribed language has "than unchastity with beasts and animals."

33. The text has *stadt* in place of *standt.*

34. Carlstadt quotes Ps 94:11 in a slightly altered form, *quibus iuravi in ira mea, si introibunt in requiem mea.* In the NRSV this is Ps 95:11.

35. While it is possible to read Carlstadt's meaning into the passage in John's Gospel, a more likely text would have been 1 Sam 16:7.

36. The marginal notation, Jn 3, and the reference in the text, Jn 4, are both correct, since both refer to the spiritual nature of God.

37. The NRSV reads, "whom I serve with my spirit . . ."

38. This is likely an allusion to Jn 4:21.

39. The Latin of 1 Cor 6:12 reads, *Ut [sed] ego sub nullius redigar potestate[m].*

40. Several texts in John's Gospel could have been in Carlstadt's mind for this quotation. Jn 3:18 or 3:36 are the likeliest.

41. The NRSV reads, "Whoever disobeys the Son will not see life."

42. Carlstadt probably has in mind the general tenor of chapters 10-12 and no particular verse.

43. This is a rather free rendition of the passage in Isaiah 1.

44. The term used is *orenkreben.*

45. Carlstadt's text from Num 30:6 differs slightly from that in the NRSV.

46. Carlstadt probably draws this inference on the basis of 1 Thess. 5:21 (test everything).

47. Carlstadt has transferred the husband-wife relationship of the Deuteronomic Code to the relationship of God and the believer.

48. An allusion to the aggressive methods Pope Innocent III, 1198-1216, used to promote crusades, especially the notorious Children's Crusade. However, it is not clear from the context whether Carlstadt meant King Eneric, 1196-1204 or King Andrew II, 1205-35.

49. Probably merely a general reference to the practice of encouraging pilgrimages to Rome after crusading activities had lost their allure.

50. Carlstadt's emphasis is slightly different from that in the RSV. There Num 30:9 reads, But any vow of a widow or of a divorced woman, anything by which she has bound herself, shall stand against her.

51. The term is *zymlich.*

52. Drawing on 1 Sam 25, Carlstadt uses Nabal, the name of Abigail's husband, as a term of derision.

53. Num 30:16 in the Vulgate reads, *"Portabitipse iniquitatem suam."* See NRSV Num 30:15.

54. George Reich was a rich merchant from Leipzig whose sympathies toward Carlstadt caused Duke George of Saxony to have him investigated.

55. Carlstadt cites Gen 2:17, without giving the textual reference.

56. Except for one proverb, *"Was sich gleicht, das kriegt sich,"* most German proverbs say the opposite of what Carlstadt claims here. See W. Körte, *Die Sprichwörter und sprichwörtlichen Redensarten der Deutschen.* Hildesheim: G. Olms, 1974 and H. Beyer, *Sprichwörterlexicon.* Munich: C.H. Beck, 1985.

57. Fraticelli, Piccards, Waldenses, and Hussites were called *Grubenheimer* because they allegedly lived in caves. Immoral activities were often ascribed to sectarians like them. We cannot establish the source on which Carlstadt bases his reference. See Grimm, Deutsches *Wörterbuch,* vol. 12, p 620.

58. We have not located the passage Carlstadt might have had in mind, except that he might have been thinking of Mt 5:28.

Chapter 4

1. Count Wolfgang von Schlick, brother of Christoph von Schlick controlled the silver-rich Bohemian mining area which bordered on Saxony. Carlstadt seems to have been on good terms with this branch of the Schlackenwerther family.

2. January 20 is St. Sebastian's. In 1522 the Friday after was Jan. 24.

3. *Heusser gotis* literally means "houses of God." The term is still preferred to *Kirche* in some parts of Germany.

4. Carlstadt may have in mind his sermon of 1521 *Von empfahung des heiligen sacraments [On receiving the Blessed Sacrament]*, cf. Freys/Barge, 76-80 or else, the booklet *Von den Empfahern: zeychen und zusag des heyligen Sacraments fleysch und bluts Christi* [Regarding the Recipients, the Signs and the Promises of the Holy Sacrament of the Body and Blood of Christ], cf. Freys/Barge, 54-58.

5. The Feast Day of the conversion of St. Paul is January 25.

6. Carlstadt draws on Hos 9 and 10, paraphrasing rather freely.

7. Carlstadt probably means Wilsnack in Mark Brandenburg and Grimmental near Meiningen.

8. A not-so-veiled allusion to Dr. Hans Ochsenfahrt of Leipzig whom Carlstadt addressed in a separate tract published at about the same time as the current document, cf. Freys/Barge, 90-92. The reference to the donkey is less clear, though it has been conjectured by Jaeger that Carlstadt meant Emser.

9. The NRSV translates Carlstadt's "hope" as "trust."

10. A reference to Gregory VII, 1073-1085 who was believed to have been the initiator of the so-called Gregorian Reforms. Their impact began with the papal election decree of Nicholas II and extended to the First Lateran Council, 1123. The *Dictatus Papae*—some twenty-seven propositions regarding papal primacy—do come from Gregory VII.

11. The text reads *eynnhemen.*

12. This is Carlstadt's own formulation which he derived from the tenor of the entire chapter.

13. Epiphanius, Bishop of Salamis, corresponded with John, Bishop of Jerusalem. This letter is from 394 C.E..

14. Carlstadt cites from Erasmus' 1516 edition of Jerome's works. It is a translation of a letter by Epiphanius to John of Jerusalem. The letter is translated in *The Nicene and Post-Nicene Fathers*, Series Two, VI, Letter 51, especially p. 88f.

15. This is a rather free rendition of Isa 44:9-18. Carlstadt misunderstands the intent of verse 20 which reads "and he cannot save himself or say, "Is not this thing in my right hand a fraud?"

16. Carlstadt continues to paraphrase Isa 44.

17. "And there is none beside me" is not found in Isa 44.

18. A legendary martyr/saint from about the middle of the third century whose reputation for having carried the Christ child gained him increasing prominence in the Western church since about the fifth century. He was regarded as the patron saints of travelers and had alleged powers of preventing sudden death.

19. "*Christoffore sancte virtutes sunt tibi tante qui te mane videt de nocte ridet or vivet.*" Wandering minstrels in the fourteenth century and later employed raucous songs such as the one cited here in which they ridiculed the serious matters they studied in their respective schools.

20. *Frombd fewr* or *fremd feuer;* hence, alien or unholy fires.

21. Such as the oft-cited Pope Gregory and, during Carlstadt's time, advocates for retaining images in churches, like H. Emser and J. Eck.

22. Carlstadt uses the phrase "*gottis schuler sein,*" reminiscent of Schwenckfeld's notion of the school of Christ or God.

23. The entire chapter, rather than a particular verse, would lead Carlstadt to ascribe this saying to God.

24. This is one of the rare instances in Carlstadt's tracts where he gives two biblical references for the same text.

25. Both Luther and the RSV translate Ezek 6:9 somewhat differently. However, the force of the passage has been retained by Carlstadt.

26. Carlstadt arranges the material in Ezek 16 to suit the flow of his argument.

27. It is not clear whether or not Carlstadt refers to the excessive feasting which was often associated with celebrations of the saints' days, or with baptisms and other religious festivals.

28. Carlstadt seems to have been instrumental in redefining the status of "beggars" in the city of Wittenberg which developed the Wittenberg Beutelordnung. For similar developments in Zurich, see Lee Palmer Wandel, *Always Among Us: Images of the Poor in Zwingli's Zurich*, Cambridge, U.K.: Cambridge University Press, 1990.

29. Actually, Mt 25:41-45.

30. Frequently in his writings, Carlstadt refers to Christ as "the Truth." He does not, however, use the masculine pronoun in this connection, but remains grammatically correct by employing the feminine pronoun referring to "die Wahrheit."

31. Although Carlstadt does not explicitly say so, his argument seems directed against professional begging in the name of religion. The points he makes seem to be aimed at mendicants.

32. A legal term which indicates that no further action or charge against a debtor was permitted; all outstanding debts were thus canceled.

33. Here and occasionally elsewhere, Carlstadt uses the singular form *endchristen*—likely a variant of antichrist—to refer to the arch enemy of Christ. Similar usage is found in Patristic writers and in the New Testament. Throughout Christian history such designations were given to people in power who abused their positions of leadership with disastrous results for those they governed.

34. Carlstadt uses *Bruderschafften*, not *priesterschaften*, to indicate the communities of religious whose communal property was to be used for the alleviation of poverty in places such as Wittenberg and wherever monastic houses were to be dissolved. Lietzmann takes this to be an indication that the Zwickau manuscript of the Wittenberg Poor Relief Order gives the original wording.

35. The two locations have not been identified, but may refer to Bohemian localities.

36. "Far" might stand for Franciscan, but the author's intended meaning is not clear.

37. An unidentified opponent of radical reforms in the town of Lausigk, near the city of Leipzig.

38. Carlstadt likely means Grossenhain in Saxony.

Chapter 5

1. See Z I, 214-248, *Eine freundliche Bitte und Ermahnung an die Eidgenossen.*

2. St. Sebastian's is January 20.

3. This is presumably the first Sunday after Christmas.

4. In keeping with English usage and his own preference, we spell Carlstadt's name with a "C" but refer to the town of his birth with a "K."

5. Carlstadt uses the term "Vorsteher" rather than "Prior" or "Abt."

6. Misprint for *sparsas.*

7. Let Christians intone the invincible praises of Martin.

He brought back to Christ the scattered flock and reconciled the errant sinners.

The tyrants suppressed the books of this great man, but Martin, the lord of life, survives and rules.

Announce to us, O truthful, just, and pious Martin, the doctrine of Christ who lives and continuously revives glory.

Christ, my hope, raised the angelic witnesses, Paul and the Evangelists, shunning Rome as if it were Gomorrah.

We should rather believe one truthful Martin than the whole mob of the papists.
We know that Christ was truly reborn through Martin; you, O God, do guard him for us.
A sequence to be prayed by the Lutherans in honor of the arising Christ.

Chapter 6

1. The full title is, *"Was gesagt ist: sich gelassen. Unnd was das wort gelassenhait bedeut und wo es in hayliger schrifft begriffen."*

2. Jörg Schenck of Schleusingen, a town halfway between Erfurt and Schweinfurt, was probably not known to Carlstadt who wrote this reply to Schenck's query under a pseudonym.

3. As in the previous document on Gelassenhait, we will mention the German terms once and subsequently offer a variety of synonyms in translation to indicate the nuanced use Carlstadt made of the term.

4. An anonymous publication from around 1430 which reflects the mystical notions of Meister Eckhart. Following the example of Luther, who published a complete edition of this work in 1518, many others made reprints of the booklet which appeared in the early sixteenth century. The tract is still read as devotional literature.

5. A large territory settled by Germanic tribes since before the birth of Christ. A unified political entity from about 1473 onwards, the March of Brandenburg was governed by Margrave Joachim I, during Carlstadt's years in the area 1499-1535.

6. An interesting reflection on the variety of regional usage at a time when uniformity in speech had not yet been attained by peasants.

7. Mt 19:29.

8. Mt 19:5.

9. From *desero*—to sever one's connection; *renuncio*—give notice; *dimitto*—to send apart, dismiss respectively. In these terms the active as well as the passive quality of the term Gelassen is suggested.

10. 1 Cor 6:17.

11. Ex 20:3.

12. Deut 6:4ff.

13. Carlstadt uses an older version whose reading according to modern sources is uncertain. The RSV translates Ps 2:11, "Serve the Lord with fear, with trembling kiss his feet."

14. Carlstadt's citation seems to be incorrect. The only text that comes close to his paraphrase is in Job 4:5.

15. Gen 8:21.

16. An echo perhaps of Jer 15:10; 20:14.

17. As so often in his writings Carlstadt here paraphrases a rather complex text, almost beyond recognition.

18. The NRSV translates Isa 5:21 as follows: "Ah, you who are wise in your own eyes, and shrewd in your own sight!"

19. Carlstadt reads notions into this text which are not sustained by the original.

20. Mt 19:26.

21. 1 Cor 1:20.

22. The section heading reads "Gelassenheit in Gelassenheit."

23. A reference to the widespread practice of purchasing exemptions from fast laws and to the selling of indulgences.

24. Not identified. Carlstadt may have had in mind Eccl 7:18 or Prov 1:32 or Isa 1:16.

25. Lk 14:33.

26. Carlstadt may have had Mt 20 in mind.

27. The NRSV has "wealth" in Mt 6:24.

28. Mt 10:28.

29. As the two subsequent references would indicate, Carlstadt uses the term *Hadermetzen* to indicate unacceptable behavior among Christians who quarrel over

temporal matters, thus neglecting the far greater spiritual dimension of the human person.

30. The NRSV does not support Carlstadt's reading.

31. The close relationship in German of *gehn lassen*—to let go—and of *Gelassen sein*—being calm, resigned, or laid back—is significant. The author's exact intention is therefore difficult to determine.

32. The notion of the *eingedruckte vermahnung* puts Carlstadt close to Spiritualists like Sebastian Franck who would resonate well with the idea that each individual has some of the truth, like an inner blueprint, as it were.

33. A hint of dualistic thinking according to which all human actions may be divided into things of the flesh (carnal matters) and things of the spirit. His sound Christian orientation does not allow Carlstadt to be too dogmatic on the matter, however.

34. The term *gebresten* used here and Zwingli's *bresten*, by which the latter means the human inclination toward or aptitude for sin, sound very much alike. A careful analysis of similarities and/or differences in the respective meanings of the term as used in Saxony and Zurich should be most enlightening.

35. This may be an allusion to the fact that "boasting" in one's yieldedness leads to spiritual pride. Hence, yieldedness or detachment, if an end in itself, brings about one's spiritual death.

36. In other words, passively and actively.

37. Carlstadt's very poignant phrase is *"ungelass der Gelassenheit."*

38. Probably Mt 10:39.

39. Jn 5:42.

40. The author uses *myden, bulgen,* and *unden*—terms which may also be found in the writings of Thomas Müntzer.

41. Along with other radicals, Carlstadt has come to suspect and even dismiss higher education as harmful to a Christians's spiritual integrity. "Die Gelehrten, die Verkehrten"—the scholars are perverters—became a watchword in Anabaptist circles, among them Hans Denck. While Carlstadt, for a time, divested himself of all academic attainments and honors, he was to return to academic life when he settled in the city of Basel in 1534.

42. *Von manigfeltigkait des ainfeltigen ainigen willen Gottes* [The Manifold Singular Will of God], was published in the spring of 1523 in Cologne. A second printing appeared in Augsburg. See Freys/Barge, numbers 102/103 and this volume, document 8 below. The text we used is from Augsburg.

43. The booklet is the *Missive von der allerhöchsten Tugend Gelassenheit, [Tract on the Supreme Virtue of Gelassenheit]*, first printed in Wittenberg in 1521 and extant in several editions. See Freys/Barge, numbers 38-42 and this volume, document 1, above.

44. Assur=King of Assyria, a semi-mythical god/king. Reference to him is made in Isa 10:5-19 where, on account of his arrogance, he is brought low by God.

45. *Sündlich* may be a mistake for *stündlich* [hourly] which would fit into Carlstadt's sequence, *täglich, Stündlich, augenblicklich.*

Chapter 7

1. *Gestrackt* suggests directness, unconditional reliability.

2. Literally: In der Aschen erstickt.

3. *Lust mit unlust zudempfen.*

4. The reference is to Luther and to all who oppose Carlstadt who perceives himself to be a true Israelite.

5. One of the characteristics of Anabaptists and radicals was their effort to live by the ethical implications of the Sermon on the Mount, Mt 5-7. Carlstadt's argument in defense of one of his publication breaks is here based on that ethic and shows him seriously trying to be a kinder person. Cf. Alejandro Zorzin, *Karlstadt als Flugschriftenautor*. Göttingen: Vandenhoeck & Ruprecht, 1990.

6. A Zorzin, op. cit. p. 111, among others has pointed out George Spalatin's influ-

ence on and attempted interference with Carlstadt's Wittenberg printer Rhau-Grunenberg as early as 1518 or 1519. This passage may well be an allusion to such activity which obviously irked him.

7. *Verordnen* does not necessarily have the formal connotation of ordaining, but does denote being commissioned or delegated.

8. This is possibly a paraphrase of the high priestly prayer of Jesus in Jn 17.

9. Acts 1:8.

10. This perception is recorded in 2 Cor 1:21f.

11. Carlstadt must have in mind Acts 16:6-7, "And they went through . . . having been forbidden by the Holy Spirit to speak the word in Asia."

12. Although Carlstadt speaks of Titus in the example, he quotes from Paul's letter to Timothy.

13. This seems to be the closest in wording to Carlstadt's quote. Several other passages, none of which is exactly like the quote, could have been in the writer's mind.

14. Obviously a blending of a number of diverse sayings as if they had been given as one statement.

15. Carlstadt seems to be mistaken in this marginal note. Luke 9 does not mention purgation through seven fires, though there are several biblical passages that he might have cited in support of his argument.

16. Mt 10:38; 16:24; Mk 10:21; Lk 14:24 would be suitable passages from which Carlstadt may have drawn this quote.

17. These words echo Paul's in Rom 7:19.

18. See Heb 12:12.

Chapter 8

1. Mt 26:39.

2. Mt 10:39.

3. Obviously paraphrased by Carlstadt.

4. The text in the microfilm copy at my disposal is illegible at this point. If the citation of Isa 62:2 is correct, then the line should read "you shall be called by my name."

5. Carlstadt sets out some of the notions regarding the nature of sin which were current at the time. We have not been able to identify his sources.

6. Carlstadt summarizes the indictment against Israel spoken by the prophet in the name of God.

7. Carlstadt's text and the passage in Luke do not correspond.

8. The text reads literally *"gswylt ynen der bauch"*—their bellies get bloated.

9. Paraphrasing Jn 14:2ff and Mt 17:20f.

10. See Ps 18:26. Sebastian Franck, especially, picked up this notion and developed it in his *280 Paradoxes*, suggesting that God is to everyone what that person is prepared to make of God.

11. Quoting Mt 10:37.

12. *Handschrift.*

13. Mt 25:42. Carlstadt collapses this saying of Jesus with the one in Mt 24, but cites only the latter.

14. The text has *frefferey* instead of *fresserey.*

15. This is an obvious typographical error. The passage cited is from Rom 7:25.

16. Meant is St. Paul.

17. This passage is from Rom 7:24.

18. In order for this statement to make sense, "not" must be inserted.

19. The text has *mais* instead of *wais* which is undoubtedly the correct reading.

20. Carlstadt challenges scholastic theology which made these subtle distinctions in order to get around the vexing problem of God's responsibility in sinful human actions which, because of his omniscience, he would have known, yet because of the freedom of humans, did not prevent.

21. The German reads, *Und wil eingeben.*

22. Carlstadt totally misunderstands the thrust of Ps 124:1-3 which asserts that "If it had not been the Lord . . . then they would have swallowed us alive, when their anger was kindled against us."

23. Probably an echo of Rom 9:22 or of 2 Tim 2:20.

24. Jn 13:34.

25. Mt 25:40f.

26. An allusion to the waiting described in Jer 9, but Carlstadt obviously combines a number of biblical passages.

27. The quotation comes from Gal 2:20. Carlstadt clearly agrees here with the baptismal understanding of the Anabaptists of his day. He affirms their theology of spiritual regeneration without guile.

28. Carlstadt confuses Sihon, King of the Amorites (Deut 2 and elsewhere), with Shimei, son of Gera, 2 Sam 16 and 19.

29. The RSV translates Ps 116:11 as "Men are all a vain hope."

30. *Eigenbegierde* is difficult to translate. While conceit is weak, egomania is too strong. Self-love may be appropriate, as long as it does not contradict the biblical injunction to love one's neighbor as oneself.

31. Not identified. Probably Ps 33:12, "Happy is the nation whose God is the Lord," or 53:6.

32. *"Fide stabilimus legem"* and *"Fide antiquamus legem."* For a similar statement see *On the Removal of Images*, document 6 above.

33. The quote is a paraphrase of the text in Jeremiah.

34. The term he uses is *"tzu der letze gesegnen."*

35. The text mistakenly has *feynd*—enemy.

36. The text reads 2 Esd 7—an indication that Carlstadt used the Greek version at this point. The intended reference then is to the book of Nehemiah.

37. *Loesung.*

38. 1 Pet 3:19.

39. Mercurius is the Roman god of merchants, shepherds, and rogues. He is the son of Zeus and the mermaid Maia. He distinguished himself from birth by his swiftness and cleverness. In Greek mythology he was known as Hermes.

40. Unidentified. Carlstadt may have meant Mt. Hebron.

41. The Feast of St. Gregory is January 2.

Chapter 9

1. In November 1524 Carlstadt's *Ob man gemach faren, und des ergernüssen der schwachen verschonen sol* was published through a Basel printshop. It was dedicated to the city clerk of Joachimstal, Bartel Bach. See Freys/Barge, number 138 and chapter 11 in this volume.

2. The text does not go to the extent of suggesting the possibility of killing the neighbor out of love for God.

3. The RSV reads, "Wait for the Lord."

4. The German has *"biss uff ire klarheit"*—a phrase borrowed from the language of mysticism—which means until it is purged of all dross and appears in its clearest possible form.

5. A similar notion is found in the 1522 publication *On the Removal of Images.*

6. The marginal note mistakenly gives 2 Chr 20.

7. *"leydlichkeit."*

8. The marginal note mistakenly has 1 John.

9. The marginal note has Deut 4.

Chapter 10

1. Bartholomew (Bartel) Bach was city clerk of Joachimstal. He had given Carlstadt a picture of Pope Calixtus and seems to have been on good terms with the Reformer.

2. The color of the tassels in Num 15:37 is blue.

3. frum.

4. 2 Cor 6:14ff.

5. Lk 14:26.

6. Mt 10:5.

7. Acts 21:26.

8. Gal 3:1-5. Carlstadt paraphrases; he adds the word "circumcised" to "works of the law."

9. The pun band/bund—bond/covenant does not work in English.

10. Deut 16:18.

11. 1 Cor 6:9f. and 10:7ff.

12. The term in the text is *maul* which, on occasion, is used figuratively for mule—traditionally seen to be a dumb animal. Why Carlstadt places the horse in the same category is not clear.

13. Ecclesiastes 3:1ff., not 9, as indicated in the margin.

14. *"so ruget die hand."*

15. Carlstadt recalls his more detailed argument on this issue in "On the Removal of Images" of 1522.

16. The reference is not in the chapters cited.

17. The passage is in 1 Cor 10:23. The RSV has "lawful" instead of Carlstadt's "fitting" *[zimen]*.

18. See Gen 37:7; 1 Kings 7:25; Num 21:8f.

19. The allusion to Ezek 32:7 is somewhat puzzling. Carlstadt seems to suggest that the imposition of rules and regulations and the enforcing of severe taxation by those who should be advancing the cause of the poor in fact sets them back.

20. No booklet by that name is extant. Carlstadt probably means *Von den zweyen höchsten Geboten,* first published in Strasbourg in 1524. See Freys/Barge, No. 121 and this volume, chapter 9 above.

21. Carlstadt probably has in mind Lk 17:1 or Rom 9:33.

22. Isa 44:9; 18.

23. Likely an echo of Deut 17:7 and 25:12.

24. Mt 5:29ff.

25. Carlstadt refers to Jerome Emser and to a reply he had written to him. Publication was suppressed by the Wittenberg censors. But see "On the Removal of Images," chapter 4 above.

26. From October/November 1524 onward, Carlstadt calls Luther and his followers the new papists, accusing them of harsh measures and of suppression of the spirit in ways reminiscent of the old papists.

27. Here Carlstadt thinks of Pope Gregory VII whose notion of images being the picture books of the laity he ridiculed in "On the Removal of Images." Here, as there, the reference should have been to the Gregorian Reforms.

28. The Hertzsch reprint of this text erroneously repeats the line *"grossen schaden thun mochten/wie vil mehr müsten."*

29. Ex 23:32f.

30. Not identified.

31. The RSV reads "Asherim" for Carlstadt's "bushy trees" and mentions "graven images" where Carlstadt writes "burn their gods."

32. Carlstadt cites Isa 44 rather loosely and gives it an interpretation that is not readily apparent from the reading of that passage. See his use of this passage in chapter 4 above.

33. There is no internal indication which booklet Carlstadt had in mind. He may have meant the booklet *On Faith and Unbelief,* published in Basel and Strasbourg respectively toward the end of November. See Freys/Barge number 71.

Chapter 11

1. Although Carlstadt is writing the names of the dialogue partners, we will use ab-

breviations as indicated throughout this booklet.

2. We have not identified the source of this saying.

3. An elliptic quote from Aristotle, the source of which we have not been able to identify.

4. A Zorzin, *Karlstadt als Flugschriftenautor*, (Göttingen: Vandenhoeck & Ruprecht, 1990), suggests that Hertzsch may have mistakenly inserted the wrong page at this point. He should have inserted A4 v, in other words, Hertzsch 40:33-41:25. In our translation the relevant section to be inserted here would then be p. 358: "Gem: That's why I speak of the humanity of Christ." up to p. 359: "Vic: I still don't understand." Since it would require a careful comparison of extant copies of the booklet, the sequence Hertzsch established was retained in translation.

5. It is next to impossible to catch the derision achieved by this bastardization of the term *pfaffe*—priest in the form of a verb.

6. He does translate, but merely from Greek to Latin, still leaving his dialogue partner ignorant.

7. That is grammatically wrong, of course. Carlstadt is at his ironical best in this argument.

8. Jn 14:26.

9. 1 Thess 1:6; 1 Cor 4:16.

10. Acts 10:47.

11. 1 Cor 11:29.

12. Carlstadt probably means the Roman lawyer Mutius Scaevula Quintus—author of some eighteen volumes of civil law. He is credited with having defined *definitiones* and *regulae*. As an adviser of young Cicero, he hated radicalism and adhered to Stoic philosophy.

13. *hützelprediger.*

14. Ps 22:22.

15. The term here means "let go" or "surrender." In a different context *"sich auf jemanden verlassen"* would mean "to trust someone"; hence, to let go of one's own position.

16. Is Carlstadt suggesting here that the term *verlassen* as he intends to use it is not readily grasped by everyone?

17. The text we used does not have "cup."

18. Rom 10:9.

19. 1 Cor 11:26.

20. Acts 2:42.

21. An obvious attempt to belittle the solemn processions behind ornate monstrances which were said to contain the host and which had to be adored by the laity with bowed heads and appropriate signs of reverence. Processions of this kind were frequent in Carlstadt's days on all religious festivals as well as in anticipation of disasters. Monstrances were carried about city streets or into fields to secure them against disasters such as hail storms, crop failures, the ravaging of the plague, etc.

22. In Greek mythology the god of the sea who possessed powers of prophecy and transformation. Anyone who was able to get the better of him in wrestling would receive prophecies regarding the future.

23. Men in holy orders were tonsured. To protect their bald heads against exposure to the sun, heads would be oiled from time to time; hence, Peter's reference to besmirched heads.

24. The term used is *Schein*. In the dialogue that follows Carlstadt skillfully uses the several nuances (light, appearance, or pretense) to make a point.

25. The account of the death and raising of Lazarus is found in John's Gospel, chapter 11. In 11:41 we read, "And Jesus lifted up his eyes and said, Father I thank you." It is the fact of this thanksgiving being the same as that spoken over the bread and the cup that Peter alludes to.

26. He is attacking the scholastic understanding of the presence as well as Luther's

"in, with, and under" notion of the real presence.

27. The tabernacles which contain the host; hence Peter's immediate rejoinder, "your jails."

28. Carlstadt puns on the Latin *similis* and the German *Semmel* to make a playful and somewhat silly point—undoubtedly to show up the futility of such line of argument.

29. It is all right to touch.

30. It's right to throw stones.

31. This should probably be Peter; the text seems to be in error.

32. A trick question. Peter tests Gemser's orthodoxy regarding the unity of body, soul, and spirit on the one hand, and pertaining to the undivided nature of Christ in his post-resurrection state, on the other. The ensuing dialogue will make the complexity of a bodily presence of Christ in the sacrament apparent to the point of appearing to be absurd.

33. The booklet was probably published at Basel in the fall of 1524 and reprinted in 1525 by an unknown publisher. See Freys/Barge, numbers 124, 125.

34. The Carlstadt tract with a title closest to the one announced is his *Erklerung des 10. Kapitels Cor 1* of 1525.

35. Two printings of this work are known. They appeared in Basel in 1524 and Strasbourg in 1525. See Freys/Barge, numbers 129, 130.

36. Carlstadt may have had in mind, *Von anbetung und ererbietung*, published by three presses between 1521-22. See Freys/Barge, numbers 68-70.

37. *Wider die alte und newe papistische Mess.* See Freys/Barge numbers 131-134.

Chapter 12

1. Ex 20:8ff.

2. He means the Ten Commandments.

3. The reference should be to Deut 23:4-5 where it is the enemy's beast that should be helped up.

4. In "Regarding Vows" of 1522, chapter 3 above, Carlstadt discusses this text in detail.

5. We are unable to establish the booklet Carlstadt had in mind.

Chapter 13

1. An English translation of Luther's *Against the Heavenly [Celestial] Prophets* of 1524 may be found in the multi-volume edition of Luther's Works published since 1955 by the Muhlenberg Press, Philadelphia.

2. Luther's attack is *Wider die himmlischen Propheten.* See WA 18:37ff.

3. While Carlstadt's response is primarily directed to statements made by Luther in his tract against Carlstadt, exact citations cannot be given in this translation.

4. The abbreviation D. L. for Dr. Luther is Carlstadt's. We have retained his usage except when it was not readily apparent what the abbreviation meant.

5. The booklet *Expositio super Augustini librum de spiritu et litera (Exposition of Augustine's Book on the Spirit and the Letter)* was published in Wittenberg in 1518. Freys/Barge, number 12, thought the booklet lost. However, it has been rediscovered and was published by E. Kaehler in 1954.

6. None of the extant booklets has exactly this title.

7. He likely means a 1523 sermon which was published in 1524 with the title *Von den zweyen höchsten Geboten.* See Freys/Barge, number 121 and our translation, chapter 9 above.

8. Carlstadt likely has in mind his *Missive von der allerhöchsten tugent* gelassenhait of 1520/21 or *Was gesagt ist sich gelassen*, published two years later. In both of these, he speaks of the old Adam as essentially overcome in the "yielded person." See this volume, chapters 1 and 6 above.

9. Since Carlstadt's description of titles is not precise, the booklets he refers to are difficult to identify.

10. See WA XVIII, parts 1 and 2, pp. 37-214.

11. Isa 62 in the NRSV does not warrant this reading.

12. The proverbial saying Carlstadt employs is *"Du habest allezeyt einen rauch und dampff des Euangelij geschriben."* Nonetheless, Carlstadt strongly implies that Luther is improving on the lawgiver Moses. He can hardly conceal his sarcasm.

13. He probably means his publication of 1524 "Von den zweyen höchsten gebotten der lieb Gottes und des nechsten." See our volume, chapter 9 above.

14. As frequently elsewhere, Carlstadt paraphrases rather than translates the text.

15. Carlstadt paraphrases an important section in Ezekiel which details God's dealings with his chosen, but belligerent people.

16. Carlstadt uses *safft* which alludes to the life-giving substance derisively.

17. As we noted above, this was one of Carlstadt's earliest works, published in January/February 1518.

18. The author uses the term *lustig* in the sense of *lüstern*.

19. Meant is the entire Pentateuch, generally referred to at the time as the books of Moses.

20. *Schwad* has several meanings. Here it likely refers to gaseous substances in mine shafts which cause death.

21. Carlstadt uses the term in the sense of an *ordo salutis*.

22. In modern German the term *Kegel* means bowling pin. At the time of Carlstadt it was also used to denote a child born out of wedlock.

23. Persons—likely Franciscans or preachers—in Orlamünde and in neighboring communities with whom Carlstadt had some quarrel or another.

24. Carlstadt may have in mind his publication of 1523, *Wie sich der gelaub und unglaub gegen dem liecht und finsternis halten* (How Faith and Unbelief Stand in Relation to Light and Darkness). See Freys/Barge, 139.

25. These are communities in the vicinity of Orlamünde. We have given their modern spelling.

26. The person cannot be identified. Hertzsch suggested that Carlstadt may have meant D. Glatz, his successor.

27. 1 Cor 12:3.

28. Carlstadt arrives at his version of a theology of regeneration which, though different in some details, corresponds with the thinking of Anabaptists like Denck and Menno Simons and radicals like Schwenckfeld.

29. Carlstadt once again seems to suggest a position in support of believers baptism.

30. Carlstadt echoes Rom 5:3.

31. He likely means his own publication of a sermon he preached on the eighteenth Sunday after Trinity in 1523, *Regarding the Two Greatest Commandments*, see chapter 9 above.

32. *"Übergebung eygner seele"* is likely another way of expressing Carlstadt's notion of Gelassenheit.

33. Carlstadt makes a clear distinction between internal, i.e., true spirituality, and outward or external religious manifestations of religion which he sees as false unless they are motivated from within.

34. Carlstadt defends his decision to wear the clothes of a commoner which Luther had criticized. In return, he mocks Luther for not quickly discarding his monk's clothing, even though he had distanced himself significantly from medieval church practices.

35. *The Sachsenspiegel* is an early thirteenth-century legal codex prepared by the nobleman Eike von Repgow. It is one of the most influential prose works in Middle Low German.

36. See chapter 12 above.

37. Carlstadt's anger at the injustice perpetrated against him is clearly apparent from these harsh words against Luther who, rather than the peaceable Christ who rides on a donkey into Jerusalem, appears like the horned beast of the book of Revelation and shows the low level of intelligence generally attributed to mules.

Chapter 14

1. The term Carlstadt uses is "princes."
2. It is difficult to render *auffrürer* in English. Insurrectionist, rebel, revolutionary are probably too strong.
3. Carlstadt refers here to the Mühlhausen peasant uprising with which Thomas Müntzer became involved. He was captured, tried painfully, and executed. Carlstadt is, of course, right in his claim not to have been party to Müntzer's schemes.
4. Carlstadt wrote Thomas Müntzer on 19 July 1524. The people of Orlamünde followed with a letter of their own to the people of Allstedt. For both letters see Peter Matheson, ed. and tr., *The Collected Works of Thomas Müntzer*. Edinburgh: T & T Clark, 1988, pp. 91-94.
5. *vermessene Anmutung.*
6. Not identified.
7. Carlstadt employs the legal term *negativam facti.*
8. Literally: *"die auch nicht in ydermans augen gangen sind"*—who also did not walk in everyone's sight.
9. The place likely is Taubertal, a small community on the River Tauber.
10. The noun is missing from the sentence. "Peasants" is our insertion.
11. An allusion to Lk 15:1ff.
12. The text merely has a capital F. That he likely meant "princes" is presumed from what follows in the conclusion of the letter.
13. June 24.

Chapter 15

1. Gottheit.
2. The German text has *"den ihren Gott hat verheissen."*
3. Carlstadt has adapted somewhat to the Swiss usage by employing *prästen* in place of *gebresten*—a term by which Zwingli spoke of the human inclination to sin. This sentence would suggest, however, that Carlstadt did not adopt Zwingli's meaning.
4. This clearly is indicative of Carlstadt's acceptance of the Chalcedonian Definition, which asserts that Jesus Christ was fully man and fully divine, both natures coexisting in him without mingling.
5. *"die ungehorsame alle erfüllte."*
6. The text seems to be flawed at this point. The context would suggest that "world" may have been intended.
7. *prästen.*
8. Another text reads "Herren" instead of "hearts."

Appendix A

1. See Barge, *Karlstadt*, vol. II, especially pp. 312-315.
2. According to the editors of WA VIII, the proverbial saying which Luther must have had in mind is *"Trau nicht, so bleibt das Ross im Stall"* [do not trust and the horse remains in the stable].
3. *sich zu recht erbeut.*
4. See WA 18,434. The editors point out that Duke George of Saxony objected to this statement by Luther. As a result, he warned the Elector John to be wary of Luther.
5. *"Der gemeyne man."*
6. Wander's collection of proverbs lists the saying as, *"Den viele fürchten, muss viele fürchten."* See WA XVIII, 437 n 3.
7. *poffel.*
8. Luther may think here of the petition in the Lord's Prayer, "and deliver us from the evil."

Bibliography

A.   Carlstadt's Tracts included in this volume

1. 1520 *Missive von der allerhöchsten Tugend Gelassenheit*

2. 1521 *Von Anbetung und Ehrerbietung der Zeichen des Neuen Testaments*

3. 1521 *Von Gelübden underrichtung Andres Bo. von Carolstadt, Doctor*

4. 1522 *Von Abtuhung der Bilder und Das keyn Bedtler unther den Christen seyn sollen*

5. 1522 *Sendbrief D. Andreas B. von Karlstadt meldend seiner Wirtschaft*

6. 1523 *Was gesagt ist: Sich gelassen, und was das Wort Gelassenheit bedeutet, und wo es in heiliger Schrift begriffen*

7. 1523 *Ursachen das And: Carolstat ein zeyt still geschwigen. Von rechter unbetriglicher beruffung*

8. 1523 *Von Mannigfaltigkeit des einigen Willen Gottes. Was Sünde sei. Andreas B. von Karlstadt, ein neuer Laie*

9. 1524 *Von den zweyen höchsten gebotten der lieb Gottes und des nechsten, Mathei 22*

10. 1524 *Ob man gemach faren und des ergernüssen der schwachen verschonen soll in sachen so gottis willen angehn*

11. 1524 *Dialogus oder ein gesprechbüchlin von dem grewlichen unnd abgöttischen missbrauch*

12. 1524 *Von dem Sabbat und gebotten feyertagen*

13. 1525 *Anzeyg etlicher Hauptartikeln christlicher Leere in wölchen Doct Luther den Andresen Carolstat durch falsche sag und nachred verdechtig macht*

14. 1525 *Entschuldigung D. Andres Carlstads falschen namen der auffrür so yhm ist mit unrecht auffgelegt*

15. 1534 *Ueber die Menschwerdung Christi. Karlstadts Zürcher Abschiedspredigt*

B. Secondary Sources

Bernhardt, Joseph. *Eine Deutsche Theologie*. München: Hermann Rinn, n.d.

Beyer, H. *Sprichwörterlexicon*. Munich: C. H. Beck, 1985.

Dykema, Peter A & Oberman, Heiko A. *Anticlericalism in Late Medieval and Early Modern Europe*. Leiden: E. J. Brill, 1993.

Egli, E. *Actensammlung zur Geschichte der Zürcher Reformation in den Jahren 1519-1533*. Zurich: 1879.

Furcha, E. J. "Zwingli and Carlstadt" in *Fides et Historia*, 1993.

Harper's Bible Dictionary. New York: Harper, 1958.

Hasse, Hans-Peter. "Zum Aufenthalt Karlstadts in Zürich (1530-1534)," in *Zwingliana* XVIII/4+5 (1991/1), pp. 366-388.

Hertzsch, Erich. *Karlstadt und seine Bedeutung fur das Luthertum*. Gotha, 1932.

————. *Karlstadts Schriften aus den Jahren 1523-1525*. Halle: Max Niemeyer, 1956.

Kempis, Thomas à. *Of the Imitation of Christ*. New York/London: 1909.

Körte, W. ed. *Die Sprichwörter und sprichwörtlichen Redensarten der Deutschen*. Hildesheim: G. Olms, 1974.

Kriechbaum, F. *Grundzüge der Theologie Karlstadts*. Hamburg: 1967.

Luther, Martin. *Luther's Works*. American Edition, Philadelphia: Fortress Press.

Mangrum Bryan & Scavizzi, Giuseppe. *Karlstadt, Emser, and Eck* on Sacred Images. Toronto: Dove House, 1991.

The Nicene & Post-Nicene Fathers, Second Series, vol. VI, New York, 1893.

Pater, Calvin A. *Karlstadt as the Father of the Baptist Movement*. Toronto: University of Toronto Press, 1984.

Pettegree, Andrew. *The Early Reformation in Europe*. Cambridge: U.P., 1992.

Sider, Ronald. *Karlstadt's Battle with Luther*. Philadelphia: Fortress Press, 1978.

Stayer, James & Packull, Werner, eds. *The Anabaptists and Thomas Müntzer*. Toronto: Kendall/Hunt, 1980.

Wandel, Lee Palmer. *Images of the Poor in Zwingli's Zurich*. Cambridge: U.P., 1990.

Williams, George H. *The Radical Reformation*. 3rd edition, Kirksville: SCS Conference, 1992.

Zorzin, Alejandro. *Karlstadt als Flugschriftenautor*. Göttingen: Vandenhoeck & Ruprecht, 1990.

Scripture Index

Name and Place Index

Subject Index

The Editor

Dr. E. J. (Ed) Furcha has been professor of church history at the Faculty of Religious Studies, McGill University, in Montreal since 1980. From 1968-73 he held the same position at the Vancouver School of Theology. His special area of interest is the sixteenth century and, in particular, the life and works of Schwenckfeld, Zwingli, Hans Denck, and Sebastian Franck. He has translated and/or edited numerous volumes on these radical reformers, being frequently published by Pickwick Publications and Edwin Mellen Press, among others.

A former high school teacher, Furcha served pastorates in Canada, Switzerland, and the United States before and after his ordination in the United Church of Canada in 1963. He is in demand as guest preacher, lecturer, and interim pastor.

An avid amateur musician, he is a dedicated poet, a sometime dramatist, and a passionate outdoor woodsman.

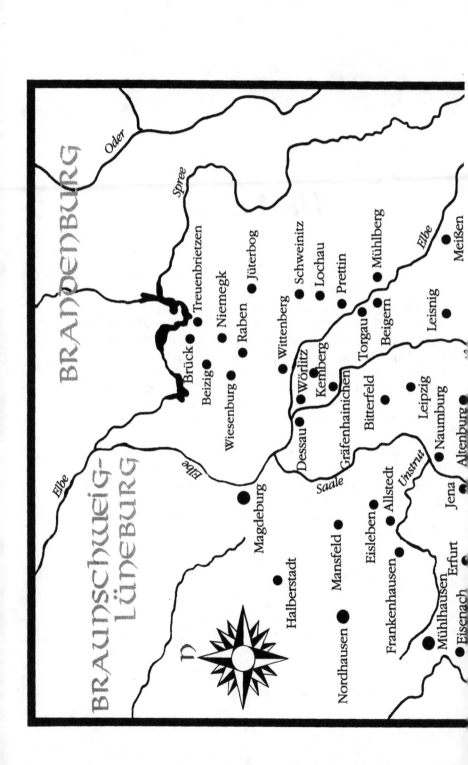

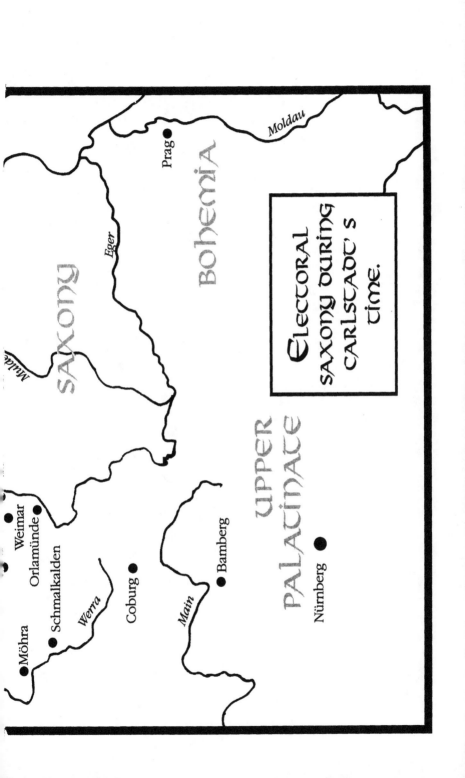

Electoral Saxony during Carlstadt's time.

Saxony

Bohemia

Upper Palatinate

Moldau

Eger

Mulde

Prag

Weimar

Orlamünde

Schmalkalden

Möhra

Werra

Coburg

Bamberg

Main

Nürnberg

CPSIA information can be obtained
at www.ICGtesting.com
Printed in the USA
LVHW081025011119
636048LV00009B/209/P